W9-AYF-153

A CENTURY'S JOURNEY

A CENTURY'S JOURNEY

How the Great Powers Shape the World

———◆———

Stanley Hoffmann (France)

Josef Joffe (Germany)

Robert Legvold (Russia)

Robert J. Lieber (Great Britain)

Michel Oksenberg (China)

Robert A. Pastor (United States)

Kenneth B. Pyle (Japan)

EDITED BY ROBERT A. PASTOR

BASIC
BOOKS

A Member of the Perseus Books Group

Copyright © 1999 by Robert A. Pastor

Published by Basic Books,
A Member of the Perseus Books Group

All rights reserved. Printed in the United States of America. No part of this book may be reproduced in any manner whatsoever without written permission except in the case of brief quota-
tions embodied in critical articles and reviews. For information, address Basic Books, 10 East
53rd Street, New York, NY 10022-5299.

Designed by Heather Hutchison

A CIP catalog record for this book is available from the Library of Congress.
ISBN 0-465-05475-7

99 00 01 02 /RRD 10 9 8 7 6 5 4 3 2 1

CONTENTS

PREFACE

T HE END OF THE COLD WAR has brought neither peace on earth nor, for that matter, goodwill to mankind. But it has brought a relaxation in strategic tensions, an opportunity to concentrate on social and economic problems, and considerable confusion about the world. To those who were comfortable interpreting all the world's events in terms of victories or defeats for the United States or the Soviet Union, the contemporary world is a tangle of contradictions. Today anti-American fundamentalists can burn a U.S. flag and eat American hamburgers and not get indigestion.

Globalization seems to be compressing the world and making it more homogeneous, but at the same time the world seems to be tearing itself apart. Grand theories explain both the unifying pressures of technology and democracy and the fragmenting power of religion and ethnicity. Each set of theories seems to be at war with the others, but they share one idea: that the great powers, and indeed all nation-states, are relics of a bygone era. On that point, we disagree.

We have come together to write this book for a number of reasons. First, we believe that states—and, in particular, England, France, Germany, Russia, the United States, Japan, and China—have been the principal actors on the international stage throughout this century and that they are likely to remain so as far as we can see into the next century. Second, we think the first and best step toward understanding the next century is to learn how these states drew the contours of the international system in the twentieth century. This is not a new idea, but lately it has been discounted by those who believe the world is so different from the past that history is of little use.

The new theories addressing why the world is shrinking or fragmenting offer penetrating insights into new forces in international politics and economics. Many of these new phenomena have altered the way that states define their interests, but we believe it is a mistake to confuse the power of these new forces with that of governments. States set the rules, and in the twentieth century they have changed the rules of the game from a world of empires to one of markets.

We realize that some readers might be reluctant to taste a broth mixed by seven foreign policy cooks. However, no single scholar could have prepared a soup as rich and about so many countries as this. I am fortunate to be joined by such respected scholars, each an authority on the country he writes about. Our task was to extract the essence of each national experience, the tasty morsels that offer a sense of where the country has come from and where it is tending. In reviewing the foreign policies of an entire century, the authors provide additional flavor by using styles that will help the reader enter the mind of each nation—whether the solid diplomacy of England, the anxieties of France, the realpolitik of Germany, the tangled web of the three Russias, the exuberant idealism of the United States, the channeled ambition of Japan, or the historical burden of China.

We selected the ingredients that would define each country and shared our recipes at the same time. We discussed outlines and presented our draft chapters to a conference at Harvard University. This conference allowed us to test our ideas and to permit the themes to coalesce. We kept writing drafts until we concluded the entire soup was better than the sum of the individual contributions.

My own career during the past twenty-five years spans some of the changes in the world that this book chronicles. I have worked four years on the National Security Council, recommending strategies to advance U.S. interests in the world, and more than a decade teaching, writing, and managing international programs at a nongovernmental organization (NGO), the Carter Center.

My experience in trying to mediate a conflict in just one country— Nicaragua—during the span of a decade illustrates the metamorphosis in the international system during that period. In 1978–1979, as the national security adviser to the president on Latin America, I worked with the State Department to try to negotiate a democratic transition between the dictator Anastasio Somoza and the moderate opposition. Our efforts failed, and the Sandinista National Liberation Front marched into Managua on July 20, 1979. A decade later I returned to Managua as a representative of an NGO and persuaded the Sandinista leader Daniel Ortega and the leader of the opposition to invite the Carter Center to monitor and mediate the transition to democracy. What was not possible for the U.S. government during the Carter and Reagan administrations was successful with the help of an NGO.

In the world taking shape at the end of the millennium, there are roles to be played by NGOs that were not conceivable two decades ago, but the way to understand their role is not to think that countries are less important. One hundred years ago, many incorrectly thought that nationalism would be far less influential than new ideas like socialism, fascism, and communism. Similarly today, NGOs contribute ideas, but governments knit these ideas together with other interests into a national interest.

As one who has spent most of a career working on issues related to the developing world, I am sensitive to those who would view a book on the great powers as flawed for overlooking the aspirations of the vast majority of countries and people in the world. Our book concentrates on the journey of seven countries in the twentieth century, but much of that history reflects their grudging recognition of the forces of nationalism expressed in the growing assertiveness of small and middle-powers. Nonetheless, there is no denying that the great powers have had a diproportionate influence shaping world politics in this century, and that is why we have chosen to write a book on them rather than on the foreign policies of 185 nations. We explain in the first chapter why we narrowed our study to the seven countries.

We owe much to many in the preparation of this book. Joseph S. Nye Jr., dean of the John F. Kennedy School of Government, and Jorge Dominguez, professor of government at Harvard and director of the Weatherhead Center for International Affairs, invited me to Harvard in the fall semester of 1998 as the Ralph Straus Visiting Professor. That was an outstanding opportunity to use the intellectual resources of the university to test our theses. The Weatherhead Center sponsored a conference, which I cochaired with Wellesley College professor Robert

Paarlberg, whose thoughtful comments on many drafts of the project qualifies him as a virtual contributor. At the conference we reviewed early drafts of the chapters, and we were fortunate to have the following people offer detailed comments: Emanuel Adler, Graham Allison, Robert Art, Robert Blackwill, Jorge Dominguez, Leslie Gelb, Akira Iriye, Carl Kaysen, Ernest May, Louise Richardson, George Ross, Robert Ross, Tony Smith, Raymond Vernon, Ezra Vogel, Stephen Vogel, Celeste Wallander, and Philip Zelikow. Aaron Lobel and Kelle Tsai provided superb rapporteur's summaries, which helped improve the next draft of the chapters. Rosaline deButts helped organize the conference. We are also very grateful to the following people for reviewing individual chapters: Dusko Doder, Fraser Harbutt, Alan Hendrickson, Michael Klare, Yawei Liu, Robert S. McNamara, Henry Nau, Victoria Nuland, Tom Remington, Dan Reiter, Christian Tuschoff, and Ellen Rafshoon, who also assisted in the research. We have benefited from the help of skillful research assistants, including James Gillespie, Jonathan Bell, Jason Mack, Jonathan Weisner, and Zaryab Iqbal.

I am grateful to the authors for their comments on the introductory and concluding chapters. Bob Lieber deserves special thanks not just for commenting on all the chapters but because I relied on his advice for every part of the project, and he was always available and wise. Tim Bartlett, our editor, saw the need for the book early, but his greatest contribution was his editorial suggestions and direction in sharpening the thesis of the book. Katherine Delfosse's careful editorial suggestions made the entire book more readable and, I hope, enjoyable. Finally, I owe more than I can acknowledge, let alone pay, to my children, Tiffin and Kip, for tolerating still another book, and to my most perceptive and devoted critic, my wife Margy.

The students at Emory University who took my course, "Foreign Policies of the Major Powers," asked if there would ever be a book that would do justice to the subject. This is the answer.

Robert A. Pastor
June 1, 1999

1

♦

THE GREAT POWERS IN THE TWENTIETH CENTURY

From Dawn to Dusk

ROBERT A. PASTOR

THE TWENTIETH CENTURY draws to a close with a musty scent of dejá vu. A war in the Balkans set western Europe and the United States against the Serbs and their Russian friends. There is a sense that we have seen this war before. In fact, every citizen of the twentieth century has seen a conflict in the Balkans, but, using the prism of their generation's trauma, each would interpret the contemporary conflict differently.

To some, the conflicts in the Balkans seem like a slow-motion repetition of the first world war—of old empires dragging new ones into an abyss with little understanding of the local causes or their global consequences. To those whose world-view was defined by World War II and the Cold War, NATO's defense of western values is the reason for its intervention. And, finally, those who see the post–Cold War world as torn by a "clash of civilizations," of Christians against

Muslims, would see ethnic groups fighting to defend their cultural identities.

Yet none of these three interpretations captured the most recent crisis in Kosovo. Empires were not at war, and the United States led the West, rather than avoided the conflict, as it did in 1914. NATO was established to deter or prevent Soviet domination of Europe, but the Soviet Union no longer existed. Finally, western Europe did not fight the Muslims of Kosovo; it defended them. Only the brutality connects the century's conflicts in the Balkans.

In the past century, as throughout history, mankind has witnessed the rise and fall of great powers and the dissolution of empires. What makes the end of the twentieth century unique is that for the first time in history, there are no empires or colonies. The great powers negotiate rules, which constrain all of them. They don't seize each other's land. They pursue their interests with each other in international organizations rather than in gunboats. They have all signed treaties affirming a single set of human rights principles, and indeed, most of the great powers went to war in Kosovo for those humanitarian reasons. They focus more on gaining access to markets than on securing resources. They spend more for social security than for weapons. They coax warring ethnic groups to make peace. The three European powers seek unity and harmony with each other rather than alliances and war against each other. All these changes arise from the fact that the great powers pursue different goals at the end of the century than at the beginning, and the new goals have shaped a different world.

The very concept of "great powers" seems to belong to the nineteenth century—a time when monarchs ruled empires, dispatched mercenary armies to control their dominions, and played the "great game" of imperialism against each other. In 1901, when England buried its longest-reigning monarch, Queen Victoria, the world's royalty came to pay their respects. Most of them were related: Kaiser Wilhelm II of Germany and Tsar Nicholas II of Russia were the Queen's nephews. Yet just three years earlier, Wilhelm had decided that Germany would build a fleet to surpass England's, and seven years earlier, Nicholas had approved a secret alliance with France aimed at containing Germany. Each such decision by a single individual, without public debate, was a step toward the Great War.

Like the other monarchs of the day, Victoria was devoted to imperialism. But she was popular in England in large part because she understood that an emperor could no longer rule England's empire. She reduced her role to a symbolic one, and freely elected leaders governed. Thus in England the regal pageantry was more form than substance. But in Germany, Russia, China, Japan, Turkey, and Austria-Hungary emperors ruled, and they defined their era by the colonies and territories they acquired.

Today, elected leaders, not monarchs, govern all of the great powers, although in China the elections are controlled by the leadership of the Communist Party. Still, the principle is almost universal that legitimate power derives not from divine right nor naked threats but rather from the consent of the governed. About one-third of the governments in the world do not practice this principle, but, of those, only a handful reject it.

None of the great powers rules the world. But of the 185 members of the United Nations, seven countries are responsible for half of the world's trade, two-thirds of the world's output, and nearly three-quarters of the world's defense expenditures. The great powers are still defined in terms of their ability to influence or respond to events far beyond their borders. They still shape the world, but in much more subtle and indirect ways than they did at the beginning of the century. The principal goal of the great powers is to advance the economic and social interests of their people, and their leaders recognize that achieving that goal requires an international system that promotes trade and investment and contains and tries to resolve conflicts. The United States is the only superpower today. But where political and economic goals predominate, superpower status is less important than it was 100 years ago, when the great powers were carving up the world. Indeed, the enduring power of the United States derives as much from the institutions it established at the end of World War II as from its wealth or weapons.

As the goals of the great powers have changed, so too have the ways they pursue these goals. Military and economic power are so profoundly different from their 1900 equivalents that they have not simply altered the ways wars are fought or avoided. The very meaning of "power" and the game of international politics have changed. Consider the following:

- One present-day nuclear submarine has more firepower than all the world's armies possessed in 1900. Yet both the United States and the Soviet Union, which possessed 93 percent of the world's nuclear weapons, were defeated in costly local wars by poor developing countries.
- Of the world's 100 greatest economies, fifty-one are companies and forty-nine are countries. One of those companies— General Motors—produced nearly the same amount of goods and services in 1997 as did all of Europe in 1900.[1]
- One fiber optic cable can carry more information in a minute than all the world's telegraph and postal services could haul in the entire year 1900. Television brings every world crisis into the living rooms of billions of people, but most care more about the cost of living than atrocities half a world away.

Some of the ends and the means of foreign policy are new, but the seven major powers have not changed. At the dawn of the twentieth century, three countries—the United States, Japan, and Germany— emerged from isolation or internal division to challenge the great powers of the nineteenth century. Although Japan and Germany were vanquished in a war at the century's midpoint, all three were dominant again as the century drew to a close. The United States, Japan, and Germany—in that order—had the strongest economies and the highest military expenditures on the eve of the twenty-first century. France and England had declined from their imperial perches of 1900, but their economies, armed forces, and permanent seats on the UN Security Council still qualified them to be in the select group. Russia and China have experienced the most extreme swings in power during the century, but both must still be considered world powers because of their permanent seats on the Security Council and their impact on the world.

The thesis of this book is that states* are still the principal actors in the international system, but the way they define their goals and the world in which they seek to achieve them has *fundamentally*—though not completely—changed over the past 100 years. They continue to compete, but in a game unlike the contest for colonies in 1900. Today they pursue social and economic goals that require interstate cooperation and adherence to international rules. Although security concerns have diminished, they have not vanished, and each power is free to defend its interests. To understand the prospects for war or peace, prosperity or economic depression in the twenty-first century, we need to understand how and why the great powers altered their goals and the system.

What accounts for these changes? The United States arrived on the world stage at the turn of the century with a set of revolutionary principles that rotated the old system almost on its head. If these principles had not been backed by U.S. power, they could not have prevailed. If the United States had flexed its muscle without the principles, it might have replaced some of the old imperialists, but it would not have dismantled imperialism.

Albert Einstein mused at the dawn of the nuclear age that everything had changed except our ways of thinking. Similarly, our views of foreign policy have not adjusted to the century's journey. We continue to fear "another Munich" or "another Vietnam," but the threats of the future bear little resemblance to the traumas of the past. Moreover, historical metaphors sometimes blind us to new opportunities. Let us examine some new ways of looking at the current political landscape, thinking of these as new maps.

---

*The term *state* is often used interchangeably with "nation" and "country." They are related but distinct. A *state* is a political unit, the principal one in the international system. It includes a people, a territory, and a set of governing institutions. A "nation" is a group of people with a shared language, culture, and history. A "country" is the territorial component of the state. The Soviet Union was a state and country composed of many nations. [For a brief discussion of these terms, see Lowell W. Barrington, "'Nation' and 'Nationalism': The Misuse of Key Concepts in Political Science," *PS: Political Science and Politics* (December 1997), pp. 712-716.]

Six Maps of the Post–Cold War World

The international political landscape is so confusing in the aftermath of the Cold War that some leaders pine nostalgically for the old bipolar world in which every event could be described as a success or failure by the United States or the Soviet Union. Without clear landmarks dividing the world into East and West or North and South, scholars and policymakers have had to find new ways to define the world. One school of thought, with many variations, contends that the era of the nation-state, like that of dinosaurs, has passed and that twenty-first-century maps should discard it as a fossil. There are many other explanations. Let me summarize six of the most influential perspectives:

1. **Globalization**. Advances in technology and communications coupled with the rising power of multinational enterprises have globalized politics and economics and reduced the role of the state. Kenichi Ohmae asserts that this "irreversible" process is leading "to a genuinely borderless economy" and improved standards of living for all.[2]

2. **Clash of Civilizations**. The new international order is defined by struggle between civilizations rather than by global integration. Samuel P. Huntington identifies nine major civilizations: Western, Latin American, African, Islamic, Sinic, Hindu, Orthodox, Buddhist, and Japanese. "The rivalry of the superpowers," he argued, "is replaced by the clash of civilizations." Economic integration will not homogenize these cultures; they will remain distinct and irreconcilable.[3]

3. **New World Order**. The end of superpower rivalry allowed the UN Security Council to play the role that its designers intended: to take "collective measures for the prevention and removal of threats to the peace" and encourage respect for human rights. The UN coalition that drove Iraq from Kuwait marked the birth of a "new world order."[4] And the new world order has appeared just in time, since globalization has reduced states' ability to manage effectively transnational activities. Only some

form of global governance can deal with problems of proliferation of weapons of mass destruction, financial volatility, massive
flows of refugees, trade disputes, or genocide.[5]

4. **The Democratic Peace**. World politics is a function of domestic politics, and peace depends on the spread of democratic
values and regimes. Democracies do not fight one another, at
least after they are consolidated, and so the principal threats to
world peace occur among dictatorships or between dictatorships and democracies.[6]

5. **Pan-Regions**. Technology has compressed distances, and
since 1947 international agreements have dismantled most trade
and investment barriers. The result, however, has been not one
world but three: Trade within each of three pan-regions—
Europe, North America, and East Asia—has increased much
more rapidly than trade between them. Each of these pan-
regions is led by a dominant power: the European Union (EU)
by a unified Germany; North America by a predominant United
States; and East Asia by Japan, but increasingly contested by
China. As Figure 1.1 shows, these three regions account for
about 80 percent of the world's product and trade.[7]

6. **States**. The international system has changed in profound
ways, but states remain its most important actors. As always,
the great powers have a greater capacity to influence the character and to shape the rules of the international system, but all
states have a voice and a vote in the international organizations
that apply the rules over a wide domain of activities.

Each of these maps of the world emphasizes certain landmarks and
omits others. The *globalization* thesis highlights the increasing integration of the world economy and the homogenization of products,
tastes, and even ideas. World trade has grown three times as fast as
world output since World War II,[8] and the principal instrument of this
growth has been the multinational enterprise (MNE), like Ford,
Disney, or Shell, with operations in many countries. Only a few
thousand MNEs now account for close to half of the world's industrial
output and trade.[9]

FIGURE 1.1   The World's Three Main Regions: Indicators, 1996

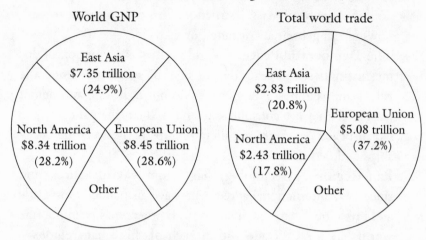

World GNP

East Asia
$7.35 trillion
(24.9%)

North America
$8.34 trillion
(28.2%)

European Union
$8.45 trillion
(28.6%)

Other

Total world trade

East Asia
$2.83 trillion
(20.8%)

European Union
$5.08 trillion
(37.2%)

North America
$2.43 trillion
(17.8%)

Other

Source: World Bank, *World Development Indicators* (1998).

Notes: Total trade is total of exports and imports of goods and services. *North America:* Canada, Mexico, United States (population 388 million). *European Union:* Austria, Belgium, Denmark, Finland, France, Germany, Greece, Ireland, Italy, Luxembourg, Netherlands, Portugal, Spain, Sweden, United Kingdom (population 373 billion). *East Asia:* Brunei, China, Hong Kong, Indonesia, Japan, Malaysia, Philippines, Singapore, South Korea, Taiwan, Thailand (population 1.72 billion).

Globalization is a natural starting point for thinking about the contemporary world. The rapid flows of goods, services, technology, and capital among states tie countries together and compel people, firms, and governments to either adapt, compete, or fall behind.[10] Global competition has forced companies to specialize more, which has provided consumers with more choices and with higher-quality and/or cheaper products.

On the negative side, nations pay a price in increased vulnerability and dependence on foreign companies. A country that wants to supplement its domestic savings with foreign capital must keep its budget balanced and its currency stable. If it doesn't, foreign capital will flee as quickly as it arrived. Economies lifted by foreign capital can suddenly collapse when it departs, as Mexico discovered in December 1994 and East Asia discovered in July 1997. The discipline of the market has always been unforgiving, but the magnitude of the flows and the speed of money's entrance and exit is new.

In 1971 Raymond Vernon, then a professor at the Harvard Business School, wrote that MNEs had contributed significantly to the welfare of the world but that they put "sovereignty at bay" because they are "not accountable to any public authority that matches it in geographical reach."[11] Others have argued that globalization has reduced the power of the state by compellling governments to compete against each other to attract scarce foreign investment by using tax incentives and cheap labor. The evidence, however, doesn't support the argument that the state is weak and endangered. In the industrialized countries the percentage of gross domestic product (GDP) going to government expenditures has nearly tripled since 1960, to roughly 50 percent. In developing countries the percentage nearly doubled during the same period, to about 28 percent. In other words, in relation to the size of its economy, the state in the richer countries is twice as large and growing faster than in the poorer countries. An increasing proportion of government expenditures involve financial transfers to the aging or the infirm. Globalization might be shrinking the world, but governments are growing bigger, and they are responding to a wider array of popular needs.[12]

States have reduced trade barriers, and this has facilitated global integration. But this has not occurred because states are the passive agents of MNE interests. Quite the contrary, Raymond Vernon argued that in the 1990s the problem of the MNEs is not that they are jeopardizing sovereignty but that states are regulating and constraining them and thereby diminishing global welfare.[13]

The trend towards global homogenization often evokes a backlash in groups or states that feel alienated or disenfranchised and fear losing jobs or dignity. The road toward globalization is not straight. Every trade barrier that is dismantled puts firms at risk, creating pressures for protectionism. The spread of U.S. popular culture through movies and CNN provokes reactions from fundamentalists, ethnic chauvinists, or ordinary people who fear a loss of autonomy.[14]

Samuel Huntington's argument—that the new divisions of the world are defined by *struggle between distinct, irreconcilable civilizations*—deepens our understanding of the cultural roots of this reaction to globalism and to U.S. power. His thesis is particularly cogent in explaining the Islamic worldview. Yet one cannot help but question the significance of culture clash in international politics when the worst conflicts in this century have occurred within rather than between civilizations. Two of the world's most barbaric twenti-eth-century wars occurred within the single civilization Huntington refers to as "Western." As the Cold War was becoming less relevant, the worst conflict occurred within the Islamic world, between Iran and Iraq. In the first decade of the post–Cold War world, the worst case of genocide occurred within the African civilization, in Rwanda and Burundi. Religion is a central element in defining "civilizations," and yet the Christian crusades against Islam pale in their intensity and in the number of deaths when compared to the wars between Catholics and Protestants and between Sunnis and Shiites.

The *new world order* has several different faces, some of them old. International economic institutions established in the aftermath of World War II—such as the World Bank, the General Agreement on Tariffs and Trade (GATT), and the International Monetary Fund (IMF)—have lifted dozens of countries out of poverty, expanded global trade, and prevented a global financial collapse and depression. Other intergovernmental organizations (IGOs) and nongovernmental organizations (NGOs) have emerged to protect human rights, eradi-cate disease, promote development, mediate conflicts, and encourage disarmament.

Has the end of the Cold War freed the United Nations to be all that President Franklin Roosevelt wanted it to be? During the Cold War each superpower wanted to prevent the other from using the UN for its purpose, and the result was UN paralysis. There is no question that the end of superpower rivalry has permitted the UN Security Council to play an increasingly active role in many of the world's conflicts. Of the forty-nine peacekeeping operations launched by the UN Security Council since 1948, thirty-six—roughly three-quarters—were ap-proved in the decade after the Cold War ended. The entire UN sys-tem has been rejuvenated, and the creation of new institutions like the International Criminal Court may improve the prospects for global governance.[15]

International institutions are important actors in the contemporary world stage, and the treaties they enforce obligate and constrain their members. The World Trade Organization (WTO), which replaced GATT, sanctions governments that increase their trade barriers. The European Union enforces the maze of agreements among its fifteen members to permit the free flow of trade, capital, and labor. But preventing war and making peace, particularly within countries, have proven far more difficult for the United Nations and regional organizations to achieve than cutting tariffs by their sister organizations. Setbacks in Iraq, Angola, Bosnia, and Sierra Leone led one writer to conclude, "In the last year of the century, the newer, saner world order confidently anticipated when Communism collapsed a decade ago is nowhere to be seen. International organizations from the United Nations and NATO to an embattled West African peacekeeping organization seemed powerless."[16] These setbacks should remind us not to confuse the tool with the mechanic. International institutions can only address a crisis if the great powers choose to collaborate, as they did in the Gulf War. If the great powers view their interests as incompatible, then the door of the UN Security Council is closed.

The United States has always been ambivalent about whether it wanted to strengthen or limit the United Nations. Its position at any given time depended, not surprisingly, on whether it viewed a specific action as serving its interests. Even in the case of the Gulf War, President George Bush did not consult the United Nations in making his decision to drive Saddam Hussein from Kuwait; he decided first and then sought international legitimacy and support. President Bill Clinton's request in July 1994 for a UN Security Council resolution to restore constitutional government to Haiti was similarly motivated: It was intended not to strengthen the United Nations but to support a U.S. initiative. In the case of Kosovo, NATO decided to begin the bombing of Serbia without United Nations authorization because of the opposition of Russia and China. In brief, the new world order bears some similarities to the old one.

The *democratic peace*—the idea that democracies do not fight each other—suggests that the critical division in the world is between democratic and nondemocratic regimes. A burgeoning literature has tested and refined this thesis, developing variations including the proposition that new fragile democracies might be more bellicose than dictatorships[17] and that narrowly based democracies might fight with more broadly based ones.[18] Recent empirical research suggests that the prospects for peace are enhanced as democratic governments join international organizations and trade more with each other. From 1950 to 1985, when all three variables—democracy, IOs, and trade—were present, the probability of violent conflict was reduced by 72 percent.[19]

The spread of democracy to 117 countries in the world in the last few decades is significant for two other reasons besides inhibiting governments from fighting each other. Governments that are elected by their people in a free environment are more civil and responsive to their people than those that are not, and second, democratic governments are more likely to act collectively in defense of global norms of human rights and democracy.[20]

The *pan-region* perspective visualizes the world in terms of three groups of states. With more than forty years of experience in trying to harmonize trade, investment, and domestic policies, the European Union is the most integrated of the three regions. It has created a new currency (the Euro) and aspires to coordinate its foreign and defense policies. The North American Free Trade Agreement (NAFTA), which took effect in January 1994, doubled trade and dramatically expanded investment among Canada, Mexico, and the United States in five years. East Asia does not have a regional grouping comparable to the EU or NAFTA, but the Association of Southeast Asian Nations (ASEAN) was established in 1967 to promote economic cooperation, and it now includes ten southeast Asian countries. The cool relationship between the region's two main powers—Japan and China—makes it difficult to conceive, let alone negotiate, a free trade area. In the meantime, Japanese foreign direct investment has begun to connect the region.

Despite concerns that each pan-region could become an exclusive trading bloc, the major country within each pan-region is too dependent on world trade to permit this to happen. The two issues of most concern to the pan-regions are to deepen integration by harmonizing policies and to enlarge the regions by including countries on their peripheries. The European Union signed an agreement with twelve Mediterranean countries to establish a free trade area by the year 2010, and it has begun what undoubtedly will be long and difficult talks aimed at integrating the countries of Central and Eastern Europe. In December 1994 the United States joined thirty-three other countries in the Western Hemisphere in a pledge to begin negotiations toward a free trade area by the year 2005. Finally, Asia Pacific Economic Cooperation (APEC), a group of twenty-one countries, agreed to establish a free trade area on both sides of the Pacific by 2020. These deadlines are optimistic, but they indicate that the countries within each region believe that their growth depends on trade and that is growing faster within each pan-region than between them.

These five worldviews seem to suggest that the era of the nation-state is passing because of the rapid erosion of sovereignty by cultural disintegration, global integration, supranational regulation, or interstate combination. But a closer analysis permits one to see the central role played by states in each of these views, as many of their proponents would acknowledge. For example, though he asserts that cultural variables are the most important for explaining state behavior, Huntington also recognizes that "states remain the principal actors in world affairs," and the conflict scenarios he develops at the conclusion of his book involve struggles between states, not civilizations.[21] Thomas Friedman writes that superpowers are being replaced by supermarkets, but he argues that because of globalization and open borders, states matter more, not less, in making the rules and enforcing them. "The hidden hand of the market will never work without a hidden fist. . . And the hidden fist that keeps the world safe for Silicon Valley's technologies is called the U.S. Army, Air Force, Navy, and Marine Corps."[22]

The *democratic peace* rests on the foundation of states. The pan-regional map is also composed of states, with one state in each region predominating. The United States accounts for nearly 90 percent of the gross product and 73 percent of the trade in North America. Japan accounts for 70 percent of the gross product and one-third of the trade among the ten nations of East Asia. And Germany accounts for 23 percent of the gross product and 28 percent of the fifteen-nation European Union.[23]

In the nineteenth century, nationalism seemed a far weaker political idea than liberalism or socialism, but *all three found expression principally within states*. Nationalism infused states with energy and direction, sometimes positively, sometimes destructively. Similarly, by the end of the twentieth century, the interests and preferences of states are being redefined by globalization, identity, and democracy, and by new actors (NGOs, MNEs, IGOs) promoting these interests and ideas.[24]

Although IGOs, such as the European Commission or the WTO, are increasingly important in a widening band of issues, their power stems from agreements between states. States must weigh carefully the costs of violating an agreement, but they always retain the right of self-defense. States join regional organizations because their leaders calculate that the benefits exceed the costs. "States," Robert O. Keohane and Joseph S. Nye Jr. remind us, "continue to command the loyalties of the vast majority of the world's people."[25] But in a world in which growth is sustained by trade, investment, and new technology, integration is a better defense than autarchy.

These six maps are not mutually exclusive. Indeed, if they were translucent and placed on top of one other, they would provide a thicker description of a multidimensional world. For example, they would help us understand the interrelationship of economic integration and cultural reaction. To explain the spreading impact of the Asian financial crisis, one might borrow insights from globalization or contrast the effect of the crisis within and among the pan-regions. To evaluate the successes or failures of the United Nations in the crises in Rwanda or Bosnia, one could refer to the new world order thesis.

States are still the pivotal actors in the international system, but each of the other perspectives adds to our understanding of the terrain on which states maneuver to defend themselves or to advance their interests. Which states are the most important? To answer this question, we need to define power and then identify the countries that have it.

Power and Its Champions

"Power" is an elusive term. In his attempt to define it, Joseph Nye Jr. first compared power to the weather—easier to talk about than to understand—and then to love—"easier to experience than to define or measure."[26] If power is defined in traditional military terms as the capacity to crush an enemy, then nuclear weapons are the main indicators, and the United States and Russia are still the world's two most powerful countries. If power is defined as a country's capacity to produce goods and services, then gross domestic product (GDP) is a better indicator, and the world is led by a triad of the United States, Japan, and Germany.

The concept of power has changed over time. In the seventeenth and eighteenth centuries it was widely believed that the governments that could enlist and feed the most soldiers and tax the largest population would win the wars, so power was often equated with the size of a state's population and the amount of land it had under cultivation. In the nineteenth century, industry and railroads were more important sources of power than agriculture or the size of territory. Russia had a larger population than Germany but was weaker because it lacked the latter's modern railroads and industrial structure.

From the first textile and industrial revolutions through the chemical, nuclear, and information revolutions, whichever country developed a new technology or knowledge or possessed the resources on which it depended found itself ahead of the power curve. Britain's invention of the steam engine and its abundance of coal gave it a head start in the industrial revolution. Moreover, certain kinds of states were better able to exploit particular stages of industrialization. The Soviet Union, for example, was able to harness the power of central planning to develop massive steel, chemical, and capital equipment industries, but its command economy proved to be a liability in the computer era. Japan learned the hard way that using an army to secure oil and coal, as it did in the 1930s, was far more costly and less effective than relying on the market and technology, as it did five decades later.

Current conventional wisdom holds that state power derives from economic growth and technological innovation.[27] Technologies become a source of power if they can compress time, distance, or space. The Internet is the most powerful new technology because it transmits knowledge and information to more people, faster, cheaper, and easier than any existing means of communication. From 1988 to 1998, the decade in which the Internet grew to widespread use, it stimulated an entire industry and, by 1998, accounted for about one-third of U.S. economic growth.[28]

The Internet and information power expand the capacity of individuals and NGOs to influence foreign policy and international politics. There is no better example of this than Jody Williams, a young woman working from a modest home in Vermont. In just six years, through the Internet, Williams organized a coalition of 1,300 NGOs in sixty countries that drafted an international convention to ban the production, storage, and use of land mines worldwide. Despite the opposition of the United States, Russia, and China, the NGOs mounted such a successful lobbying campaign that representatives of 122 countries signed the convention in Ottawa in December 1997. Williams won the Nobel Peace Prize for her role in organizing it. A public entrepreneur used a new technology to further an international norm: This is a new kind of power in a new age.

How one defines power influences one's perception of the shape of the world, and vice versa. In a world of autarchy and protectionism, land is a source of power. Land is less important in a world of free trade, and a small state like Singapore or an island nation like Japan can be wealthy and powerful. As Richard Rosecrance has noted, our understanding of the meaning of power has changed as the world has moved from the "territorial state" to the "trading state" to the "virtual state," where information and virtually all factors of production are mobile.[29]

State power is generally visualized in terms of "hard power"—military forces, population, economy (GDP, trade), territory, and natural resources.[30] The beauty of "hard power" variables is that they can be measured, and they are universally recognized as indicators of power. But we need to pause and consider a number of questions before leaping to the conclusion that a country with plenty of hard power can automatically get its way. First, are variables comparable, one to another? China's army is ten times as large as Japan's, but its economy is one-sixth as large. Which country is more powerful? Second, can variables be weighted and combined to come up with a single index of power? Adding population to military expenditures is like mixing apples with ball bearings. And third, what is the "conversion ratio" for determining the amount of hard power necessary to change an adversary's position? Robert Dahl's oft-cited definition of power as the ability to get others to do what they otherwise would not do[31] does not answer this question. Without knowing an adversaries' initial preferences or motives for changing, there is no way to tell whether the use of power is decisive. Hans Morgenthau dismissed the search for motives as "futile and deceptive."[32] And in computing this "conversion ratio," where do we fit such intangible factors as nationalism? As the Vietnamese and the Afghanis proved, intangible factors can be strong enough to defeat the most awesome military machines.

Nye improves on Dahl's definition conceptually by distinguishing between hard power and "soft power," which he defines as "indirect or cooptive . . . getting others to want what you want."[33] Soft power derives from persuasion or attraction. The Germans did not force Chile in the nineteenth century and China in the early twentieth to accept their military advisers; Germany was asked to send advisers because Chilean and Chinese leaders thought the German army was an effective model.

Of course, soft power is intangible and impossible to measure. But there are surrogate indicators of a country's attractiveness. Japan's soft power stems from its reputation as a technological leader, which developed gradually over two decades, beginning in the late 1950s. U.S. soft power is evident in the one million immigrants and 500,000 foreign students who are attracted to the United States each year. They are signs that people want to live in and learn from the United States. The popularity of U.S. movies and of CNN reflect U.S. cultural influence.

In contemplating whether to come to the aid of the French in their war against the Vietnamese Communists in 1954, President Dwight Eisenhower recognized that "an asset of incalculable value" to the United States was its standing "as the most powerful of the anti-colonial powers." This "moral position of the United States," he concluded, "was more to be guarded than the Tonkin Delta, indeed than all of Indochina"[34]—a wise assessment of one dimension of U.S. soft power.

In the late 1950s, the Soviet Union's apparent success in transforming itself from a poor Third World country into the second-greatest power influenced Third World leaders searching for alternative models to that of the West. Fidel Castro acknowledged that Soviet success in space with *Sputnik* and the apparent "missile gap" in their favor attracted his interest, thus changing the course of Cuban history. The relationship between hard and soft power has not been explored adequately, but it seems that a country's success makes it more attractive as a model, which in turn reinforces its image as a great power.

Over the course of the century, such universal norms as self-determination have become forces constraining states. The development of an international regime on human rights has compelled states to defend their actions at annual meetings of the United Nations in Geneva and in other forums. The power to define norms may be as important in the next century as the power to draw the boundaries of colonies was in the last.

The more we have tried to understand "power" the harder it has been to grasp. But we can make some useful distinctions. First, we can identify military and economic indicators of hard power, even if we can't easily compare or aggregate them. Second, nationalism and international norms have made the use of physical force more costly, and soft power has grown in importance. Finally, there are no simple answers to the questions of what kinds of power are most likely to be effective in compelling or persuading an adversary, even in war, but especially in peacetime or in negotiations.

What Constitutes a Great Power?

By almost any of the indicators of hard and soft power, it is not hard to identify the seven great powers. The three traditional categories of power are size (population and territory), economy, and military power. (See Table 1.1.) As the century closed, the United States was the preeminent power in virtually all categories, but it shared its lead in the economy and military spending with Japan and Germany, and in military personnel and weaponry with Russia and China. Great Britain and France were members of the nuclear club and ranked from fourth to seventh in most of the economic and military areas. A united European Union surpassed the United States in all economic indicators and came in second or third in the military areas.

TABLE 1.1 Ranks and Shares of Traditional Power Resources, 1990s[1]

	United States	Japan	Germany	France	Britain	Russia	China	European Union[2]
Basic Resource								
Population (1995)	3rd 4.7%	8th 2.2%	12th 1.4%	19th 1.0%	17th 1.0%	6th 2.6%	1st 21.2%	3rd 6.6%
Territory (1994)	4th 7.1%	59th 0.3%	60th 0.3%	46th 0.4%	76th 0.2%	1st 13.2%	2nd 7.3%	7th 2.4%
Economy								
GNP (1995)	1st 25.2%	2nd 18.7%	3rd 8.7%	4th 5.5%	5th 4.0%	14th 1.2%	7th 3.0%	1st 30.1%
Manufacturing (1995)	2nd 22.6%	1st 25.4%	3rd 11.7%	4th 5.9%	7th 3.7%	8th 3.1%	5th 5.3%	1st 33.8%
High-tech Exports (1986)	1st 21.0%	2nd 20.0%	3rd 16.0%	5th 8.0%	4th 9.0%	– –	– –	1st 33.0%[3]
Merchandise Exports (1995)	1st 12.1%	3rd 9.2%	2nd 10.8%	4th 5.9%	5th 3.1%	15th 1.7%	10th 3.1%	1st 38.7%
Military								
Nuclear Weapons (1996)	1st 46.8%	– N/A	– N/A	3rd 2.9%	5th 1.7%	2nd 46.1%	4th 2.5%	3rd 4.6%
Military Expenditures (1993)	1st 41.0%	2nd 5.9%	3rd 5.4%	4th 5.3%	5th 5.1%	6th 4.3%	7th 4.1%	2nd 21.5%
Military Personnel (1996)	2nd 6.7%	22nd 1.4%	15th 1.6%	12th 1.8%	24th 1.0%	3rd 5.7%	1st 13.2%	2nd 9.1%

[1] Rank is the country's rank as compared to the rest of the world. Share is the country's population (or GNP, etc.) as a percent of the world's total.

[2] European Union is the combined total of Austria, Belgium, Denmark, Finland, France, Germany, Greece, Ireland, Italy, Luxembourg, the Netherlands, Portugal, Spain, Sweden, and the United Kingdom.

[3] High Tech Exports of the European Union in 1986 is only the combined total of France, Germany, and the United Kingdom.

Source: World Bank, *World Development Indicators, 1997* (Washington, D.C.: IRBD, 1997); NRDC, *NRDC Nuclear Program*, (www.nrdc.org); Singer, J. David and Small, Melvin. National Material Capabilities Data, 1816–1993 (Computer File), Ann Arbor: ICPSR, 1996.

To what extent does this picture of power in the 1990s reflect longer trends? A ranking by similar indicators in the mid-1980s would have shown the Soviet Union first or second in all the military and most of the economic categories.[35] Soviet power, which seemed so formidable, collapsed in a few short years. Power was redistributed after the Cold War just as it had been after both world wars.

Let us examine the long-term trends in several indicators of power. Beginning with population, Europe's decline is most noticeable. The three European powers—Germany, Britain, and France—ranked fourth, seventh, and eighth in 1900 and eleventh, sixteenth, and eighteenth in 1995. The European Union as a whole, however, ranked third in 1995, just below China and India, which together accounted for about 38 percent of the world's population. Until its dissolution, the Soviet Union ranked third, a place now filled by the United States, the only major industrialized country whose population continues to expand at a moderate rate; about half of U.S. population growth is due to immigration.[36]

China's and Russia's armed forces have been larger than other nations' for most of the century because of their large population and territory and because of internal and external threats. On the eve of both world wars, the U.S. armed forces were small, ranking eleventh, below even Romania and Spain. After World War I (in 1920) the U.S. Army ranked fifth, and in 1950 it ranked third. Unlike the United States, which caught up after entering the wars, Japan and Germany built their militaries beforehand. Germany had the second largest armed force in 1914 and 1940; Japan was eighth in 1914 and seventh in 1940. Great Britain and France fell between the two. After World War II the three European governments and Japan reduced their armed forces, so they ranked from fourteenth to twenty-fifth. (See Table 1.2.)

Economic indicators show the resilience of the Japanese and German economies. Within fifteen years of their defeat in World War II, Germany and Japan had recovered to become the fourth and sixth largest economies, respectively. By 1980 Japan had leaped over Germany and both had surpassed France and England, and by 1990, with the decline of the Soviet Union, they were second and third. In 1990, after its third enlargement, the 12-nation European Community

TABLE 1.2   Active Duty Military Personnel: Rank and Share

	1850[1]	1900[2]	1914[3]	1920	1930	1940	1950	1960	1980	1990	1995
Russia	1st 30.0%	1st 19.7%	1st 18.8%	1st 27.1%	2nd 9.5%	1st 14.7%	1st 24.7%	1st 18.3%	2nd 14.4%	1st 13.0%	3rd 6.1%
China[4]	–	2nd 17.2%	6th 6.5%	2nd 12.8%	1st 19.9%	3rd 7.0%	2nd 23.0%	2nd 16.5%	1st 18.2%	2nd 11.6%	1st 12.8%
United States	19th 0.7%	11th 2.2%	11th 2.4%	5th 3.1%	6th 3.4%	11th 1.6%	3rd 8.0%	3rd 11.7%	3rd 8.3%	3rd 7.8%	2nd 7.1%
India	–	7th 3.7%	7th 3.3%	6th 2.9%	11th 2.2%	16th 0.05%	9th 2.0%	7th 2.7%	4th 4.5%	4th 4.8%	4th 5.5%
France	2nd 15.1%	4th 10.7%	4th 11.2%	4th 3.1%	3rd 8.6%	6th 3.4%	7th 3.4%	4th 5.2%	10th 2.0%	13th 1.8%	10th 2.2%
Germany	6th 4.5%	3rd 10.8%	2nd 12.2%	16th 0.9%	15th 1.3%	2nd 11.6%	–	15th 1.6%	10th 2.0%	12th 1.8%	17th 1.5%
Britain	4th 6.9%	6th 8.4%	5th 7.6%	7th 2.7%	9th 2.8%	5th 3.6%	4th 4.0%	8th 2.6%	16th 1.3%	19th 1.2%	25th 1.0%
Japan	–	13th 1.5%	8th 4.3%	3rd 5.3%	10th 2.8%	7th 3.4%	–	17th 1.3%	23rd 1.0%	20th 1.0%	24th 1.0%
European Union	–	–	–	–	–	–	–	*4th 9.8%*	*4th 7.8%*	*3rd 9.0%*	*2nd 10.1%*

[1] Data for 1850, 1950–1993 and for all years on European Union is from J. David Singer and Melvin Small, op. cit.

[2] For 1900 and 1914, percentage of total is rough approximation.

[3] Data for 1914–1940 and 1990 is from Singer-Small, op. cit.; Department of Defense, *Selected Manpower Statistics, Fiscal Year 1997* (Washington, D.C.: Department of Defense, 1997); *World Almanac and Encyclopedia*, 1900, 1914, 1920, 1930, 1940 (New York: Press Publishing Company, New York World, 1900–1940), for 1995, U.S. Arms Control and Disarmament Agency, *World Military Expenditures and Arms Transfers, 1996* (Washington, D.C.: Government Printing Office, 1997).

[4] Manpower estimates for China particularly should be regarded as approximations.

had a combined gross national product (GNP) that edged ahead of that of the United States.[37]

The trends in world trade reveal much about the distribution and variation of world power in the twentieth century. (See Table 1.3.) Great Britain dominated world trade from the middle of the nineteenth century to the eve of World War II, when it was overtaken by the United States. Germany and Japan became powerhouses in trade before World War II, but they did not recover their prewar strength until 1980, when they moved into second and third places. With Germany in the pivotal trading role, European Union exports and imports were more than twice those of the NAFTA countries.

The triad of the United States, Japan, and Germany also dominates the world of research and development—an indicator of future technological prowess—with the United States spending $168.5 billion in 1997; Japan, $75.1 billion; and Germany, $37.4 billion. Japan, however, leads the field in the numbers of patent applications.[38]

As the twenty-first century begins, these three powers—the United States, Japan, and Germany—have global interests, but an increasing share of their wealth comes from the regions they lead. The two most important trading partners for the United States are its neighbors in North America. An expansion of NAFTA to the entire hemisphere would create a region with twice the population of the European Union and with a comparable market. Germany is the EU pivot. Japan and China are still competing within an inchoate but increasingly connected East Asian region.

Another important source of power, particularly in the post–Cold War era, are the five permanent seats on the UN Security Council, whose holders have the right to propose and, more significantly, to prevent UN peace-keeping operations. Each of the great powers except Germany and Japan holds a permanent seat. These seats are another example of how the meaning of power has changed over time. During the Cold War the United States and the Soviet Union were viewed as the two most powerful states for many reasons, but their UN veto was not one of them. The United Nations was not a consequential actor on security issues. As the UN Security Council has become a critical instrument for legitimizing interventions, the votes of

TABLE 1.3 Trade[1]–Rank and Share

	1850	1900	1913	1920	1930	1939	1946	1960	1980	1990	1995
United States	3rd 18.0%	3rd 12.4%	3rd 11.8%	2nd 20.4%	2nd 11.4%	1st 21.8%	1st 27.7%	1st 12.7%	1st 12.5%	1st 13.0%	1st 13.5%
Germany	–	2nd 12.7%	2nd 13.0%	9th 2.8%	4th 8.1%	3rd 9.7%	–	3rd 8.9%	2nd 9.3%	2nd 10.8%	2nd 9.5%
Japan	–	5th 4.9%	14th 1.7%	7th 2.9%	5th 4.9%	4th 5.7%	–	8th 3.5%	3rd 6.8%	3rd 7.5%	3rd 7.7%
Russia	4th 4.4%	8th 3.3%	6th 3.9%	24th 0.5%	18th 1.6%	22nd 0.8%	14th 1.9%	5th 4.6%	10th 1.9%	10th 3.2%	17th 1.4%
China	–	12th 1.6%	13th 1.9%	6th 3.0%	33rd 0.5%	17th 1.0%	36th 0.3%	23rd 1.0%	22nd 1.0%	15th 1.7%	11th 2.8%
Britain	1st 48.4%	1st 21.9%	1st 17.7%	1st 24.0%	1st 12.6%	2nd 15.8%	2nd 11.3%	2nd 9.5%	5th 5.5%	5th 5.9%	5th 5.0%
France	2nd 26.3%	4th 11.3%	4th 10.1%	3rd 7.2%	3rd 9.6%	5th 5.2%	4th 5.5%	4th 5.4%	4th 6.3%	4th 6.3%	4th 5.6%
Italy	–	9th 2.8%	9th 3.1%	14th 1.8%	8th 4.0%	9th 2.6%	9th 2.8%	9th 3.4%	6th 4.5%	6th 5.0%	6th 4.4%
European Union[2]	–	–	–	–	–	–	–	1st 24.8%	1st 35.0%	1st 39.7%	1st 39.2%
NAFTA[3]	–	–	–	–	–	–	–	–	–	–	2nd 18.0%

[1] Trade is total of exports and imports of goods and services divided by 2.

[2] European Union in 1960 is the combined total of Belgium, France, Germany, Italy, Luxembourg and the Netherlands. By 1980, Denmark, Ireland and the United Kingdom are included. By 1990, Greece, Portugal and Spain are added. In 1995, Austria, Finland and Sweden are added.

[3] NAFTA in 1995 is the combined total of Canada, Mexico and the United States.

Source: Banks, Arthur S. CROSS-NATIONAL TIME SERIES, 1815–1997 [Computer file]. Computer Solutions Unlimited, Binghamton NY: Computer Solutions Unlimited [producer and distributor], 1998; International Monetary Fund. *Direction of Trade Statistics Yearbook.* IMF: Washington D.C., 1985.

all five permanent members have become more valuable. Any great power that wants the United Nations to act must secure the votes or acquiescence of the permanent members. As their votes gain in value, countries might trade them like legislators swapping votes.

But like any other institution, the United Nations is more than a reflection of its members' current interests; it is also a prisoner of the moment it was established. In 1945 Japan and Germany were defeated and excluded from the United Nations. Today, when economic and technological prowess carry more weight than armies as signs of great power status, the countries with the second and third largest economies in the world—Japan and Germany—still lack permanent seats in the Security Council.

What conclusions can one draw from the indicators of power? Until World War II, world power was concentrated in Europe. Germany was the ascending power that catalyzed a coalition against it. Although Great Britain could no longer rule the seas, British diplomats skillfully used their declining assets to continue to play a balancing role. The Soviet Union recovered slowly from its revolution and World War I, but it was able to mobilize its population in war and subsequently in peace to lift the country to the second rank of power before collapsing in the century's last decade. The United States had the economic power to rank first since the beginning of the century, but its military potential was tapped only after it was drawn into the two world wars. The United States did not retreat from power after World War II or after the Cold War, but despite its preeminent position it displayed considerable ambivalence about global leadership.

In Asia, Japan followed a trajectory similar to Germany's. After World War II it devoted its energies to economic growth and technological development and raced ahead of the Soviet Union to become the second economic superpower. Whereas Russia rose and then declined, China followed the opposite trajectory. The twentieth century was not kind to China: The turmoil of foreign intervention, revolution, civil war, and the Cultural Revolution made it more a victim of global politics than an actor. But in the last twenty years of the twentieth century China's spectacular growth gave the country a new sense of confidence, perhaps even an aggressive urge to reshape parts of Asia.

Even a cursory analysis of the indicators of power would identify these seven states as the world's major powers. India, with the world's second-largest population and as a democracy (albeit a fragile one), could be considered an eighth great power; indeed, India decided to test nuclear weapons partly in order to be considered a great power.

Why, then, does India not merit a chapter in this book? First, this book surveys foreign policy throughout the twentieth century. India was a colony for half the century, and it suffered civil war and multiple border conflicts for much of the rest. Second, a "great power," by definition, exercises an important influence around the world. Although India's impact on the southern part of Asia is substantial, its influence beyond that radius is trivial. At one point it played a major role in the Non-Aligned Movement, but that organization's impact has been limited. Third, India's economy has been weak and its trading capacity small. If India's economic growth accelerates and sustains a growth rate of 10 percent or more for two decades, and if it maintains and deepens its unity, then it could be a great power in the twenty-first century.

Other states might join or supplant the great powers in the twenty-first century. The most obvious candidates are now considered regional powers; their influence in their own regions is considerable, possibly exceeding that of the major powers. In Latin America, Brazil, Argentina, and Mexico are regional powers; in Africa, Nigeria and South Africa; in the Middle East, Iraq, Iran, and Egypt; and in Asia, India, Indonesia, and Pakistan have influence beyond their borders. A book that focused on each region would no doubt deal with each of these powers, but this is a book about the world's great powers.

Comparing Foreign Policies

Each chapter synthesizes a century of foreign policy in a particular country by describing and explaining both continuities and changes, the constraints within which decisionmakers worked, and their legacy. Each author has sought not to predict future policies but to extract from the country's journey those themes that might foreshadow the country's future direction.

Henry Kissinger dramatically described the challenge facing Winston Churchill as he maneuvered between Franklin Roosevelt and Joseph Stalin to create a stable structure of peace in the closing months of World War II: "Trapped between Wilsonian idealism and Russian expansionism, Churchill did his best, from a position of comparative weakness, to vindicate his country's ancient policy—that, if the world is not to be left to the strongest and the most ruthless, peace must be based on some kind of equilibrium."[39] This wonderfully concise interpretation of a pivotal moment in international politics assumes that all one needs to know about a country's foreign policy is in the mind of its leader. If a country's foreign policy were no more than a leader's preferences, then each country would adopt and abandon a highly personal foreign policy with each change of government, and a century would yield a broken field of different policies. But leaders do not make policy in a vacuum. Even one of the world's most determined warriors, Napoleon, admitted: "Men are powerless to secure the future; institutions alone fix the destinies of nations."[40] And the institutions within a state are influenced by numerous internal and external factors.

In order to track the foreign policies of the great powers, we need a definition of foreign policy, and we need to know what variables influence it. Foreign policy is the instrument by which a state defends or advances its interests. A nation's foreign policy goals are generally ranked, from vital to desirable, as (1) national security, that is, the defense of its borders and the prevention of external manipulation of its internal affairs; (2) the pursuit of its economic interests and welfare; (3) the defense and spread of its values or culture; and (4) the implicit or explicit effort to make other nations more like itself.

These goals are straightforward (with the possible exception of the last). Countries, like people, tend to be more comfortable in the company of others like themselves. Weak countries can rarely translate this preference into reality, but richer, stronger countries export their models, either directly, as imperial powers did in the colonial era, or more subtly, through such cultural exports as advertisements and movies.

By and large, the more vulnerable a country is, the more it is concerned about its national security. Paradoxically, the wealthier a country is, the more it spends on defense, because it has more money to spend and more assets to protect. Once a country secures itself against most threats, it devotes more time to advancing its economic, cultural, and moral goals through statecraft or diplomacy; military power, both threats and actions; economic aid, sanctions, trade, and investment; propaganda and public relations; and cultural exchanges.

In the chapters in this book, we do not remove individual leaders from the policymaking processes of their nations. Instead, we begin with the assumption that as individuals make policy they interpret and define their state's interests, drawing from or being influenced by two sets of determinants: those intrinsic to a country and its environment, and those characteristics of a country or its economic and political system that are not permanent, such as its institutions, leaders, and ideas.

Intrinsic

In a study examining the foreign policies of the major powers in the 1930s, Jules Cambon began his chapter on France with a simple assertion: "The geographical position of a nation is the principal factor conditioning its foreign policy—the principal reason why it must have a foreign policy at all."[41] Geographical facts are the most compelling. Countries change their leaders, their political systems, and their economic policies, but they cannot change their geography, and thus geography or geopolitics has long been the point of departure for studies of foreign policy or world politics.

Policymakers and analysts can readily explain why island nations like Great Britain or Japan need to build strong navies to protect their shores. Similarly, Russia and China have always had large armies to protect their long borders. Because it sits in the middle of Europe, Germany needed to be wary of invasions from both directions. And the United States, flanked by two oceans, could afford to be isolationist in the nineteenth century.

A second intrinsic factor is a country's natural endowments. A country endowed with ample natural resources is, ceteris paribus, stronger and less vulnerable than one without. But resources are relative and contingent indicators of wealth or power. Oil, for example, was not an asset until the late nineteenth century, and some economists would argue that it has been a liability for countries like Nigeria, Venezuela, and Indonesia, which allowed themselves to become completely dependent on this single commodity. Moreover, a lack of resources does not automatically dictate any particular policy. In the 1930s some Japanese argued that their country's lack of mineral wealth required a militarist foreign policy. Five decades later, some Japanese argued that their lack of mineral wealth required that they spend their scarce resources not on national defense but on technological research. In short, the presence or absence of natural resources affects a country, but there are any number of possible foreign policy responses to the availability of resources.

The people who inhabit the state are a third intrinsic factor. No one would dispute that a people's historical or cultural traits affect the character and direction of a country's foreign policy, but the precise connection is not clear. Ethnically homogeneous countries, like Japan, may be more unified and purposeful than a state composed of many nations, like the United States, but that is not always the case. Japan had a clear strategic vision throughout much of the century, except for immediately after World War II and in the 1990s. U.S. policies fluctuate, but during crises few countries have been as unified as the United States. It is also easy to believe that the stereotypical characteristics attributed to a people or race—for example, that the British are enterprising; the Germans, disciplined; Russians, stolid—might produce different foreign policies, but the literature on the subject is ambiguous.[42] The harder question is whether these characteristics are permanent or transitory, real or perceived stereotypes.

U.S. foreign policy has always been influenced by what Theodore Roosevelt described as "hyphenated Americans"—German-Americans, Anglo-Americans, Jewish-Americans—that is, Americans who retain an attachment to the homeland of their ancestors. In the late nineteenth century, the two major political parties fought for the allegiance of Irish immigrants, who were concentrated in politically "swing" cities, by criticizing the British. Jewish-Americans have long had substantial influence on U.S. policy toward Israel; African-Americans shaped U.S. policy toward apartheid in South Africa; and

Cuban-Americans affected U.S. Cuban policy. The absence of immigration in Japan has no doubt deepened its insularity, and the presence of North Africans in France and Muslims in Russia has heightened the sensitivity of their foreign policies toward Islamic conflicts abroad.

A state is influenced not only by intrinsic factors but also by its place in the international system. Each state must assure its own security. This realist framework asserts that geography and a balance of power are the determining variables in a country's foreign policy.[43]

Although the intrinsic factors—geography, natural resources, and people—are not static, by and large they still provide an enduring continuity. Thus intrinsic factors, along with the international system, are helpful in explaining the constancy and coherence in a country's foreign policy, but they are not very helpful in explaining the changes.

Institutions, Leaders, and Ideas

"Foreign policy is the face a nation wears to the world," wrote Arthur M. Schlesinger Jr. "The minimal motive is the same for all states—the protection of national integrity and interest. But the manner in which a state practices foreign policy is greatly affected by national peculiarities."[44] The factors that offer the richest and most diverse explanations for a country's foreign policy are internal but not permanent. They include all the characteristics—institutions, leaders, and ideas— that define the nation and make it different from others and from itself at different times.

Since Aristotle, political analysts have used the concept of "political culture" and ideology to explain why nations organize their politics and aim their external policies in different directions. Some argue that the economic system—whether it depends on small businesses, large MNEs, or state corporations—determines a country's foreign policy. In the 1920s in the United States, small businesses pressed successfully to raise tariffs. But as U.S. companies and banks became competitive internationally, the U.S. government reversed the policy.

Others believe that the political institutions or regimes matter more. In the United States, foreign policy is often the product of the pushing and pulling between Congress and the president. When a country is divided sharply by social class, race, ethnicity, or religion, these cleavages influence both the direction and the coherence of its foreign policy. A change in regime has an even more profound effect on the direction of a country's foreign policy, as one can see in the cases of Germany, Japan, and Russia in the twentieth century.

Leaders like Woodrow Wilson, Joseph Stalin, Mao Zedong, and Adolf Hitler have undeniably affected their countries' foreign policy. The decisionmaking process, the role of interest groups, public opinion—these too are important. Much of the foreign policy literature aims to demonstrate the utility of each of these in explaining a country's foreign policy.[45]

One important and subtle factor shaping a nation's foreign policy is how a generation interprets a key traumatic event of its recent past. Losing a war is the greatest trauma. Bitter over its loss in World War I, Germany fell prey to a Hitler who sought revenge. But even the winners of a long, tragic war are likely to be traumatized by the experience. The horror of World War I led the British and the French to draw the lesson that they must try to avoid war at all cost. Those lessons produced a different mistake. The English and the French signaled passivity to Adolf Hitler in Munich at a moment when a more forceful response could have restrained him. The United States also drew the wrong lesson. Congress, believing that the nation had been pushed into World War I by bankers and arms manufacturers, passed laws to prevent a second occurrence. But the effect of the Neutrality Act was to tie the president's hands and delude the Japanese and Germans into thinking that the United States would not interfere with their global ambitions. In both cases, the governments made new mistakes based on the lessons they drew from history.

The public has long had a fascination with the great powers. Paul Kennedy identifies the primary reasons for the rise and fall of the great powers over the past 500 years.[46] Our purpose in this volume is not to travel Kennedy's path but, rather, to address different questions: How did each of the major powers define their interests in the twentieth century, and what does that tell us about their paths in the next century? We will tell the story of each country's foreign policy in the twentieth century and identify their underlying factors.

In August 1914 no European leader thought the war would last more than a year or two. On December 6, 1941, no American leader predicted the attack the next day that would radically change U.S. foreign policy. As the twenty-first century dawns there will be many predictions, but the unanticipated changes that occurred in this century should warn those making them. We cannot predict events. Instead, using a panoramic sweep of the entire century, we will try to explain how history is likely to shape the foreign policies of the great powers and how these powers are likely to shape the world.

2

◆

GREAT BRITAIN
Decline and Recovery

ROBERT J. LIEBER

O N THE EVE OF THE TWENTIETH CENTURY, it was not the
United States, China, Japan, Germany, or a uniting Europe that
stood as the foremost military, economic, and cultural power. Instead,
after a century in which it had amassed an empire of unprecedented
scope, Britain remained the world's preeminent country. In 1900 the
scope of Britain's influence and its imperial scale bore comparison
with the Roman Empire at the dawn of the first millennium. Indeed,
in its geographic reach—to Asia, Africa, and parts of the Americas and
Oceania—the Pax Britannica substantially exceeded the Pax Romana.

The United Kingdom (UK), with a population of just over 40 million people, ruled fifty colonies with a total population of more than
345 million and a land area of 11.6 million square miles[1]—ninety-six
times the size of the UK itself. At its peak the British Empire covered
a quarter of the population and land area of the entire world. In an age
of imperialism, the British Empire dwarfed its competitors in size and
extent. Not only did Britain control a far larger number of colonies
than any of its imperial competitors, but the population and land area
under its control actually exceeded the totals of France, Germany,

Portugal, the Netherlands, Spain, Italy, Austria-Hungary, Denmark, Russia, Turkey, China, and the United States *combined*.[2]

The combination of its island location and far-flung imperial interests shaped Britain's grand strategy, that is, its overall approach to foreign policy based on vital interests, potential threats to those interests, and decisions on how to use available resources of economic, military, and political strength to protect these interests.[3] The strategy aimed to achieve two fundamental objectives. One was to maintain sea lanes to even the most distant portions of its empire. This led Britain to establish bases and seek control of strategic locations linking it to India and required commitments in the Mediterranean, the Suez Canal, and the Persian Gulf, among other locations.

The other fundamental objective of British grand strategy had developed over the centuries. This was to prevent any one country from dominating the European landmass, in the belief that any power capable of doing so would have amassed the resources and strength to threaten the British Isles themselves. In order to pursue this foreign policy objective Britain acted as a balancer, throwing its weight onto the scales to oppose the rise of any such continental power. It thus acted with other European countries against Spain in the sixteenth and seventeenth centuries and later against France in the eighteenth and early nineteenth centuries. But skillful British diplomats sought to avoid becoming ensnared in "continental entanglements." As the astute British foreign minister Lord Castlereagh expressed this in the years after the Napoleonic Wars, "Our true policy has always been not to interfere except in great emergencies and then with commanding force."[4]

By the latter part of the nineteenth century, however, the seeds of Britain's twentieth-century decline had already been planted. Britain had pioneered the industrial revolution and was still wealthy and influential, but its economic dominance was increasingly challenged by the United States and, especially, Germany. Indeed, the rise of Germany would make it harder to avoid the costly continental entanglement dreaded by British statesmen. In the decades to come, the problem of relative decline in economic power and military strength, the slowly but ineluctably rising forces of nationalism, and the difficulty of competing with powers of continental size and population would gradually erode the basis of empire and make the twentieth century for Britain very different from the nineteenth.

For much of the twentieth century, British foreign policy would be a constant struggle to adapt goals to diminishing capabilities, a daunting problem that Paul Kennedy called "imperial overstretch."[5] It is thus the task of this chapter to assess how Britain ultimately came to manage that decline while maintaining an influence and world role extending far beyond what her population and size would otherwise have seemed to dictate. In one of the great sagas of the past 100 years, Britain endured two world wars, the loss of empire, the Cold War, and wrenching social and economic upheaval. Despite this odyssey, by the eve of the twenty-first century she emerged with a vigorous and significant international role.

Demography and Culture

Britain's ascendancy in the centuries before 1900 was a remarkable achievement. The country possessed limited land area, and the United Kingdom today is smaller than the state of Oregon.[6] In the seventeenth century it had a population of only 4 million people, in contrast with such larger neighbors as France, with 16 million people, and Spain, with 8 million. Yet as an island off the northwest coast of the European continent, Britain enjoyed a series of geographical advantages that along with its social, political, and cultural attributes helped make it an early leader in industrialization, economic growth, and the building of empire.

Though it was not rich in natural resources, Britain's reserves of coal and iron and its relatively favorable agricultural climate provided initial assets. Moreover, its compact size, relatively homogeneous population, and especially its island status enabled it to avoid invasions (at least after 1066) and freed it from the necessity of maintaining a large standing army. By contrast, continental European countries incurred huge costs from their military expenditures. For example, the Spanish monarchy actually went bankrupt twice in the sixteenth century (in 1557 and 1597) and imposed such heavy taxes that it badly damaged its commercial life and triggered the collapse of agriculture and rural depopulation in some areas.[7]

England's geographical position and its need for a navy to defend the islands and to trade for necessary goods and resources provided a stimulus to world exploration and imperial expansion. In an era before the steam engine, railroads, and the internal combustion engine, movement of people and goods by sea, river, and canal was often the most efficient, and few places in the British Isles were far from the coast or from navigable waterways—the interstate highways of their day.

As early as the Elizabethan Age, England under the monarchy of Queen Elizabeth I (1558–1603) had established itself as a major maritime power and had successfully warded off the naval power of Spain, most notably in the Battle of the Spanish Armada (1588). In the 1600s this naval strength helped England establish itself in the Caribbean, the American colonies, Canada, and India.

Britain had developed a substantial middle-class base of artisans, yeoman farmers (small independent landholders who acquired early political rights), merchants, and then entrepreneurs. Their presence helped to foster a relatively benign internal political climate, at least in contrast to much of continental Europe. Though sometimes bloody struggles took place, a tradition of restraint on royal power dating back to the Magna Carta of 1215 created the foundations for constitutionalism and the rule of law. The Protestant ethic encouraged independent intellectual and scientific inquiry and a climate in which individual entrepreneurship and commercial development could flourish with less interference than in countries with traditions of royal or religious absolutism. It is not surprising that the industrial revolution began in Britain in the mid-18th century, thus providing the country with a lead in technology and the dynamism to expand its influence over large parts of the globe.

The human and intellectual dimensions of this development contributed greatly to the rise of Britain and its empire. These included the development of a well-educated and self-confident elite with exceptional diplomatic skills and the spread of mass literacy in the population as a whole. Together, these factors contributed to the growth of industry, the spread of the English language, and Britain's eventual international primacy.

Social and cultural dimensions can be double-edged. The durability, tenacity, and self-confidence that marked Britain's institutions and characterized its elites were also coupled with a certain insularity and amateurism. An anecdote that Claude Cockburn, a prominent journalist, told about an encounter his well-bred father had just after the end of World War I conveys the flavor of this mind-set:

> A friend told him there was a good job going as chief of some international financial mission to look after the finances of Hungary. Perhaps he would like that? My father asked whether the circumstances of knowing almost nothing about Hungary and absolutely nothing about finance would be a disadvantage. His friend said that this was not the point. The point was that they had a man doing this job who knew all about Hungary and a lot about finance, but he had been seen picking his teeth with a tram ticket in the lounge of the Hungaria Hotel and was regarded as socially impossible. My father said that if such were the situation he would be prepared to take over the job.[8]

Britain at the start of the twentieth century was not without serious internal problems as well. Disputes over political participation, including demands for Irish independence, female suffrage, working-class rights and conditions, and aristocratic privilege and power would all prove to be subjects of major political conflict.

The Trauma of Imperial Decline

Britain, it was said, had no permanent allies, only permanent interests. In prior centuries this had led it to intervene on the European mainland whenever a rising power seemed to be on the verge of dominating the continent. Previously these threats had come from Spain and then France. In the early years of the twentieth century, however, it was the power of a united and dynamic Germany that became more ominous.

Beginning with its unification in 1871 under the leadership of Prussia, Germany increasingly challenged Britain for leadership not only in Europe but globally. In land area, population, technology, economic development, and military strength, Germany more and more overshadowed its neighbors. As a result, a continental counterbalance was no longer possible without the committed presence of Britain.

Though population and economic data are not the only indications of a nation's power, the signs of Germany's rise were increasingly evident. In 1870 Germany's population of 40 million was already greater than that of Britain or France. By 1914 its population had grown to 65 million (an increase of 62 percent), outpacing both Britain, which grew from 31 million to 45 million (a rise of 45 percent), and France, whose population remained nearly stagnant. (See Table 2.1.)

Similar trends were evident in the economic realm. For example, Germany's steel production in 1880 was barely half the level of Britain's, but by 1900 it had surpassed it and by 1914 Germany was producing more than double the steel that Britain was. (See Table 2.2.)

As Germany surged in population and industrial might and began to challenge Britain's dominance on the high seas and in its far-flung colonial empire, Britain responded by seeking to build alliances with former adversaries and by undertaking a costly program to expand and strengthen its naval forces. British diplomats established an increasingly close alliance with France and with the autocratic and backward tsarist Russia. By 1907 a pattern of European alliances was not only established but was becoming dangerously rigid, with Britain, France, and Russia linked in the Triple Entente against Germany, Austria-Hungary, and Italy in the Triple Alliance.

Impact of the Great War

The outbreak of World War I in 1914 proved to be catastrophic for Europe, and the war was to have profound consequences for Britain. As the British foreign secretary Sir Edward Grey said prophetically at the time, "The lamps are going out all over Europe; we shall not see them lit again in our lifetime." In the four years of bloody trench warfare that followed, the major combatants suffered massive losses in

TABLE 2.1   European Populations (millions)

	France	Germany	Great Britain
1870	36	40	31
1900	39	56	41
1914	39	65	45

Source: Quincy Wright, *A Study of War* (Chicago: University of Chicago Press, 1942), Vol. 1 (pp. 670–671), as cited in Anton W. DePorte, *Europe Between the Superpowers* (New Haven: Yale University Press, 2nd ed., 1986), p. 13.

TABLE 2.2   Production of Steel in Europe (millions of tons)

	France	Germany	Great Britain
1880	0.39	0.73	1.32
1900	1.57	6.46	4.98
1913	4.69	17.60	7.79

Source: Ingvar Svennilson, *Growth and Stagnation in the European Economy* (Geneva: United Nations Economic Commission for Europe, 1954), p. 260, as cited in DePorte, *Ibid.*, p. 13.

men killed and wounded. Over the course of the war Britain suffered some 1 million dead and millions more wounded. It is no exaggeration to describe the war as having destroyed an entire generation of the country's best young men.

The impact of the war went well beyond the vast loss of life. Britain was demoralized by the war's human toll and the subsequent loss of confidence in national leaders and ruling institutions. The country was burdened by the huge financial costs incurred in the war, and British politics were marked by bitter recriminations about the causes of war and the strategy with which it had been fought. There was criticism of the judgment and competence of military leaders, who had persisted in using the tactics of an earlier age, ordering disastrous human-wave assaults of British troops across battlefields saturated by machine-gun and artillery fire, at such places as Ypres, Passchendaele, and the Somme.

British diplomacy was unable to achieve a stable peace in the aftermath of the war. An increasingly isolationist U.S. Congress refused to ratify the Versailles Treaty and with it U.S. participation in the League

of Nations. Relations with a series of French governments were difficult, and British foreign policymakers often tended to treat the French
more as competitors than as essential allies against a potentially resurgent Germany. Meanwhile, other major countries in Europe became
alienated from the postwar settlement: Russia under the revolutionary
regime of the Bolsheviks, Italy under the fascist dictator Benito
Mussolini, and Germany under the weak and debt-laden Weimar
Republic and especially under Adolf Hitler from 1933 onward.

For its part, Britain was further weakened by social turmoil. The
outbreak of war in 1914 had actually forestalled potentially explosive
domestic confrontations. Perhaps the most important of these was
over class issues. The increasingly well-organized trade union movement and its Labour Party demanded improved welfare for the working class and changes in the country's rigid and deeply entrenched
class structure. By the end of the war, Labour had supplanted the
Liberal Party as the chief opposition force in British politics against
the dominant Conservative Party. Labor strife came to a head with a
nationwide General Strike in 1926. The collapse of the strike after
months of confrontation left an enduring legacy of bitterness and social division.

The Irish issue also had divided the country on the eve of World
War I. The problem of Ireland was of long standing, and the growing
possibility of Irish home rule or even independence for all of Ireland
elicited a strong reaction on the part of the large Protestant minority
in Ulster (Northern Ireland) and their supporters in England. In 1912
most of the Protestant population of Ulster signed a pledge to resist
home rule, which for them meant submission to the majority Catholic
population of the island. An increasingly well-armed movement, the
Ulster Volunteer Force, grew to some 90,000 men by 1914. When the
Liberal government of Prime Minister Herbert Asquith sought to
proceed, it met bitter opposition from the Conservative opposition,
the British military officer corps, and even King George V. Indeed,
the government faced a mutiny by army officers when in March 1914
it tried to send troops to protect arms depots in Ulster.[9] Meanwhile,
bitterness ran so deep on the Irish Catholic side that some Irish favored Germany over Britain in the war, on the principle that the en-

emy of my enemy is my friend. Indeed, during Easter week of 1916, in the midst of one of the bloodiest phases of World War I, Irish rebels staged an armed uprising in Dublin.

Depression and Appeasement in the Interwar Period

During the 1920s and 1930s Britain found itself increasingly embattled, and social friction at home was further exacerbated by the impact of severe unemployment and poverty during the Great Depression. This domestic weakness and the memory of the terrible casualties suffered in World War I made it hard to sustain a strong foreign policy vis-à-vis Germany. The peace of 1918 and the League of Nations meant to sustain it were slowly unraveling while regimes opposed to the European status quo gained strength. As fascists took power, first in Italy in 1922 then Germany in 1933, and with the Spanish civil war of 1936–1939, there was consensus neither within Britain nor with France and other democratic countries on whether to pursue a strong policy of opposition to these rising powers or to seek to accommodate them through a policy of appeasement.

The growing strength of Nazi Germany presented an ominous challenge. But without the active involvement of the United States in the European balance, Britain faced a difficult task in effectively containing Hitler. Military cooperation with France and the Soviet Union did offer a potential counterbalance to German power. But Stalin was deeply suspicious of the West, and the British themselves were divided on the proper course of action, with some members of the Conservative elite and government seeing the Soviet Union as the greater threat. Cooperation with France proved to be awkward both because there were a series of weak governments in Paris under the Third Republic and because British governments tended to consider French policies too punitive toward Germany.

As Nazi Germany became an increasingly grave threat to the countries of Europe, British governments were unable or unwilling to provide the kind of support for France that might have contained Germany and prevented a new world war. In March 1935 Hitler rejected the disarmament provisions of the Versailles Treaty. In 1936 his troops occupied the Rhineland, which Germany had previously pledged to leave demilitarized under the treaties of Versailles and Locarno. The British government, however, was unwilling to support the French in resisting these moves, and the German actions went un-opposed.

As Hitler expanded German power within Europe, he continued to meet an indecisive Western and British response. In the aftermath of World War I, European leaders had sought to build a new interna-tional institution, the League of Nations, to replace the system of al-liances that had so ignominiously failed to prevent the Great War. Instead, the League's members, through a system of collective secu-rity, would cooperate in opposing any new threat to the peace. Despite a number of modest successes in the 1920s, the League could not implement an effective collective security policy. Its impotence became obvious when it failed to act decisively either against Japan's aggression in East Asia or when Italy attacked Ethiopia in December 1935. With the United States remaining outside the League, the Soviet Union was alienated from it, and with the fascist powers posing an increasingly grave threat to their neighbors and the inter-national system, the League proved incapable of providing an alter-native either to individual state actions or to traditional alliances. The League's members, whatever their attachment to its declared purpose, almost invariably gave higher priority to their own national and state interests.

As the threat posed by Nazi Germany continued to grow, Britain, under the Conservative government of Neville Chamberlain, embraced a policy of appeasement. Treating Hitler as a misunderstood national-ist and vilifying those who favored a stronger policy, Chamberlain and those supporting his policies sought to ward off another war by accom-modating Nazi Germany's demands. The severest test of the policy, and of England, came in 1938 over Czechoslovakia. In April and May of that year Hitler demanded that Czechoslovakia relinquish its west-ern region, the Sudetenland, in which 3 million ethnic Germans lived. At first, with the support of France and Russia, the Czechs were pre-pared to resist. When the British government reluctantly confronted the Germans as well, Hitler temporarily retreated from his demand, but he set an October deadline for resolving the crisis.

In the succeeding months Prime Minister Chamberlain acted to undercut the French and to force the Czech government to accede to Hitler's ultimatum. The British role proved to be pivotal: Without the firm support of Britain, France feared to face war alone against Germany; the Soviet Union was unwilling to risk war without France; and the position of the Czechs was hopeless unless they were supported by one or more of the great powers. In September, despite agreement by the Czech government to meet the Sudeten German demand for local autonomy, Hitler intensified his threats of war. With the crisis at its peak, the British and French prime ministers flew to Munich to meet with Hitler and Mussolini in a last desperate attempt to avoid war. On September 30 the allied leaders capitulated to Hitler's demands. Chamberlain returned to London, claiming to have achieved "peace for our time,"[10] but the Munich agreement had disastrous results. Czechoslovakia was ruined by the accord. The Sudetenland was ceded to Germany, and Hitler seized the remainder of the country six months later. The anti-Nazi alliance was discredited, and the Soviets signed a nonaggression agreement with Germany in August 1939. With Hitler's invasion of Poland on September 1, 1939, World War II had begun, but England and France were now in a far more dangerous position.

After the British suffered traumatic defeats early in the war, Chamberlain's position became untenable. On May 10, 1940, he was finally replaced as prime minister by Winston Churchill, who had led a group of some forty British Conservative members of Parliament opposed to appeasement. Britain under Churchill displayed remarkable tenacity, managing to rescue its encircled army from the port of Dunkirk, standing alone against Hitler after the defeat of France and the Nazi occupation of western and central Europe, and withstanding German efforts to bomb the country into submission or to launch an invasion in the autumn of 1940. But despite Britain's courage and resolve and despite some 400,000 wartime deaths, the war was won only with the entry of the USSR and the United States.

Problems of Adjustment to the Postwar Era

During World War II Churchill maintained an extraordinarily close relationship with President Franklin D. Roosevelt. Together with Stalin, these leaders made crucial decisions determining the fate of entire countries and peoples. Britain thus appeared to emerge from the war as one of the Big Three victorious powers, working closely with the United States in creating key postwar institutions, including the United Nations, the World Bank, the International Monetary Fund, the General Agreement on Tariffs and Trade (GATT), and the North Atlantic Treaty Organization (NATO), and it was logical that Britain should take its place as one of the five permanent members of the UN Security Council.

Britain had maintained its status by virtue of its wartime role and the fact that it was still an imperial power and was at the head of a Commonwealth of more than 450 million people. However, although it seemed to be one of the world's great powers, the entire foundations of this status were crumbling. There were deep-seated internal and external reasons for this decline, which was to continue unabated for the next four decades.

First, the bases for Britain's strength were ebbing rapidly. The costs of the war had forced the liquidation of much of the country's income-producing assets. Britain was nearly bankrupt, and its economic situation became so perilous that the government implemented bread rationing in July 1946—something that it had not had to do during the entire war and that the minister of food had declared in 1939 to be "the last resort of a starving nation."[11] By the end of 1947 most important foods were rationed or controlled in some form, and rationing was not completely phased out until controls on meat and butter were lifted in July 1956. During the bitter winter of 1946–1947, the British government informed the United States that it could no longer afford to carry the burden of aiding Greece and Turkey, both of which were under serious pressure from the Soviet Union. This announcement provided an important catalyst for the Truman Doctrine, the Marshall Plan, and what soon became U.S. postwar leadership of the Western world, but the initial impetus for these actions stemmed from Britain's own decline.

Although the post-1945 Labour government did preside over the creation of a relatively successful welfare state, Britain's economic weakness was becoming more and more evident. In July 1947, under pressure from the United States, the British tried to implement immediate currency convertibility. The attempt was both premature and very costly, and convertibility had to be suspended just five weeks later. After a series of unsuccessful efforts to sustain its overvalued currency, Britain was finally forced to devalue sterling from $4.00 to $2.80 in September 1949.

Second, much of Britain's claim to world power had rested on the size and population of its empire. But in the postwar environment decolonization and the dissolution of empire came with remarkable rapidity. Although the British Empire had actually gained in territory and population as a result of World War I, acquiring control of areas in Africa that had been held by Germany and in the Middle East that had been under Ottoman rule, the edifice of empire was already being challenged in the interwar period. Nationalist pressures began to build in India, which had been the "jewel" in England's crown, and they would ultimately culminate in complete independence a generation later.

Decolonization began in South Asia, with India and Pakistan in 1947 and Burma (now Myanmar) and Ceylon (Sri Lanka) in 1948, and took place in Palestine (Israel) later in that year. The process accelerated in the late 1950s and early 1960s as former colonies in Africa and Asia gained their independence. Despite periods of violence, Britain largely avoided the costly and traumatic colonial wars of the kind that embroiled France in Indochina (1946–1954) and Algeria (1954–1962). The British also successfully transformed much of their empire into a voluntary Commonwealth association. This perpetuated links with newly independent countries, many of which maintained ties to the British legal, educational, and financial systems and retained the English language. The Commonwealth could not, however, take the place of the empire. Ironically, the symbolism of this transformation helped to mask the real decline in Britain's imperial power and to delay a necessary adjustment in Britain's world role. Certainly, the Commonwealth remained for some British politicians and the public an alternative to Europe.

Third, after the war the balance of power quickly shifted away from the countries of Europe and toward the U.S. and Soviet superpowers. By 1947, with the onset of the Cold War, Washington and Moscow became the key decisionmaking centers and London took on only a secondary importance as a key U.S. ally. Strategic military power was now based on continental-sized economies, populations, and armies and on increasingly vast nuclear arsenals. Although the British did develop their own nuclear capability (albeit with a degree of American cooperation), the UK lacked the size and resources of the United States or the USSR.

Fourth, the effect on Britain of the growing globalization of the international economy was increasingly evident from the 1960s onward. As their former adversaries and neighbors recovered from the ravages of war, the British increasingly found themselves straining to remain competitive with Germany and Japan and even with France and Italy. Reliance on ties to the Commonwealth, the fact that its political and economic system had survived the war, an antagonistic climate of relations between labor and management, and a tradition-bound culture all worked to retard Britain's adaptation to a rapidly changing international economy.

British leaders were especially slow to join the movement toward closer European unity. In the immediate postwar period, Winston Churchill, no longer prime minister but as head of the Conservative opposition, offered rhetorical support for the building of a united Europe. But he saw Britain as a great power on the level of the United States and the Soviet Union and as the head of important Commonwealth interests, and thus he conceived of Britain's role as that of sponsor or well-wisher, not full participant. The Labour government of Prime Minister Clement Attlee (1945–1951) was even less disposed to commit itself to Europe, particularly because it did not want to risk interference with its efforts to build a welfare state and managed economy. In early 1949 the French foreign minister, Robert Schuman, had approached Britain about the creation of an organization to place the key coal and steel industries of Western Europe under a common authority with supranational powers. Ultimately, this European Coal and Steel Community would become the nucleus of the European Common Market. British leaders, however, were unwilling to contemplate such a step, and when Schuman announced his proposal in May 1950 Attlee rejected the idea, objecting in particular to its preconditions that participant nations pool resources and consent to a binding authority.[12]

Despite seeming to have a more positive orientation toward Europe, Churchill and the Conservatives were no more willing than Labour to commit Britain to the European unity effort after they returned to office in November 1951. They thus refused to join the proposed, and ultimately abortive, European Defense Community of 1951–1954. Then, in 1955, they failed to recognize a historic turning point in the creation of Europe. Though they were invited to a June 1955 meeting in Messina, Italy, with the foreign ministers of France, Germany, Italy, and the Benelux countries to begin talks on establishing the European Common Market, the Conservative government sent only an observer from the Board of Trade (and withdrew him from the talks in November). Neither British political leaders nor the public seemed to appreciate that the Europeans were taking a profoundly important step toward merging their economies and developing important new political institutions. Indeed, the House of Commons paid almost no attention to the subject until July 1956, more than a year after the Messina talks had begun. Not only a widely held skepticism about European schemes but imperial nostalgia and the special relationship with the United States influenced these attitudes and choices. The effect was to retard Britain's adaptation both to the creation of an integrated Europe and to a globalizing world economy.

The Long Process of Adaptation

The reasons for Britain's imperial decline were deep-rooted and structural in the sense that they stemmed from underlying causes that could not readily be reversed by conscious policy decisions. Britain's slowness to adapt and to play a more active role in Europe was summed up by a former U.S. secretary of state, Dean Acheson, who said in December 1962 that Britain "has lost an empire and has not yet found a role." He observed, "The attempt to play a separate power role, that is, a role apart from Europe, a role based primarily on a 'special relationship' with the United States, a role based on being head of the Commonwealth . . . is about played out."[13]

The hesitation of British leaders to adapt to the country's diminished postimperial role was evident in the tenacity with which they had adhered to what Winston Churchill called the "three circles" concept, which most British leaders at least implicitly shared until at least the late 1950s.[14] Britain's international position was said to be unique because it was located at the intersection of three geopolitical groupings, or circles. The first circle was the Empire and Commonwealth, which it headed; the second was the United States, with which England had a "special relationship" in its role of intimate ally and senior adviser, or "Greece" to America's "Rome"; and then third was the European continent, to which Britain was related by geography and history.[15]

Both the three circles concept and the illusion that Britain could still act independently as a great world power received a stunning blow in the Suez crisis of 1956. During the summer of that year, after a series of hostile statements and threatening actions, President Gamal Abdel Nasser of Egypt nationalized the British-owned Suez Canal. Prime Minister Anthony Eden saw Nasser's seizure of the canal as a threat to Britain's vital interests and a danger to its sea routes to India and the Persian Gulf. In his suspicion of Nasser, Eden appeared to draw a parallel with the rise of Hitler, and he concluded that firm action rather than compromise or appeasement was required.

On October 31, 1956, after secretly coordinating measures with Israel, Britain and France launched a combined attack to regain control of the Suez Canal. Although the operation succeeded militarily, it was a political debacle for Britain and France. Amid widespread international criticism of the invasion, the United States and the Soviet Union both condemned the operation in the UN Security Council.

The Soviet leader, Nikita Khrushchev, went so far as to threaten missile attacks, and the Americans applied financial pressure at a time when the British pound was already seriously weakening on world markets and England was beginning to face fuel shortages brought on by closure of the canal. Under political and economic duress, the British and French governments capitulated, and on December 3 they announced that they would remove their forces from the canal region.

In the aftermath of this humiliation Prime Minister Eden resigned. He was replaced by Harold Macmillan. The entire Suez expedition had been a fiasco. It was evident that Britain no longer had the ability to carry out a major foreign intervention unilaterally and against the wishes of the United States. More than eleven years after the end of World War II and almost a decade after the start of the Cold War and the decolonization of India, it had become painfully apparent that Britain no longer possessed the capacity to act with the independence and autonomy of a great world power.

Imperial nostalgia, slowness to adapt to a rapidly changing world, and economic and social stagnation at home came under growing political attack within England. The process also unleashed major cultural ferment, as movies, plays, novels, and the arts took up these themes, for example, in the work of a group of playwrights and movie directors known as the "angry young men."

Conservative Prime Minister Harold Macmillan sought to adapt to Britain's declining power status. The most important of his initiatives was the 1961 application for membership in the European Common Market. The decision represented a radical departure from past British policy, which had been summed up in Churchill's phrase that Britain was "in but not of Europe." It was taken not only against the opposition of those Conservatives who preferred to emphasize the connection with the thirty-one other members of the Commonwealth or the tie with the United States but also in the face of the growing antagonism of the Labour Party, whose leader, Hugh Gaitskell, was to argue that the country must not turn its back on a thousand years of British history.

Ironically, after its long delay in coming to accept that it might act as part of Europe, Britain found the path to membership long and difficult. In January 1963 President Charles de Gaulle of France vetoed Britain's application on the grounds that it was not yet sufficiently European. Only a decade later, in 1973, after additional reversals and the resignation and death of de Gaulle, did Britain finally gain entry.

The veto provided yet another blow to Britain's prestige and morale, not least because of the growing realization that it had little choice. Its much-revered symbolic role as leader of the Commonwealth did not represent a viable alternative. The members of the Commonwealth had fewer interests in common than did the European nations, and most were finding other alternatives to their economic and political reliance on the UK. The grouping was too limited to encompass even Britain's full range of interests. In addition, though the United States still remained close, it was becoming increasingly clear that the United States preferred to see Britain inside the European Community rather than outside it. Moreover, closeness to the United States was no guarantee that Britain's needs would receive priority. For example, in December 1962 the Kennedy administration stunned the Macmillan government by canceling the Skybolt missile program upon which London had been basing the future development of its independent nuclear deterrent. As a hastily agreed alternative, the United States agreed to provide the Polaris submarine-launched missile. This arrangement provided additional evidence of Britain's dependence on the United States, and it was one of the elements leading to de Gaulle's veto a month later.

Throughout the 1960s and 1970s, Britain continued to suffer from a series of reversals at home and abroad, all pointing to the problem of decline and the difficulty of adaptation. Britain's economic performance and average annual growth rates continually lagged behind the performance of its competitors in Europe and Asia. The cumulative effect was that a country that had once had one of the highest per capita annual incomes in the world saw its comparative living standard decline to the level of Italy's over the course of a generation.

Part of the reason for lagging economic performance was attributable to the policies of "stop-go." Whenever Britain's economic growth rate began to accelerate, the country began to import goods at a faster rate, which threw the balance of trade and payments into a deepening deficit. But because both Conservative and Labour governments were determined to preserve the exchange rate of the pound, governments were often forced to tighten monetary or fiscal policies in order to slow the rate of growth, improve the balance of payments, and thereby ease pressure on the exchange rate. This policy choice was driven not only by economic considerations but by political ones. The pound was seen as a national symbol, and it was believed that devaluation would be taken as a sign of weakness. Many of the members of the Commonwealth were committed to maintaining their financial reserves in sterling rather than in dollars, and to devalue would be to break faith with the group of countries Britain claimed to lead.

In the end these efforts proved futile. In November 1967 Harold Wilson's government, which had spent three years defending the pound, was forced to devalue from a rate of $2.80 to $2.40. Only with the onset of floating exchange rates after 1971 did this issue finally become less of a drag on British economic performance, but by then the country had paid a huge cost in lost growth, and it had to withdraw British forces from "East of Suez" (the Persian Gulf, Malaysia, Singapore) from 1967–71.

Conflicts between government and the trade unions also adversely affected Britain's economy and its international role. For example, the Conservative government of Edward Heath, which had taken office in 1969, clashed bitterly with the miners' union during the most critical period of the 1973–1974 energy crisis. The confrontation and strike led to power blackouts and further damaged the economy. It also contributed to the Conservative defeat in the 1974 election, but Labour nevertheless inherited the continuing problem of maintaining full employment and a welfare state in the face of a competitive international marketplace, continuing pressure from the unions for higher wages, and work rules restricting employer flexibility in the use of labor.

Britain's weak economic performance, coupled with the global emergencies of 1973–74, left the country vulnerable to balance of payments problems and pressures on the exchange rate. Inflation ran as high as 26 percent in 1975. In a particularly humiliating moment in 1976, the Labour government was forced to seek a substantial loan from the International Monetary Fund and to accept reductions in its public spending as a condition for support.

Even with floating exchange rates, the onset of North Sea oil production (1.6 million barrels per day in 1979, or 80 percent of its oil consumption), and membership in the European Community, financial problems could not be avoided. In an increasingly globalized international economy, Britain was vulnerable to large and rapid capital movements. In October 1990, in recognition of the growing importance and priority for the country's European role, Britain joined the European Monetary System's Exchange Rate Mechanism (ERM), which linked the exchange rates of eleven of the European Community member countries. However, the huge internal costs of German unification and a large budget deficit in the Federal Republic led the German central bank (Bundesbank) to impose a steep interest rate increase in July 1992. These measures were taken for reasons internal to Germany, but they had an immediate impact on its neighbors, including Britain.

Higher interest rates attracted funds to Germany, where they could earn greater returns. This left Britain, France, Italy, and others facing unpleasant choices. Because the deutsche mark was not being revalued upward and because their membership in the ERM prevented them from allowing their exchange rates to float, they were forced to raise interest rates to keep their currencies from dropping below the ERM targets. These rate increases, however, dampened business investment and slowed their economies, thus increasing unemployment. At the same time, speculators began to sell these currencies and buy deutsche marks, betting that governments would eventually have to devalue in order to lower interest rates and restimulate their economies. The Bank of England and other European central banks were forced to intervene in exchange markets, committing huge sums in an ultimately futile effort to defend their currencies. In September 1992 Britain withdrew from the ERM and lowered its interest rates, but only after spending billions of pounds in the effort to keep sterling within the agreed rates of the ERM.[16]

In the military realm, at the beginning of the 1990s, and despite continuing defense expenditures equivalent to more than 4 percent of gross domestic product (GDP), a figure substantially greater than for

Germany (2 percent) or Japan (1 percent), Britain found it necessary to purchase the submarine-launched Trident missile from the United States.[17] This decision once again demonstrated the limits of Britain's independent nuclear deterrent and its degree of dependence upon the United States.

The Thatcher Era and the British Revival

In the British general election of October 1979 the Conservative Party, under the leadership of Margaret Thatcher, defeated the Labour government of Prime Minister James Callaghan. Thatcher stepped down after winning successive general elections in 1983 and 1987, and by the time her successor John Major was finally defeated by Tony Blair in May 1997,[18] the United Kingdom had experienced a profound change in its economy and society and in the means of dealing with the problem of decline.

The Thatcher era is best understood in contrast to the previous thirty-five years of postwar British governance. In 1945 the Labour Party under Clement Attlee defeated Churchill and the Conservatives. In the next five years Attlee and Labour went on to carry out a peaceful social revolution and to establish a comprehensive welfare state and managed economy. These measures helped to meet long-standing needs of the British public that had not been adequately provided for in the past. Labour also began the process of decolonization, which was carried through by the Conservatives after 1951, and it committed Britain to a firm alliance with the United States and NATO in the Cold War. A generation later, however, Britain's economy had become stagnant, its industries were uncompetitive, the relations between labor and business were embittered, its balance of payments was in chronic deficit, and its international stature was much reduced. The postwar prime ministers, Attlee, Churchill, Eden, Macmillan, Home, Wilson, Heath, and Callaghan, had managed Britain's decline but had been unable or unwilling to match the economic growth of Germany, France, and Japan or to arrest the erosion in Britain's relative standing in the world.

The statistics of Britain's economic performance in the postwar decades are especially revealing. In 1960 Britain's gross national product (GNP) per capita ($1,357) exceeded that of its leading European competitors, France ($1,336) and Germany ($1,300), and was nearly three times that of Japan ($463). Just twenty years later, however, in 1980, Germany ($13,410) and France ($12,300) had far surpassed the UK ($9,080), and even Japan ($9,400) had edged ahead.[19] This remarkable change was the cumulative effect of different economic growth rates. For example, from 1960 to 1973 real GNP per capita increased in Germany by an annual average of 4.8 percent, in France by 5.7 percent, and in Japan by 10.5 percent. By contrast, the figure for Britain was just 3.2 percent. In the 1970s the British performance was even worse: From 1971 to 1981 its growth averaged a mere 1.4 percent per year, compared with 2.5 percent in Germany, 3.1 percent in France, and 4.8 percent in Japan.[20]

In contemplating this dreary performance, and following the ideas of her influential adviser Keith Joseph as well as those of free market economists such as Friedrich von Hayek and Milton Friedman, Thatcher was determined to remake both the Conservative Party and the country. In doing so, she broke with the long tradition of Tory paternalism that previous leaders of her party had embodied.[21] Slowly at first and then with increasing momentum after her reelection in 1983, she implemented sweeping measures of privatization and deregulation, reduced taxation, and cut government spending.[22] Among the watersheds during her years in power were the denationalization of huge and inefficient enterprises, particularly British Telecom and British Steel, and their ultimate transformation into efficient and competitive enterprises, and the "Big Bang" (massive deregulation of Britain's financial sector in the City of London). Before being ousted in late 1990 by Conservative members of Parliament opposed to her rigid personality and in some cases to her policies, she had achieved a revolution. Under her successor, John Major, and then Tony Blair after Labour took power in May 1997, the changes begun by Margaret Thatcher brought substantial improvements in economic productivity, competitiveness, and employment. As evidence of this, by early

1999 the unemployment rate in the UK was 6.3 percent, far below the figures for her principal European competitors, Germany (10.5 percent), France (11.5 percent), and Italy (12.0 percent).[23]

Thatcher's foreign policy also reflected a more assertive and nationalistic approach than that of her immediate predecessors. The most dramatic event took place in April 1982, when Argentine dictator General Leopoldo Galtieri sent troops to seize control of the Falkland Islands. This territory, 400 miles off Argentina's Atlantic coast, had been the subject of periodic controversy but had been under British sovereignty since 1833. Although both the UN Security Council and the European Community condemned the invasion, their resolutions did not carry any means of returning the islands to Britain. Instead, Thatcher reacted assertively, dispatching a naval task force 8,000 miles to the South Atlantic, where, in late May and June after several weeks of sometimes heavy fighting, the British retook the islands. The dramatic British intervention provided a powerful demonstration that British foreign policy could involve more than an unremitting retreat from the outposts and bases of the old empire. Moreover, the Falklands War provided an unexpected stimulus to Thatcher's popularity after her difficult first years as prime minister. In 1983 she and her Conservative Party won a decisive reelection against Labour under the inept leadership of Michael Foot (whose election manifesto came to be described as the longest political suicide note in history).

In Europe, Britain under Thatcher continued to act as a close partner of the United States, supporting the U.S. deployment of Pershing II missiles in 1983 to offset Soviet SS-20s in Eastern Europe and providing air bases for the Reagan administration's reprisal against Libya in 1986. Britain did not uncritically support the United States, however. In 1983 the Thatcher government did not support the U.S. military intervention in Grenada. More important, it opposed the Reagan administration's attempts to block construction of a natural gas pipeline from the Soviet Union to Western Europe. When the United States sought to impose restraints on foreign subsidiaries of U.S. firms and even on European companies holding U.S. licenses, British officials condemned the measures as an "unacceptable extension of

American extraterritorial jurisdiction."[24] Thatcher explicitly rejected the Reagan effort to halt the construction, observing, "I feel very strongly that once you have made a deal you ought to keep it."[25]

Thatcher was, however, quick to take a firm stance against Iraq after Saddam Hussein's forces invaded Kuwait on August 2, 1990. She urged a strong policy upon President George Bush, and British armored forces and aircraft played an active military role in Operations Desert Shield and Desert Storm.

Thatcher's nationalism and her opposition to state intervention in the economy led her to take an increasingly uncompromising position against efforts to deepen and extend the European Union (EU). During the period of her prime ministership she pressed aggressively for a readjustment of Britain's contribution to the European Community budget, criticized the Brussels bureaucracy, and fought an increasingly strident campaign within the Conservative Party against those favoring closer integration with Europe. In a widely cited October 1988 speech she said, "We have not successfully rolled back the frontiers of the state in Britain only to see them reimposed at the European level with a European superstate exercising a new dominance from Brussels."[26]

Thatcher's successor, John Major, continued many of her policies, though he projected a softer style. Nonetheless, on Europe he maintained her legacy, refusing to join with eleven other countries of the EU in establishing European Monetary Union or to adopt the euro as a common currency. Attitudes toward Europe emerged as one of the issues in the May 1997 election that returned Labour to power after eighteen years of Conservative rule. Ironically, one embittered pro-European Conservative attributed the party's 1997 electoral debacle to its anti-European stance and blamed Margaret Thatcher, criticizing the policy of "Euro-rejectionism" as "based on a mixture of arrogance, self-indulgence, and self deception."[27]

When Tony Blair took office Britain was on the verge of relinquishing Hong Kong, its last significant vestige of empire. At midnight on June 30, 1997, the colony reverted to China, ending an era of British rule that had begun in 1842.

Blair and "New Labor" had won a huge electoral victory, but the new prime minister did not seek to reverse the course set by the preceding Conservative governments. Instead, having fought successfully to change long-standing Labour Party policies, Blair's government continued and even accelerated programs favoring modernization, adaptation, and competitiveness. Blair called this new orientation for both Britain and the Labour Party the "Third Way." Though he only vaguely defined the term, it designated a desire to move beyond, in Blair's own words, "an old left preoccupied by state control, high taxation and producers' interests and a new laissez-faire right championing narrow individualism and a belief that free markets are the answer to every problem."[28] The change in Labour's orientation marked the culmination of a struggle that had begun when Hugh Gaitskell sought to remove the commitment to nationalization (Clause Four) from the Labour Party's constitution before his death in 1963.

As Samuel Beer observed, both Thatcher and Blair embraced a type of liberalism that broke with deep-seated and relatively collectivist party traditions. Thatcher rejected Tory paternalism, with its roots in traditional concepts of deference and noblesse oblige. Blair has moved away from the Labour Party's commitment to socialism and the values of a more organic and communitarian society. Both emphasized the rights of the individual, and Blair stressed not the older Labour and socialist ideals of equality of condition but the liberal ideal of equality of opportunity.[29]

Under both Major and Blair Britain also continued to play a leading role at the United Nations as one of the five permanent members of the Security Council. This activism was evident in its active participation in seeking solutions to the Bosnian problem (1992–1998) and in its support for U.S. efforts to enforce Iraqi compliance with the UN weapons inspection regime. But Britain's long-standing hesitation about deeper integration with Europe reduced the influence it might otherwise have been able to bring to bear. For example, the Thatcher government had only limited influence in shaping the arrangements for Germany at the end of the Cold War, and the Blair government found itself playing an awkward role when it held the EU presidency and had to preside at meetings to decide on arrangements for the European Monetary System and the euro.

Britain's half-century of withdrawal from empire was also marked by a distinctive shift in trading patterns toward Europe and the United States. Whereas in 1956 only 25 percent of British trade had been with Europe and just 9 percent with the United States, by 1996 Europe's proportion had doubled to more than 51 percent, and that of the United States had climbed to 12.4 percent. (See Table 2.3.) What is remarkable about these numbers is that despite the huge increase in Asian economic activity during this thirty-year period, and even before the economic crisis of 1997–1998, Asia's share of British trade actually dropped by a third, from 21.3 percent in 1956 to just 14.2 percent in 1996. The evidence of these numbers is that postimperial Britain has become much more European and Atlantic.

These data are also increasingly reflected in British attitudes. A March 1998 Gallup Poll revealed that although 70 percent of the public took pride in the fact that Britain had once had a great empire, 50 percent said Europe was now most important to Britain; 25 percent, the United States; and fewer than 20 percent, the Commonwealth.[30]

Conclusion:
Britain in the Twenty-First Century

Britain's twentieth-century saga provides a remarkable tale of decline and renewal. Its economic and political power eroded through most of the century, and rejuvenation came only in the final decade-and-a-half. After a long and difficult transition, Britain has achieved major economic change and at the same time has adapted to the end of empire, maintained selective conventional and nuclear capacities, skillfully played an influential diplomatic role in Europe and at the United Nations, and maintained the special relationship with the United States.

The roles of Thatcher and Blair exemplify Marx's dictum that "men make their own history, but they do not make it just as they please."[31] These British leaders, acting within inherited constraints, made fundamental choices in their parties and as prime ministers. In doing so,

TABLE 2.3   British Trade With Major World Regions (percentage of British Trade)

	1956	1996
European Union	25.2	51.2
United States	9.1	12.4
Asia	21.3	14.2
Rest of World	44.4	22.2

(Trade equals merchandise imports plus exports.)

Source: Data from IMF and British Board of Trade, as reported in *The Economist*, 3 January, 1998, p. 56.

they benefited from the British electoral system, which turned their electoral pluralities into huge parliamentary majorities. This gave them more freedom to implement their policies than U.S. presidents and many European and Japanese leaders enjoy.

On the eve of the twenty-first century, Britain's trajectory is much more promising than might have been anticipated at any time in the first eight decades of the twentieth century. Language and culture, economic vitality and competitiveness, a prominent (albeit grudging) role in the large and developing European Union, a robust special relationship with the United States, an active and important presence as a permanent member of the UN Security Council, a power projection capacity by virtue of its ability to dispatch small but well-trained military forces to distant locations, the international influence afforded by both a nuclear deterrent and a long tradition of adroit diplomacy—all have enabled Britain to adapt better than many of its midsized competitors. Germany, France, and Japan might have been expected to be more dominant, but all of them face persistent internal problems (France and Germany are carrying large, expensive welfare states and face regulatory barriers to economic adaptation; Japan suffers from governmental or bureaucratic paralysis and stalemated economic policies).

In a century of imperial decline, the elements of this remarkable renewal have been diverse, and they include more than economic rejuvenation. In part, despite the loss of an empire, Britain was able to sustain an important international role by virtue of its language and culture. The late-twentieth-century U.S.-led revolution in information technology has made English even more globally ubiquitous than at the height of the Cold War. The computer revolution, the Internet, satellite communications, and the global spread of trends in the media, entertainment, and mass culture have combined to give English an unprecedented international reach as *the* international lingua franca on the threshold of the twenty-first century. A small but telling example of this was evident in the first meeting of Germany's newly elected Chancellor Gerhard Schröder and President Jacques Chirac of France: They found themselves having to communicate in English, their only common language.[32]

Britain's role in creating the post–World War II international institutions has guaranteed it a place among the major powers, most obviously as one of the five permanent members of the UN Security Council. Moreover, any calculation of power involves not only an absolute but a comparative dimension, and Britain has benefited in its relative standing from circumstances limiting the comprehensive strengths of its major competitors. By dint of the still enduring legacy of World War II, Japan and Germany remain to some degree inhibited in exerting the kind of international influence their economic strength, population, and historical weight would otherwise suggest, and neither possesses the nuclear weaponry nor the power projection capacity that continue to give Britain an international influence in strategic and military realms. Britain's special relationship with the United States also has proved to be more durable than seemed to be possible just a generation ago. This too has stemmed from multiple causes: the British willingness and ability to cooperate with the United States across a wide range of foreign policy issues, the assets the British still retain, the inability of the European Union ("dithering and indecisive," in Tony Blair's words[33]) successfully to create an effective common foreign and security policy as an alternative to U.S. leadership, the lack of other powers able to play this role across the full range of issues, and the durable commonalities of language and history.

Finally, though it was far from obvious for most of the century, the British themselves have proved, after all, to be skillful at preserving and adapting their assets. In 1900, at the dawn of the twentieth century, Britain's leaders saw their national interest bound up in sustaining the country's unsurpassed but vulnerable imperial role. This had led them into rivalries with their European imperial competitors in Africa and dictated determined efforts to maintain the passage to India, control of the Suez Canal, long-standing commitments in the Persian Gulf, and a series of far-flung imperial outposts. In the two world wars, the British found themselves fighting bloody and exhausting struggles to prevent the domination of the European continent by a hostile power that threatened both their vital interests and even, in the case of Nazi Germany, their national existence. The human and economic toll of those wars, together with the economic stagnation of the interwar period, left Britain ill-equipped to face the post-1945 world. With the gradual liquidation of the empire in the postwar years, however, Britain's definition of its interests slowly but steadily changed, a change symbolized, for example, by its withdrawal from most of its outposts "East of Suez" after 1970.

For an entire generation—encompassing the third quarter of the century, essentially until after the coming to power of Margaret Thatcher in 1979—Britain experienced a steady decline in its world role and competitiveness. During this period the British relinquished virtually the entire empire that had given them global stature; they saw their economic growth and wealth fall behind those of Japan and their chief European competitors; and they were slow to engage both a burgeoning European unity and an increasingly globalized international economy.

Yet on the edge of the twenty-first century, Britain managed to stabilize its global role, rejuvenate its economy, achieve an effective presence within the European Union, and reassert a more active and confident international presence as one of the world's half-dozen leading powers. In effect, under the Conservative prime ministerships of Thatcher and Major and then under the New Labour leadership of Blair, the British redefined their national interest. They now saw their national interest increasingly in terms of adapting Britain to compete successfully in a globalized world economy, while at the same time streamlining the welfare state and altering or even discarding features of British politics, economy, and society that no longer served their purpose. Not all these changes were without risk. For example, the

Blair government set in motion a process of devolution for Scotland and Wales in order to reduce governmental centralization and to provide for local autonomy in these once-independent lands. However, there is a distinct risk that rather than satisfying local desires and undercutting the pro-independence Scottish National Party (SNP), devolution could ultimately create momentum for the full-fledged independence of Scotland and its 5 million people. The future of Wales and its 3 million inhabitants might also then become uncertain, and with possible changes in Ulster's relationship to the Irish Republic, the existing United Kingdom, with its population of 59 million people, might ultimately be reduced to the land area of England alone and a population of fewer than 50 million.

Overall, Britain in the twentieth century experienced the subtle interplay of divergent influences: its position in the global arena, its own location and intrinsic characteristics, and the evolution of its society and economy. These were mediated (both well and badly) by its leaders and most-influential figures, particularly David Lloyd George, Neville Chamberlain, Winston Churchill, John Maynard Keynes, Clement Attlee, Harold Macmillan, Harold Wilson, Edward Heath, Keith Joseph, Margaret Thatcher, and Tony Blair. Indeed, two of the three most recent prime ministers have been among the most successful of the century. Thatcher, notwithstanding her faults, has been described by *The Economist* as "Britain's outstanding peacetime leader of the twentieth century."[34] And though his record has been far more brief, Tony Blair has had one of the most auspicious beginnings of a British head of government in several decades.

The British experience provides an object lesson in political economy on the grand scale: Outcomes are shaped by the interplay of both politics and economics. Those who would dwell on only one of these dimensions at the expense of the other cannot hope to gain a full understanding of what has taken place; nor can they appreciate the probable future course that Britain is poised to take in the twenty-first century.

3

❖

FRANCE

Two Obsessions
for One Century

STANLEY HOFFMANN

A S THE NINETEENTH CENTURY CAME TO A CLOSE, France had two dominant worries as an actor on the world stage. It has the same two worries a century later. One is Germany, which in 1871 had achieved unity as a nation by defeating France and annexing Alsace and part of Lorraine. The other, a related but wider and less precise concern, is the fear of decline, a fear that pervaded the writings of Maurice Barrès and the ideology of the Far Right and prodded the "anxious patriotism" of young men such as Charles de Gaulle (born in 1890). The complicated story of French foreign policy from 1898 is the story of the strategies French leaders have followed to deal with its powerful neighbor to the east and with the forces threatening France's rank and status in the world.

In 1898 France was one of the major players in world affairs. Being both an Atlantic and a Mediterranean power, it had built a mighty navy. The presence of a powerful and often hostile Germany on its eastern border—a border with no natural barriers—had a double effect on French policy. France was demographically weaker than Germany and was afflicted by a falling birthrate. After its defeat in the War of 1870–1871 it had instituted compulsory military service in order to build as vast an army as possible. And because Germany had encouraged the young Third Republic to compensate for its defeat not by seeking revenge against a formidable rival but by overseas expansion, France had become the second-largest colonial empire. Just as Berlin had hoped, France repeatedly clashed with the largest, Britain, from Egypt to Fashoda.

Though France was only the fourth industrial power—after Britain, the United States, and Germany—in the last years of the nineteenth century it had entered an era of growth, with increasing industrial investments, production, and prosperity. Thanks to abundant resources of coal and steel and an agriculture that employed more than 40 percent of the active population, France could congratulate itself on its "equilibrium"—even though agricultural productivity was poor and protectionism had deprived rural France of any pressure to modernize. Although it was not self-sufficient, France was less dependent on foreign trade than were Britain and Germany and was therefore less eager to conquer markets or to invest abroad. Most of its investments were political, aimed, for instance, at bolstering France's ally Russia. (After the Kaiser "dropped the pilot"—that is, Bismarck—he had clumsily allowed Russia to fall into France's eager arms.) France was also blessed with a homogeneous population: a mix of ethnic groups (recently replenished by abundant immigration from Italy) blended in a melting pot of assimilation and national integration as powerful as that of the United States. There were a few autonomists left in Brittany and Corsica, but most Corsicans sought jobs in continental France, and Breton peasants pushed their children into schools where they would learn in French, not Breton patois.

These intrinsic factors meant that the France of the beginning of this century had to be doubly vigilant: Its German neighbor was no longer ruled by Bismarck, who, having unified his country, for twenty years played an acrobatic game aimed not only at averting an anti-German coalition but also at preserving peace in Europe. And it needed to protect its far-flung empire, particularly the most precious part of it, Algeria, which was, administratively, carved into three French *départements*. The two worries merged when Wilhelm II decided to challenge French ambitions in Morocco.

France had the good fortune of being able to face these worries with a political and social system that had many flaws but, on balance, provided far more strength than weakness. The parliamentary Republic suffered from a rather chaotic party system—the only truly organized one was the Socialist Party, which achieved its unity only around 1905—and consequently from brief, shaky, and weak coalition cabinets. But the Radical Party—another twentieth century creation, far less disciplined than the Socialists—was the balance wheel of the regime until 1940. It stayed almost constantly in power by shifting alliances with the Left and the Right. Tensions between the urban proletariat and the vast constellation of French bourgeois and petits bourgeois were often violent, but the bulk of French industry was made of small and middle-size firms whose personnel was barely unionized. The working class, for all its distrust of bourgeois political institutions—a distrust that the dominant union, the Confederation Generale du Travail (CGT), turned into a dogma—nevertheless voted for political parties that were fervently Republican.

This, indeed, was one of the two great strengths of France: It had a political regime that enjoyed the broad support of the both the peasants and the workers. The peasants appreciated both the right to vote and the social stability provided by the Republic. And the great Socialist leader Jean Jaurès reminded the workers of all they owed the regime: political freedom, the vote, and free primary education. In less than thirty years the Republic had produced a broad consensus around a liberal, lay democracy, largely through its "lay missionaries," the school teachers. To be sure, its militant anticlericalism (revived by the Alfred Dreyfus case), its liberal and democratic principles, and its weak system of government were an anathema to much of the Right, which included a significant part of the bourgeoisie and (mainly urban) petite bourgeoisie.

But France's second strength was that both Republicans and non-Republicans (that is, Monarchists and temperamental Bonapartists) shared one overriding value: patriotism. There was a handful of "antipatriots" on the Far Left. And some on the Far Right, notably around the shrill anti-Republican and nationalistic newspaper *L'Action Française* of Charles Maurras, denounced the Left, especially the Socialists, for being insufficiently patriotic, too eager for a transnational proletarian peace, and too critical of the excesses of colonialism. But almost all agreed on the duty of national defense, on the duty to protect the French nation from invasion and aggression. The counterrevolutionaries who still deplored the Revolution of 1789 had after 1880 become nationalists; the heirs of the Revolution had always been intensely patriotic. And so the schools of the Republic as well as the private schools run by the Catholics all injected into their young charges a fervent love of *la patrie*, strong enough, when challenged from abroad, to overcome social and ideological divisions, as French behavior in 1914 demonstrated.

The fear of Germany and the fear of decline converged sufficiently to suggest a diplomatic strategy to much of the French political class, and certainly to the Quai d'Orsay: creating a coalition capable of containing Germany and of checkmating the Austro-German alliance. Russia had already been enlisted. After Fashoda, and thanks to the Kaiser's blunders and Admiral Alfred von Tirpitz's challenge to British naval supremacy, the British moved closer to France, concluded the Entente Cordiale, and supported Paris against Berlin in the two Moroccan crises of 1905 and 1911. This strategy of containment and deterrence was not without its critics, mainly on the Left. If we leave aside the Socialist hope that peace would be forced upon the rival governments by an alliance of the French and German proletariats, the alternative strategy was to accommodate and effect a reconciliation with Germany (this strategy was popular in some business and financial circles). Before 1914 the main champion of this last strategy was the Radical Joseph Caillaux; but the concessions he made to the Germans in 1911 were unpopular both in Parliament and in the country, and between 1911 and 1914 there was something of a nationalist revival among the young. In reaction against Caillaux's "appeasement" of the Germans, Raymond Poincaré, a statesman from Lorraine who saw Germany as the main threat to France's security and status, was elected president in 1912. It was not the last time that those two alternative strategies would clash.

Between Grandeur and Decadence
(1914–1939)

Rather than discussing only the turning points, I will mention also the turning periods that brought major changes to France's situation, policies, and key worries.

The first such period is that of World War I. After the murder of Archduke Ferdinand in Sarajevo, the French government had to decide whether to back its Russian ally, whose determination to stop Austria-Hungary from destroying Serbia risked igniting a war between the two rival alliances, or whether to try to hold Russia back. We do not know what Poincaré told the tsar and his ministers when he visited St. Petersburg in July 1914, but it is clear that France's leaders put the preservation of the Russian alliance first among France's priorities. Despite Jaurès's pleas that peace be given every possible chance, the nation rallied behind the view that those responsible for the crisis were the two central European empires: Austria-Hungary because of its provocative ultimatum to Serbia and Germany because of its support for Vienna. The French felt that the war, when it came, was a just war of national defense and that any other policy would have made Germany the hegemon in Europe and ended France's alliance system. After Jaurès was assassinated by a nationalist, his party joined the "sacred union" around *la patrie*. France's performance during that atrocious war was nothing short of extraordinary. Even though the main industrial areas of the north and northeast were occupied by the Germans, France provided arms for its own forces and for those of Britain and later the United States. Even though French casualties were huge and French top commanders were often foolish, France bore the brunt of the fighting, at least until the arrival of the U.S. army. Even though parliamentarism showed its familiar flaws, when the national consensus showed signs of strains—exhausted soldiers mutinied in early 1917 after the monstrous losses at Verdun, some Socialists regretted their choice of nation over class in 1914 and turned their eyes toward events in Russia, and Caillaux and a few other politicians began to consider peace by compromise—Parliament turned and gave full powers to the formidable Georges Clemenceau. Poincaré and Clemenceau, former adversaries, cooperated for France's victory.

France's situation after the war was a delicate and perilous mix of highly visible strengths and dangerous weaknesses under the glittering surface. On the one hand, France was now the dominant power on the continent. It had achieved its revanche: Alsace-Lorraine was French again. Germany was partly dismembered, disarmed, and in political turmoil. A newly independent Poland was a protégé of France, which helped it ward off a Bolshevik invasion. France had new allies among the new states of central and southeastern Europe. Not without creating sharp tensions with its British allies, France expanded its empire by obtaining a mandate over Syria and Lebanon, as well as over parts of the former German empire.

On the other hand, France's victory had been incredibly costly. With almost 1.5 million soldiers killed, France's demographic situation had worsened drastically. The French currency had been weakened by the huge costs of war and reconstruction. Reflecting on the spectacle of the colonial powers fighting each other and inspired by the Russian Revolution, nationalists raised their heads and their hopes in various parts of the empire from Morocco, where the French had to fight bloody battles, to Indochina. The two national anxieties had not vanished: Germany was wounded, not seriously enough to cease being a threat but seriously enough to want to undo the indignities of the Versailles Treaty, which had blamed Berlin for the war. The first test of strength went badly for France. Its occupation of the Ruhr in 1923, caused by German procrastination over reparations, failed both because of German resistance and because there was little outside support for France. Indeed, the lesson both of the Great War and of such subsequent events as the Versailles negotiations and the Ruhr affair was that France could not achieve its national goals alone. At Versailles Woodrow Wilson and David Lloyd George had resisted

French pleas that Germany be dismembered. Clemenceau's alternative—an iron-clad security guarantee from London and Washington—sank along with Wilson. In the 1920s the French found that the British and American business interests were more eager to help the German economy than to extract reparations from it. Furthermore, the British refused to guarantee the borders of the states east of Germany or to turn the League of Nations into an effective instrument for collective security against eventual German aggression. France was diplomatically worse off than it had been in 1912 or 1913. Its Russian ally was gone, replaced by a Bolshevik regime that denounced all capitalist states, tried at first to foment revolution abroad, and when this failed, switched to a policy of "Socialism in one country." Socialism in Russia turned out to be compatible with a rapprochement with Germany, thus demonstrating that a power could be both verbally revolutionary and effectively revisionist and that revisionist powers gravitate toward each other. Italy, which had become a French ally in World War I, was disgruntled by its failure to gain support for its expansionary plans after 1918, and when Mussolini seized power he joined the revisionist camp. Britain, axiomatically playing its old balancing game, seemed more worried by French continental predominance than by the possibility of an eventual German revival. The only reliable French allies—in Eastern Europe—were liabilities: They added little strength to France's and created obligations that could become a drain on France's strength.

France had become a status quo power. Preserving the status quo, however, required resources that France no longer had. At the systemic level, the containment of Germany—or a policy aimed at obliging Berlin to carry out the provisions of Versailles concerning Germany's borders, disarmament, and reparations—required a coalition that France could not assemble without the two major powers that were on leave, the United States and the USSR. Above all, the internal determinants of French behavior were no longer a plus and in fact had become a huge minus. The population was exhausted by its effort and its losses, and veterans associations proclaimed the motto "Never again." The regime continued to demonstrate its flaws, but this was a period that required strong governments to deal with financial and diplomatic troubles. The broad Republican consensus was being weakened by a new Communist Party that ate into the Socialists' working-class electorate and by various new fascist parties and leaders on the Right. The Communists heaped scorn on all the symbols of patriotism: the army, the flag, the empire. The fascists posed as nationalists but asserted that the defense of the nation's interests required an authoritarian regime.

Thus it is not surprising that from the 1920s until Hitler's ascent to power France seemed to oscillate between two policies. One—represented by Poincaré—was aimed at keeping Germany down, at putting security above the disarmament of the victors that had been conditionally promised at Versailles, at squeezing reparations from Berlin. It ran into two formidable obstacles: the lack of external support, and the effects of the Great Depression on Germany (effects that Chancellor Heinrich Brüning in particular skillfully used to resist French demands). The other policy, pursued by Aristide Briand, aimed at a reconciliation with Germany through accommodation on reparations, an early evacuation of the territories occupied by France, and a quick return of the Saar to Germany. But opinion was not ready for this "appeasement" (a word Briand was the first to use). And though Briand's strategy used reconciliation as a means to achieve French security—in France's weakened circumstances—some of Briand's allies, such as Senator Pierre Laval, were more willing to concede primacy in Europe to Germany if this was the price to be paid for avoiding another war.

Hitler's rise to power, his hypernationalism, and his onslaught on the Versailles Treaty and on democracy ought to have strengthened the advocates of containing and deterring Germany, which was now officially bent on revanche and on destroying the post-1918 European order. For a brief period Foreign Minister Jean-Louis Barthou tried to galvanize France's allies, to improve relations with Italy, and to begin a rapprochement with Russia. But he was murdered in 1934 along with Yugoslavia's king, and this was the end of the policy of resistance. Pierre Laval, who succeeded Barthou, courted Benito Mussolini by promising to let him have a part of Ethiopia, and he signed a mutual aid pact with Moscow—but signally failed to implement it.

What happened was a nefarious combination of unfavorable systemic and internal factors. At the systemic level, any French attempt at "encircling" Nazi Germany would run into two obstacles. Mussolini—worried by Hitler's designs on Austria—might have joined a coalition if he had been given his way on Ethiopia, but there the logic of balancing power collided with the logic of collective security: The former designated Hitler as the main threat to the system; the latter required resistance to aggression by anyone. Britain and France went far enough in following the League principles to alienate Mussolini, but not far enough to defeat him. The second obstacle was the fact that Russia was an embarrassment as a potential ally: It was as much a revolutionary, totalitarian power as was Nazi Germany. That fact would not have stopped the kings of France from seeking Russia's help against Hitler, as Colonel de Gaulle told his worried, devout mother, but it did give pause both to the British and to the French center and Right. Moreover, some of France's Eastern allies saw Russia (even a non-Communist Russia) as a threat. Poland, especially, feared Russia and sought a rapprochement with Hitler. With weak or dubious allies on Hitler's other front, France was left with only one strong partner, Britain. But Britain's policy, alas, consisted of putting the brakes on France and trying to appease Hitler.

I have mentioned the distrust of the Soviet Union among the French political class. In the worst imaginable domestic conditions, France was facing the colossal threat of a fanaticized Germany. France suffered from a conjunction of acute (interstate) war fatigue and intense internal strife. The Republic was plagued by corruption and by a collective inability to deal with the effects of the depression in terms other than Hoover-like, deflationary orthodoxy, which failed. At the same time, an increasingly antiparliamentary radicalized Right had rioted and threatened the regime in February 1934. The result was a swing to the Left in the elections of 1936, but the Popular Front government of Léon Blum was partly incapacitated by the division on economic policy between Socialists and Radicals and was faced with the rabid hostility of the Right. Hence this drama: A profound pacifism prevailed among at least half the members of the Socialist Party, among many Radicals, and in the non-Communist unions. To that, one now had to add the conversion to a policy of appeasement of a great part of the previously patriotic and anti-German Right, both parliamentary, like the party of Pierre Etienne Flandin, the foreign minister of early 1936, or antiparliamentary, like L'Action Française.

The conversion of the Right was often rationalized as having been dictated by French weakness (especially its demographic weakness). Yet it was primarily dictated by a desire to finish off the domestic adversaries of the Right—the Socialists and Communists—and to introduce a dose of authoritarianism into the regime before, perhaps, confronting Hitler. Unlike in pre-1914 France, class struggle this time did affect opinions on foreign affairs profoundly, and the representatives of the working class, in its parties and unions, were themselves split by pacifism and by anticommunism (especially in unions whose leadership had recently been taken over by Communists).

The fear of a new war, the conviction among the workers that preparing for it could jeopardize the social conquests of the Popular Front (for example, by increasing the workload again), the worry among many bourgeois that a second war could lead to a French version of the Russian revolution—all of this was bad enough. The old patriotism that had led to the "sacred union" of 1914 was dead (pacifism was especially strong among schoolteachers).

To make matters worse, though it was impressive in parades, the French army was—so to speak—a drag. It had drawn from the Great War one overriding lesson: "Fire kills," and a defensive posture was best. This coincided with the mood of the country and led to the building of the Maginot Line, but it stood in firm contradiction to the imperative of protecting Hitler's potential victims in the east and in Belgium, that is, of being able to save France's continental allies. Moreover, France's corps of professional soldiers was meant only to train and to lead the conscripts, which in turn meant that in a crisis there was no stance between passivity and quasi-general mobilization. Finally, not only was there no *armée de métier* (professional army), despite de Gaulle's argument for it, but the leadership grievously underestimated the role of tanks and planes.

All of this accounts for France's diplomatic decline from 1933 on. There was a turning point: the German reoccupation of the

Rhineland in 1936. A weak French government, on the eve of legislative elections, followed the "English governess." It proclaimed that it wouldn't allow German guns to threaten Strasbourg, but it essentially did nothing because the military chiefs said they could stop the rather meager German forces Hitler had sent toward the French border only by a huge mobilization. This demonstration of impotence threw Belgium back into neutrality. The Popular Front governments of Blum and Edouard Daladier had the sense to begin rearmament, but they were so handicapped by the factors I have described that they pursued appeasement: They failed to intervene in the Spanish civil war, and they betrayed their Czech ally at the Munich conference. In both cases British pressure (as it had in the Rhineland crisis) and domestic divisions prevailed over the realistic analysis of the French heads of government. They had no illusions about Hitler. And yet it was only after Munich that Blum became willing to confront the pacifists in his party, and Daladier was saddled with a foreign minister, Georges-Etienne Bonnet, who was not an appeaser by necessity like himself but an appeaser by conviction à la Laval.

Hitler's brazen violation of the Munich agreements and his destruction of Czechoslovakia in March 1939 put an end to the diplomacy of appeasement. Britain and France committed themselves to the protection of Poland, but that very commitment, and all the domestic factors already listed, made an alliance with the Soviet Union almost impossible. Desultory negotiations in Moscow ended when Stalin, via Vyacheslav Molotov, signed his fateful pact with Hitler, via Joachim von Ribbentrop, and thus sealed the fate of Poland and of the Baltic states. France had failed to stop either the huge internal and external increase of German power or Hitler's destruction of the order of Versailles.

Falling, Rising, Stumbling, Leaping (1940–1958)

I now come to another crucial turning period: that of World War II. France's crushing defeat in five weeks (indeed, militarily in less than a week); the humiliating terms of the Armistice; the division of the country into a zone annexed by Germany, an area under German occupation representing more than half of the metropolitan territory, and an area left to French rule—all of this represented the nadir of the French nation-state. With more than 1.5 million soldiers in German prisoner of war camps, the new French regime in Vichy was left with only two assets: its fleet, which it felt was more threatened by its British ex-ally than by the Germans, and its empire (but Indochina was quickly put under de facto Japanese "protection"). The Republic committed hara-kiri and transferred power to a coalition of defeated and aging soldiers and of appeasers led by Laval. For all intents and purposes, one of the great powers had become a satellite of Hitler.

The story of the two Frances of 1940–1944 has been told too often to be repeated here.[1] It is only necessary to remind the reader that in the beginning there was a paradox. The regime that enjoyed the support of the great majority of a shell-shocked population (10 million took to the roads to flee the invaders) embraced an unpopular policy of "collaboration" with a ruthless and contemptuous victor. Different yet convergent calculations led to the collaboration: For some, like General Maxime Weygand, it was a way of slowly rebuilding strength so as to carry some weight in case of a deadlocked war or in case of a final German victory; for others, like Laval, it was a way of minimizing German wrath and, perhaps, of being allowed to get a small share of the spoils. The two calculations converged on resignation to loss of status. De Gaulle, an almost unknown rebel with no power other than his lucidity and will, claimed—from London—that he was the legitimate voice of France. His mission was nothing less than the restoration of France's power, integrity, and status, even though he was, objectively, as dependent on Winston Churchill's good will as Vichy's premier Philippe Pétain was on Hitler's.

Vichy wasted its few assets and lost its domestic support by a morbid combination of concessions to Germany—which often anticipated and surpassed Nazi demands in the hope that Hitler would feel obliged, in counterpart, to bolster Vichy's "sovereignty" (he didn't)—and domestic persecution and repression that escalated as internal resistance grew. De Gaulle achieved his main objectives: He protected the integrity of France and its empire, and France was among the war's main victors, despite Soviet indifference, U.S. hostility, and British ambivalence. One of the greatest feats of statecraft in French history, it was accomplished by a politically inexperienced temporary general. But de Gaulle was endowed with a formidable sense of power that led him to harness the volatile, dispersed, and divided fragments of the Resistance for his, that is, France's, purposes. And he was endowed with an even more formidable inflexibility on essentials that he translated whenever necessary into a nuisance power that obliged others to deal with him.

As a turning point, 1945 deserves a special mention. This was the year in which the French were called upon to participate in the signing of Germany's capitulation and in the occupation of Germany, in which they were made one of the five permanent members of the UN Security Council, and in which they reasserted their presence and authority in Saigon. But it was also the year in which they were not invited to join the Big Three at Yalta and Potsdam—a sharp reminder of the demotion of Europe, which had become an object for other actors, and of France especially. In that same year the French had to crush, brutally, an Algerian revolt in Sétif and to yield under British pressure to demands for independence in Syria and Lebanon, and they found Ho Chi Minh solidly in control of Hanoi.

De Gaulle, steeped in the realpolitik tradition, tried to resolve the "German question" once and for all by calling for the dismemberment of the enemy, and he tried to ensure against its eventual revival through the traditional means of an alliance with the Soviet Union and an intensive program of French rearmament. But his call was not heeded. And Stalin, obsessed with military might as the yardstick of power, did not take France seriously. As for French rearmament, its costs exceeded French means, and Socialist and Communist opposition to de Gaulle's priorities was one of the two main factors that led him to resign abruptly in January 1946. The other factor was his inability to influence the formation of a weak new constitutional system by the constituent assembly whose election he had engineered.

When the Fourth Republic emerged from the long torments of constituent assemblies and popular referendums, the tripartite coalition of

Socialists, Communists, and Christian Democrats that had been shaped by the Resistance faced France's two anxieties in drastically transformed circumstances. It quickly became clear, in 1946, that Germany's future was going to be a major stake in the Cold War that began between East and West. The Soviets' lack of support for French claims on Germany (along with France's enormous needs for economic assistance) pushed French decisionmakers into the Western camp. Britain and the United States were no more favorable than was Stalin to French desires for revenge across the Rhine, but Paris thought it could influence the Anglo-Saxon approach to Germany, if only through obstruction. Moreover, the majority of the French saw in the USSR a threat that had to be taken seriously, given the links between Moscow and the French Communist Party. Thus the coalition broke up, and the Communists were ousted from the government in the spring of 1947. A country that needed military assistance in case of trouble against both a revived Germany and an expansionist Soviet Union could not afford the neutrality that many intellectuals advocated.

Having made a fundamental choice, the politicians of the "Third Force" (the parties situated between the Communists and the Gaullist Rally de Gaulle launched in 1947) faced France's two nightmares with more handicaps than assets. They tried to obstruct and delay the Anglo-American plans for Germany's economic rehabilitation and for the creation of the Federal Republic of Germany, but this entailed isolation and frustration, as French diplomats discovered in 1947–1949. And France's world status was threatened in two ways. Choosing the Western camp meant accepting U.S. preponderance. Britain found out in 1946–1947 that for all its heroic stance in the war it could no longer be an equal of the new superpowers. France's need for military protection against both Germany and Russia led its leaders to conclude that they had to accept third place in the Western alliance that the Marshall Plan and the North Atlantic Treaty were shaping. They fell behind the U.S. leader, and they also fell behind a much-weakened Britain, which was playing the card of the "special relationship" with Washington to keep the position of the privileged lieutenant. The other threat to France's status was the anticolonial challenge that dragged the French into repression in Madagascar, Morocco, and

Tunisia and into two tragic and interminable wars, first in Indochina (1946–1954) and then in Algeria (1954–1962). For the heirs of the Resistance, firm believers in the unique virtues of French colonialism, the choice was between the status quo and limited reform, not between the status quo and independence. But repression was counterproductive. The wars proved to be unwinnable (militarily in far away Indochina, politically in Algeria) as well as divisive at home, where many argued that France's liberal and democratic traditions required the end of colonialism.

Thundering in the wings, de Gaulle charged that the leaders of the Fourth Republic were betraying French interests by allowing London and Washington to drag them toward a revival of a prosperous German state and by failing to preserve the empire's integrity. But the leaders had only a weak hand to play. Decolonization was pushed by Moscow, popular in Washington, and accepted as inevitable in London. France was essentially isolated. Nor did France have the military strength to challenge the Anglo-American domination of the integrated North Atlantic Treaty Organization (NATO) that emerged from the shock of the Korean War. Once again, unfavorable systemic factors were reinforced by bad internal ones. The party system, less fluid than it had been under the Third Republic, was complex enough to again require coalition cabinets, whose weakness was increased by proportional representation (always the enemy of strong government) and by the fact that the Communist and Gaullist oppositions represented between a third and two-fifths of the National Assembly. Cabinet crises and "immobilism" were thus guaranteed. Stubborn resistance to Washington's hegemony was ruled out (several of the parties received U.S. funds). Stubborn resistance to decolonization was assured.

And yet the hapless Fourth Republic did not botch everything. The brief but important consensus of 1944–1947 turned France into a welfare state (a major factor, over time, in softening class conflict) and into a dirigiste economic system. The state could thus play a dominant role in France's reconstruction and modernization through nationalizations, planning, and the control of credit. Cabinets came and went, but a remarkable cohort of civil servants saw to it that the protectionist, cramped, rural, and petit bourgeois France of the past was replaced by an effective industrial society, devoted to the cult of growth rather than "equilibrium." This major, indeed revolutionary, change in goals resulted from the meditations on the causes of decline that had obsessed both the Free French and the Resistance. The new Ecole Nationale d'Administration that de Gaulle had created in 1945 produced a formidable corps of bureaucrats who saw themselves as the guardians of the public interest. After 1941 French demography had turned around. A massive migration of rural workers into the cities provided industry with the manpower it needed. Thus France offset its loss of power abroad with an increase in internal power. Under the Fourth Republic the decisions were taken to launch an ambitious program of nuclear energy and to move toward a nuclear bomb.

The squabbling politicians of the Fourth Republic were not the main architects of this impressive modernization (although they put in place the civil servants who performed it and provided the means to carry it out). But they certainly were the architects of another great undertaking: European integration. Robert Schuman's decision in the spring of 1950 to adopt Jean Monnet's design for a supranational European Coal and Steel Community was a switch from the old policy of anti-German steadfastness to its recurrent alternative, a policy of reconciliation. It was also an imaginative and profoundly innovative leap beyond the traditional methods of interstate relations. It appealed to very different strands of thought: realists concerned with limiting German sovereignty in key areas, functional federalists impatient to solve concrete problems in transnational, technocratic ways, and idealistic federalists eager to make war among Europeans impossible and to transcend the shibboleths of national sovereignty. It conceded equality to Bonn, yet it encased Germany in a construction of friendly containment.

That those shibboleths could not be easily ignored was demonstrated both by the fierce opposition to the Schuman plan on the Far Left and on the Right and, above all, by the saga of the European Defense Community (EDC). Jean Monnet invented the European Defense Community as a way to accept the German rearmament that the United States wanted after the outbreak of the Korean War, while still avoiding any revival of a purely German army and high command. Equality, here, meant giving up the independence of the French army in order to prevent an independent German army. Given the importance of the national army as a component of nationhood, this was too bitter a pill to swallow. The long debate highlighted France's predicament. EDC was tabled by the National Assembly, and the substitute invented by Anthony Eden and Pierre Mendès-France preserved the French army while putting the new German one into the straitjacket of NATO integration—not a bad deal, except that it reinforced Western Europe's subordination to Washington.

It was obviously wiser to push European integration back on the economic track (where it also had the merit of opening France's borders to competition). The Treaty of Rome created Euratom and the Common Market—the last diplomatic achievement of the Fourth Republic (and a rather paradoxical one, for although Monnet's mind was concentrated on Euratom rather than the Common Market and although the debate in the French National Assembly dealt far more with the former, it had only a dim future). The Rome treaty confirmed that a solution to the Franco-German quandary was being sought in a mix of reconciliation and transcendence. But didn't the leap into Europe imply eventual resignation to the decline of France as a sovereign power, as an autonomous state?

Defiance and Accommodation
(1958–1989)

The year 1958 was another turning point. The Fourth Republic collapsed, overthrown by the settlers and the army in Algeria. Like its predecessor, it tried to safeguard the appearances of legality by transferring power to a military man; but this time the man was de Gaulle. What followed was the most exciting, if not the most successful, episode in French foreign policy in this century.

Germany and decline had haunted de Gaulle all his life. The sixty-seven-year-old man who came back to power in 1958 had drastically revised his views since 1945. He pursued the policy of reconciliation with Germany that the Fourth Republic had adopted (and he could have argued that he had never ruled out). He gave it an intensely personal turn through his friendship with Konrad Adenauer. But in two important ways he modified what the politicians of the 1950s had done. He distrusted supranational enterprises because they threatened to subordinate France to *apatride* (stateless) bureaucrats and to curtail French freedom of action. And he wanted to submerge Franco-German equality in European affairs, that is, in a *"Weltpolitik"* that only France, not the Federal Republic, could wage. This renationalization of reconciliation resulted from his conviction that France's struggle for status, rank, and grandeur required free hands and a global activism *(tous azimuts)*. (Indeed, should Germany ever again become a threat, France had to be able to return to a coercive policy, for instance to an anti-German coalition with the Soviet Union if necessary.)

De Gaulle gave a planetary dimension to the struggle for grandeur. On the one hand, it required strength at home. Modernization was accentuated (and extended especially to agriculture, thanks to the alliance between the dirigiste state and a new generation of reformist farm leaders). Many had feared de Gaulle would pull France out of the Common Market. Instead, he used it to accelerate France's economic transformation and to provide its farmers with safe markets. Thus both free trade for industrial goods and European protectionism for agriculture became the engines of France's economic growth. Also, in de Gaulle's design, although the Common Market was composed of U.S. satellites (except for France!), it could slow down or resist U.S. economic pressures. The nuclear force became a symbol of modernization, a crucial component of power, and a mark of superiority over Bonn. Above all, de Gaulle gave France what it had lacked for more than a century: a regime that was both democratic and effective, with a strong executive that no longer depended on party maneuvers—a kind of synthesis of France's monarchic and Republican traditions.

On the other hand, he challenged the existing international order, both because it reduced France's role to that of a dependent of the United States and because it subjected Europe to the designs of the two superpowers (which allowed him to pose as the champion of European as well as French independence). He thought that France, no longer a "mastodon," would be much better off in a multipolar world and thus proceeded to confront both superpowers, especially, after the Cuban missile crisis, the one he saw as dominant, the United States. (But he did not jeopardize U.S. military protection against the Soviets.)

De Gaulle acted as if Germany was still a major concern but no longer an enemy. Therefore, the new enemy threatening France's position in the world was the United States. He recognized Communist China, to which both superpowers were hostile. He masterfully used the "myth of Yalta" as a rallying point for those who wanted to liberate their countries from the grip of the superpowers, and since ending Europe's division required ending the Cold War and the superpowers' "blocs," he made himself the champion of détente. He tried to submerge the Common Market into an intergovernmental European entity—*"l'Europe européenne"*—capable of defining its own military and diplomatic policy. In world economic affairs there was only one superpower, and so he attacked the supremacy and privileges of the dollar and called for a return to the gold standard. He made France an actor in the Middle East, in Vietnam, in Latin America, and even in Canada. And he tried to square the circle by championing the decolonization of the former French empire while preserving France's influence there.

It was a grand design. Judged by its objectives, it failed. French-led détente did not shake the order of Yalta. France's partners in the European Community wanted supranational institutions and a close alliance with the United States. The dollar remained the world's dominant currency. The French "community" that was to replace the empire did not last (although French influence did). The chaotic events of 1968 in France and the Soviet reaction to the Prague Spring in the same year were serious setbacks for de Gaulle.

And yet in two respects he was extraordinarily successful. He gave the French a pride and self-confidence they hadn't had in many years, and morale is a significant component of power. Although the multipolar world he wanted failed to emerge, he masterfully exploited the possibilities that the bipolar order provided to a state in France's position: the possibility of challenging that order while benefiting both from U.S. protection and from the division of Germany that the Cold War preserved; the possibility of both staying in the Atlantic Alliance and stepping outside the integrated machinery of NATO; the possibility of being the Federal Republic's partner and supporting its right to reunification while also calling for a "European" solution of the German problem that amounted to subordinating Germany's future to the will of the victors of the war against Hitler. De Gaulle boosted French power and status within an international system he had tried in vain to change, and his presence, prestige, eloquence, and sense of drama were a major, albeit temporary, component of that power and status. His unique diplomatic style, both imperious and magisterial, a mix of blitzkrieg maneuvers and Olympian encyclicals, was both a reflection of his personality and an instrument in his pedagogy of power and pride.

In consequence, of course, deflation occurred when the great actor left the stage for the second and final time. Prosperity—under de Gaulle both a national objective and a means to grandeur—now became the supreme goal. Global activism was curtailed. The mix of nuclear autonomy and collaboration with NATO and of reliance on U.S. protection and pursuit of détente with Moscow continued. But the locomotive of détente was now driven in Europe by Willy Brandt's West Germany and in the rest of the world by the Nixon-Kissinger team, which distrusted Brandt. De Gaulle's hostility both to supranationality and to Britain's entry into the European Economic Community (EEC) (he saw Britain as a U.S. Trojan horse) had paralyzed the EEC. To revive it, his successor, Georges Pompidou, had to allow Britain's membership, thus assuring that there would be no "l'Europe européenne" and also that the enterprise, far from gaining new dynamism, would spend ten years haggling over the terms and financial effects of Britain's entry. The Yom Kippur War and the oil crisis that followed confirmed U.S. preponderance in the Near East and the determination of France's European partners to follow U.S. leadership in order to mitigate the effects of the oil crisis.

On the whole, Pompidou and Valéry Giscard d'Estaing kept France on Gaullist tracks, but it wasn't clear that these led anywhere. Giscard and his friend Helmut Schmidt took a few policy initiatives in the European Community, but he otherwise seemed to be more an observer than an actor in world affairs.

François Mitterrand, in his first term in office (1981–1988), made three important decisions. In 1983 he encouraged the Bundestag to endorse the placement of U.S. missiles on German soil, which could be seen either as a break with de Gaulle's anti-Atlanticism or as an orthodox balance of power move at a moment when the Cold War and the Soviet military threat seemed to be getting more intense. In the same year, he had to choose between, on the one hand, the pursuit of Leftist economic and financial policies that could require exchange controls and trade restrictions, and on the other, the preservation of France's commitments to the EEC. In choosing the latter he acknowledged that French domestic autonomy had been sharply reduced in a world of economic globalization and European integration and that prosperity seemed more likely through full engagement in these processes than through Keynesianism-in-one. Participation in an open world capitalism and in the Common Market made it too costly for France to pursue policies incompatible with its partner's. And so the Socialists turned around, and away from dirigisme.

Indeed, Mitterrand's third decision was the *relance* (raising of stakes) of European integration after the financial conflict between Margaret Thatcher and the EEC was resolved in 1984. Mitterrand, and French officialdom, had concluded that France's future was Europe and that power in the world was less attractive, or less possible, than influence in a European Community in which France had major assets and on which its prosperity largely depended. Jacques Delors, having left the French Finance Ministry for the presidency of the EEC Commission, joined Mitterrand, Thatcher, and Helmut Kohl in promoting a single market and in making it possible for the EEC members to reduce drastically the number of issues requiring unanimous decisions. The struggle against decline became equated with the buildup of a Europe in which the component nations had to pool ever widening chunks of their sovereignty.

Post–Cold War Anxieties
(1989–1999)

The years 1989–1992 constitute another turning period in French foreign affairs, and they present us with one more paradox. The "order of Yalta" collapsed; the Cold War ended; the division of Europe vanished. This was exactly what French leaders—Mitterrand as well as de

Gaulle—had called for. But it did not usher in a new multipolar age, and it did not serve French interests. Indeed, French fears were revived.

It was one thing to encase a Federal Republic, politically handicapped by historical memories and by partition, within a European structure in which France, with its *force de frappe* (nuclear force) and its diplomatic activism, had strong advantages. It was another suddenly to have to deal with a reunified Germany, no longer on the dangerous border between two camps but in the center of a reuniting continent, endowed with a population and an industrial machine much bigger than France's, in an era in which economic power matters more than unusable weapons. It was a formidable challenge and the return of a nightmare.

De Gaulle had foreseen German reunification and envisaged a way for the great powers to manage it. But the initiative was seized by Bonn. The fading Soviet Union, far from trying to control the conditions of Germany's resurrection as a single state, accepted Germany's and the West's terms in exchange for financial assistance. Mitterrand wavered and toyed with the idea of a new balance of power policy that would appeal to Russia's interests and to Thatcher's anti-German feelings to contain Germany. Much to Thatcher's dismay, Mitterrand decided for continuity: The policy of providing a European and friendly framework for Germany would be preserved and even accelerated. Kohl was willing and eager to reassure Germany's neighbors. This led to the Treaty of Maastricht of 1991 and to the plan for a single European currency. Moreover, the French soon realized that their fears of a German domination of Europe were excessive and premature. Germany had been hit as hard as had France by unemployment and the slowdown of economic growth, and the financial, economic, and psychological costs of reunification turned out to be far in excess of Kohl's expectations.

Nevertheless, the policy of taming the tiger by sharing a gilded cage with it raised the major and difficult questions of France's decline as an autonomous actor. The end of the Cold War failed to bring about the demise of the Soviet and U.S. blocs. The superpower France had tried to engage as a way of balancing U.S. hegemony had disintegrated in 1991. NATO not only survived, more under U.S. leadership than ever, but even prepared to expand, thus extending the U.S. grip to the central and eastern parts of the continent. Moreover, the tight-ening of European integration in the new European Union (EU), the expansion of majority rule within the EU, and the constant enlargement of the EU's scope stirred the indignation of the champions of French national sovereignty and freedom of action. Mitterrand rashly called a referendum on agreeing to the Treaty of Maastricht; the yes vote prevailed only by a hair. The European enterprise undermined or dismantled such hallowed French institutions and practices as monopolistic public services, a central bank devoid of independence, and the sovereignty of French law. Many Frenchmen on the Left and on the Right became convinced that the fundamental wager behind France's German policy since 1950—that the leap into Europe would actually strengthen France's position and serve the national interest, that Europe would be a means to national ends—was being lost and that the "means" had become a boomerang. At Germany's insistence, the monetary union pushed by France required budgetary restrictions and a tight credit policy. But the budgetary restrictions threatened France's social safety nets and the credit policy prolonged high unemployment. In this sense, the resurrection of a strong Germany and the *engrenage* (grinder) in which France is caught in the EU have cracked the domestic consensus on French foreign policy that de Gaulle had largely achieved. Europe divides both the Left and the Right.

The fear of decline is nourished not only by the changes in Europe but also by domestic and by systemic factors. The modernization of France in the late 1950s and 1960s required an influx of foreign workers. Once growth slowed down, the presence of immigrants from North Africa and from black Africa fed the xenophobia of those who saw in this invasion a threat to national identity. Before it exploded from its own internal divisions, the National Front had become the second-largest party on the Right, and its shrill appeal to racist prejudices has deeply influenced official policies on immigration, naturalization, and asylum. The anxiety about French identity has also been heightened by globalization. On the one hand, the French morosely count the handicaps French industry and services face in the global competition: They have too little dynamism abroad, they have been too sluggish in embracing the information age, there are too few "world-class" big enterprises and there is too little innovation among the smaller ones, and so on. On the other hand, this global competition, relentlessly pushed by the United States, creates fears that French producers and workers will be submerged by products from cheap-labor countries and put out of business, and fears that French culture and cultural goods (such as films) are being bulldozed by the English language, by Anglo-American mass culture, and by Hollywood. Thus French resistance to U.S. schemes for universal laissez-faire continues.

Eager to build a strong EU, if only in order to prevent the "rena-tionalization" of German foreign policy, France has called for a common foreign and security policy. Eager to preserve a margin of independence in world affairs, France has clung to the principle that the EU's decisions must be unanimous and has attempted to maintain autonomous policies in many parts of the world. The requirement of unanimity helped paralyze the EU in the handling of the Yugoslav tragedy, so that once again, belatedly, the United States had to be the "indispensable nation" in putting an end to the Bosnian war. The au-tonomous policies have largely been fiascoes: In the Arab-Israeli con-flict the United States has pushed France (and Europe) aside; in Africa the French backed too many dictators, especially in Zaire and Rwanda, and so have lost ground and feel crowded out by Washington; in the Gulf War the French desire to operate both in al-liance with the United States and Britain and with a margin of dis-tinctiveness failed diplomatically and militarily.

The twentieth century has seen the suicide of Europe as the core of world affairs because of two gigantic and insane wars. The first was the result of a failure to stop the infernal machine of alliance commitments and military timetables, and the second was the result of a failure to stop the demon of hatred and destruction who was dismantling the European order. In retrospect, the French sometimes wonder if de Gaulle might not have been right in suggesting that he may have writ-ten the last pages of France's greatness. The empire is gone, and since 1940 France has not been a major player. However, the balance sheet of these 100 years is not as bad as it seems, or as they think. At home, the French have a flexible and effective system of government; they are still the fourth economic power (ahead, now, of Britain); despite the deep division over immigration the integration of foreigners is actually proceeding; the problem of France's meritocracy is not whether it is mediocre but whether it is too stable, too hierarchical, and too narrow. The hatchet of anticlericalism has been buried, and the issues of poverty and "exclusion" are being addressed. Abroad, even if participation in the European Union obliges France to share its powers with its partners, it is probably the sanest possible response to the predicament of France and of Europe, and it is certainly the most constructive way of handling the inevitable fact of Germany's presence next to France—a fact neither recurrent wars nor, as the World War II collaborationists proposed, accepting once and for all Germany's preponderance was able to manage.

To be sure, among the elites there is a nostalgia for the days when France was a great power. Opinion polls show that the public realizes that those days are gone but also, to paraphrase de Gaulle again, that relative decline does not mean resignation to mediocrity. What is missing at present is a leader capable of exploiting in France's favor the opportunities provided by European integration and reunification (the French—indeed, the EU's—response to the latter has been timid and dilatory, largely for narrow economic reasons), by globalization, by the fact that the only superpower has formidable handicaps of its own, and by France's own assets. France's hard power includes a military force that is both useful to France and an asset for Europe insofar as it is both nuclear and (increasingly) geared to interventions abroad, and an economy with a productive agriculture and some strong industrial sectors (telecommunications and transportation). Its soft power includes considerable bureaucratic and diplomatic skills, which have been invaluable for France in the EU; a culture that remains influential; and such domestic assets as patriotism, a determination not to fade, and solid institutions. It is unsafe for a political scientist to predict the course of the twenty-first century, but for the near future, continuity is the most likely course.[2]

Looking Backward and Forward

I began and ended with continuity. But I have also shown multiple discontinuities, with both systemic and internal causes. The systemic discontinuities are the result of the very different international contexts in which France has had to face its two obsessions. The internal ones consisted in different regimes, in the ups and downs of political leadership, and in the highs and lows of domestic unity and morale. These discontinuities manifested themselves in three ways: variation in the hierarchy of enemies (Germany was *the* enemy before 1940; from 1945 to 1958 Germany and the Soviet Union were both seen as threats; after 1958 the United States was often seen as at least as much a menace as a protector); variations in allies (Russia and the United Kingdom before 1914, a rather unreliable United Kingdom between the wars, the United States as a bulwark against both Germany and the USSR after 1945, and now Germany); and variations in foreign policy goals (security dominated everything until the late 1940s; from the mid-1950s on prosperity became at least as important, and the fear of decadence focuses on economic decline; today security and prosperity share the stage with the preservation of national identity).

There were also discontinuities between the choices French leaders have made over the century, even in regard to the same problems. Concerning their German predicament, they have practiced antagonism (before 1914, from 1914 to 1924, and from 1945 to 1949), interstate accommodation (by Caillaux, Briand, and de Gaulle), submission (the policy of collaboration in 1940–1944), and what I have called transcendence through European integration. Faced with a fear of decline, they have practiced denial (in the 1920s and, with respect to the empire, in the beginning years of the Fourth Republic), resignation (in the 1930s and under the Vichy regime), what might be called a "soft landing" policy of making the best accommodation possible (during the Fourth Republic and after de Gaulle in the Fifth), and last but not least, defiance: I refer to de Gaulle's policy of not going gently—or at all—into the good night, and of being both the overgrown Tintin and the modern Cyrano of France ("Je sais bien qu'à la fin vous me mettrez à bas qu'importe, je me bats, je me bats, je me bats [I know that you'll crush me at the end— never mind: I'm fighting, I'm fighting, I'm fighting]").

The agenda for the beginning of the twenty-first century is European integration. It is the perfect example of France's predicament. On the one hand, it is useful both as a protection against an unfettered Germany and as an insurance against decline; it provides France with an avenue for leadership, with a buffer against the United States (for instance in the World Trade Organization), and with opportunities for economic growth. However, it risks dismantling the armature of France, its state, whose restoration and strength were de Gaulle's life aims. If that happens, France may be left with a society traditionally dependent on the state and yet still poor in voluntary associations capable of replacing it, a society hanging, so to speak, between a French state much reduced in sovereignty and power and a European "state" of weak, not very democratic, and not always very effective institutions.

The continuing weight of the trauma of 1940 is likely to mean that France will not be passive either in the struggle against decline or in the not-so-hidden contest with Germany. It is also likely to impose limits on the degree to which France will accept federalization of the EU, for even among French "European integrationists," the legacy of the trauma is the Gaullist motto "Never entrust the fate of the nation to others." On the other hand, outright defiance is unlikely: Most Frenchmen think its benefits are dubious and its costs excessive (as they already appeared in 1981–1993), and there are no de Gaulles on the horizon. Thus, France's most likely course is one of persistent "transcendence" with respect to Germany and of accommodation to the present international system, given the relatively modest weight of France (Giscard noted that France represented 1 percent of the world population), the heavy weight of France's entanglements, and the increasing importance of the transnational aspects (public and private) of world affairs. Indeed, one of the main reasons for the EU's impotence in the strategic and diplomatic arena—its habit of depending on the United States and the division in the EU between the French, who resented it, and the other states, who embraced it—may fade away as Tony Blair's Britain turns more forcefully toward Europe and as the United States becomes more willing and eager to share its "burden of responsibility" with Europe. In the foreseeable future Europe will not be France writ large, as many French leaders had hoped, but French policy will continue to be largely Europeanized—in pursuit of France's persistent concerns.[3]

4

GERMANY

*The Continuities from
Frederick the Great
to the Federal Republic*

JOSEF JOFFE

HARDLY ANY OTHER NATION's foreign policy has fluctuated as widely and wildly as Germany's. Nor has any other major European power shown so many different political and territorial faces to the world. And few are the countries whose history contains so many broken threads. Yet there is one strand that binds the grand strategies of modern Germany together from the Prussia of Frederick the Great in the eighteenth century to the Berlin Republic on the threshold of the twenty-first: the curse of geography. Whatever shape Germany assumed, it was always stuck in the heart of Europe with vulnerable frontiers in a dangerous neighborhood. There was France in the west, Russia in the east, Austria-Habsburg in the southeast, and Britain looming across the North Sea.

At best Germany was strong enough to hold off one of them. But no matter how mighty, it was always too weak to prevail against all, and hence it faced the eternal strategic nightmare: a multifronted war fought in, over, or against the European center. So all of German grand strategy has faced a permanent problem: how to banish the "nightmare of coalitions," as Bismarck called it—whether by diplomacy, alliance, or hegemonic war. Germany's elusive geographical identity set it apart from Britain, France, or Spain, Europe's prototypical nation-states. Prussia, an upstart kingdom, conquered and then *became* Germany—when Bismarck unified Germany in 1871, fusing twenty-five smaller entities into the "Second Reich."[1] In the twentieth century Germany has suffered six radical changes of political personality: from the Wilhelmine Empire (1871–1918) to the Weimar Republic (lasting until 1933), from Hitler's "Third Reich" (1933–1945) to its two successor states, the Federal Republic of Germany (FRG) and the German Democratic Republic (GDR), and back again to a reunified Germany in 1990.

Modern Germany's foreign policy—from Frederick's to the Federal Republic—has been no more stable than its political regimes. It has run the gamut from impotence to overreach, from alliances with either flank to not-so-splendid isolation at the center, from almost total victory over Europe in 1942 to total defeat by a global coalition in 1945.

Prussia and the Problem of German Grand Strategy

The best place to start is the Prussia of Frederick the Great, who stands at the beginning of Germany's road to power. In 1740, the just-crowned twenty-eight-year-old attacked Austrian Silesia (part of present-day Poland). This war, the War of the Austrian Succession, quickly expanded into a general European melee. Frederick managed to hold on to his Silesian booty. But with it came an enduring predicament, for he never managed to extricate himself from the permanent conflict with Habsburg. "Austria has not forgotten Silesia," he wrote in 1752, "and Maria Theresa will march to the attack in order to recover Silesia as soon as she has consolidated her domestic affairs and restored her army."[2]

The Habsburg Empire, aching for revenge, had an obvious incentive to forge an alliance with France to outflank Prussia from the west. The trap was sprung during the Seven Years' War (1756–1763), triggered by Franco-British rivalries in North America. Both antagonists began to cast around for Continental allies. Frederick joined Britain, and France found a natural ally in Austria, which had the Silesian account to settle with Prussia. Russia too weighed in on the Austrian side. The Franco-Austrian alliance treaty of 1757 noted the necessity to reduce Frederick's power "within such boundaries that he will not in the future be able to disturb the public tranquility."[3]

The "public tranquility" was but a metaphor for the European status quo. The traditional powers suddenly faced an unsettling intruder in their midst, and so Frederick found himself surrounded by a coalition of European powers. Supported only by British subsidies and by the North German princes, Prussia had to hold off Austria, France, Russia, Sweden, Saxony, and the Catholic princes of what had been the Holy Roman Empire.

By 1761, when Spain joined the fray, the Seven Years' War seemed about to bring the Prussian parvenu to an early demise, but Frederick was saved by a stroke of good luck. In 1762, Empress Elizabeth of Russia died. She left the throne to her husband Peter III, who pulled out of the war. One year later, it ended amid the general exhaustion of all combatants. Frederick again managed to hold on to Silesia. It was *das Mirakel des Hauses Brandenburg*—a sheer miracle that saved the House of Brandenburg.[4]

But Frederick's miraculous escape did not dispose of the trap itself. The "nightmare of coalitions," as Bismarck called it, was still there, posing the *existential* problem for all future German foreign policy. Nor did Germany ever succeed in cracking the predicament, all the way to Hitler's regime. For none of Frederick's successors could undo the curse of geography that had placed Germany in the heart of Europe.

The rise of Frederick's Prussia was inseparably tied to conquest, and so, one century later, was the ascent of Bismarck's Germany. What Silesia was for Prussia, Alsace-Lorraine was for the Second Reich: the grand theft that turned neighbors into permanent enemies. The struggle against Habsburg dominated all of Frederick's life (he died in 1786), and the Wilhelmine Empire could never pacify France after the War of 1870–71. Frederick and his heirs sometimes succeeded in defending their conquests, but never in having them legitimized. This is another way of highlighting Germany's congenital vulnerability. Bismarck's Germany has been called only a "semi-hegemonic"[5] power; Frederick's Prussia was no more than a "semi-great" one. It lacked the overseas resources of imperial Spain, the population and territory of France or Austria, and the trading wealth and geographical insulation of Britain.

Endemic vulnerability spawned a peculiar temptation that would shape another continuity of German grand strategy. Exposed frontiers and a relatively narrow territorial base naturally favored offensive maneuvers, in which surprise, speed, and the concentration of forces had to carry the day. In the nineteenth and twentieth centuries the strategic offensive hardened into dogma. To break permanently free of encirclements (largely of Germany's own making), Wilhelm II and Adolf Hitler *initiated* what Frederick and Bismarck had feared most: a two-front war against both east and west. This is what the Second Reich did in 1914 and what Hitler did, in stages, in 1939 and 1941. Though Hitler was initially more successful than the Kaiser, both in the end had to retreat under the onslaught of their many enemies, particularly Russia and the United States. In short, Germany's offensive capabilities regularly exceeded its defensive ones.

Grand Strategy
from Bismarck to Wilhelm II

At first sight, the contrast between Frederick and Bismarck could hardly be starker. Whereas the Iron Chancellor's diplomacy looks like a paragon of stability, Frederick's maneuvers epitomize the vaunted flexibility of an age when princes and potentates were supposedly free to define their stakes and place their bets unencumbered by domestic forces and national passions.[6] These differences, however, ought not to obscure the underlying continuities. In the short term Frederick could change allies, conclude separate peaces, even carve up Poland

with his archenemy Maria Theresa. But Habsburg remained Frederick's lifelong obsession.

The continuities in German history emerged here. Bismarck's Prussia drove the Austrians out of Germany in the war of 1866, completing what Frederick had started, and it was the victorious 1870–1871
war against France that allowed Bismarck to sweep a recalcitrant
Bavaria into the "Second Reich" proclaimed in Versailles on January
18, 1871. The spoils of that war, Alsace and Lorraine, embroiled Germany in a permanent conflict with France.

A. J. P. Taylor has labeled this process of expansion and unification
the "Conquest of Germany by Prussia."[7] It was Prussia that spear-
headed the drives against Austria and France, triggering the wave of
national fervor that swept the south German states into the union. It
was the king of Prussia who became emperor of the Second Reich.
And it was the black and white colors of Prussia (combined with the
red of the Hanseatic League) that served as the imperial flag.

But this new Germany would also inherit Prussia's endemic insecurity, even though it was vastly larger and more powerful. As Austria
had for Frederick, France became Bismarck's lasting security obsession. He wrote in 1874, "Nobody ought to harbor any illusions; peace
will end once France is again strong enough to break it."[8] Bismarck
remained entangled in a permanent conflict of Germany's own making. In Bismarck's words, Germany had to be "*toujours en vedette* [al-
ways on guard]" against the "*cauchemar des coalitions* [nightmare of
coalitions]."

In order to dispel that nightmare, with one foe—France—already in
place, Bismarck followed the strategy limned in the famous "Kissinger
Diktat." His goal was the creation of a "universal political situation in
which all the powers except France need us and, by dint of their mutual relations, are kept as much as is possible from forming coalitions
against us."[9] Such a strategy posed a stupendous agenda. To keep Germany's flanking powers apart required an impassable barrier between
east and west, with Germany as "guardian at the gate," as arbiter and
gatekeeper of east-west relations. Nevertheless, this is precisely what
Bismarck attempted to do, and he set the model for modern German
foreign policy.

In Bismarck's words, Germany had to act as the *"Bleigewicht am Ste-haufmännchen Europa,"* as the dead weight in the tumbler doll that was Europe—an ambitious task. It meant that Germany had to manage the conflict-laden European balance from the center. At a maximum, Germany had to contain the forces that drove Russia and Austria toward collision in the Balkans, that might embroil Britain and Russia in the arc of crisis from Turkey to Afghanistan, and that could tempt Britain, Russia, or Austria to look for help from France. At a minimum, these clashes on the periphery had to be kept from engulfing the heart of Europe.

But the would-be manager of Europe was also its central problem. As the London *Times* editorialized on September 7, 1876, "We feel that an enormous power for good or evil has risen up somewhat suddenly in the midst of us, and we watch with interested attention for signs of its character and intention." Initially Bismarck tried to keep his hands free. He used the classic techniques of nineteenth-century diplomacy—mediation, compensation, diversion—in order to keep the other powers both busy and beholden to Berlin. A perfect example of Bismarck's early style was the Congress of Berlin in 1878, where the chancellor bestrode the stage in the role of the *"ehrlicher Makler"* [honest broker]."

The issue was a classic late-nineteenth-century, three-way conflict, among Britain, Austria, and Russia in the Balkans and the Near East. The Russians had just scored a victory against Turkey (1877–1878), and its rivals Britain and Austria refused to condone it. Bismarck's technique was both to bind the wound, and thus prevent an all-European war, and at the same time to keep it festering in order to tie the antagonists down at a safe distance from Germany. To divert the French, he kept encouraging them to expand into Tunisia.

Yet Bismarck soon learned the perils of brokerage. In Berlin, with the chancellor presiding, the British forced the Russians to disgorge many of the gains they had won from Turkey. The Russians then demanded compensation in southeast Europe, which Bismarck could not grant them for fear of alienating his Austrian ally. Prime Minister Disraeli returned home satisfied and convinced at last that Germany was "saturated," "pacific," and "conservative."[10] But the Russians felt betrayed by Bismarck, for whom they had benevolently held the ring during the Franco-Prussian war of 1870–1871.

Successful mediation requires invulnerability or superior power. Bismarck's Germany, though "semi-hegemonic," had neither. Bismarck must have grasped immediately the futility of trying to emulate England, the grand master of the balancing game, without Britain's invulnerability. Instead, after the Congress of Berlin, Bismarck contracted a case of lasting "pactomania." The centerpiece of the system was the 1879 Dual Alliance with Austria, which bound each to aid the other against an attack from Russia. Two years later, that axis was embedded in a revived Three Emperors' League, in which Germany, Austria, and Russia each guaranteed benevolent neutrality in a war with a fourth power, that is, France. At the same time, the imperial trio tried to smooth over Austro-Russian quarrels in the Balkans and Near East by making any change in the status quo contingent on tripartite agreement.

These maneuvers added the "Saburov Rule" to the logic of the Kissinger Diktat. As Bismarck told Saburov, the Russian ambassador in Berlin,

> You all too often fail to appreciate the importance of being in a party of three on the European chessboard. This is the invariable objective of all cabinets, and of mine above all. All politics can be reduced to this formula: Try to be in a threesome as long as the world is governed by the precarious equilibrium of five great powers. That is the true protection against coalitions.[11]

By 1883 Bismarck's alliance system covered half of Europe. Serbia and Romania were drawn into the Austro-German orbit by subsidiary alliances in 1881 and 1883. Italy joined Vienna and Berlin in the Triple Alliance concluded in 1883—a mutual defense pact essentially directed against an "unprovoked attack" from France. Finally, after the Three Emperors' League collapsed under the pressure of Austro-Russian rivalries in the Balkans, the shaky capstone of the structure was set in place in 1887: the Reinsurance Treaty with St. Petersburg, which was a mutual (and secret) pledge of benevolent neutrality in case either party suffered an unprovoked attack from its most likely foe—Germany from France, and Russia from Austria. Even by the rough standards of realpolitik, that was a most duplicitous move because Austria was Germany's best ally.

Later historians have attacked Bismarck for casting over the continent a net of contradictory and mutually stalemating alliances that were bound to be useless in case of war. That is true, but it is beside the point. Bismarck constructed his system not in order to aggregate strength but to *devalue* it. Like subsequent German leaders from Gustav Stresemann to Konrad Adenauer, Bismarck dreaded the marriage of Germany's flanks; unlike Wilhelm II and Hitler, he dared not attempt to overwhelm them. Hence he created the web of entangling fetters and counteracting commitments that came to a center in Berlin like spokes on a hub; it would preserve the precarious peace by making war itself impossible. If none could move without being tripped by that net, each would stay in place, as would the European status quo so profoundly destabilized by that enormous but merely "semi-hegemonic" power of the Second Reich.

A few months after Wilhelm II dismissed Bismarck in 1890, Paul Kayser, the head of the Foreign Office's colonial section, noted, "After a quarter of a century of genius, it is a real blessing to be able to be as homely and matter of fact as other governments."[12] Bismarck's successors, starting with Friedrich von Holstein, the éminence grise of the Wilhelmstrasse, certainly lived up to that sigh of relief. The first blow against complexity was struck when the new regime refused to renew the Reinsurance Treaty with Russia on the correct reading that this secret compact conflicted with Germany's alliance obligations to Austria and Romania. Wily, even devious though Holstein was, he could not see the virtues of inconsistency. The new chancellor, Leo von Caprivi, was heard to confess that he simply could not keep several balls up in the air at once as Bismarck had done.

To the Russians, however, the new simplicity was a threat, especially since Holstein was an inveterate Russia-hater and an advocate of alliance with Britain, Russia's bitter foe. The Russians concluded that German grand strategy was moving against them. Worse still were the effects of nonrenewal on Russia's archrival Austria. As the Russian foreign minister, Nikolai de Giers, noted, "Through the dissolution of [the Reinsurance Treaty] Vienna has been liberated from the wise and well-meaning, but stern control of Prince Bismarck."[13] It was a perceptive comment. When Bismarck tried to inveigle Wilhelm I into the Dual Alliance with Austria, he used the since-famous argument that every alliance had a rider and a horse, meaning a partner who directs and one who follows. As de Giers had foreseen, Germany did not stay in the saddle; the Austrian horse took the bit in its teeth and dragged the rider into World War I despite half-hearted bridling attempts. Snubbed by Germany, Russia turned to Europe's other great revisionist power, France. Two years after Bismarck's dismissal in 1890, France and Russia signed a military convention that blossomed into a full-blown alliance in 1893.

But Germany was not yet completely surrounded by powers allied against it. The missing link in the chain of encirclement was Britain. Britain might have been an ideal ally for Germany: It had no territorial interests in Europe, it was linked to the Kaiser by ties of family, and the Hohenzollerns were not yet competing seriously with them for colonial glory.

Why this did not happen was nicely outlined in a famous memorandum written in 1907 by Sir Eyre Crowe, then a middle-level official in the British Foreign Office. He thought there were two possible interpretations of German foreign policy, which by then was meddling in Africa, both north and south, and in the Middle East via the notorious Baghdad Railroad and was consequently making Britain ever more nervous. Either the Kaiser was aiming at European hegemony and maritime ascendancy, in which case England's very existence would be threatened, or "all her excursions and alarms, all her underhand intrigues do not contribute to . . . a well-conceived and relentlessly followed system of policy." Crowe concluded that in the end it did not matter. Whatever Berlin's true intention, the relentless growth of German material power would feed Germany's ambition, turning the country into a "formidable menace to the rest of the world," even if there were no "malice aforethought."[14]

Crowe's point was that the nature of the European stage—the distribution and dynamics of power—mattered more than the intentions of the actors. And the distribution of power was shifting with a vengeance. From 1871 to the eve of World War I, German coal output rose sevenfold, approaching par with Britain. Steel production grew tenfold, and exports leaped by a factor of almost five.[15] Wilhelm II's personality may have exacerbated the problem Germany posed for the rest of Europe, but it did not create it. The Kaiser's prodigious ambitions were hardly matched by his talents; more than just vainglorious, he was perhaps even a bit demented. But the real issue was neither the psychology of the emperor nor Germany's lagging democratic evolution.[16] The key problem was that Wilhelm's antics in the Near East and in Africa both highlighted and reflected the dramatic increase in Germany's power. The historical pattern was certainly familiar: Riches beget their own ambitions. Eventually steel, pig iron, and coal would be forged into swords; eventually the wherewithals of power, just by being there, would engender their own purpose.

In 1898—a critical year—Wilhelm's "new course" and *"Weltpolitik"* were married to the First Naval Bill, which was clearly directed against Britain. If there were any doubts of Germany's ambitions, they were dispelled by 1904 when Germany began to build a new class of battleship that was bigger, better protected, and more heavily armed than anything in the British arsenal. Not coincidentally, in 1904 Britain's "splendid isolation" began to come to an end. In 1904 Britain and France settled their ancient colonial differences (they had almost come to blows in Fashoda in 1898), and three years later France managed to bring about reconciliation between the traditional archrivals Britain and Russia. Seventeen years after Bismarck's dismissal, his League of Peace was dead, and Germany's encirclement was complete.

Why? Because the balance of power, the invisible hand of European politics, was at last exerting its influence. Merely by coming into existence, the new Reich had shaken the balance of power to its very foundation. Bismarck understood this far better than did the *Weltpolitikers* who succeeded him. His convoluted and duplicitous maneuvers had been intended not only to immobilize his country's most likely foes but also to contain Germany itself. Self-containment, however, was not the game of the epigones. They saw only that Germany was rapidly overtaking the rest of Europe by almost any measure of material power, and they thus thought that Germany at last deserved a "place in the sun": not only a permanent seat at the great power table but also a bigger share of the winnings. But the more it clamored, the more resistance it mobilized.

Hence the temptation. As early as 1871, the chief of the Prussian General Staff, Helmuth von Moltke, had begun to plan for a two-front war against France and Russia, hitting Russia first. In late 1887, at the very end of his career, he pushed for preemptive war against Russia. Bismarck dismissed the idea with the quip that he did not want to commit "suicide for fear of death." When Alfred Count Schlieffen became chief in 1891, he proposed to reverse the sequence and strike at France first. This two-phased attack was enshrined in the fabled Schlieffen Plan of 1905, which laid out Germany's strategy on the eve of World War I: attack first in the west, then, after vanquishing France, in the east.

Gallons of ink have been spilled on the question of responsibility for World War I. Today it is clear that Germany was not solely responsible, at least not in the sense of the "guilty" verdict delivered at Versailles in 1919. But once the *cauchemar des coalitions* had come into being, one response was both tempting and compelling: to strike at both flanks before they could converge on the center. Furthermore, the new dynamics of warfare—nicely captured in the French dictum *La mobilization, c'est la guerre* ("Mobilization means war")—made a first-strike strategy even more alluring. The French army should be destroyed before the Russian one was fully mobilized.

But Germany was not the only country tempted by war. With the balance of power so thoroughly unhinged by the rise of the Reich and the decline of three once-mighty empires—Turkey, Austria, and Russia—all of Europe was being seduced by the lure of war into a feeling that they should just "get it over with." So many conflicts had accumulated since 1815; and a hundred years later, Germany was in the center of most of them. "In Bismarck's days, this never would have happened," mused a Russian diplomat. "What did happen was the result of Germany's novel ambition to grapple with a task more stupendous than that of Bismarck—without a Bismarck."[17] In 1914, Germany faced a coalition of all the European powers, just as it had in

1761 when Frederick the Great suddenly found himself surrounded by an all-European coalition, with Germany, a tottering Habsburg at its side, up against Britain, France, and Russia. This time, however, there was no escaping from the trap, and so defeat in 1918 drove home the existential problem of German grand strategy: The country in the middle was always better on the offensive than on the defensive, and though it was strong enough to hold off any single power it was too weak to defy them all.

The Strategies of the Weimar Republic

When the new German Republic signed the armistice on November 11, 1918, not a single alien soldier had set foot on German soil. The Central Powers were in fact holding front lines running southward from Brussels to Basle in the west and from Riga to the Black Sea in the east. The magnitude of Germany's defeat was driven home six months later in Versailles. In the west, Alsace and Lorraine were returned to France, and the cities of Eupen and Malmédy were ceded to Belgium. In the north, Schleswig was given to Denmark. In the east, Memel was cut off and given to newly independent Lithuania. West Prussia, Posen, and Upper Silesia (in 1921) became Polish.

Germany's territorial losses, apart from its colonies, amounted to only 13 percent of its lands, yet as a result Germany lost one-quarter of its hard coal and three-quarters of its iron ore assets.[18] The left bank of the Rhine was to be occupied for fifteen years and demilitarized forever. The Weimar Republic was allowed a small army of 100,000 men, but no air force or heavy weapons. Finally, Germany was to pay the bill for the war: 226 billion marks (roughly four times the German gross domestic product of 1913).

The verdict of Versailles was no more unjust than the brutal peace Germany had imposed on an exhausted revolutionary Russia in Brest Litovsk just the year before. Yet in terms of Europe's postwar order, the peace was but a warm-up for the next war, since Germans of all persuasions immediately rallied against the conditions. Bismarck had unsettled the European status quo by fusing many small German states into one; now the Weimar Republic threatened the status quo by its birth. Craving what it had lost, it was a revisionist power from day one—though it had neither the muscle nor the means to make changes.

It found itself in a familiar predicament. Surrounded by implacable victors, the republic had to break the encirclement that had proved the Reich's undoing. Gustav Stresemann, foreign minister from 1923 to 1929, put it thus: "First of all, we must get the strangler off our neck. Therefore, German foreign policy . . . will have to maneuver [*finassieren*] and to dodge any lasting commitments."[19] Handicapped by impotence, imposition, and reparations, he faced an all but impossible task.

Two years into the life of the young republic, the noose began to retighten. When Berlin refused to accept the reparations bill, France occupied the cities of Düsseldorf, Duisburg, and Ruhrort in Germany's industrial heartland. Eager to cage Germany in from all directions, the French concluded alliances with Poland and the "Little Entente" (Czechoslovakia, Yugoslavia, and Romania). In March, Britain and the Soviet Union signed a trade agreement, and that was followed by rumors of secret Franco-Soviet talks. Where was Germany to break the ring? The logical place was Communist Russia, the other great pariah power of Europe.

Prime Minister David Lloyd George of Great Britain set the stage in Rapallo, a resort town near Genoa. Export-dependent Britain wanted an international conference to rekindle trade. The centerpiece was to be a Western consortium, including Germany, that would manage and profit from the reconstruction of Russia. It was the first attempt at economic détente with Moscow, but the Soviets were loath to deal with a united capitalist front. Thus, on the way to Italy, the entire Soviet delegation stopped in Berlin to negotiate a separate treaty with Europe's other outcast. Under the Treaty of Rapallo, signed on April 16, 1922,[20] diplomatic relations between Moscow and Berlin were to be resumed immediately, and both would drop reparations claims. Each would give the other most-favored-nation treatment in trade. Finally, Moscow and Berlin promised to consult each other in case their "economic needs" became subject to such "international regulations" as the consortium. In short, the Rapallo Treaty sought to ban each nations' worst fears by enjoining both from entering into separate economic agreements with the West.

The Rapallo Treaty was another variation on an archetypal theme. In Rapallo the Germans perceived a stark and simple problem: Once again, they were facing the key members of the earlier anti-German coalition. Worse, the British and the French were conducting secret talks with the Russians, offering them the carrot of reparations from Germany under the Versailles Treaty. So once more the Germans were haunted by the *cauchemar des coalitions*, and they saw preemption as the way to exorcise it.[21] Even better, by grabbing the initiative the losers of World War I might become players again. E. H. Carr clearly exaggerated when he complained that Germany could now "maneuver freely between east and west, playing off one against another [and] extorting concessions from the one by threatening to fall into the arms of the other, and always keeping its own choices open."[22] The Rapallo Treaty was above all the first breach in the ring of encirclement that had closed on the eve of World War I. The Germans showed the Soviets that an alliance was necessary if the Soviet Union was to stave off a united capitalist front, and they showed the West that they were not helpless waifs but, rather, indispensable partners against Soviet Russia. The Rapallo Treaty was the first step toward transforming the curse of geography into a strategic blessing (the advantage of the "interior lines," in the military vernacular). The Germans had managed to interpose themselves as a wedge between Russia and the West.

What the treaty had limned, Foreign Minister Stresemann, perhaps the most brilliant of German diplomats, would execute to perfection in the following four years. The next step was the Locarno Pact of 1925. Though the Germans had cracked the wall in the East by establishing privileged relations with the Soviets, the wartime alliance between Britain and France still needed to be ruptured. This time the French set the stage. Recognizing the soaring costs of their Ruhr incursion and the Anglo-American resentments it was generating,

France magnanimously proposed to withdraw, but only if Britain extended a new defense pact. That, of course, would be a death blow to Stresemann's strategy for breaking out. In his own words, he "wanted to forestall the formation of a new Entente which was to be based on a three-way pact between France, Britain and Belgium under Chamberlain's leadership."[23] If France was going to manipulate the German threat in order to lure back Britain, then Stresemann would play the card of sweet-minded pacificity. And so he solemnly reaffirmed to both Britain and France Germany's new western borders. For good measure, these borders were to be guaranteed by Britain.

Why would the revisionist suddenly preach self-denial? For one thing, such a virtuous move would rob the French of their strongest argument for a renewed British alliance. Second, it would mute the urgency of France's outflanking alliances in Eastern Europe. With France and Britain propitiated, the Weimar Republic could focus its revisionist ambitions on Poland, to which it had been forced to cede the largest chunk of its lands.

Stresemann's stratagem worked brilliantly. At Locarno, Germany concluded a treaty with France and Belgium that reaffirmed their mutual borders as they had been redrawn in Versailles. All three agreed to forego the use of force and to submit all disputes to arbitration. In addition, Britain and Italy were to guarantee French and Belgian borders militarily. But Stresemann stubbornly refused to agree to the new borders in the east, and he got away with it. The status quo in the east was merely shored up by arbitration treaties with Poland and Czechoslovakia.

These barren terms hardly do justice to the German strategic victory. By renouncing revisionism in the west, Stresemann had merely traded away a non option. How could the quasi-disarmed Weimar Republic have wrested Alsace-Lorraine from France? But in exchange for next to nothing, Germany had acquired an implicit British alliance—with Italy thrown in for good measure—against France. Britain and Italy were now bound to defend Germany against French attack, even against a replay of the Ruhr invasion. That was the end of the Franco-British Entente. Stresemann had also created a malleable status quo in the east, for there were now "borders of different dignity and sanctity in Europe."[24] With the Rapallo Treaty in 1922 Germany broke the encirclement, and with the Locarno Pact of October 2–16, 1925, it disrupted the Anglo-French alliance.

The French game now shifted toward the League of Nations. The heart of the League was collective security: If any member were to be attacked from any quarter whatsoever, even from within the League itself, the other members would rally in its defense. That was the lofty principle; in practice, the French saw the League as a status quo alliance against the two revisionist states, Germany and Soviet Russia. Russia had lost Poland and the Baltic states, and Germany had been forced to cede West Prussia—the "Corridor"—to the new Polish state. Poland was now part of that anticommunist cordon sanitaire in eastern Europe. France had concluded alliances in the early 1920s with the Eastern European nations in order to encircle Germany and to contain revolutionary Russia. But securing the cordon sanitaire required at least passage through, if not the collaboration of, Germany. If the Weimar Republic could be chained to the collective security obligations of the League of Nations, France could separate Berlin from Moscow and use Germany as a springboard for an anti-Soviet intervention in eastern Europe.

So before and during Locarno, France pushed hard for Germany's entry into the League, which it saw as a system that would both constrain and harness the energies of its archenemy. The Soviets caught on immediately. If the Soviets were excluded, Germany's entry would turn the League into a Western alliance against them.[25] The Soviet Union therefore returned to a preemptive diplomacy à la Rapallo that presaged Soviet post–World War II *Westpolitik:* In the 1950s the Soviets would seek to forestall West Germany's integration into the West by offering reunification-cum-neutrality; in the 1920s they offered to push Poland "back . . . to its ethnographic frontiers." Translated, this read, "We shall help you reconquer your lost lands in the east."

Lest Germany turn a deaf ear, Moscow resumed diplomatic relations with France in October 1924, and just prior to the meetings in Locarno Foreign Minister Georgi Chicherin of the Soviet Union paid a demonstrative visit to Paris. Germany was being squeezed in a classic flanking maneuver. Lesser minds might have been frozen in despair, but Stresemann not only broke the vise, he welded the pieces into a solid strategic base. To thwart the French attempt to use Germany against the Soviet Union, Stresemann simply pleaded impotence, confronting France with the facts of Versailles. Had not the victors stripped Germany of its military might? How then could Germany assume the risk of going against Soviet Russia? Ergo, France would either have to lift the military constraints on Germany or concede to Germany a special status in the League scheme.

France made the obvious choice. Given their overwhelming fear of German rearmament, they would rather swallow watered-down German obligations in the League. When Germany joined the League of Nations, it was granted the symbol of great power status, a permanent seat in the League Council, yet it did not bear the risk of having to join a Western intervention against the Soviet Union. Berlin was obliged to participate only if that was "compatible with its military situation and takes into account its geographical position."[26] This proviso spelled the best of all possible worlds: a wide margin of choice and a special role in East-West affairs. Germany was now *of* the West but *with* the West only at its discretion.

Nor was this the end of Stresemann's breakout strategy. On April 25, 1926, Stresemann recruited the Soviet Union into the German orbit. Under the Treaty of Berlin, the Rapallo compact was to "remain the basis of relations between Germany and the USSR." Both states were to "maintain friendly contacts" about "all political and economic questions" of mutual concern, and they bound themselves not to participate in economic sanctions directed against either. The core was Article 2: "Should one of the contracting parties, despite its peaceful behavior, be attacked by a third power or several third powers, the other . . . shall observe neutrality for the complete duration of the conflict."[27] This was continuity par excellence—practically a rewrite of Bismarck's Reinsurance Treaty of 1887.

Eight years after its defeat in World War I, Germany had vastly improved on the strategic position of the Second Reich. Though Germany lacked the Reich's military muscle, Stresemann had accomplished Bismarck's dream: The "nightmare of coalitions" had evaporated, and the ancient curse of geography had turned into a first-class strategic asset. The victim of encirclement had become the master of European diplomacy. It was allied to East *and* West, and it was needed by both. It could forestall Western intervention against the Soviet Union and it could play a dependent USSR against the West. Neither East nor West could move against the other without German cooperation.

The relationship between Germany's flanking powers was controlled by Berlin, which had thus in effect acquired a veto power over East-West relations. Europe's conflicts were suspended around the hub of Berlin. Together, the treaties of Locarno and Berlin spelled out the twentieth-century implementation of the Kissinger Diktat: All the powers depended to some extent on Germany and were constrained by their own dissensions from allying against it.

The Hegemonic Temptation Revisited

Like Wilhelm, Adolph Hitler succumbed to the temptation that has always been part of Germany's strategic predicament: to try to banish the "nightmare of coalitions" once and for all by striking out in all directions. Had he been a "normal" German leader, as Britain's appeasement advocates originally perceived him, he would have built on the exalted strategic position bequeathed by Stresemann. He would have continued to unravel Versailles, regained part or all of the lands amputated in 1919, and perhaps even secured for Germany once more the role of overseeing East-West relations in Europe. But for Hitler, the European setting clearly favored Germany. The United States was no longer part of the balance; nor was the Soviet Union, which was content to watch the capitalist powers lunge at each other's throats. France was isolated from Britain and entranced by a Maginot Line mentality that defined safety in terms of a concrete-and-cannon wall along its German border. And Britain, until 1939, saw succor in propitiating "Herr Hitler's" legitimate grievances.

Of course, Hitler was not a revisionist who accepted the basics of Europe's balance of power but a revolutionary who wanted to overturn it. Nor was he a "normal" hegemonist like Charles V or

Napoleon I, for in 1939 he unleashed not only hegemonic war but also racial and genocidal war for which European history offers no precedent. Nonetheless, for all of his demented uniqueness, part of Hitler was also firmly embedded in the classical logic of German grand strategy that had animated Moltke and Schlieffen and their like.

On August 11, 1939, just a few weeks before he attacked Poland, Hitler confided, "All my endeavors are directed against Russia; if the West is too stupid and too blind to grasp this, I shall be forced to seek an understanding with the Russians, beat the West and [finally] turn with all my forces against the Soviet Union."[28] And this he did. First he neutralized Soviet power through the Non-Aggression Pact of August 24, 1939, one week before the invasion of Poland. In May 1940 he struck at France, subjugating the country within six weeks. Then he started bombing Britain as a prelude to invasion.

Yet like Moltke in 1914, who had hurried two critically important army corps to the eastern front before France was vanquished, Hitler did not finish the job on the west before attacking the Soviet Union in the summer of 1941. Hitler's Wehrmacht, like the Kaiser's army, now found itself caught in precisely the two-front war that Hitlerian strategy was intended to banish for good. But here the precedents and analogies end. For unlike Wilhelm II, indeed, unlike any would-be conqueror of Europe since Charles V, Hitler fought not one but two wars: one for strategic hegemony and the other for racial hegemony. And he had to win the former before he could turn to the latter, which was industrial genocide.

"Danzig is not the object that matters,"[29] Hitler openly admitted in May 1939. The appeasement-minded great powers still thought Hitler was seeking merely to undo the land distributions of the Versailles Treaty, in this case the separation of Danzig and East Prussia from the main body of Germany. His real intent was a European empire with lebensraum for German colonizers in a subjugated East that extended as far as the Urals. The core empire would be secured on the periphery by African possessions and a large blue-water navy. This would put the Third Reich alongside the United States and the empires of Britain and Japan in a quadripolar world. Eventually, in the next generation, the struggle for global hegemony would come down to two contenders: Germany and the United States. The struggle was not just for Europe but, ultimately, for the whole world.[30]

Nor was Nazi Germany intent just on conquering space; the lands had to be cleansed of Jews, Poles, and other "subhumans," and the Jews of Europe were to be totally annihilated. Genocide became the consuming obsession overwhelming every other purpose as the war's fortunes turned against Germany after 1942. Why else would Hitler continue to allocate ever more precious resources—rolling stock and military personnel—to feeding the gas chambers in the east rather than to stopping the onslaught of the Red Army? Why else, in 1945, did he order the "death marches" from Auschwitz and the other camps into the Reich if not to continue the slaughter at a safe distance from the invading Russians? Clearly, genocide trumped everything else, even the very core purpose of all strategy: the defense of the national space. Only after the Allies had conquered every square inch of that national space did the twin war against the world and the Jews end.

The enormity of Nazi Germany's goals were mirrored in the enormity of its defeat. One of the first things the victors of World War II did was to abolish Prussia—the entity that had launched Germany's climb to great power status—as a state and as a name. Quadripartite rule followed, and then sevenfold dismemberment.[31] In 1945, after unleashing a war that had claimed 55 million lives, Germany had little to look forward to but indefinite subjection and punishment.

Adenauer and the Politics of Dependence

Considering the depth to which Germany had fallen, Konrad Adenauer, chancellor of the Federal Republic from 1949 to 1963, did better even than Stresemann at returning Germany to the world stage. Like the first, the second republic was both impotent and revisionist, both a prey and a threat—not a promising combination. Worse, West Germany could not count on the fluid milieu of the 1920s, which saw power progressively drained from the system with Britain and the United States turning away from the Continent and Soviet Russia retracting into postrevolutionary consolidation. Indeed, Bonn had to act in the most rigid setting Europe has ever known: a system divided into two immutable blocs and polarized around two overweening super-powers. Yet merely ten years after the most catastrophic collapse since Carthage's, West Germany had shouldered the occupation regime, re-gained sovereignty, and reentered the community of nations as linch-pin of the West's Cold War coalition.

Since *Schaukelpolitik* ("policy of maneuver and balance") in the man-ner of Weimar was not an option in the rigidly bipolar system of the Cold War, Adenauer opted for a diametrically opposed technique: He became a compulsive committer and joiner. As sovereignty and secu-rity could only be had from the three Western powers, commitment to the West was like a down payment that would instill trust and move the victors to loosen the occupation regime. But the real payoff would come from a more subtle strategy, and then at a very low price: not from calculated submission but from voluntary integration.

For the Federal Republic, integration within Western Europe and later the Western alliance was a high-profit venture because it traded nonexisting potential rights for actual even if partial sovereignty. Un-like the other Western European nations, West Germany did not give up sovereignty, but with each step toward economic integration it achieved a bit more communal self-determination. Since integration was predicated on the equal subjection to common rules, self-abnega-tion became the condition of self-assertion. As such, Adenauer's strat-egy was exactly the reverse of the early Europeanists such as Jean Monnet, one of the founding fathers of the European Community. The "Functionalists" saw integration as inexorably spreading the sol-vent of national sovereignty because each step in any one area would force nations to integrate more sectors. Adenauer, however, reversed the logic, using each concession by West Germany as a lever for prying off yet another lien on the country's sovereignty.

When the West, in the late 1940s, insisted on reparations and in-ternational controls on the iron and coal industries of the Ruhr Valley, Adenauer complied, but he proposed that the FRG join the Interna-tional Ruhr Authority, and thus the controlled became one of the con-trollers. When France moved to detach the iron-rich Saar from West Germany, Adenauer countered with a call for complete Franco-

German union.[32] Afterwards, he was a most enthusiastic supporter of the European Coal and Steel Community (ECSC), the forerunner of the European Economic Community and European Union (EU). If the French, as they had in the early 1920s, wanted a grip on Germany's energy and steel sector, the classic backbone of war, Adenauer was willing to let them have it, but only within an institution of equals.

The game was to transmute the constraints imposed by the victors into controls voluntarily accepted by all. Also, for a prostrate country, membership in *any* international body bestowed not only the trappings of equality but also the real chance to influence events. Rarely has a country pursued hard-nosed realpolitik so effectively in the guise of goodness as did West Germany in the 1940s and 1950s.

It is doubtful whether the Federal Republic's founding father would have succeeded so brilliantly without the first violent eruption of the Cold War: North Korea's attack on the south in the summer of 1950. "Without power," Adenauer was to reminisce years later, "one cannot conduct policy. Without power, our words will not be heeded."[33] Just a few months after the Federal Republic's founding in 1949, Adenauer had already proposed rearmament, evoking angry protests at home and abroad: "Germany should contribute to the defense of Europe in a European army under the command of a European headquarters."[34] But by dramatizing the worldwide contest between the United States and the USSR, the North Korean invasion turned West Germany from a vanquished ward into a first-class strategic asset. Only a few months later, in September 1950, the United States decided to rearm West Germany, which would fundamentally change the bargaining relationship between Bonn and the West.

Five years later, the occupation regime was lifted, and a rearmed and all-but-sovereign Federal Republic was admitted to the North Atlantic Treaty Organization (NATO) as result of a grand bargain struck between Bonn and the West in 1954.[35] Looking at the deal in some detail will elucidate how Adenauer's *Westpolitik* fits into the larger scheme of German foreign policy in the last two centuries.

On the surface, Adenauer's gift to the West was a seemingly straightforward policy of submission. First, the Federal Republic accepted stringent limits on its sovereignty, leaving all rights pertaining to

"Berlin and Germany as a whole" to the three Western powers. Second, Bonn would raise half a million troops and integrate them wholly into NATO. Third, it renounced nuclear weapons and pledged itself to a strictly defensive stance. Notably, Bonn would "never have recourse to force to achieve . . . reunification."[36] To guarantee compliance with these resolutions, Bonn accepted several hundred thousand Western troops on its soil, which evidently had the dual function of holding off the Soviets and keeping the Germans on their best behavior.

In exchange the FRG gained a remarkable position in Europe that would recall the strategies of Bismarck and Stresemann. On their part the United States, Britain, and France agreed that only the Federal Republic was "entitled to speak for Germany" as a whole. This made Bonn the successor to the Reich and denied the legitimacy of its "counterstate," the German Democratic Republic, which been founded by the Soviets shortly after the birth of the Federal Republic. Second, the West agreed that the "final determination of boundaries" must await a *freely* negotiated settlement. This was a most precious prize. In effect, the West was refusing to accept the permanence of Germany's territorial losses in the east while reassuring Bonn against another imposed peace treaty. Third, the Big Three vowed "to achieve by peaceful means their common aim of a reunified Germany enjoying a liberal democratic constitution like that of the Federal Republic and integrated within the European Community."[37] That was a resounding "no" to the Soviets, who were forever pushing for a neutralized Germany under Four-Power supervision. Reunification would occur only on Western terms and within the West.

At first sight, this deal appears both unrealistic and provocative. It enshrined a revisionist agenda toward the East that was more demanding even than Weimar's. As such, it was destined to turn Bonn into a lasting target of Soviet and Polish hostility, and it made the GDR an object of dubious standing. But the grand bargain was continuity par excellence, and the key prize of Adenauer's strategy. By striking the 1954 deal, Adenauer had shown himself to be a worthy disciple of Bismarck and Stresemann. By limiting his own options, he had reduced those of the West even further. The West was now bound to ostracize Bonn's counterstate, the GDR, and to refuse to ratify

Moscow's and Warsaw's territorial gains. The West could now pursue one end only: a reunified Germany under "liberal," "democratic," and "integrated" auspices. In other words, there would be no more impositions by the unified Four Powers, as there had been at Potsdam. The Big Three were bound to deal with the East only on West German terms. Like Stresemann, Adenauer had acquired a veto power—though a borrowed one—over East-West relations.

Nor was this all. With the Cold War heating up, Adenauer proceeded to squeeze even more benefits out of the West's rising demand for Bonn's manpower and strategic space. To the legal bones of the 1954 settlement he added the muscles and sinews of practical day-to-day diplomacy by forging an additional set of fetters on Western policy known as the *Junktim*, or the "policy of linkage."

Under that policy, the Western powers bound themselves to put reunification at the top of any diplomatic agenda with Moscow. Germany became the peg on which everything else was to be hung, be it European security arrangements, détente, or arms control. The linkage stratagem was well chosen, because once Bonn had joined NATO, the Soviets changed course. If the Soviet Union could not have a neutralized Germany, the second-best option from their point of view was a Europe where both *their* Germany and the redrawn borders in the East were permanent. Adenauer's *Junktim* was the obvious counterfoil: If the West and the Soviet Union wanted to deal, that was fine—but only as long as any agreement proceeded in lockstep with reunification-qua-*Anschluss*. That, of course, was out of the question in the zero-sum game of the Cold War. But Adenauer's insistence on linkage meant that if there was no reunification, there would be nothing else—no détente, no new Potsdam, no settlement imposed on Germany by the victors. As long as they were chained to this iron ball, the Western powers could not move where Moscow tried to drag them.

That was the true thrust of Adenauer's *Westpolitik:* to win a veto on East-West relations. At home, alliance with the West was sold to a skeptical electorate and a hostile Social Democratic opposition as the royal road to reunification—variously named "rollback" or "policy of strength." But reunification certainly was not the highest-priority item on Adenauer's agenda. To begin with, unity was the most unrealistic of West German objectives. Germany was the "prize, the pivot and the problem of European politics."[38] And given the zero-sum nature of the Cold War contest, neither side would voluntarily relinquish its half of the prize. Whichever superpower absorbed all of Germany would score an unacceptable victory over the other. Nor could the prize be taken by force, since nuclear weapons entailed costs that dwarfed the value of any conceivable prize in the European arena.

The only alternative to separate possession of Germany was a neutral Germany. For good reasons, the West was not interested. A neutral Germany would have bottled up the Atlantic Alliance behind the Rhine and would hand the strategic and psychological advantage to a Soviet Union straddling both Asia and Europe. Also, neutralization raised all the uncertainties of the ancient "German problem." If the nation in the middle were neutral and disarmed, how could it be kept disarmed and still safe from domination? If it were neutral and armed, how could it be kept neutral and prevented from dominating the rest? Bipolarity and partition had defused both risks in a novel and stable way. It protected Germany not only against others but also against itself.

But what about West German interests? Why did Adenauer refuse to grasp the opportunity to have unity plus neutrality, which the Soviets offered in the early 1950s? In the first place, Adenauer hardly had any other choice than to cast his lot with the West.[39] Playing East against West as Stresemann had would have tightened the occupation regime or, worse, reactivated the wartime coalition. If there was anything worse than partition, it was unarmed neutrality.

The real problem of West German policy transcended the antinomy between community and unity. The real crux was once more the ancient obsession of German foreign policy. Adenauer forcefully articulated the problem in a 1953 interview that captured the articles of faith and fear on which all his diplomacy was based:

> Potsdam signified nothing but: Let us strike a bargain at Germany's expense . . . Bismarck spoke about his nightmare of coalitions against Germany. I have my own nightmare: Its name is Potsdam. The danger of a collusive great power policy against Germany has loomed since 1945, even after the Federal Republic was established [in 1949]. Escaping from

this danger zone has always been the true purpose of [my] foreign policy.[40]

Binding the Federal Republic's fate to the West would fetter both the East and the West. Apart from delivering sovereignty and security, integration would undercut the "nightmare of Potsdam" by drastically limiting the West's options toward its former Soviet ally. The real thrust of Adenauer's *Westpolitik* was bluntly driven home by Franz Josef Strauss (minister of defense from 1956 to 1962) when he parried the eternal (and logical) Opposition complaint that reunification required agreement with all the four occupying powers. True enough, he said, yet it created "a constellation which makes a Four-Power bargain at our expense impossible."[41] Since the West was treaty-bound to honor West German claims and since Moscow was just as adamant in demanding ratification of its conquests, there was no deal to be had. Because a revisionist solution to the German problem had become the *conditie sine qua non*, détente, arms control, and cooperation had become hostage to Bonn's veto. The "open status quo" was now thoroughly locked and bolted, and the keys lay in the hands of West Germany.

Again, the Kissinger Diktat had triumphed. Adenauer had crafted a political situation in which other powers were prevented from forming coalitions against Germany. Adenauer had actually accomplished more than either Bismarck or Stresemann had. He too had turned Germany into a barrier to anti-German collusion, but by chaining the West to Bonn's claims, by turning the German problem into *the* stumbling block of a postwar settlement, he had managed to "Germanize" the international politics of Europe.

Returning to the Center: Willy Brandt, Helmut Schmidt, and *Ostpolitik*

Adenauer's masterful policy contained one fatal flaw. Unlike Bismarck, he had no autonomous weight; his veto power was derivative, resting on leased strength. His role as arbiter required the West's continued willingness to accept Bonn's conflict with the Soviet Union as its own and to subordinate its own policy to a German orthodoxy that in essence said, "No détente without national unity." Furthermore, Bonn's successful exercise of its veto depended on the Soviet Union meekly submitting rather than attempting the obvious: splitting the German ward from its Western guardians.

By the end of the 1950s neither the United States nor the USSR was willing to have its relationship Germanized. In 1958 Moscow decided to test the limits of Bonn's veto by instigating the Berlin Crisis. Moscow's main message was the obverse of Adenauer's: "No stabilization without ratification" (that is, of the war's territorial and political verdict). Nor was the United States ready to honor the German veto indefinitely, especially after its brush with nuclear war over Cuba in 1962. With the main purpose of U.S. policy—Bonn's integration into NATO—accomplished, the United States felt it was now time to deal with the larger perils of the Cold War.

With its leased veto power running out, Bonn had to go along or go it alone. And the nightmare of isolation was hardly less oppressive than the "nightmare of coalitions." As the United States, Britain, and France went off to Moscow, bypassing the German guardian at the gate, Bonn had to adapt and relocate. In the words of Willy Brandt, the Social Democratic chancellor from 1969 to 1974, Bonn had to make sure that "détente did not pass around, or over, Germany."[42] But it is a powerful testimony to the continuity of grand strategy that Brandt's "new *Ostpolitik*" would part with orthodoxy only to end up in a position where Bonn could *again* act as arbiter of East-West relations in Europe.

The New Ostpolitik

Continuity certainly informed Brandt's arguments. During the ratification debates on the 1970 treaties with Moscow and Warsaw—the core of the New *Ostpolitik*—he told the Bundestag, "An anti-German coalition was Bismarck's as well as Adenauer's nightmare. We, too, face this problem, and we should make sure that our own policy does not turn this problem into a liability."[43] The problem was obvious enough. Adenauer's truncation of foreign policy—pacification in the West, revisionism in the East—had served the country brilliantly as long as the West accepted Germany's conflict with the Soviet Union as its own. Once these chains were broken, the FRG could not sustain the game. Willy Brandt's New *Ostpolitik* was launched in earnest in late 1969, a few months after Soviet-American détente was formally inaugurated with the Strategic Arms Limitation Talks (SALT).

Within three years the European stage was transformed beyond recognition. Bonn moved from the trenches of the Cold War to the gates of Moscow, becoming the Kremlin's favorite European interlocutor. The vehicles of reconciliation were three treaties—with the Soviet Union, East Germany, and Poland—that amounted to a virtual settlement of World War II, twenty-five years after the fact. The treaties with Moscow and Warsaw (signed on August 12 and December 7, 1970) certified the "inviolability" of the territorial status quo in the East, buttressing it with a renunciation-of-force pledge.[44] The de facto recognition of the GDR was formalized in the Basic Treaty of December 21, 1972.[45]

With these treaties the Federal Republic all but relinquished its old claims while gaining a remarkable new role. Brandt, the Socialist, had heeded Bismarck's counsel "never to sever the tie to St. Petersburg." By dispatching its separate conflict with the East, the Federal Republic deftly fused reconciliation and realpolitik—as had Stresemann at Locarno in 1925 and Adenauer in 1954, when they settled with the West. Both Stresemann and Adenauer had labored under a security deficit, and both had tried to close the gap by propitiating Russia. Even Adenauer had paid homage to this rule early on by resuming diplomatic relations with Moscow only months after Bonn's accession to NATO in 1955. When Brandt decided to legitimize Moscow's postwar conquests, he was merely continuing the policy of "reinsurance."

But the new *Ostpolitik* involved more than reconciliation and reinsurance. Its underlying logic was nicely summed up by Herbert Wehner, the Social Democratic Party's (SPD's) parliamentary leader: "At best you can stand on one leg, but you can't walk on it."[46] The acquisition of a "second leg," ending the truncation of foreign policy, not only allowed mobility in the East but also relieved pressure on

Bonn's "Western leg." By dropping its revisionist claims toward the East, the FRG also shed its excruciating dependence on the West. Bonn could further diminish its dependence on the West by appeasing Moscow. With Moscow no longer pressing so hard on West Germany, Bonn could reduce its demand for security from the West.

Germany's demand curve shifted downward and became more elastic; that is, Bonn could live with less security and would therefore pay less for it. Brandt's successor, Helmut Schmidt (chancellor from 1974 to 1982) later proudly held up the fruits of the new *Ostpolitik*. "Our margin of maneuver," Schmidt told the Bundestag in 1975, "has been extraordinarily enlarged." The Eastern Treaties have "largely . . . liberated our country from its role as [a] client" who kept craving "yet another pledge of assurance from his patron powers." Moreover, "our treaties with Moscow, Warsaw, [and] East Berlin . . . have greatly reduced the numerous reasons we had in those days to seek—and to beg for—continuous reassurance."[47] Standing on "two legs," the Germans no longer needed to cling to either power.

But how was Germany to use its newfound freedom, especially since Brandt's *Ostpolitik* had apparently dispensed with reunification as an operational objective and given the Soviets what they had demanded ever more rudely since the mid-1950s. Aware of Bonn's lost veto over East-West relations, Brandt reversed Adenauer's formula, under which evolution in Europe had been contingent on reunification. Brandt put détente first and unity after: "Progress toward German unity can occur only to the extent to which overall East-West relations are fundamentally improved."[48] Détente, once the Beelzebub of West German diplomacy, became an unwritten article of Germany's constitution when Bonn began to seek a solution to the nation's problem via the long, "systemic" detour of loosening bipolarity.

This seemingly profound break with Adenauer's policy actually ended up *reinforcing* continuity because West Germany returned to the position *Ostpolitik* had seemingly vacated: that of playing the arbiter in East-West relations.

The true purpose of self-denial and détente-mindedness was precisely the *transformation* of the undesirable status quo the Eastern treaties had just validated. The fundamental goal—to undo what the war had wrought in Central Europe—remained the same. The strategy was no longer to pursue "rollback" through a "policy of strength"; rather, it was to achieve revisionism by reassurance.

Propitiation and cooperation would relax the Soviet Union to the point where it would feel secure enough to loosen its imperial grip over Eastern Europe. Allowed a longer leash, equally mollified Eastern European regimes—above all in East Berlin—might then feel free to grant a larger measure of liberty to their subjects. The goal was a setting in which the East German regime would lower its guard and grant ever more interaction between the FRG and GDR. Trade and travel would soar; instead of growing apart, the two German states would grow together again. In the longer term, the attenuating partitions would make reunification a de facto reality or an unnecessary formality.[49] More ambitious *Ostpolitikers* like Brandt's crafty confidante Egon Bahr harbored even bolder dreams. Bahr was not so much anti-American or pro-Soviet as a classically German nationalist. If the Cold War could be laid to rest if Europe no longer had to labor under a strategic threat and the imposition of the superpowers, then an all-European security system could shoulder aside the logic of blocs and zero-sum politics. With bipolarity receding to the edges of Europe, the center, rid of its dependencies, would at last be free to determine its own fate. Germany would be confederated or perhaps even reunited, but at any rate it would be back in the central role.

The problem of accomplishing such dreams was twofold. First, such a subtly balanced strategy of reassurance and "subversion" could only flourish in a permissive milieu. It required "loose" rather than "tight" bipolarity, in which bloc discipline was low and regime confidence was high and in which the Soviet Union would not feel the need to brandish its power because its imperial sensitivities were respected by everyone. Second, the agenda was very ambitious under the best of circumstances. If relaxation through reassurance was the key, then a détente-minded West Germany was not enough; everybody would have to live by the logic of *Ostpolitik*. Détente *über alles* had to transcend Germany; its maxims had to serve as a categorical imperative for the entire West. In short, détente had to be Germanized.

And so we return to the theme of continuity. In a way, all of German grand strategy has tried to Germanize East-West relations because geography never granted Germany the luxury of isolation that Britain and the United States enjoyed. Bismarck's intricate alliance system made the Second Reich the hub to which all the major relationships had to converge like so many spokes. Stresemann crafted the Locarno-Berlin system to place the Weimar Republic between the West and Russia. Adenauer Germanized Cold War strategy by entangling the West in his "no reunification, no détente" dogma. Though Brandt reversed the course, the thrust was the same: His *Ostpolitik* would only work if everyone stuck permanently to détente. Again Germany had to play the gatekeeper.

What had been merely latent in Brandt's *Ostpolitik* became dramatically explicit under his successor Helmut Schmidt once he was embroiled in the turbulence of "Cold War II" (the resurgent tensions between East and West in the late 1970s and early 1980s). The new chapter was driven by the intervention of the Soviet Union's proxy, Cuba, in Africa, the Soviet invasion of Afghanistan, the Reagan counterchallenge, and the six-year battle over Soviet SS-20s and U.S. Pershing II missiles in Europe from 1979 to 1985. Cold War redivivus, threatening to refreeze what détente had so painstakingly thawed, inevitably inflicted the heaviest penalties on the Germans. And the FRG suffered twice—as a state and as a (half-)nation—because its fortunes were so tightly tied to a cozy East-West climate. As Brandt put it in 1981, at the height of Cold War II, "Today, we and other Europeans face the problem . . . of how to keep the deteriorating relations between Washington and Moscow from spilling over into Europe."[50] Yet the United States, trying to harness its allies to the cause of neocontainment, demanded loyalty, not neutrality. As a result the West Germans were confronted with the deadliest bane of their diplomacy: a choice between their Western obligations and their Eastern mission.[51] On the one hand, to defy the United States was impossible; Schmidt could not face the Soviet Union alone. But neither could he allow the United States to drag Bonn into its global quarrels with Moscow without sinning against every commandment of *Ostpolitik* and provoking Soviet retribution. To avoid either choice, Schmidt was forced into a role that no German government—from Bismarck onward—has been able to carry off for any length of time.

Schmidt at first instinctively tried to straddle the conflict and to withstand the pull of either superpower. Then he tried to play the role of intermediary and mediator. To save German *Ostpolitik* he had to save European détente, and to achieve both he had to prevent the two superpowers from renewing the Cold War. Schmidt took a page out of Bismarck's book. Putting himself forward as "honest interpreter of Western policy," he proclaimed, "We have an important role to play in [saving superpower dialogue], both toward our friends in the United States and toward the Soviet Union."[52] In the aftermath of the Afghanistan invasion, the notion of the "honest interpreter" (echoing Bismarck's offer to play the "honest broker" between Britain and Russia) became part of Schmidt's standard repertoire. But Bonn was singularly ill-equipped to sustain the role of bridge and brace. The problem was ancient: The country *of* the middle would end up *in* the middle, not as a mediator but as one of the stakes. Though the clash between the great powers had been triggered on the periphery (from Angola to Afghanistan), the contest inexorably returned to its traditional locus, Europe. The critical question was again control of Germany, the country at the fulcrum of the East-West balance, a country too weak to hold its own and too strong to be left alone.

It was precisely in Europe that the Soviet Union was trying to inflict a major defeat on the United States by executing a two-pronged "decoupling" strategy. First, by holding out the promise of a separate détente to Western Europeans, Moscow hoped to gain their benevolent neutrality, if not active opposition, to the U.S. plan to turn NATO into the forward bastion of neocontainment. Second, by defining Western Europe's refusal of U.S. Euromissiles as the true test of détente-mindedness, the Soviets sought to thwart what the United States saw as the very symbol of U.S. power restored. And it was in West Germany, the focus of all pressures, where the battle would be decided.

Had Schmidt presided over a "semi-hegemonic" country, he might have succeeded. As Bismarck had convened the Congress of Berlin,

Schmidt might have convened a "Congress of Bonn," to broker the conflict between the United States, the heir of Britain, and the Soviet successors of the tsars. Yet the European stage had irretrievably changed. The great powers did not take their complaints to "Berlin"; instead, Schmidt traveled to Moscow in the summer of 1980 to plead his case before the Politburo. The Kremlin did not relent. Though the chancellor tried to persuade Leonid Brezhnev to dismantle the SS-20s, the Soviets refused to accept nuclear parity in Europe.[53]

At the same time, Bismarck's latter-day disciple collided with the Iron Chancellor's classic injunction—the Saburov "party of three" rule. The latter-day translation read, "Do not oppose both of your two most important allies—France and the United States—at the same time." Schmidt's brokerage task became even less likely to succeed when France recognized that without Germany to the east, the independent stance advocated by Charles de Gaulle would degenerate into mere posturing.

The turning point was the transfer of power in France from the centrist Valéry Giscard d'Estaing to the Socialist François Mitterrand in 1981. In the face of the Soviet military buildup (particularly the SS-20 missiles, which threatened to devalue the modest French deterrent) and Bonn's apparent eastward drift, Mitterrand hastened to link hands with the United States and undo the Continental Entente that had allowed Schmidt to defy the more blatant pressures from Washington. The Soviets had "upset the military equilibrium in Europe," he proclaimed upon assuming office. "I will not accept this, and I agree that we must rearm to restore the balance." Without the French prop, the center could not hold. To defy the United States was one thing; to sustain a simultaneous conflict with Paris would overtax Bonn's resources.

The conflict also so battered Schmidt's domestic position that the foreign crisis and internal opposition conspired to unseat him from the chancellorship in the fall of 1982. The man who would have defied the strictures of the European system ended up being felled by them. As he was pursuing his desperate tightrope act, his own Social Democratic comrades threw him off balance. When it became clear that they would rather live with the Soviet SS-20s than support counterdeployment, Schmidt lost his last weapon against the Soviets as well as his credibility in Washington. Indirectly, his defeat abroad led to his ouster at home. Seeing that Schmidt was no longer in control of his own party, now dominated by the pacifist left, his Free Democrat coalition partner bolted and helped elect Helmut Kohl, a Christian Democrat, chancellor on October 1, 1982.

A System Destroyed and a Nation Restored: Helmut Kohl and His Successor

Schmidt's failure to Germanize détente reflected the oldest of Germany's problems. Though forced by geography to play the hub, the country has been too weak or too vulnerable to sustain the game for any length of time. At the end of his tenure, the would-be mediator was losing the trust of his French and U.S. allies while failing to influence the Soviets.

His conservative successor Helmut Kohl (chancellor for sixteen years, from 1982 to 1998) immediately absorbed the lesson of Schmidt's fiasco. As Bismarck had after the Congress of Berlin, he understood that mediation required superior weight, invulnerability, or the consent of others. Yet at the height of Cold War II, the superpowers were not interested in Bonn's brokerage. The issue was still the balance of power in Europe, and Germany, the country in the middle, again became the biggest stake of the contest.

Just as Bismarck switched from balance to alliance after counting the meager profits of mediation, Kohl too fell back on the Saburov Rule and hastened to patch up the frayed U.S. and French connections. Since the acceptance of U.S. medium-range nuclear missiles was the ultimate test of loyalty, he staked his political life on their deployment in West Germany. When he called an early election in March 1983, after only half a year in power, the electorate showed they agreed with his policies by returning his coalition with a resounding margin of 53 percent. On November 22, 1983, the Bundestag confirmed the government's pro-missile choice; the next day, the systems began to arrive in West Germany.

Once it had secured its ties with its Western allies, the Kohl government began to define a less ambitious role for itself. "In my view," the chancellor mused, "it is a hoary illusion to believe that the relationship between . . . the GDR and the Federal Republic of Germany can really improve while the global political climate remains at subzero temperatures." For *Ostpolitik* to flourish, the larger setting had to be right, and the power to shape it was not Germany's alone. Wolfgang Schäuble, the cabinet-level director of the Chancellor's Office, added, "Any estrangement from the Atlantic Alliance would render the Federal Republic incapable of conducting a *Deutschlandpolitik* and *Ostpolitik* deserving of the name."[54] But that principle merely refocused attention on the German dilemma; it did not dispatch it. So in the same breath, Kohl's confidante paid tribute to the legacy bequeathed by Brandt and Schmidt: "The effects of partition for [our] people" must be "rendered more tolerable." Bonn must not "provoke the GDR" but must engage it in "dialogue and cooperation." Nor could Soviet sensibilities and interests be ignored, and an *Ostpolitik* "that would try to circumvent Moscow could not succeed."[55]

So when the Reagan administration tried to enlist the Europeans in the Strategic Defense Initiative (SDI), a program that would shelter the West behind an antimissile shield, Bonn signed on only symbolically in deference to strident Soviet opposition. In 1988, when the United States sought to modernize its short-range nuclear missiles in Europe, Kohl's foreign minister Hans-Dietrich Genscher craftily talked the subject to death. This again evaded Moscow's ire and positioned Bonn ever so subtly as a useful partner of Soviet policy.[56] As the Cold War began to wind down for good after Mikhail Gorbachev's accession to power in the Soviet Union in 1985, Bonn was again ready to resume the role its station in the European system dictated. Germany would be in and of the West, but it would reach out to the Soviet Union, which held the key to East Germany and Eastern Europe. Such a finely tuned game could only flourish in a climate in which East-West tensions were low and neither side would try to exact an exclusive commitment from the Germans. Precisely this logic had animated the two previous Social Democratic chancellors, Brandt and Schmidt, before Cold War II knocked the stage out from under them.

That a conservative friend of the United States like Kohl would resume that game was a powerful testimony to the enduring systemic imperatives operating on the Federal Republic.

Kohl was luckier than Schmidt; this time the conditions were right. The beginning of the end of Cold War II arrived when Soviet leader Mikhail Gorbachev met with Ronald Reagan at the Geneva Summit of 1985. Détente II was formally declared at the Washington Summit of December 1987, when the United States and the USSR concluded a treaty eliminating worldwide the intermediate-range nuclear forces (INF) that had been at the heart of the superpower contest in the 1980s. Dispatching them all, the Washington Treaty signaled what Bonn had craved since bipolarity had tightened in the late 1970s: a modicum of harmony between the two great powers.

Ironically, the bell was beginning to toll for the GDR just as the two German states had accepted each other's permanence and legitimacy. Europe's political tectonics began to shift in 1989, and within a year the architecture of partition had all but collapsed. Soviet expansionism in the 1940s had spawned NATO and cemented the division of Germany and Europe. Conversely, the retraction of Soviet power, initiated by Gorbachev in the late 1980s, overturned the Cold War system in a matter of months.

Presumably, Gorbachev lost his Eastern European empire in a fit of absentmindedness. Presumably, he had intended not to relinquish but to reform Moscow's Communist bastion between the Bug and Elbe Rivers. But once he dropped the old guard in Prague, Sofia, East Berlin, and Budapest, he reaped a revolution that revealed the enormous, irreducible weakness of the regimes Stalin had installed in the late 1940s. In the autumn of 1989 Communist regimes in Eastern Europe fell in quick succession, and hundreds of thousands gathered in the cities of the GDR, at first to demand democracy ("*We* are the people") and then to demand unity ("We are *one* people").

Communist regimes in Eastern Europe simply evaporated. On October 18, 1989, Erich Honecker, the GDR's president and party chief, was ousted by his own comrades, who were hoping to save the GDR and Communist rule with new leaders and modest reforms. Curiously enough, the Kohl government also implicitly assumed that a reformed East Germany would continue to exist. On November 28 the Kohl government enunciated a Ten-Point Plan that was still predicated on two German states. Accordingly, the plan merely foresaw a "contractual community" between the two states that would eventually mature into a confederation. Yet in the meantime, the postwar order in Germany had literally collapsed, appropriately enough in the very place that had been the focus and symbol of the Cold War. The Berlin Wall was breached on November 9 by jubilant Berliners, and that was the beginning of the end of the GDR.

With the constraints of the postwar system crumbling, tens of thousands crossed into West Germany, threatening to turn the GDR into a hollow shell. Governmental authority simply dissolved, and the GDR economy was grinding to a halt. Ironically, reunification was now *forced* on a Federal Republic that previously had dispensed with the dream. Willy-nilly, fabulously rich "Bonn Inc." was forced to rescue a bankrupt, failed "Prusso-Marx."

But before reunification could be completed, the two states' external stockholders had to be satisfied. The United States, eager to assure a European future with a democratic and Western-oriented Germany, was the first to support the reunification process. Skillfully running interference for Bonn, Washington persuaded Paris and London to stop their delaying tactics, and at the same time it blocked a host of Soviet designs, ranging from Germany's dual membership in NATO and the Warsaw Pact to unification outside of NATO.[57]

Bonn was willing to pay a hefty price for reunification. First, the FRG reduced the armed strength of united Germany by 40 percent, to 370,000 men (down from 495,000 in the FRG and 140,000 in the GDR). Second, united Germany reaffirmed the renunciation of nuclear weapons pledged by the FRG in 1954. Third, neither NATO forces nor NATO nuclear weapons would be deployed in what had been East Germany. Fourth, united Germany renounced all territorial claims against Poland and the former Soviet Union. Fifth, the Russian withdrawal (completed in 1994) was sweetened with 12 billion deutsche marks (then $8 billion). Finally, Gorbachev and Kohl, in a July 16, 1990, meeting in Stavropol, signed a treaty that promised cooperation and joint crisis management. In a wonderful testimony to continuity, Article 3 echoed Bismarck's vaunted Reinsurance Treaty of 1887: "If one of the two states should become the target of aggression, then the other side will give the aggressor no military aid or other support."

From Moscow to Maastricht

This second "Reinsurance Treaty," coming 103 years after the first, represented the older continuity of German grand strategy: No matter how deeply committed Germany became to another power, it preserved the "tie to St. Petersburg," which would diminish Germany's dependence on its primary ally while keeping the flanks from uniting against the center. Another compact, the Treaty of Maastricht signed by the fifteen members of the European Union on February 7, 1992, reaffirmed a more recent continuity: Its main element was European Monetary Union (EMU)—the introduction of a common currency, the euro. The euro would at first coexist with the various national currencies, but by January 1, 2002, francs, marks, guilders, lira, and so on were to be history, replaced by euros and cents.

There was a strategic impetus behind the Treaty of Maastricht and EMU. Perhaps the hour of its birth should be rendered thus:[58] The place is the library of the Elysée Palace, the time is early March 1990. Only three people are present: François Mitterrand, the French president; Helmut Kohl, the chancellor of soon-to-be reunited Germany; and, since neither speaks the other's language, a faceless interpreter.

Mitterrand is in a melancholy mood. Over the last several months, ever since the collapse of the Berlin Wall in November 1989, he has tried every diplomatic stratagem to stop, or at least brake, the quickening pace of German reunification. But to no avail. Glumly, he stares into the fire as his friend Helmut says all the right things.

"Look, François, this time it won't be like Versailles in 1871, when the new Reich was proclaimed on the ruins of French pride. We have Franco-German friendship; we have the European Union; our forces are completely integrated in NATO; we don't even have our own general staff."

Mitterrand continues to stare into the fire. Then, he bursts out: "Bon, Helmut, c'est ce qu'on va faire [that's what we'll do]. You get all of Deutschland, if I get half of the deutsche marks."

The point of this imaginary scene is that the euro is above all a political currency. It was born out of an abrupt and wrenching transformation of world politics: Moscow's capitulation in the Cold War that suddenly revealed the true power relationships on the Continent. In a few months, on October 3, 1990, Germany would be "whole and free" again, as George Bush had put it; once united, the country would also shed the ancient dependencies that had tied two-thirds of it, the Federal Republic, to France.

But like Bismarck, Kohl understood the precarious position of Germany—about to become the dominant power in Europe again by dint of population, GNP, and central strategic location. Like Adenauer and Brandt, Kohl knew that Germany was too weak to stand alone but too strong to be left alone. The lesson of the past 100 years was practically bred into his genes: When Germany, its power untrammeled, struck out on its own, it reaped ever greater disaster. Yet when it was safely encased in communal institutions, when its power was "socialized," so to speak, it flourished beyond belief. Self-abnegation was the price of self-assertion, and community the condition of leadership.

Germany's Cold War chains were about to drop off, and so Kohl sought to reassure France and the rest of Europe by replacing the Cold War bonds with those forged by integration. The deutsche mark was the very symbol of German primacy. What better way to soften its edge than to multinationalize the country's currency? By way of the euro, Germany proposed to tie itself down. To the French, invaded thrice by Germany in the space of a lifetime, the euro offered perfect compensation. The French had lost the War of 1870–1871 and had emerged from World Wars I and II as nominal victors only, watching helplessly as their postwar containment strategies withered within a few years. And now, in 1990, the last constraints on Germany would melt away. On October 3 the Federal Republic would expand by one-half while gaining complete sovereignty of united Germany. Kohl's gracious offer of the deutsche mark as the foundation for a European currency was a godsend for France.

On Germany's part, this act of self-containment was, like all previous partings with autonomy, a condition of self-assertion. German power would lose its edge but not its purpose if Europe's institutions embodied German interests writ large. And so it was with monetary union.

To begin with, the "convergence criteria"[59] of EMU reflected the German priority of monetary stability. Second, EMU is run by the European Central Bank, located in Frankfurt, which is practically a copy of the Bundesbank. Third, EMU was chained to the Stability Pact, a German invention, that prescribed monetary and fiscal discipline not only during the run-up to the introduction of the euro (1993–1998) but forever more. Fourth, and perhaps most fundamentally, monetary union reflected sound German economic interests. As the strongest trading power in Europe, Germany has an obvious stake in stable exchange rates within a market that takes two-thirds of German exports. That interest had already driven the European Monetary System (EMS), the forerunner of EMU that Schmidt established in 1979. Since the 1960s, the deutsche mark had relentlessly appreciated against the dollar (from DM4.20 to about 1.70 at century's end) and against key European currencies (except the Swiss franc). A rising currency forever threatened German export surpluses, the very engine of the economy. Embedded in monetary union, however, Germany would no longer have to take the brunt of such revaluation pressures. While rising collectively against the dollar, Europe's currencies would remain locked to each other. Hence Germany would not suffer a loss of competitiveness vis-à-vis its European neighbors.

Monetary union, the greatest surrender of sovereignty yet, was not such a big sacrifice for the largest power in the system because the player who shapes the rules profits most from the game. And Germany profited twice from EMU, politically and economically. By Europeanizing the deutsche mark, the very symbol of German primacy, EMU reassured France and the rest of Europe about the suddenly unshackled giant in their midst. But by Germanizing the rules of monetary union, Kohl and his finance minister Theo Waigel made sure that Europe would become a formalized deutsche mark zone in everything but name. The region's largest economy and exporter would benefit most from a system in which revaluation pressures would push up not the deutsche mark alone but everybody together, and in which Germany's European competitors could no longer manipulate their exchange rates for gain.

After Bipolarity:
No Threats, No Temptations

For Germany, the system has been destiny. Regimes have come and gone, yet whatever their coloration they had to act on an unyielding stage. Whether called political geography, geopolitical reality, or the structure of power, one thing never changed: Germany's location in the heart of Europe. Its size and might waxed and waned, but even in the best of circumstances it never moved beyond "semi-hegemony." At its strongest it could defeat any rival, but it could never defeat all of them together. That fact was foreshadowed by Frederick's calamities in the Seven Years' War and conclusively demonstrated by the two world wars.

Hence the monster of encirclement has overshadowed all of German grand strategy. Germany both suffered and sometimes profited from its central position. But whether ruled by absolutist kings or Social Democratic chancellors, whether resorting to balance, alliance, or hegemonic war, Germany had to live with the eternal problem of vulnerable frontiers and powerful neighbors on both flanks.

At no time was the system more Germany's destiny than during the four decades of bipolarity. The Cold War reduced Germany's options and maximized its constraints. It forced upon (West) Germany a commitment to the West that was unprecedented in the nation's history. Still, two Cold War factors reinforced the time-honored imperative of reinsurance in the East: First, presiding over the most exposed country of the NATO Alliance, every Bonn government has sought an additional margin of safety by partial propitiation of the Soviet Union. Second, the Soviet Union was not only the greatest threat to Germany but also its greatest potential benefactor, for reunification was Moscow's alone to give or withhold.

Yet when the Soviet Union collapsed on Christmas Day 1991, Germany's ancient structural dependence on both the East and the West vanished overnight. This sea change has transformed Germany's strategic geography on the threshold of the twenty-first century. Never before has Germany enjoyed such a propitious strategic situation. Volker Rühe, defense minister from 1992 to 1998, could not have put it more succinctly: "Now, we are encircled only by friends."

For the first time since the founding of the Bismarckian Reich—indeed, since Prussia's rise—the rules of the international game *favor* Germany. Unity was accomplished not by "blood and iron" but with the consent of *all* the great powers. Unlike the Germany of Frederick and Bismarck, the Berlin Republic need not guard against permanent enemies. Unlike the Weimar Republic, it does not have to play East against West. Gone is the unique dependence that chained Adenauer to the West, and so is the pressure to pay tribute to the East that bedeviled Brandt, Schmidt, and even Kohl, the most Western-minded of Adenauer's successors. The classic obstacle course of German foreign policy was simply flattened along with bipolarity in the early 1990s, leaving behind the smoothest of playing fields.

The point is that, as far as the eye can see, Germany faces no strategic threat—an absolute novelty in its history. To assure its security, Germany need not even rattle sabers, let alone unsheathe them. To gain status Germany need not clamor for a "place in the sun" and thus provoke those whom it is trying to impress. To assert power, Germany does not have to send panzers into wars it could never win. Freed from the specter of war, the post–bipolar game favors those whose chips are dominated in the currency of economic power—or, more generally, in "soft power."[60] The clout wielded by Europe's no. 1 economy was nicely demonstrated by writing the rules of the European Monetary Union and establishing a central bank modeled on its own. In such a game, encirclement and the "nightmare of coalitions" have lost their meaning. Though rivalry persists even among the best of friends, the competition is inherently peaceful, and cooperation is encased by the expanding institutional framework of the European Union.

It has been said (since Immanuel Kant) that democracy is the father of peace. In the German case, the statement should be reversed: Benign international systems favor peace and democracy. The most chauvinistic nation of this century has become as aggressive as a sloth. Why? First of all, democracy flourishes best in a setting where safety is assured, and authoritarians profit most when they can manipulate external threats for the sake of maximal power at home. Thus the amazing democratic miracle of postwar Germany cannot be separated from the mighty deterrent wall on the Elbe River that was manned by U.S. troops and reinforced by nuclear weapons until the Russian/Soviet army departed homeward in 1994. In a stable no-threat environment, this miracle will surely endure. Second, history has seared an indelible lesson into Germany's collective consciousness. Whenever the country tried to go it alone, it reaped ever larger disaster, as it did in 1914 and 1939. Yet when it sought safety and influence in community—from NATO to the European Union—it flourished.

The habits learned in the latter part of this century will not soon vanish, especially because they serve Germany even better in a post-bipolar system low on threats and high on options. Whatever the country needs can be acquired most safely by harnessing winning coalitions within the institutional framework of Europe that is spreading eastward via the enlargement of EU and NATO. Nor are these shackles likely to become too onerous, because the constraints created by these communities are the very condition of Germany's self-assertion. For from these constraints flows reassurance, shortening the shadow of power this newly liberated Germany casts over the rest of Europe.[61] This moral has been well internalized. Reunited Germany had to be dragged, not bridled, by its NATO allies to dispatch combat forces—for the first time since World War II—into the Bosnian theater in 1995.

Reunified Germany is in a position Germany has never before enjoyed: comfortable with its possessions and unchallenged by its neighbors, no longer needing to be on guard against the ambitions of others and against threats of its own making. In so benign a setting grand strategy has a high ratio of options to constraints, a ratio that is nicely reflected in the sprawling, postmodern structure of German foreign policy in the 1990s.

What are the main girders of Germany's new foreign policy?

The first is *the tie to the security of NATO and the U.S.*, which discharges a triple function. The U.S.-led alliance serves as insurance against danger from the East, either from a resurgence of the Russian threat or from Russia's descent into chaos. Furthermore, the United States has been the indispensable organizer of "out of area" operations (in Bosnia, in the Kosovo conflict, and in the Persian Gulf). Finally, as in the past, the Atlantic anchor reassures not only Germany but also its neighbors by taking the sting out of Germany's power and the country's centrality in the European balance.

The second is a *continental option*, embodied in Germany's special relationship with France. Like the Atlantic tie, this axis was also forged in midcentury, when West Germany needed France as legitimizer and secondary protector. Germany's demand for security from France has vanished, and its need for legitimization by the French has dwindled, but the two countries' interests continue to dovetail. Each of the two regards (and manipulates) the other as an indispensable partner in the leadership of Europe and as a latent counterweight against the "last remaining superpower."[62]

A third element in German foreign policy, an element that helps Germany limit its dependence on France, is its *tie to Britain*. Some German interests—like freer trade or the eastward extension of the EU and NATO—are better served by London (and the Hague) than by Paris, which is perennially pushing for tighter Western European combinations as a balance against the United States. Following the Franco-German model, Bonn and London have instituted regular bilateral consultations.

The fourth is the traditional *Russian connection*—though greatly scaled down because Moscow now has very little with which to blackmail or to bribe Germany. In the past, West Germany's exposure to Moscow's armed might and Moscow's control over the pace and intensity of inter-German relations required a goodly measure of propitiation on West Germany's part. With Soviet power gone and Germany reunified, it is now the fear of Russian weakness—the specter of a "Weimar Russia"—that makes for solicitous (and worried) attention.

Fifth, because the Russian connection is so uncertain, the *stabilization of Germany's Eastern European hinterland* is an immediate task. Germany has been more eager than most to extend Western institutions eastward. This strategy makes sense economically and geographically. Economically, these countries function for Germany much as Mexico does for the United States: They are next-door neighbors with wage to productivity ratios that will continue to stay favorable compared to Germany's levels, the highest in the world. Their markets are ideally suited for penetration, but that requires political stability. Hence Germany is in the forefront of those who would attach the east-central Europeans to the EU and NATO, though they are taking care not to do so too blatantly for fear of alienating Russia.

Of course, these five elements do not add up to a coherent whole. The French connection does not harmonize with the Atlantic one, and the central European strategy clashes with the remaining two, reassuring Russia and maintaining homogeneity in the EU for the purpose of "deepening" the community and protecting it against cheap competition, above all in agriculture.

Other things remaining equal, Germany will therefore pursue a strategy of diversification, balance, and compensation, trying to give unto Peter without taking from Paul and to evade exclusive commitments. Above all, and in the absence of a strategic threat, Germany will try to do what it knows best: to play out the advantages of being a soft power actor while eschewing for as long as possible the ways of a traditional great power and the use of force. And why not? If a country is surrounded only by friends, it will seek to keep them. If it enjoys a setting emptied of the threat of war, it will labor hard to preserve it. For this is a wondrous system indeed: permissive, peaceful, and reasonably protected from the turmoil that continues to grip the rest of the world.

But there is a twist, a continuity that endures above and beyond the vanished strategic threat. Precisely because the system has been Germany's destiny, all German statesmen from Bismarck on have tried to Germanize the system: to structure it in ways that favor German purposes while constraining the options of others. Bismarck sought to Germanize the European system by making the Reich the center of all Europe's major strategic relationships. Stresemann crafted a system based on the Treaties of Locarno (with the West) and Berlin (with Russia) that made both sides beholden to the Weimar Republic in their dealings with each other. Adenauer Germanized the West's policy toward the East, and so, with a different thrust, did Brandt. Schmidt acted out that reflex, too: Unable to insulate the European center from the fallout of the Cold War, he strained to mute and mediate the conflict of the strong to protect the fortunes of his own nation. Nothing could exemplify the primacy of the system better than reunification. Before reunification could happen, bipolarity had to collapse, and it had to collapse in the right way, without violence and war. So it was not enough just to pursue German interests; in order to advance them, Kohl had to work on the European system first: pacifying Paris, compensating Moscow, and winning over Washington as sponsor and shepherd.

The obvious pitfall, which has survived the strategic threat that dominated the first forty years of the Federal Republic's existence, is overreach. Precisely because Germany is so beholden to system dominance, it will always try to dominate the system itself—to structure it in ways that favor German interests. To structure Germany's milieu in favor of German interests evidently became easier on the eve of the twenty-first century when bipolarity, partition, and Germany's legitimacy deficit eroded. It was no surprise, then, that at least the style of German policy changed when Kohl left the stage in the fall of 1998. Also, his successors, Social Democratic chancellor Gerhard Schröder and Foreign Minister Joschka Fischer of the Green Party, hail from a different generation. They came of age in the mid-1960s, with no personal memory of Nazism and World War II.

To begin with, the new chancellor took on the EU in the manner of Margaret ("I want my money back") Thatcher. Schröder told his neighbors that in the past, "compromises in Europe were achieved because Germany paid for them. This policy has reached its end." To reduce Germany's financial contributions to the EU, Schröder coolly threatened to "postpone," that is, block, the EU's eastward enlargement.[63] With a touch of resentment, Schröder noted, "All of our EU partners may forcefully pursue their interests; only we Germans apparently must not do this."[64] His finance minister Oskar Lafontaine called for the upward "harmonization" of EU taxes on the simple premise that Germany's high-tax environment could not endure as long as commercial rivals like Britain and the Netherlands exacted far lower rates from business. The Green ecology minister, Jürgen Trittin, pushed for an energy tax and the closing of all nuclear power plants in Germany.

Yet none of these goals could be achieved by Germany alone; continuity reasserted itself even in the face of systemic and generational discontinuity. The "harmonization" that Lafontaine demanded required the Germanization of the EU's tax policy. Nor could Germany bring about antinuclearism in one country, because it was bound to France and Britain by long-term contracts under which spent German fuel was reprocessed in La Hague and Sellafield. When Foreign Minister Fischer demanded that NATO formally renounce nuclear first-use, he was attempting to Germanize NATO strategy, a sally that would have been inconceivable during the Cold War.

Given Germany's peculiar position, Europe must be persuaded to accept the country's interests as its own. Sometimes, as in the case of the European Monetary Union, Germany's interests *are* those of Europe, and so the European Central Bank becomes the Bundesbank writ large. In other cases this dynamic generates the familiar problem of ambitions outpacing power. So the system remains destiny—but with a benign twist.

At no time has the system delivered so many blessings to the country in the middle as it has on the verge of the third millennium. Hence this Germany, the country that has profited most from the post-1945 international system, will deal far more tenderly and responsibly with the world than did its predecessors in the first half of the twentieth century. This means that Berlin will be more likely to inject German-made public goods into the system than to try to squeeze benefits out of it. In other words, it will act more responsibly than does the world's second most powerful economy, Japan. Nor is this just a matter of goodness. Though Schröder started out in 1998 by trying to blackmail the EU into reducing Germany's dues, he soon came to view Germany's net contribution of DM22 billion (about $12 billion) in the proper perspective: The sum simply paled when compared to the enormous profits the EU's largest trading power extracts from the unified market.

Will this benign structure hold? Only one thing is sure. Bipolarity has vanished, and autonomy is growing. It is the Long Peace, the longest in the history of Europe, that eclipsed traditional power politics in the second half of the twentieth century. And this glorious era rested not just on democracy and integration but also on the pillars that secured both of these good things.

One pillar was the U.S. security guarantee, which spared the Europeans the necessity of devising autonomous security policies, a classic cause of conflict among nations. The other was the military stalemate that rendered unthinkable the use of force. One of these—bipolarity—has already collapsed. The other—the U.S. umbrella—has outlived the peculiar historical circumstances that gave rise to it. The Atlantic Alliance has endured and indeed expanded to include Poland, the Czech Republic, and Hungary at a time when it should have disappeared along with the strategic threat that spawned it in 1949. So the best parts of the postwar system—economic and military community—continue to endure. But why should this wondrous system last forever? If and when it changes, so will Germany's destiny, now more richly blessed by history's fortunes than at any time since Prussia's sudden rise to power.

5

THE THREE RUSSIAS

Decline, Revolution, and Reconstruction

ROBERT LEGVOLD

WHAT THREAD BINDS TOGETHER the foreign policy experiences of Imperial Russia, Soviet Russia, and the new Russia? What can be said to relate today's Russia—shorn of an empire central to its identity for a half-millennium, a Russia that is weak and muddled—to the expanding, tyrannized Russias of Nicholas II and Stalin? The tie is not in a single core set of goals—not, as many have suggested, the search for warm water ports and possession of the Black Sea Straits, not the drive to dominate what Halford Mackinder called the Eurasian "heartland" or short of that, to control the politics of eastern and central Europe, the physical intersection of Russia with Europe's other great powers.[1] On the contrary, on more occasions and for more years than not over the last 300 years, Russian behavior has only weakly responded to these impulses. Nor can the thread be found in a dominating relationship or a compelling dread. At times Russia's engagement in the outside world has been heavily shaped, even monopolized, by great rivalries (Peter the Great's with Sweden, nineteenth-century Russia's with Great Britain, and the postwar Soviet

Union's with the United States). In the larger scheme of things, however, these too were episodes rather than regularities. The longest of them, the conflict between Russia and Great Britain, lasted from 1853, when the Crimean War broke out, to 1907, the year of the Anglo-Russian spheres agreement. The U.S.-Soviet rivalry was shorter but left a more important legacy, not simply because it held sway only yesterday but because it more thoroughly penetrated all aspects of each country's foreign policy.

Nor does Russia's periodic sense of mission constitute a link across history. Important though its influence has at times been, the oft-alleged continuity among Russia as the "third Rome," pan-Slavism, and Bolshevik messianism misrepresents reality. To cite Martin Malia, when the monk Philotheus of Pskov described Muscovy at the fall of Constantinople in 1453 as the third and final Rome, he had in mind "not the power of the Muscovite state, but the purity, the 'right teaching,' of Muscovite Christianity."[2] Pan-Slavism, which gathered momentum in the last third of the nineteenth century, originated in circles outside the imperial court. It never became the official purpose of the imperial Russian state, and it stirred as much unease as enthusiasm among the monarch and many senior officials. Only Bolshevism created a true fusion of the state with a messianic idea. While a turning point of great consequence and one to which we will return, this merger represented discontinuity rather than continuity.

If the thread is not the Russian mission, then might it not be the allied theme of Russian exceptionalism? Russians have persistently seen their culture and values as distinctive, requiring or permitting an alternative path to modernity, and providing a superior lead for civilization. From Fyodor Dostoyevsky to Aleksandr Solzhenitsyn, they have declaimed the "Russian idea," prizing the country's spirituality, commitment to the collectivity over untrammeled individualism, and, when most idealized, cultural harmony.[3] Russian exceptionalism, however, exerts its influence in tension with an alternative self-image that since the first third of the nineteenth century has juxtaposed Slavophiles to Westernizers. While the character of the two camps has changed over time, the stakes have not. Then and now the basic dispute is over the right relationship to a particular civilization, notably, the West.

So persistent have been the effects of Russia's sense of difference that it comes close to being the thread for which we are looking. If it fails in this role, it is because over time it has changed too much in its very essence. In the eighteenth century the roots of Russian exceptionalism grew from events, as Peter forcibly imposed Western models on a resistant society and in the process engendered strains of opposition that endured well into the next century, and, some would insist, to our own day. But in the nineteenth century Russian exceptionalism was also transformed into a consciousness. It resolved among the intelligentsia into competing images of Russia's past and promise: Slavophiles stressed Russia's unique values (and value), and Westernizers emphasized Europe's values (and attraction). In 1917 the wheel turned again when Lenin's revolution obliterated that contrast and advanced instead an exceptionalism founded not on ambivalence over the West and its values but on Russia's perfection and transcendence of those values. Russian exceptionalism remains a powerful part of the historical legacy, casting a conspicuous shadow over current events in ways to which we will return.

It also relates directly to the feature that does figure in all of Russia's international history, the thread that does tie one period to the next and one Russia to the next: the turbulence surrounding Russia's location within the international system. Like Japan, Russia's place in the prevailing international order has set its foreign policy apart at virtually every stage of its modern history. In his chapter in this volume, Kenneth Pyle contends that for Japan place has usually meant face, understood as the power that yields respect and safety among the industrialized Western states. The Russian quest to resolve its relationship to the international order of the day, in contrast, has taken many forms, nearly always vexed and nearly always on a continuum whose one end is alienation.

Peter brought Russia *into* the European international system during the long years of the Northern War with Charles XII's Sweden (1700–1721), but he did not make it *of* the system. Even in its decisive phases, the Northern War was a sideshow to the main event, the War of the Spanish Succession (1701–1713), in which Europe's major powers occupied themselves with the ambitions of Louis XIV's France. By defeating Sweden, then one of Europe's major powers, establishing Russia's influence on the Baltic Sea, and giving it a dominating voice in

Polish affairs, Peter rendered his country incontestably a new factor in European politics. Yet Russia continued to be seen as an alien threat. Rather like the Ottoman Empire, it was considered to be outside the mainstream of Continental politics. As one British official put it,

> Germany and the entire North have never been in such grave peril as now, because the Russians should be feared more than the Turks. Unlike the latter, they do not remain in their gross ignorance and withdraw once they have completed their ravages, but, on the contrary gain more and more science and experience in matters of war and state, surpassing many nations in calculation and dissimulation and gradually advancing closer and closer to our lives.[4]

Nor did Peter appear to see the axis of his diplomacy as being fully or even primarily confined to the emergent European system of Westphalia and Utrecht. Throughout his reign, he looked south with nearly equal intensity. Though his wars and near wars against the Turks often affected and were affected by events in Europe, they remained nonetheless a separate preoccupation. And even though his covetous policies in the Baltics were partly intended to further his hopes for an expanded commerce with Europe, Europe scarcely occupied the whole of his attention in this regard. He also dreamed of the great profits to be had in trade with Persia, central Asia, and India and thought they warranted efforts to strengthen Russia's role in the Persian-controlled Caucasus, which led to the last of his military campaigns, the 1722–1723 war with Persia.

By the end of the eighteenth century, as a result of Russian expansion into the Black Sea region during Catherine the Great's reign and of Catherine's role in carving up Poland, Russia was a regular and key player in the European-dominated international order. Yet Russia's outward thrust and the dynamic of its relations with Europe's other major powers constituted the system's core ambiguity. The problem traced back to what made Russia truly different. This was neither its self-image nor, as might be imagined, its domestic political and social order (at least, not for much of the eighteenth century). Rather, Russia's difference lay in the nature of its frontiers.

In the international system of the eighteenth and nineteenth centuries, Russia and Great Britain were "flank powers." Britain, however, clearly defined the western reaches of Europe, in part because Britain in Europe, as opposed to the British Empire elsewhere, had little concern over frontiers. Russia, in contrast, not only confounded Europe's eastern limits but greatly complicated Europe's international relations by its policies in the formless or decaying frontiers encircling an expanding Russian Empire.

Long before Catherine, Russia's ambitions and maneuverings at the soft edges of the Ottoman Empire and in the debris of a once powerful Polish Empire had entangled it in the calculations of Europe's leading states. However, its conquest of Crimea and the shift in the power balance in the south from the Ottomans to the Russians in the wake of two successful wars against Turkey transformed what had been distant depredations into direct threats to others' basic interests in the Mediterranean, particularly those of Great Britain. Similarly, though Russia's role in the first partition of Poland (1772) was largely as an accessory (having triggered Austria's and Prussia's desire for compensation by its gains in the 1768–1774 Turkish war), Austria and Prussia also hoped to contain Russia by the deal. The last two partitions—in the 1790s, the final one obliterating Poland from the map— were very much at Empress Catherine's instigation. Like Russia's other aggrandizing moves, however, they were more a function of opportunity, the norms of the day, and the working of the European balance of power than of an inherent, irresistible Russian impulse to expand.

Then and long after, Russia's actions at the edges of its empire complicated, usually prejudiced, and sometimes dictated its place within the international system. Throughout these years its leaders struggled to manage and often to exploit the challenges raised in the south by the slow demise of the Ottoman Empire and in the west by the decrepitude of an independent Poland and later by the rebelliousness of a subjugated Poland. The collapse of the Austro-Hungarian Empire after 1914 might have accentuated the problem for Lenin's new Russia, but the Bolshevik regime was far too weak to meddle seriously in the enlarged inchoate stretch between Russia and a now-diminished

European international system. It could only encourage from the sidelines the quickly extinguished revolutions in Hungary and Bavaria and, in 1920, attempt disastrously to export revolution to Poland at bayonet's point. In contrast, after World War II, Stalin's imperious handling of the Soviet frontier with Europe launched the Cold War. Eastern Europe henceforth formed the point of departure for and the key underpinning of the Soviet engagement in a vastly altered bipolar international system. The collapse of the Soviet empire in 1991 posed the issue of frontiers anew. Both to the south and the west, Russia's frontiers had shrunk to pre-Petrine dimensions, but Russia's approach to them and its way of handling the threats and opportunities arising within them and promised to define Russia's position in the contemporary international order as much as ever.

Russia's problematic place in the international system has depended not only on the interplay where the system physically meets the empire. From Catherine's day forward, it has also stemmed from the growing difference between the way internal and external politics conjoined in Russia versus the way they came together for other major powers. When Catherine invaded Poland on the way to the second partition in 1793, she did so to quash the "spirit of insurrection and innovation," inspired by the Jacobinism of contemporary France.[5] Whatever her intellectual attachment to the French philosophes (and theirs to her), the French Revolution was an anathema. From then until Imperial Russia passed from the scene in 1917, it could find no way to make peace with the ideas and political influence of 1789. Throughout the nineteenth century, Nicholas I and his successors labored hard and unremittingly to contain their effects and, when the traces of 1789 erupted in renewed revolution in the early 1820s, 1830, and 1848, to crush them, if need be by military force.

For the first three decades after the victory over Bonaparte, hostility to liberalism reinforced Russia's partnership with Prussia and Austria. By the last half of the century, however, the latter two had begun transforming their conservative monarchies to accommodate the new forces, leaving Russia again alone. Russia's reactionary political order not only generated foreign policy requirements increasingly at odds with the agendas of Europe's other major powers, but made of trends abroad an extension of its own internal fears and passions. Other states and other political movements came to constitute a threat not only by what they did but by what they were. France's Louis Philippe, "the king of the barricades"; the Frankfurt Assembly of 1848; the Hungarian Republic of Lajos Kossuth—all represented a challenge derived from what Russia could not tolerate in its inner world. As Nicholas's foreign minister, Count Karl Robert von Nesselrode, said, coming to the aid of Frederick William IV of Prussia in resisting democratic inroads or of Emperor Franz-Joseph in crushing Kossuth's republic was not simply a matter of mutual security but of Russia's "internal tranquillity."

What made Russia different in this instance and what made its impulses perverse within the international system were not its readiness to interfere in the internal affairs of other states; it was no more guilty of that than were most of its European counterparts. Rather, its difference lay in the attempt to subordinate trends in other societies to the imperatives of its own domestic order.

In the Soviet period the Bolsheviks carried this deformation to an extreme. Starting from a notion of the world that judged states good or evil by the nature of their domestic orders, they reduced the dynamic of international politics to a function of the socioeconomic character of the states involved. They transformed threat into a function of a state's identity rather than of its intentions or behavior. In the postwar period, Soviet security within its own alliance system rested not on shared international interests or convergent foreign policies but on domestic political orthodoxy. Like their tsarist predecessors 100 years earlier, they reached for the sword when liberal change in neighboring societies impinged on their sense of well-being: in Berlin in 1953, Hungary in 1956, and Czechoslovakia in 1968.

Russia's dislocation within the international system, however, should not be taken for divorce from the system. For three centuries Russia has been a key player in the system. On rare but important occasions, it has even been one of its architects. Such was the case at the end of the Napoleonic Wars. Alexander I not only assumed a central role in constructing the intricate balance of power underpinning the postwar order, he and his successor made it a priority to preserve their collective handiwork for decades after. True, as he was inclined to argue by the first meeting of the European Alliance at Aix-la-Chapelle (1818), collaboration among the great powers should guarantee not only the territorial status quo but also a political order "based on 'wise' constitutions to be granted by the *sovereigns* to their people."[6] True, as well, he and Nicholas at times broke ranks and took matters into their own hands, as during the Greek civil war in the 1820s and in numerous other set-tos with the Turks. For the most part, however, they defined Russian national interest as living within the rules of the system and, when these were threatened, as rallying to their defense.

The other occasion when Russia was not merely a deeply involved participant but an architect of a new international system came at the end of World War II. Then, as in Alexander's day, Russia was in a dominant power position, something that has been rarely true over the last 300 years, for weakness has more often characterized its position. Indeed, within fifty years of the Congress of Vienna the shadow of Russian power had vanished, and within roughly the same number of years after the Yalta Conference the reality of Soviet power had disintegrated. While Soviet power lasted, however, Stalin and his successors were founders and co-managers of the postwar order. How they played this role introduces the last and most dramatic manifestation of Russia's historically tortured relationship with the prevailing international system.

The 1917 revolution made of Russia something it had never before been, a revolutionary state—not in Lenin's or Mao Zedong's sense but in Henry Kissinger's: That is, a state determined to overthrow the international order of the day.[7] The only other time Russia came close was during Catherine's reign. After her first victory over Turkey she devised a half-baked scheme to eliminate the Ottoman Empire and replace it with a restored Greek Orthodox empire ruled by her newborn grandson, christened Constantine for the occasion. Such would have gravely disrupted the European balance. Even in this case, however, she pursued her revisionist objective by seeking the blessing of another key player, Austria's Joseph II. Until 1917 Russia was at heart a status quo power. This does not mean that the Russians did not seek to aggrandize themselves regularly and handsomely from Peter's time to the end of the Romanov era. Their greed, however, always fell within the normal pattern of contemporary behavior and, more important, was never intended to destroy the larger order. On the contrary, more often than not they saw themselves as acting to strengthen it.

Not Lenin. The purpose of his revolution was not merely to extinguish the ancien régime at home. He intended to bring down the entire architecture of relations among states. He meant to do this not by altering a distribution of power but by obviating its significance, not by outmaneuvering other states but by undermining the means and modalities by which they acted. His was a revolution to end international relations as they had existed. Unlike Napoleon's France or Hitler's Germany, Lenin's Russia laid siege to the international system at a moment when it was itself weakest, which made the Russian challenge modest in comparison to its French and German counterparts. It also guaranteed that the international reality the Bolsheviks were bent on undoing would, in fact, be the undoing of their own inflated and misguided premises. When they accepted a separate and annexationist peace with Germany in March 1918, they were already a long way from their original revolutionary assumptions. They were also learning how to compromise and how to back and fill in the face of unfavorable circumstance, a practice that they would continue to perfect under Lenin's successors and that over time they would apply frequently, often with great cynicism.

Stalin's cynicism and his capacity to use power ruthlessly, however, was not the source of Soviet Russia's ongoing misfit within the international system. That stemmed from the Soviet Union's alienation within the system. No matter how brutal Stalin's subordination of others' revolutionary prospects to the needs of the Soviet state, no matter how un-Marxist Nikita Khrushchev's determination to inflict strategic defeats on the West in Berlin, and no matter how uninspired and mundane the foreign policy preoccupations of Leonid Brezhnev's regime, all three leaders remained united in their disbelief in the basic legitimacy of the international system. Scholars have vigorously divided over the sincerity of Stalin's commitment in the 1930s to collective security as an obstacle to Hitler's ambition, but the debate misses the point. Debate over whether Stalin wished to make meaningful the

League of Nations or the 1935 mutual assistance treaty with France, or whether he viewed them as merely a subterfuge, obscures the fact that either course was but an expedient to which he attached no inherent value.[8] As with his eventual wartime alliance with the United States and Great Britain, his choices could only be instrumental; normative choices were beside the point in a world whose preservation he could not accept.

Hence, although after victory in 1945 Stalin liked to compare himself to Alexander I, they had little in common as architects of postwar orders. Alexander helped to create a system whose premises and organization were embraced by the other great powers. Stalin shared none of the assumptions of the Anglo-Saxons with whom he helped to fashion a postwar order. The institutions and arrangements on which they agreed at the wartime conferences were for him superficial expedients rather than the infrastructure of an enduring international system. His eagerness to divide the postwar map into spheres of influence, his bald effort to regain every scrap of the lands held by Imperial Russia and then some, his preoccupation with status and rewards commensurate to those of the United States and Great Britain, and his attempt to forestall and manipulate coalitions among the other powers rested on the notion that eventually all of this would perish. He was a Russian imperialist on a scale matching any of his tsarist predecessors, but he was also a revolutionary persuaded that the forces of history had doomed his adversaries and the international order they had contrived and dominated.[9] Evidence suggests that at the war's close, although he did not rule out a prolongation of cooperation between the Soviet Union and his partners in the Grand Alliance, he viewed it as an interlude. Sooner or later the fateful dynamic within the capitalist world would lead to conflict and the next phases in the breakdown of the old order.

Those who came after Stalin continued to deviate from revolutionary orthodoxy in order to cope with such changing international realities as the appearance of nuclear weapons, the rise of nationalist challenges within their own camp, and the emergence of the Sino-Soviet conflict. Doctrine, wooden in its incantation and rubbery in its formulation, came to seem increasingly hollow as a motive force. These trends, however, failed to alter the underlying reality: Until Mikhail Gorbachev, even the most pragmatic Soviet leaders operated with a set of assumptions in which competitors were adversaries by nature, not circumstance; in which tensions were a function of social systems, not an inherent feature of international politics; and in which cooperation among states, although important, particularly in controlling nuclear arms and achieving economic benefit, was a limited and temporary expedient, not a durable and fundamental path forward.

Eventually, Russia had a third chance to be a key architect of a postwar order. Again, for the second time, it had the opportunity to do so in consensus with other great powers. And for the first time it had the chance to resolve Russia's problematic relationship to the international system. Gorbachev's foreign policy revolution had cut to the core of the Leninist conceptual universe and undone the last remnants sustaining the Soviet Union's alienation. As the Cold War ended, thanks in no small part to his efforts, he began sketching a vision for the next international order that was radically different from anything that any Russian leader had ever imagined. It was a vision far closer to Woodrow Wilson's than even contemporary U.S. leaders were ready to venture. His role in creating the new order, however, ended before it began. The collapse of the Soviet Union removed Russia as an architect and left Gorbachev's successors to wrestle with the historic problem of their country's place within the international system, a system whose shape would, again, be largely beyond their control.

Russia in the Twentieth Century

No country, not even Germany, was more scarred than Russia by the great, tragic, seminal event of this century, World War I. Russia entered the war a vast but spent empire under the absolutist sway of an increasingly brittle monarchy. It was weighed down by an increasingly impoverished but still dominant landed aristocracy and a peasantry only a few decades beyond serfdom. Russia exited the war in turmoil. The old regime had been smashed, its empire was in pieces, and a new radical revolutionary group attached to a small urban proletariat was clinging precariously to the fragments of power seized in November 1917. All around, opposition gathered. Within four months of the Bolshevik coup d'état, Lenin's fragile regime was embroiled in civil war. Disparate armies assailed it from three directions. Military forces from France, Great Britain, the United States, and Japan took up positions on Russian soil, ostensibly to fight the Germans but not above making life still more difficult for the new regime. On the fourth side, to the west, the German Kaiser's military had just extracted the painful Treaty of Brest Litovsk (in March 1918), by which the Bolsheviks conceded one-third of the empire's population together with control over Ukraine, Finland, and the Baltic and Polish territories.

Nicholas II's Russia was a doomed, dying creature, living out its last two decades trying to find minor escapes from ills its leaders only dimly understood. A reckless war with Japan in 1904, economic recession, and the growing brushfire of worker strikes and peasant disorders turned 1905 into a dress rehearsal for revolution. The tsar, having failed to quell a rising tide by violence, reluctantly agreed to an elected parliament. But it was toothless: It had no power to approve or censure the government, limited control over the budget, and no authority to monitor its implementation. Even this pitiable challenge exceeded Nicholas's forbearance. At the first excuse he dissolved the first Duma and the second Duma a year later in summer 1907. Nicholas's concessions had exposed the cracks in absolutism but had not implanted the genuine rudiments of constitutionalism.

On the eve of the war Imperial Russia was a complex of trends. On the one hand, economic growth had resumed, export trade was expanding, and some aspects of the agricultural system were being improved; on the other hand, the brief window of liberalization in religion, education, and the treatment of non-Russian nationalities that opened during the weakening of the regime in 1905 was again being closed. At the same time, the radicalization of the regime's opposition grew apace.

Making the drama more compelling, Russia's internal decline paralleled the unhinging of the nineteenth-century international order, which like Russia perished not with a whimper but a bang. At the heart of its demise was the lethal interaction of two other moribund empires—the Austro-Hungarian and the Ottoman—and the rise of a new continental power, a unified Germany. By the turn of the century Russia had turned from its Prussian/German alignment to a new partnership with France. By 1907 its new orientation would lead to a reconciliation of Russia with Great Britain. Russia, in this new configuration, scarcely sought hostility with Germany and its Austro-Hungarian partner. On the contrary, Nicholas in particular worked to the last to find some grounds for restored cooperation. But turmoil in the Balkan portion of the Turkish Empire lured the Austro-Hungarians in, out of fear that developments among the southern Slavs would infect the restless portions of their own Slavic peoples. Across the divide the Russians backed the Serbs, the object of Austro-Hungarian ire. From 1908 to 1914, in a slow dance of death, the Bulgarians, Serbs, Greeks, and Turks made war, the Austro-Hungarians and the Russians edged toward confrontation on behalf of their warring clients, and the Germans, forced to choose, chose their Austrian cousins. The British, fearing the rise of German power, and the French, fearing the failure of their alliance system, weighed in on the Russian side. Thence, when in late June 1914 a Bosnian Serb assassinated the heir to the Habsburg throne in Sarajevo, not just the Balkan antagonists but Europe went to war.

When the cataclysm was over, Russia, weak, fractured, yet arrogant in its revolutionary pretensions, had been reduced to a side issue in European politics. As at the 1815 Congress of Vienna following the Napoleonic Wars, the victors were focused on constructing an order to keep the vanquished — primarily the Germans — in line. The new Russian regime, as already noted, injected a radically different notion of international relations, but it was too preoccupied with the challenges at home to do much to bring it about. Other than a measure of rabble-rousing at the edges of the European system and among the "toilers of the East" (principally in Persia, India, and Afghanistan), the Bolsheviks had their minds mostly on loosening the noose of civil war and breaking their near-complete isolation.

One strand of their efforts concentrated on inducing the major Western powers to extend recognition, and with it aid, to an economy battered by war and by the excessively exuberant revolutionary exper-

iments of 1918–1921. The second strand focused on a backstage maneuver to forge ties with Europe's other pariah state, Germany. To the
stunned consternation of London and Paris, Lenin's emissaries did
manage to persuade the German delegation attending the 1922
Genoa conference on European reconstruction to sneak off to the
neighboring seaside city of Rapallo, where the two governments cut
their own deal.

Throughout the 1920s, however, the Soviet Union acted from a position of weakness. At home the regime toiled to rebuild a decimated
state and empire under a new, half-thought-out, and troubled economic model. Following Lenin's death in early 1924, a struggle for
power clouded Soviet politics, until in the early 1930s Stalin had
picked off a sufficient number of his competitors to seem the probable
successor. Throughout these years Soviet policy-makers struggled to
have their cake and eat it too: They sought normal state-to-state relations and trade with Europe's major powers while at the same time
their revolutionary arm, the Comintern, encouraged the formation,
development, and subordination of local Communist parties, Com-
munist-dominated trade unions, and youth organizations dedicated to
overthrowing the political orders of these same states. Insofar as
Lenin and those who survived him had a national security agenda, it
focused on the past. Hence, they feared most that the British and
French would once again try to strangle the regime with sanctions or,
worse, that they would contrive a provocation in or near the Soviet
Union as a pretext for direct intervention. Much of policy was organized, often rather circuitously and lamely, around efforts to head off
this danger.

By the early 1930s, with Stalin now firmly in the saddle, the Soviet
Union's security challenge grew larger and altogether more tangible.
The rise of Italian fascism, Japanese militarism, and German Nazism,
linked by a desire to overthrow much if not all of the existing international order, was again setting the world on the road to general war.
The aggressors were helped by confusion and illusions on the part of
Europe's other great powers. Soviet ideology biased Stalin and his colleagues to see this danger sooner than did many in the West. They
feared that whatever the "imperialist" nature of the war, their country

could not avoid being dragged in and, even worse, that the Western powers would conspire to divert the aggressors eastward. Meanwhile, amid these gathering clouds Stalin was rushing his country into a violent transformation of its agricultural base and forced-draft industrialization, followed soon by a crash defense program. At the same time, rather incongruously, he unleashed a massive, murderous purge of the Communist Party, the Soviet military, and other critical segments of society.

In the half-decade before World War II the Soviet Union simultaneously traveled two paths: One led toward collaboration with the Western democracies in hopes of containing the events and protagonists leading to war; the other began with appeasement of Hitler's Germany and concluded with the 1939 Nazi-Soviet Pact, by which the two carved up central Europe in anticipation of war. On the first path, the Soviet Union entered an earlier vilified League of Nations, just as the aggressors were exiting it; argued vainly for strengthening its sanctions; failing that, toyed with substituting mutual assistance pacts tying France to the Soviet Union and both to states lying in the corridor between Germany and the Soviet Union; and reoriented the Communist International toward antifascist resistance. On the second path, Stalin kept open his options with Berlin and sought expanded trade and other forms of cooperation. At every turn he made it plain that his choices in no way involved a moral or normative preference for the first over the second path. Thus, when the first path led nowhere—and historians disagree over how much Stalin's actions contributed to this outcome; indeed, some deny that the first path ever existed in his mind—he had no trouble shifting to the second. His deal with Hitler bought his country two years' freedom from German aggression, far less time than he had hoped. And then in June 1941, Hitler's armies were turned on his country.

The Soviet Union came out of World War II fearfully ravaged (15 percent of its population and 50 percent of its economic infrastructure were destroyed). Militarily, however, it stood astride half of Europe, emerging as one of two powers best placed to impose its preferences on the postwar order. For the first time in nearly one and a half centuries Russia was not on the losing end of a major war. Stalin made the most of victory to solidify his hold on the booty from his 1939 deal with Hitler and to reclaim territories lost since tsarist days. None of this would have produced the Cold War had he not also insisted on dictating the character of the regimes put in place in a postwar Eastern Europe.

Stalin may have wished the wartime cooperation among the British, the newly dominant Americans, and the Soviets to continue into the postwar period, but for two reasons this could not be. First, though the Soviet position in the world had changed (from being an object of international politics to an architect), the Soviet view of the world had not. This profoundly influenced the terms on which Stalin was prepared to cooperate. Second, the emergence of two great hegemons in the vast power vacuums of post-war Europe and Asia was bound to generate considerable U.S.-Soviet jostling. Combined, these factors produced a slow dynamic that eroded cooperation and hardened competition.

Not only was the Soviet Union again squarely at the heart of international politics, but the new international order for the first time in modern history was divided in two and stretched across the globe. For the first time it was an East-West order. And for the first time Russia was a power above all others save one.[10] In the initial phases of this new order, though other nations saw the Soviet Union as an expansionist power bent on controlling ever wider expanses of territory to its east, south, and particularly west, it saw itself as being on the defensive (albeit not without opportunities to probe here and there to advance the revolutionary cause, especially in Asia after the Chinese communists swept into Beijing in October 1949). The first major tests of strength between East and West, the Berlin blockade of 1948 and the beginning of the Korean War in 1950, were more the products of miscalculation on Stalin's part—driven in the first instance by a sense of vulnerability and in the second by an underestimation of U.S. commitment—than of a coherent design for inflicting large-scale strategic defeats on the West. Throughout these years Stalin's attention remained focused on Europe. In Europe his preoccupations converged. The enormous task of rebuilding the Soviet economy; girding for a military, including an atomic, competition; solidifying Soviet control over Eastern Europe; and facing the West where the fusion of its power was the most formidable all became one in Europe.

Stalin's successors started from the same base, for the backbone of the postwar order remained a divided Germany within a divided Europe. But gradually, after Nikita Khrushchev impetuously tried to force the West's hand in the Berlin crises of 1958–1961 and the 1962 Cuban missile crisis, the Soviet leadership moved the active parts of the contest to the more fluid outer reaches of the international system. The expansion of the Cold War to the Middle East, to southeast Asia, and eventually to Africa obscured the constraining effect on Soviet foreign policy of two major new developments: the impact of nuclear weapons on great power competition and the impact of nationalism and defection within communism, most dramatic in the Sino-Soviet conflict, on the Soviet camp. By the end of the 1960s the Soviet Union's renewed postwar economic dynamism had faltered, at precisely the time it had finally achieved genuine strategic nuclear parity with the United States. Thus it had strong incentives to explore a better-managed competition with the West together with enhanced economic cooperation. The early 1970s' détente with the West, however, was a spongy affair in Soviet minds and a weak constraint on Soviet behavior in southern and east Africa, where in the mid-1970s third-world turmoil next erupted. By the late 1970s détente had gone a-glimmering, and with the Soviet invasion of Afghanistan in 1979 a partial reprise of the early harsh Cold War years occurred, only now with the United States in the catbird seat in a Sino-Soviet-U.S. triangle.

Gorbachev, faced with an atrophying domestic order and frustrated by an overextended and counterproductive foreign policy, called a halt to the East-West contest as it had been variously waged over the past four decades. His revolutionary modification of Soviet foreign policy ended the Cold War even before events ended the Soviet Union.

Again the wheel had turned. Russia was back to the start: weak, reduced in size, a price-taker rather than a price-maker, and struggling to reinvent itself. Initially the leadership of this new, third Russia merged its democratic, market-oriented aspirations at home with its policy abroad. Boris Yeltsin and his first foreign minister, Andrei Kozyrev, assumed that democracy in Russia should be pursued by making Russia a part of the West. So they embraced the far-reaching innovations of the Gorbachev era and then took the next step. Russia would seek not simply to fashion a constructive relationship with the industrialized democracies but to make itself a member of their club. Soon, however, the trials of reform within Russia, the challenge of coming to terms with new neighbors and an imperial past, and the disappointments of "partnership" with the industrialized democracies ended the experiment. Russia headed in new directions, but without much of a compass other than frustrated national pride, anxiety over its troubled transition to a new order, and an awareness of a shrinking set of foreign policy options in a world less than ever subject to its influence.

Making Something of History

Contemporary Russia can no more escape this history than it can immaculately will itself into democracy or any other de novo identity. What Russia is, how its leaders think and react, and what its society expects, fears, and dreams of reflect what has been written in earlier chapters of its history. At the same time, nothing stays the same, including the world in which, for good or ill, Russia finds itself more enmeshed than ever. As surely as context gives meaning to text, the post–Cold War international setting twists and reshapes the legacy of the two prior Russias. The features of Russia's past that survive in the new Russia of our day do so in altered form and significance. History counts, but as a continually reprocessed influence.

  As the chapters in this book show, foreign policy for all states is the creature of many influences. Some are physical givens: Where a country is situated geographically, how generous its natural resources and defenses, and how vast its territory and population. Some are more organic, grown on the soil of the country, such as political culture, the mentality of a society, and what it makes of historical experience. Some derive from the nature of a country's political system and how it goes about making political decisions. And some come from the outside, from the character of the international environment, from the configuration of power among the major states, from the underlying purposes of other states, and from the primary dynamic of international relations in a given era (toward peace or war, toward more or less integration, and the primacy of economic or security concerns). Rarely, however, do these influences operate uniformly, with the same relative weight, and unmediated.

In the Russian case, these influences have merged and worked their effect through other broad phenomena. One is geography. For Russia more than for most countries, geography has been destiny, from whence comes the peculiar effect of Russia's frontiers. A second is empire, Russia's half-millennial imperial vocation. Third, Russia's long and distinctive tradition of authoritarianism weaves itself powerfully through the history of Russian foreign policy, echoing in our own day. A fourth is the process of social and political upheaval accompanying great internal transformations and often preceded by great social and political degeneration. The fifth centers on ideas and the peculiar force that ideology exercised in the first two Russias and still does in contemporary Russia, a topic already touched upon. And sixth, Russia's place in and among the great powers, for all its twists and turns, for all its ambiguities and discomforts, always constitutes the fulcrum of Russia's effort to orient itself in the outside world.

These six phenomena are the strands that in varying combination and degree have formed the larger thread introduced at the start of this chapter. Thus, while the thread constitutes an important part of the legacy viewed over the long haul of history, it is these six factors that transform the legacy into a complex, concrete reality weighing on the new Russia. They have interacted over centuries, and intensively in our own, not only to define what Russia has been as an international actor but to set the terms within which Russia now struggles to fashion a policy fitting its new circumstance. They are the forces of the past colliding with the unfamiliar imperatives of Russia's present environment, bending some, yielding to others.

Empire

Until the Soviet Union collapsed in 1991, modern observers had lost sight of what might be called its imperial essence, focusing instead on the problem of Soviet expansionism, a related but different matter.

The Soviet Union, it turned out, never *had* an empire; it *was* an empire. Like its nineteenth-century predecessor—and before that the Russia of the sixteenth, seventeenth, and eighteenth centuries—the Soviet Union, despite Stalin's monstrous engineering, could not transcend the fragility of an imperial state that failed to make of itself a nation-state. At each opportunity in Russian history to choose between turning the Russian core toward nationhood or preserving dominion over a far-flung collection of ethnically distinct borderlands, the national leadership chose to preserve dominion.[11] Stalin's formula—a federation of republics "national in form, socialist in content"—surely was intended to render the form empty and the content everything, but in the end form prevailed.

Thus the collapse of the Soviet Union was less the disintegration of a state than the decolonization of the last empire. It created for the new Russia an instant set of separate neighboring would-be states. These states were once of its own body and hence were not only a new, nearby foreign policy challenge but an emotional trial as well. Alas, for Russia, the force of decolonization does not end at its new borders but threatens the country from within. Russia too was of the empire, embodying all of its deformities and infirmities. Both factors—the end of empire and the ongoing vulnerability of Russia itself—constitute critical influences on contemporary foreign policy.

To understand why, one has to look back at the role of empire in the first two Russias. By the twentieth century the Russian empire was a largely finished work. Beginning in the middle of the sixteenth century, from its core in Muscovy, it gradually stretched eastward across the Urals and Siberia to the Pacific Ocean, flowing outward at a pace that took in an area the size of Holland every year for 150 years.[12] Catherine the Great extended Russia's sway over Poland in the west and Crimea and the Caucasus in the south in the last half of the eighteenth century; her nineteenth-century successors added central Asia and finally even ports on China's Liaotung Peninsula. For the most part the imperial enterprise came to a halt at the beginning of the twentieth century. The new century opened with Imperial Russia's defeat in the 1904–1905 Russo-Japanese War, a war caused by the reckless ambitions of adventurers in Nicholas II's entourage who plotted to bring much of north China under Russian sway even if, along the way, it required a "little war" with Japan. Russia's defeat, however, did not abruptly end imperial ambitions. In the Balkan crises leading to World War I and particularly during the war itself, its leaders put great effort into seizing control of the Black Sea straits. Here too it failed in the far larger disaster of the war. Taken together, the two failures constituted the high-water mark of imperial expansion.

The empire cracked and began to fragment in the course of the war. When Lenin and his colleagues seized power, large parts of the empire had sped toward independence (including Finland), had slipped from Russian control with the eastward advance of the Kaiser's army (notably Poland), or had become a no-man's-land of contending forces (such as the Baltic states, Ukraine, Belorussia, Georgia, Armenia, Azerbaijan, the Crimea, and central Asia). Three hundred years of empire-building had suddenly been reversed, helped by Bolshevik revolutionary exhortations for "free self-determination." Shortly, however, deeds departed from rhetoric. Bolshevik efforts to save an allied regime in Finland came a cropper, but by the end of January 1918 their siege of Kiev had driven out the newly formed Ukrainian parliament that three weeks earlier had proclaimed a "free and sovereign republic." Over the next four years the new Soviet regime gradually regathered the lost fragments of empire, often by force.[13]

The disintegration and reconstitution of empire at the end of World War I matters in our own day for two reasons: Even allowing for the ravages of the war, the disintegration of Imperial Russia testified starkly to the empire's underlying vulnerability. "For more than three centuries," Geoffrey Hosking wrote, the Russian Empire's "structures had been those of a multi-ethnic service state, not those of an emerging nation."[14] And collapse was the price paid. A "multi-ethnic service state" it remained after 1917, with first the Communist Party and then the Stalinist bureaucracy in the place of the tsar as the arbiter of service. Thus the underlying vulnerability remained as well.

In neither case did the Russians, whether high-placed or not, understand the roots of the problem, and in both cases their misreckoning colored their attitudes toward the defecting borderlands. Imperial Russia spent the last three decades of its existence in a program of vigorous Russification and centralization, trying to force the empire into a sturdier mold. It greatly intensified the imposition of the Russian language, religion, and often immigrants on non-Russian minorities in an attempt to protect the empire by grafting a single ethnic identity onto all. The effort failed, not simply because people resisted or because the policy fell short in execution but for a far more fundamental reason: Riding rough-shod over ethnicity is one thing; attempting to assimilate dominated peoples into a nation that does not exist is quite another. As Sergey Witte confessed in his 1910 memoirs, "the mistake we have been making for many decades is that we have still not admitted to ourselves that since the time of Peter the Great and Catherine the Great there has been no such thing as Russia: there has been only the Russian Empire."[15]

Ostensibly Lenin and his followers repudiated Russia's imperial past and committed themselves to emptying the "prison of nations." They pledged that through the promotion of education and the development of national elites, the nationalities would flourish. From the beginning, however, Lenin and, in particular, Stalin intended this process to lead to the merger of nations in a transcendent enterprise. In effect, the Bolsheviks sought to replace one empire with another, the Russian Empire with a Communist empire. "Marxism-Leninism internationalism in the form of Soviet patriotism," to borrow Gerhard Simon's formulation, "was designated as a sort of supra-national imperial ideology."[16] They imagined a community beyond the traditional nation-state, a value system beyond nationalism, and a new reason for being for a multinational *Soviet* state. Again, Russian nationhood was the casualty.

The idealism faded by the early 1930s, and Stalin reversed the process of de-Russification and the development of native cultural roots, substituting a forced modernization, the formation of an assimilated *nomenklatura*, and vigilance against "national deviations." Though the strategy had changed, the premises had not, nor did they until the end. Notions of "internationalism," at home and abroad, may have become an empty rhetorical shell, but nothing was allowed to replace them. Hence, in the 1970s, once the system had lost its capacity to beat its many parts into submission and then, through the exhaustion of its productive possibilities, the commitment (or at least the honest labor) of even its own minions, in the void stirred a renewed loyalty to tradition, lost national identity, and the plausibility of genuine autonomy and maybe independence. In Simon's words, "The crisis of the ruling state ideology generated a huge spiritual vacuum, which was then filled by national consciousness."[17]

Because Russia had lived so long as an empire, yet, without the Russians recognizing its underlying vulnerability, when it fell apart they were left uncomprehending. Granted, they were scarcely alone in assuming that the empire's long history, buttressed by the economic and social transformation of the republics and the creation of new Soviet institutions, had rendered the Soviet Union a permanent albeit flawed reality.[18] Still, their deeply embedded urge to consider the Soviet Union as in the nature of things made the appearance of suddenly independent states more than a surprise; they arrived as unnatural entities whose relations with Russia were something other than those of distinct and sovereign nations. Gradually, as the first decade of the post-Soviet era draws to a close, the Russians, in varying degrees of sophistication, are learning to live with the technical reality of their new neighbors' independence. As we shall see, however, even among the most moderate of them—those least susceptible to the nostalgia for empire, those most eager to put the past behind and to transform their country into a democratic, enlightened member of the international community—a deeper incredulity and skepticism continues to affect the way they think about managing Russia's role within what used to be the empire.

The legacy of empire matters to contemporary Russian foreign policy for a second, wrenching reason: Because of it, the most fundamental underpinnings of foreign policy are missing. "One cannot say that, as it stands, the post-1991 Russian Federation is really a nation-state. It is more a bleeding hulk of empire: what happened to be left over when the other republics broke away."[19] Because the agony of change daily reminds Russians of their country's own incompleteness, foreign policy proceeds from a basic insecurity over the country's capacity to survive this period intact. Foreign policy, thus, must deal not only with the hazards posed by the outside world but with the fear that the gravest threat to national security comes from within. At a minimum, this lurking self-doubt inclines Russia's elites and foreign policy makers to emphasize traditional security concerns—the risks to Russia of instability on its borders, the threat posed by outside powers thought to be bent on diminishing Russia within the post-Soviet space and establishing strategic bridgeheads of their own, and even the uncertain consequences of military balances badly tilted against Russia (as with NATO) or potentially so (as with China).

Authoritarianism

Empire, of course, is allied to authoritarianism, another crucial mediating influence on Russian and Soviet foreign policy. The fact that Russia for most of the last 400 years of its history, including nearly all of this century, has been ruled rather than governed obviously affects the nature of foreign policy making and hence its content. Russia's course for much of this time has unfolded according to the inclinations of a single autocrat or of a small oligarchy. While various figures within the government and in the tsar's entourage, and sometimes freelancing military officials or regional governors, might shape Russian actions, the process nearly always involved maneuvering to gain Nicholas's ear. Russia's blundering into war with Japan in 1904 owed to the intrigues of a self-promoting, well-connected retired guards officer named Alexander Bezobrazov, who wormed his way into the tsar's confidence. He was supported by warmongering regional military commanders, eager to force Japan to back down before Russian military power, and the minister of interior, V. K. von Plehve, eager to embarrass his bitter rival, Count Witte, then minister of finance. Witte, Count Lamsdorf, minister of foreign affairs, and General Aleksey Kuropatkin, minister of war, all regarded Bezobrazov's scheme as folly, but they were helpless to counter it. This is not to say that the bureaucracies did not crank away, adding their input to policy, or that in subsequent years impulses were not felt from other quarters, such as the conservative extremists in the second Duma.

Their effects, however, were filtered through a narrow and often capricious inner circle that rotated around the person of the monarch.

In the Soviet period, within a decade of the revolution the authorship of policy had also shrunk to a small clutch of people, themselves under the immense shadow of the autocrat. During the first years of Bolshevik power—from the signing of the Brest Litovsk Treaty in March 1918 to the New Economic Policy in 1921—foreign policy remained a genuinely contested matter, although the contest occurred mostly among personalities in the Party's upper reaches. By the middle 1920s, however, these disputes—even one as fundamental as that between Leon Trotsky and Stalin over revolution in China and relations with the Kuomintang—were ceasing to have direct implications for foreign policy and were becoming largely weapons in an internal political battle. By the end of the decade, as Stalin's grip on power tightened, differences of view even among the restricted few at the top of the Party hierarchy ceased to matter much. It is true that Soviet policy, even at the height of Stalin's domination, was never reduced merely to the whim of the dictator. Others continued to shape elements of policy, whether in managing Soviet initiatives within the League of Nations or in handling much of the detail of bilateral relations with the other major powers. Foreign Ministers Maksim Litvinov and Vyacheslav Molotov often took the lead in crafting Soviet positions.[20] But all acted in the treacherous and isolated environment of the dictator's will, and more diffuse, indirect influences from beyond simply did not penetrate their austere realm.

After Stalin's death the system acquired a more oligarchic character, but the design of foreign policy was still the monopoly of a narrow circle of Party principals. The shift, however, made room for serious policy disputes—for example, over the signing of the Austrian state treaty in 1955, the treatment of Eastern European allies during much of the 1950s, the significance of nuclear weapons well beyond the dawn of the nuclear era, the engagement with radical Third World regimes in Khrushchev's last years, the handling of the Sino-Soviet conflict from the early 1960s on, and policy toward West Germany in 1964. Such disputes buffeted policy, shaping its timing and content.

Though the essence of decision remained oligarchic to the end, slowly in the 1950s and 1960s and then more swiftly in the 1970s a wider circle of participants began to have a role at the edges of the system. Second-level figures within the Party's apparatus and the foreign and defense ministries had a say in framing the analytical context within which policy decisions were taken. Senior commentators in the media, experts in the bureaucracies (including the KGB), and well-connected academic analysts funneled assessments and ideas through the cracks into the inner sanctum.[21] Their influence, however, was never regularized, and whether or not their often sophisticated analyses had an impact depended on patronage, random openings in the discussion at the top, and the willingness of the oligarchs to listen to someone other than themselves. As soon as a topic turned urgent or fateful, however, not simply the number of participants but the entire mechanism of decisionmaking shrank to a tiny core. This was true of the decision to invade Afghanistan in 1979; it remained true in the decisionmaking under Gorbachev over German reunification.[22] The decisionmakers could be counted on the fingers of one hand.

Entwined with these prosaic features of Russia's unbroken authoritarian tradition are more elemental dimensions, carrying still costlier and harsher consequences. The hazards of unconstrained decisions, susceptible to caprice and constricted vision, have long been a special burden of Russian and Soviet foreign policy. Not only because an alternative tradition has not yet had time to grow but also because institutions and procedures to fill the void have scarcely formed, these hazards live on. They were embodied in Russia's tragic rush to war with Chechnya; they appear in the periodic off-the-cuff initiatives Yeltsin makes when traveling abroad (on nuclear weapons in France in 1996 and on force deployments on the northern flank in Sweden in 1997); they echo in the leadership's indifferent efforts to mobilize support in the Duma for key treaties, such as START II; and they are present in the failure of national leaders to build public understanding of the external challenges facing Russia.

Though its residue remains, the edifice of authoritarianism has disintegrated, and that too has its deleterious effects. Because the obverse of authoritarianism is not a well-rounded, well-institutionalized

democracy but, rather, a lack of structure, another of authoritarianism's legacies is policy incoherence. The often amorphous process by
which Russia comes to adopt positions or take actions in foreign affairs is not just the result of Yeltsin's peculiar style of leadership.
Notwithstanding a certain primacy that Yevgeny Primakov achieved
for himself and his ministry during his years as foreign minister, the
process remains open-ended, weakly institutionalized, loosely focused, and only sporadically accessible to a democratically elected parliament. Representatives of corporatist interests, from regional
governors to oil company executives, increasingly influence a range of
issues far beyond their immediate interests, from regional conflicts to
NATO expansion. Amid the organizational voids, however, their influence lacks coherent effect. This inchoate environment tends to reduce consensus to lowest-common-denominator crudities: injured
national pride, the use of sticks rather than carrots in dealing with
neighbors, and ostentatious displays of foreign policy independence.

These conspicuous traces of Russia's long experience with authoritarianism, however, mask its deeper consequences. Russia did not develop a civil society until the last third of the nineteenth century, and
what began then was abruptly cut short by the super tyranny of the
Stalin era. Two things followed, the first linked to the weight of empire. First, the state and nation never became a unified entity. Geoffrey Hosking, writing about Petr Struve, the early twentieth-century
economist and journalist and the leader of the Kadet Party, noted that
Struve believed it important to generate in both the people and the intelligentsia an appreciation for both the state and nation. "No state,"
Hosking said of Struve's view, "could survive in the modern age, let
alone pursue a successful foreign policy, without the support of national awareness. "The national idea of contemporary Russia is the
reconciliation between the authorities and the people, which awaken-
ing to its own identity . . . State and nation must organically coalesce."[23] It never did. It still has not.

The second consequence also relates to the deformed relationship
between state and society. The gulf between them produced a foreign
policy disembodied from the needs and capacity of society. One need
not go as far as those who argue that both imperial Russian and Soviet

regimes used foreign policy to compensate for their lack of legitimacy.[24] At its most extreme, the claim is that Imperial Russia's expansion into central Asia in the 1860s was inspired by an urge to shore up its sagging image in the wake of the Crimean War and, similarly, that Soviet boldness, as in the Berlin crisis of the 1950s or in Third World adventures in the 1970s, stemmed from a desire to substitute international accomplishments for missing accomplishments at home.

Short of this, it is clear that the state's divorce from society permitted and perhaps even encouraged undertakings and causes that exceeded the country's resources and, worse, jeopardized its domestic good health and progress. As Michael Florinsky said of Imperial Russia, "A country already oversized and underpopulated, hopelessly backward industrially and culturally, squandered her scant resources of men and treasure in conquests of the arid wastes of Asia and in unrewarding adventures in the Balkans"—all this to flatter "national *amour propre*," a "superficial and unreasoned satisfaction . . . purchased at the exorbitant cost of retarding Russia's political, social, and economic progress."[25]

The Soviet Union did the same. If any feature distinguished the foreign policy of the Soviet Union as it too advanced into its waning years, it was the widening gap between the foreign policy agenda that national elites continued to pursue and the nation's shrinking capacity to sustain it. Worse, Soviet leaders embarked on a policy course that actively damaged a system they sought to preserve, a prominent theme of Gorbachev once in power. Edvard Shevardnadze, Gorbachev's foreign minister, argued that not only did the tyranny of the past, the cult of personality, and the dogmatism of the regime deny the Soviet Union others' trust, they betrayed the country's ideals and devalued Soviet initiative.[26] Not only did the system's deformation warp Soviet relations with other Communist and workers' parties, it led Soviet leaders to underestimate the strength of the "progressive world community" and to overestimate the military dimension of the struggle with imperialism. But most tragically, by fostering a crude, ideologically rigid image of the enemy, it doomed the Soviet Union to squander inadequate resources on a misconceived threat, damaging rather than protecting the real welfare of the society.[27]

Authoritarianism's collapse does not mean the gulf between state and society has been corrected. Because none of the rich array of non–public policy organizations characteristic of democracies has yet emerged, because political parties remain inchoate and thus ineffectual as alternative sources of foreign policy ideas and channels of popular foreign policy attitudes, and because foreign policy expertise, where it exists, attaches itself to warring factions in the narrow circles of Moscow politics, policy takes shape in a stultified, warping arena.

State Transformation

Many phenomena filter the effects of the factors that shape a country's foreign policy. None looms larger in Russia's case than the ravages of system transformation. For much of the twentieth century the three Russias have been caught up in vast social and political upheaval. During these periods the state itself has been at stake, either in fatal decay or under massive reconstruction. At two moments, in the 1930s and in the 1990s, vast political transformation occurred alongside an attempt to replace one economic order with another. In fact, rarely in this century has Russian or Soviet foreign policy been the product of a settled political system—the unarticulated premise of analyses that look for the sources of foreign policy behavior in the processes and politics by which policy is made. And sometimes, even when the domestic setting had been more or less formed and stable, as during the eighteen years under Brezhnev, degeneration had already set in.

This means that for much of the twentieth century the background to policy was a system in crisis, crisis in the word's original sixteenth-century medical meaning of the moment when the patient moves either toward recovery or death. Most historians would agree that even before Nicholas's coronation in 1894, the old order was entering such a crisis. Much the same could be said of the Soviet Union on the eve of Gorbachev's accession to power.[28] In the case of Imperial Russia, absolutism faced the rising forces of rapid industrialization, a small but restless industrial proletariat, an increasingly organized opposition comprising revolutionary as well as liberal parties, and the debilitating effects of an ever more impoverished peasantry. In the Soviet case, the Stalinist economy under the management of a sclerosed Party bureaucracy had lost its capacity to stimulate growth or to make the transition to a postindustrial, technology-based economy.

In the first Russia, as the crisis deepened, accelerated by the regime's failures in the 1904–1905 war, Nicholas yielded to the advice of counselors like Witte and, with the October 1905 decrees, initiated reforms leading toward constitutional monarchy. Or so it seemed. But the tsar's heart was not in the effort, and even those who, like Witte, urged the change only did so because of the particular weaknesses they saw in Nicholas II and the momentary accumulation of social pressures, not because they doubted that absolutism was the better system for Russia. In contrast, Gorbachev believed in both the need for and desirability of perestroika. But ironically, rather like his earlier predecessor, he set in motion a process that he could not control and that he would not try to surmount by taking reform, particularly its crucial economic component, to a logical conclusion.

In both cases, foreign policy was a casualty of the country's growing weakness, but the effects were very different. Nicholas and many around him understood too slowly the withering of the regime's foreign policy possibilities—a myopia particularly conspicuous in the lead-up to the 1904 war with Japan and made worse by racist assumptions about Russia's chances against a non-occidental people. Nevertheless, by the war's end and from the revolutionary year of 1905, the more sober among senior foreign policy leaders began to take seriously the limits imposed by the unresolved problems at home. When, in early 1908 Foreign Minister Aleksandr Izvolsky argued against his predecessor's support for the status quo in the Balkans and commitment to cooperation with Austria, he was soundly rebuffed by his colleagues in the council of ministers. To his invocation of Russia's "historic mission in the Near East," they responded with somber reminders of the country's unreadiness for war. Said Pyotr Stolypin, "any policy other than a strictly defensive one" in present circumstances "would be the delirium of an insane government."[29] A year later, when war between Austria and Serbia again appeared imminent, the council's reaction was the same: Financially and militarily Russia was in no position to risk a war. Izvolsky's successor, Sergey Sazonov, argued for restraint throughout the Balkan crises of 1911–1913, but with decreasing success as the pressure of more impetuous voices mounted and the increasingly rigid diplomatic setting reduced Russia's choices.

Ultimately, the dynamic of international politics overwhelmed the imperative of Russia's gestating domestic crisis and marched the country into war, with predictably disastrous consequences. In contrast, at the Soviet Union's end the international environment permitted Gorbachev to act on the country's weakness. The retreats he effected in the face of the Eastern European revolution, the lopsided arms control arrangements with the United States and NATO, and the terms of German reunification were all, at one level, caused by the Soviet Union's growing internal quandary as the economy plummeted amid internally contradictory reform measures and as political control seeped away in the confusion of the leadership's half steps. Yet if the international dynamic had been as competitive as it was on the eve of World War I or if the rivalry among major powers had been rising rather than diminishing, it seems doubtful that Gorbachev and his closest counselors would have adopted—or would have been permitted by more conservative forces to adopt—the course they did.

Still more dramatic in effect are periods of state restructuring. The second Russia, born in revolution, spent much of its first decade overwhelmed by the struggle to create a new political and economic order in the place of the shattered ancien régime. Having consolidated his power, Stalin, in the new regime's second decade, unleashed a transformation far more turbulent and far-reaching than the first. At the end of the century the Russians are once more going through the trauma and ruptures of a wholesale recasting of their political and economic existence. Russia's persona and behavior abroad, as might be expected, was and is now deeply affected.

Upheaval on this scale echoes in policy on many levels, but three effects are particularly important. First, grand and troubled enterprises, such as the Bolshevik revolution, Stalin's forced industrialization, and contemporary Russia's attempt to build democracy and a modern, market-based economy, have a considerable built-in risk that they may fail. Failure does not merely entail pain or the repudiation of those who launched the process or setbacks in the outside world. It also carries the far graver risks, at a minimum, of sending the country reeling into an opposite future (into reaction rather than socialism in Lenin's case, into dictatorship rather than democracy in Yeltsin's) and, at a maximum, of tearing the country apart or setting its development back massively.

At the turn of the century, doubts persist undiminished over the likelihood the country will survive intact or escape a return to authoritarianism. Even though few Russians think either outcome is highly probable, much less inevitable, their mere plausibility casts a debilitating pall over policy. The gloom grows whenever the crisis of transformation deepens, as it did in the wake of the financial collapse in summer 1998. As a consequence, at the beginning of the twenty-first century Russian leaders must put foreign policy's normal tasks second: seeking optimal results in relations with other states, deflecting harm coming from the outside, and where possible enhancing the nation's influence, status, and material benefits beyond its borders. Their first task is to preserve the state. Russia's 1993 military doctrine assigned its defense forces a primary mission of preserving the country's territorial integrity, not against external enemies but against civil strife and internal ethnic conflict. In his last speech as foreign minister, Primakov characterized protecting the country's "territorial integrity" against the threat of separatism as "one of the major 'domestic' tasks of our diplomacy."[30]

Not surprisingly, Russia's root insecurity infects the attitudes of leaders and elites toward the international community's most powerful states, imposing on relations a special psychological burden. The actions of the United States, Germany, Japan, China, and other major European powers are never assessed only on their own terms; rather, they are treated as a source of insight into these countries' ultimate regard for Russia's survival or, at the very least, their desire to be helpful or hurtful in Russia's struggle with great internal challenges. The Bolsheviks' creed disposed them to see an irreducible and ultimate hostility in the policies of the Western powers, but the chaos and perils of the road facing them after 1917 vastly reinforced these biases. Russia's leaders at the beginning of the twenty-first century make no similar axiomatic assumption of the outside world's enmity. But they are prone to interpret conflicts of interest—particularly with the United States over such issues as the exploitation of gas and oil in the new post-Soviet states, let alone an issue like NATO expansion—as reflecting malign intent.

Second, these great transformations directly affect foreign policy by radically altering the state's power. No feature of Russian foreign policy during the Yeltsin era stands out more than the collapse of Russian power. It occurred in all domains (military, economic, and political, where alliances matter), both absolutely (measured against what had been) and relatively (measured against what others have). In this, Yeltsin's Russia was no different from Lenin's, only worse. By 1923–1924, six years into the Russian Revolution, total industrial production in the Soviet Union had reached barely half the 1913 level.[31] In the new Russia's first four years of independence, industrial production plunged 46 percent, a drop that followed a 5–8 percent decline in the Russian share of Soviet industrial production during the Soviet Union's last two years.[32] The slide continued as the country closed out the century with a further expected annual contraction of 6–10 percent.

Economic collapse, of course, is both a source and a manifestation of the state's basic enervation and, in particular, of its incapacity to mobilize resources essential to the performance of basic governmental tasks, including the design of effective foreign policy. Russia's federal government at the end of the 1990s collected less than 9 percent of a shrunken gross domestic product (GDP) in revenue, a ratio too small to sustain a national government whatever its condition.[33] The state is not only unable to ease the dislocations and pain that tumultuous economic change has caused the population, it cannot protect society from the health, environmental, and personal security hazards of a decaying infrastructure. Nor can it even preserve intact the human capital (such as its scientific community) and social capital (an education system) essential for renewal. In these respects, too, contemporary Russia parallels Soviet Russia under Lenin. And as in that earlier era, its ability to shape even its most immediate external environment suffers continually from strained resources and a limited array of tools.

Added to this is the disintegration of military power, which must also be seen as a consequence of system demise and reconstruction. For reasons largely unconnected with the turbulence of state transformation, Russia is at the same time, like Lenin's Russia, without allies.[34] Taken together, this ruination of Russian power in all its forms save nuclear weapons has inspired Lawrence Freedman to claim that "there is now no particular reason to classify Russia as a 'great power.'" Furthermore, he continued, "Russia cannot therefore expect the privileges, respect and extra sensitivity to its interests normally accorded a great power. Increasingly it lacks the clout to enforce its objections to developments it considers harmful or to take on the sort of responsibilities that can earn it international credit."[35] Much as they resent the thought, Russian elites fear its truth.

Their fear is linked to another profound consequence of great transformations. Decline gravely diminishes Russia, and not simply because its reduced power renders it weaker or because it is suddenly in the shadow of others' power. Rather, Russia ceases to be in command of its own international fate and finds itself transformed into an object of others' foreign policy. No longer does it rank among the authors of the international order, as it did at the close of World War II and for long after. Instead, at least as Russians fear more powerful states see them, it sinks to the level of a player whose role and place in the international system is set for it.

Such must have been the symbolism for the Bolsheviks of Maksim Litvinov cooling his heels in Stockholm, waiting to see whether he, their representative, would be allowed to appear before the Paris Peace Conference, where David Lloyd George, Georges Clemenceau, and Woodrow Wilson prepared to decide the fate of his country. Such was the case when the Soviets were invited to attend the 1922 Genoa conference to hear what role the British and French had in mind for Soviet Russia in the economic reconstruction of Europe. "Regretfully," said Foreign Minister Georgi Chicherin in his understated response to the three would-be hosts, it seemed to his government that "the actions of the Great Powers before the conference make it seem probable that some of the nations invited will be faced with decisions already worked out and formulated by a certain group of Governments."[36] The Treaty of Rapallo, the rabbit Chicherin pulled out of his hat, derailed Lloyd George's project, but it did not alter the essential Russian circumstance.

This sense of being an object in international politics rather than a shaper of the environment seems again to be at the back of Russian minds, except now without the compensations of earlier eras. It underlies much of Russia's reaction to the West, showing up most clearly in discussions of Russia's role in Europe and the future of NATO. In one typical example, Alexei Pushkov compared the victors' way of taming Germany at the end of World War II with their approach to contemporary Russia.[37] "Keeping the Russians out," the complement to "keeping the Germans down," no longer applies as a formula. But neither are the Russians to be incorporated. Rather, they "should be kept precisely within reach, if not allowed to raise their heads too much," allowed near enough when their assistance is needed but barred when their views are inconvenient. Lenin and his followers had as compensation a conviction that whatever Soviet Russia's current status, it had on its side basic forces that would eventually destroy its competitors. And Stalin could count on divisions among the malevolent architects of the international order of his day to offset the Soviet Union's vulnerability during the awful revolution he imposed in the 1930s. Neither form of relief exists for today's Russia.

Ideology

Samuel Huntington once wrote of the United States that it had great difficulty ceasing to be "a nation with the soul of a church" and becoming a "nation with the soul of a nation."[38] Or, as a variation on Benedict Anderson's overworked formulation, it was and remains the most imagined of "imagined communities." Essentially Russia too has been an Idea, and even more have ideas been a central influence. They have played a particularly critical role in shaping the country's encounter with the outside world. They have also distinguished one Russia from the next, without entirely perishing in the shift. In the twentieth century the fate of ideas and their impact on Russian foreign policy was particularly far-reaching and convulsive.

Whatever underlying continuities Lenin and Stalin shared with their tsarist predecessors in playing the hand geostrategic realities had dealt them, the meanings they attached to international politics, as earlier noted, were utterly different. Lenin's Russia crossed a threshold because its ideology was different not only in its content but in its very nature. The Bolsheviks did not simply reject the ancien régime—its values and organization as well as its purposes and practices—they turned their back on the entire discourse, on international politics as such. Russians under the monarchy had feared and fought liberal ideas at home and abroad. And they had acted aggressively on behalf of other ideas, such as their responsibility for defending Orthodox Slavs in the Ottoman Empire. But they always acted and thought entirely as supporters of the international order of the day. Lenin and those around him disbelieved in international politics as it was understood by every other national leadership. The gulf between the Bolsheviks and other national leaderships depended not simply on discrepant interests but on a wholly different notion of the essential dynamic among nations. Their Marxist view of the world, amended by Lenin's borrowed conception of imperialism, led them to believe that most of what had constituted international relations to that point, including war, colonialism, and *raison d'état* would perish with the capitalist order underpinning them. This deluded faith, in turn, rested on the assumptions they made about the wellsprings of national behavior, which they located in the law-governed dynamics of capitalism. They were naively convinced that revolution in the advanced portions of Europe was both inexorable and essential if the Russian revolution were to be saved. But even when this conviction faded, their more basic ways of conceiving and interpreting the world survived.

What they made of the outside world would have a telling effect on how they acted within it until the very end. And even when their actions resembled what their tsarist predecessors did or were capable of doing, the impulse behind their actions was very different. The Soviet decision to impose a revolution on Poland by military force, after Poland's 1920 offensive against Russia had faltered, may not seem so different from earlier Russian leaders' use of force to get what they wanted. The evidence suggests, however, that Lenin and his excited colleagues took the step because, as the young general who led the offensive, Mikhail Tukhachevsky, said, "There can be no doubt that if we had been victorious on the Vistula the revolutionary fires would have reached the entire continent."[39] Compounding this flight of fancy, the Bolsheviks' peculiar faith encouraged them to believe Polish workers and peasants would welcome this military handmaiden to revolution. Instead, as a sadder but wiser Lenin confessed, "In the Red Army the Poles saw enemies, not brothers and liberators. They felt, thought, and acted not in a social, revolutionary way, but as nationalists, imperialists."[40]

The lesson, however, applied to specifics, not to premises. Both before and after the Polish gambit, Lenin hewed to his view of history's plan. More than that, he and even his most cynical collaborators were often led to misgauge events precisely because of their deeper convictions. For example, the Soviets continually misunderstood the situation in Germany, from the first revolutionary stirrings in 1918 through the last twitch in Saxony and Thuringia in 1923, because they insisted on viewing developments in terms of the Russian experience.[41] In 1918 they interpreted the Kaiser's abdication, the convocation of the All-German Congress of Workers' and Soldiers' Councils, and the formation of the provisional government controlled by social democrats as the "Kerensky period" of the German revolution, and from there they spun out the analogy down through the Kapp putsch of March 1920 (which was cast as the counterpart to the Kornilov affair in Russia in August 1917).[42]

Ideology mattered not only because it tempted Lenin and his successors into (false) analogy but because it warped their understanding of crucial phenomena, such as the rise of national socialism in Germany. Stalin saw the Nazi movement as "petty-bourgeois" and the ascendancy of fascism as a sign of the country's "sharpening contradictions" and of an approaching denouement, from which the Communists would profit. On the strength of this insight he made German social democrats the enemy and the Nazis a helpful foil.[43] Through the Comintern he also had the German Communists, in effect, join forces with Hitler's movement at key points, aiding its rise to power. It was scarcely the only occasion when Stalin's reading of events, people, and forces reflected this worldview, a worldview he had inherited and then passed on.

The enduring significance of Soviet ideology, however, came less from the distorted images of political reality that it produced in Russian minds than from the particular beliefs about the world that it sustained. Marxism-Leninism, for all the cynicism and manipulation of its priests, continued almost until the end to mark for Soviet leaders the anchor points of international politics. In the process it determined what they dared to believe possible, what they saw as threats and what as opportunities, what they considered logical and necessary in their own behavior, and what they saw as the essence of the other side's motivation. The last, in particular, gave special qualities to Soviet foreign policy.

Over the years, Soviet leaders had come to have an ever more complex, even convoluted conception of who gets what, when, and how in capitalist societies. Their notions of capitalism's fate, including its economic cycles, had grown more sophisticated and hedged, and their understanding of the "contradictions" within and among capitalist states had assumed forms recognizable to an outsider. But never, until Gorbachev, did they free themselves from their basic assumptions about Western governments, about what made them tick, and, in particular, about what drove their foreign policies. The militarism they saw as inherent in the capitalist system imposed limits on what they believed could ultimately be expected from arms control. Their conception of how these societies worked gave to their "enemy image" a permanent and ultimately insoluble quality. Their definition of threat—with its strange combination of preoccupation with the military and fear of political subversion—remained inextricably tied to their view of the nature of the opposing system. Only secondarily did they relate it to the varying character of leadership. The threat, too, therefore, could only be marginally adjusted, not lifted.

Gorbachev and his political allies changed this. From the beginning, the Soviets had modified ideological tenets to accommodate new realities. But the core was always left intact. Gorbachev and the most innovative of his colleagues, people like Alexander Yakovlev, Edvard Shevardnadze, Georgi Shakhnazarov, and a half-dozen policy

planners in the International Department of the Party's Central Committee, pushed beyond. Prompted both by what they saw as the foreign policy failures of the Brezhnev years and by their concerns over
the increasingly debilitated condition of the country's economy, they
began to recast the most basic Soviet notions. Much of the change occurred unsystematically, one altered thought leading to another. The
result, however, was comprehensive change. Every dimension of the
Soviet engagement in international politics underwent critical re-
thinking: from notions of national and mutual security to the character of Soviet alliances; from the Soviet stake in regional conflicts to
the legitimacy of human rights as an issue in East-West relations;
from the nature of power in international relations, including the role
of arms, to the utility of international institutions. Ultimately even the
foundations of international politics, as the Soviets had traditionally
understood them, were thoroughly reformulated. Rather than start
from the perspective of class struggle, Gorbachev thrust this analytical framework into the background. Instead, he emphasized the interdependence of societies, the common threats facing nations, and the
distinctive contributions of different socioeconomic orders.

By so fundamentally redoing prior ideological assumptions, the
Gorbachev era left the new Russia an enormously positive legacy. In
most crucial respects, the task of breaking with hidebound assumptions and dysfunctional ideas had been largely accomplished. Many
among Russia's foreign policy elite have absorbed this legacy and
moved far beyond. In the Ministry of Foreign Affairs, parts of the
Duma, the president's entourage, the media, and academic circles
there are policymakers and analysts with a thoroughly modern appreciation of international politics, people whose way of thinking about
foreign policy problems hardly differs from the foreign policy community in the West.

If the story ended there, the outsized role of ideology in the second
Russia would cease to be relevant. Important as the changes under
Gorbachev were, however, they unfolded only in limited corners of
society. Because these new ideas dominated within the Gorbachev
regime, they had a special force. But they did not have a broad base.
The lingering shell of the old ideology survives, particularly in the

Communist Party of the Russian Federation, a relic far closer to the pre-Gorbachev Communist Party of the Soviet Union than its now long-scattered progressive wing. The Party and the many splinter groups laying claim to the same mantle are a hodgepodge of biases and views, and Gennady Zyuganov, the Party's leader, is an odd blend of Russian nationalist, and even religious sentiments together with Soviet prescriptions. They, however, all preserve preconceptions of the West, particularly of the United States, that trace directly to the Soviet period. To hear Zyuganov talk about Western purposes is to reencounter a Party ideologist circa 1952. "We have only begun to understand how the West," he said, "while talking about Russia's 'admission to civilization,' has actually been trying to remove or weaken its chief geopolitical competitor. The West has always considered historical Russia—whether the Russian Empire or the Soviet Union—to be its number one geopolitical rival."[44] He goes on, "As a rule, attempts to conquer us have been covered over by some ideological veneer. But in reality, all conquerors-to-be came to us for our land and our wealth, hoping ultimately also to enslave our souls and take away our faith."

Zyuganov, his party, and its political base are a dying element in Russian political life, but for the next decade they will retain measurable influence over both domestic and foreign policy. Indeed, if Russia's current economic crisis deepens, their influence will probably increase. More than that, they are simply an organized embodiment of patterns of thinking that extend far beyond the Party's following. Echoes of Soviet ideas attributing Western hostility to its nature rather than to conflicting interests remain widespread in the country.

A second dimension of ideational tradition raises again the issue of Russian "exceptionalism." The Bolsheviks, in embracing a view of the world that made of their revolution history's chosen instrument, were only an intense version of what had long marked Russia's distinctive sense of identity. The tendency to see Russia apart, as a force transcending a narrow national community, as a set of values and experiences incapable of being submerged in a modern materialist West or, for that matter, in the new Asia, affects far more than radical nationalists from the left and the right. Often very moderate voices struggle with the problem of locating Russia, insisting on its special role, fearing it will be allowed less.

Sergei Kortunov, a seasoned diplomat and long-time advocate of constructive relations between Russia and the West, is such an example. He starts from the conviction that the West not only fails to appreciate how essential to international stability are Russia's special spirituality and its role in the Eurasian space, but also cares little if, by its actions, it threatens both. The Russia he describes stands alone, at risk of being swallowed up in the spheres into which others—the Americans, the Chinese, the Germans, and the Japanese—will carve the world. Above all, it is vulnerable to the demeaning and self-destructive role that the West will assign it if it fails to rediscover its historic meaning.[45]

The angry suspicions of the unreconstructed right and left converge with the anxieties of the moderate but romantic middle to produce two practical consequences: First, ever more Russians, for a variety of often rather different reasons, find it difficult to resolve their conflicted notion of what their society's relationship to the West should be. Second, and of more immediate and practical significance, Russian officials and commentators too easily see in U.S. and other Western policies in the former Soviet Union an intent to displace Russia and establish their own bridgeheads of influence—whether by developing bilateral relations with prominent new states such as Ukraine, by seeking access to oil and gas, as in the Caspian Sea basin, or by developing new forms of cooperation, such as the Partnership for Peace. As a result, they are too ready to interpret interactions with Western powers in the region as strategic rivalry, a theme to which I will return.

The Thread and the Legacy

What do these vast and often sad parts of the legacy together signify for the new Russia, and how are they likely to influence Russia's historically bedeviled relationship within the larger international setting? No sensible observer can arrive at this point undaunted by the vast uncertainties surrounding the answer to these questions. One may state, as Martin Malia boldly did, that "with her Communist identity gone, and with no other ideological identity possible, she has little choice but to become, as before 1917 just another 'normal' European power, with an equally normal internal order." But how can one know, given the massive unpredictability in the context determining Russia's choice?[46] Only once before—in 1918—have the futures of international politics and of Russia itself been simultaneously in such flux. Anyone trying then to imagine how the historical legacy would shape the international behavior of Lenin's Russia in the twentieth century would almost certainly have missed the mark by a wide margin.

The last part of the twentieth century has created not one but many possible international futures for Russia in the twenty-first century, some of them extreme. Because we cannot know which of them will occur, our analytical energies are better applied to weighing the factors likely to shape them. One such factor is Russia's historical legacy. However, because this legacy is both ever changing and in many parts, the trick is to determine how the different, evolving parts, taken together, are setting the scene for what will come. Not surprisingly, the parts contain much that prudence tells us is inauspicious.

The historical legacy might be thought of as comprising three levels. First comes its ideational portion, the peculiar force of ideas and self-image. Though contemporary Russia appears to have turned its back on the Leninist worldview and therefore on the set of ideas that militated against its integration into the international system, the hole it left is being filled by alternative notions of Russian "exceptionalism," some containing the seeds of a new alienation. Whatever the source of these new notions—whether fear for Russia's existence, anger and frustration over its demeaned standing abroad, or a more positive search for a meaning with which to fill the void—many of these formulas rest on a rejection of what the industrialized powers of the West represent. When some in Russia claim that their country can and must be the bellwether of "a 'post-material' era," featuring "a 'post-economic' (*i.e.*, humanitarian) culture with different intellectual and spiritual values" and then talk of a "Russian spiritual imperium," they mean to be constructive; they want Russia to save itself by becoming a positive moral force not so much against the West as beyond the West.[47] But central to that vision is an image of a spiritually, morally, and culturally deficient West, whose most deficient member is the United States. For others this quickly becomes the point of departure. The West and its preferences and purposes are to be rejected, whether embodied in the narrow instance of a "liberal economic model" foisted on Russia or in the broad terms of an international order arrogantly designed to the West's specifications. Others then go the next step. Not only are the preferences and purposes of the dominant states of the West objectionable, but they have embedded in them a direct threat to Russia. Harming, perhaps even destroying Russia, they insist, constitutes a primary Western—or, at least, U.S.— motivation.

None of these notions has yet triumphed. They compete with newer impulses amid the chaos of contemporary Russian thought. Alas, in this competition the images of Russia as a liberal democracy patterned after Western models and committed to building a liberal international order have largely lost out. The more serious competition comes from those attuned to what they see as fundamental change in the international environment, in particular, a "universal globalization" of economy and information that is "erasing the border between foreign and domestic politics" and from which no country can hide.[48] For the business titans and their allies among policymakers and the political elite who share this view, this world scarcely requires Russia to adopt "alien" cultural and political values. Rather, in this view Russia should focus on priorities permitting it to exploit the new "economization" of international relations. Here, however, these priorities are seen to be impeded by an excessive preoccupation with lost grandeur and traditional security concerns.

None of these outlooks warms to the virtues of U.S. or Western European society. All of them condemn the danger of one state— which these days means the United States—striving for hegemony. And each in different ways advocates tough, self-seeking approaches to Russia's nearest neighbors. Still they have very different implications for the way Russia sets priorities, relates to the West, conceives its international role, and plays the game of nations.

This brings us to the second level of the historical legacy—Russia and the external world. Russia the external actor operates on two axes: The first, in proximity and priority, is Russia's relationship with the new states of the former Soviet Union; the second is Russia's relationship with the other great powers. All great powers concern themselves with the other great powers. What they do with and to one another constitutes the backbone of the international system. But for Russia the historical legacy has left the country ill-equipped to build on the past or even to learn from it.

For most of this century Russia has not had to choose among the great powers, nor has it had to struggle with the challenge of engaging any or all of them in a deeply constructive or lasting fashion, because its basic posture was alignment *against*. Of the contemporary great powers, the Soviet Union was only ever aligned *with* one, China. China from 1949 to 1958, however, was not a great power and the Soviet Union made no pretense of treating it as one. The wartime alliance among the Soviet Union, the United States, and Great Britain served a historic but narrow and momentary purpose, and it failed precisely because it contained no possibility of alignment. It might be argued that the Nazi-Soviet pact of 1939 was an exception, but, if so, it hardly yields useful lessons for the present.

What of the earlier Russia? Does not Imperial Russia provide the new Russia with 200 years' experience in the most intricate management of great power relations? In the spring of 1998, Primakov, then foreign minister, spoke on the 200th birthday of Count Aleksandr Gorchakov, his long-serving nineteenth-century predecessor. Primakov described Gorchakov as someone who had also guided Russian foreign policy during a period of great internal difficulty, when the country had been written off by others who sought to exploit its weakness to their own advantage.[49] Aside from the self-serving parallel, he stressed two other themes. First, that Russia has no "permanent enemies, but rather permanent interests." "We," he went on, "often ignored this important truth in the Soviet period with the result that our state's national interests were sacrificed to the struggle with 'permanent enemies' or to backing 'permanent allies.'"[50] We know better, he said, "We have reverted to rational pragmatism." Second, according to Primakov, rational pragmatism meant that Russia must follow a "multi-dimensional policy," tying itself to no set of states, cultivating relations equally with "the United States, Europe, China, Japan, India, the Middle East, the Asia-Pacific region, Latin America, and Africa." Gorchakov, Primakov added, "realized that without diversification of foreign contacts Russia would not be able either to surmount its difficulties or to stay on as a great power."[51]

Apart from the abuse this does to the historical record, Primakov's rendition reflects only half of the contradictory pulls that Russia feels. On a trip to India in December 1998, Primakov, then prime minister, came much closer to the spirit of Gorchakov when he proposed creating a "strategic triangle" among China, Russia, and India.[52] "Diversification of foreign contacts" was no more Primakov's motive than it was Gorchakov's and Alexander II's when they pushed for a military alliance with Germany in 1873, only to be thwarted by Bismarck, and then successfully labored to bring about the Three Emperors' League later the same year. But where Gorchakov and Alexander sought alliance in order to manage relations among allies, particularly Russia's increasing competition with the Austro-Hungarians in the Balkans, Primakov made no bones about the fact that his proposed strategic partnership was directed against U.S. "arrogance of power."[53]

Setting aside for the moment the unreality of the proposal (neither China nor India was interested), the link to Russia's historical legacy warrants reflection. In the nineteenth century Imperial Russia twice phrased its foreign policy in terms of a competition on a grand scale, first, against the ideas and influence of France, the bearer of revolution, and later against the global reach of the British Empire. For the last fifty years of its existence all Soviet policy revolved around its rivalry with the United States. To the extent that Russia again sets itself against the role and status of a great power rather than simply against specific actions to which it objects, it is following in former footsteps. This time, however, it is acting from a position of overriding weakness. Even for a vastly stronger Soviet Union, the preoccupation with countering U.S. primacy undermined a sound and sustainable foreign policy. Worse, in the nineteenth century, notwithstanding an alliance with the conservative monarchies of Prussia and Austria, Russia often found itself pursuing its agenda unilaterally. It occasionally won momentary local victories, as in the 1876–1878 war with Turkey, but in the end, rather than creating leverage against an offending great power, it turned itself into the object of great power collusion.

Much of this played out in the amorphous territories surrounding the Russian Empire. The frontier today is different, back to its mid-seventeenth-century form, but the danger exists that Russia will follow the earlier pattern. The legacy is doubly at work. First, although the empire is gone its ghost lingers. Only a small minority of the political elite believes literally in the possibility of restoring it, but a still smaller number are prepared to relinquish a special role or a right of primacy in the post-Soviet space. They are not united on the nature and degree of integration that Russia should seek nor with whom; nor do they agree on which is the better tactic for dealing with their new neighbors: the Russian knout alone or in combination with, in the Russian phrase, "honey cakes." Unfortunately, as Russia struggles to come to terms with its imperial past only the tiniest fraction argues for a third strategy of reassurance and positive incentives as the best way to advance Russian interests among the post-Soviet states. Progress toward the normalization of Russian relations with Ukraine, the Baltic States, Azerbaijan, and Georgia, based on a convincing acceptance of their independence and aided by the resolution of issues left over from the breakup of the Soviet Union, continually risks reversal. New leaders, such as Yuri Luzhkov, the mayor of Moscow and a leading candidate for national leadership, regularly appear arguing a nationalist line on many of the issues already thought to be resolved and sounding themes of wounded imperial pride.

The unresolved imperial legacy then intersects the inchoate great power legacy. The defining characteristic of the emerging international system may be economic and technical globalization, dictating the erosion of traditional security concerns and requiring schemes to enhance mutual advantage, but on the system's frontier with Russia the movement returns to an earlier time. In the minds of most Russians, the positive norms of globalization do not apply in the post-Soviet space. Instead, as they see trends, Russia is faced with a wide-ranging effort to increase Western, particularly U.S., power, in-

fluence, and presence at their expense. Promoting "geopolitical plu-
ralism" in the region of the former Soviet Union, the policy attributed
to the United States, is considered a euphemism for containing and
indeed rolling back Russia. Much of what the United States does to
promote multiple oil and gas pipelines, Ukrainian and Baltic security,
subregional forms of cooperation, and NATO expansion is seen of a
piece. In response, Russian policymakers and elites wrestle openly
with strategies and steps intended to parry the West's putative aims.
Their evolving policy in the Caucasus, including the August 1997 mutual assistance agreement with Armenia and the mix of carrots and
sticks offered to Azerbaijan, reflects this impulse. It is evident in Russia's counteroffensive in central Asia over the last two years of the
1990s and particularly in the special relationship that it is straining to
build with Kazakhstan. The Chinese have noticed and have begun to
write about it.[54] It figures in the calculations surrounding the troubled
moves toward integration with Belarus. Indeed, scarcely any dimension of Russian foreign policy is without its traces.

Incipient strategic rivalry in the post-Soviet space threatens to cor-
rupt one of the three blessings of this period in world history. For a
rare moment, we are free of the three great scourges that, alone or in
combination, have wreaked the greatest damage in the modern state
system: Nowhere in sight is there a great power with both the capacity and will to overthrow the existing international system—no Bonaparte, no Hitler. Nor, second, is there any prospect—unless it be
between the United States and China in the early part of the next century—of a rapidly ascending state openly challenging the role and position of the dominant international power. Third, for the first time in
memory, relations among the major powers of the world do not re-
volve around active strategic rivalry. The dynamic among the great
powers, for the moment, does not focus on maneuvering for political-
strategic advantage, on a preoccupation with one another's military
power, or on a tendency to define threat in military terms—with the
budding exception of strategic rivalry in the post-Soviet space.

Whether or not a full-blown contest or some other negative outcome emerges on Russia's frontier will depend heavily on the impact
of the historical legacy at the third level, where the authoritarian tra-

dition meets the drama of state transformation. This is where the contemporary context is most uncertain, for Russia stands at a crossroads. Conceivably it will slowly work its way out of its current economic impasse; new institutions capable of sustaining a viable and perhaps even democratic state will take root; it will find an economic and political compact suitable to a workable federal union. And Russia will continue its millennial existence.

On the other hand, after the lengthy economic decline of the 1990s, given the deep structural impediments to a successful economic transition and no indication that the political establishment possesses the insight or will to overcome them, and after the flow of power away from the center and out of the state, it is also conceivable that the new Russia literally will not survive. The legacy of Russia the empire in lieu of Russia the nation-state haunts the present with growing force. For in truth Russia the empire was not only fundamentally different from imperial England or imperial Holland, states with far-flung yet separate empires, it was also different from the empires with which it is most often compared—the Ottoman and Austro-Hungarian. In the Ottoman and Austro-Hungarian Empires, the empire and metropole were integral; in the Russian case, however, not only were they integral but the metropole was itself an empire. The Russian Empire was like a Russian *matrioshka* doll: an empire, within an empire, within an empire. Unless Russia can fashion viable state institutions and restore a modicum of economic vitality, there is no natural stopping point to imperial decay.

Even if the odds of Russia's extinction are low—as they for now should be regarded—its current plight leaves room for other outcomes scarcely more attractive. Russia need not perish, but, if several more years pass without the by-now secular trends of economic and social decline being halted, the country risks considerable economic and political disintegration. China too survived the revolution of 1911 as a shell, its national economy melted into fragments and its national cohesion lost to regional war-lords. Unfortunately Russia could become its modern version. Were that to happen, Russia would give new meaning to the notion of a "failed state."

Or, before Russia reaches this point, political forces may congeal in an attempt to stem the force of events by reverting to authoritarianism. It is far from clear, however, that an effective and durable authoritarian solution could be found. Instead, the great danger arises that these forces, unable to seize the commanding heights of a state endowed with intact institutions of repression, would reach and retain power by exploiting sources of tension within society and by magnifying its baser impulses. This is not the Augusto Pinochet model often discussed in Russia, but the Slobodan Milosevic example. Thus, the largest question mark in a world laced with question marks is Russia itself.

The near-impossibility of predicting Russia's future, coupled with the ongoing ambiguity of its evolving relationship with the other great powers, particularly the United States, and the still unsettled character of its relationship with the new neighboring states create an immensely broad spectrum of possibilities. They extend from a moderate Russia increasingly well-integrated into the external order to an alienated and increasingly combative Russia. And beyond that, there is a broken and collapsed Russia, a turbulent vortex in the international system.

To start where hope begins, grounds do exist for envisaging a *moderate and well-integrated* Russia. They originate with the changes in Russia itself. Although Russia has not eradicated every fragment and habit of its authoritarian past, it has largely dismantled the infrastructure needed to underpin an authoritarian system. At the same time, although Russia has not built democracy, it has legitimized the democratic aspiration as never before, even if not in the image of liberal Western democracies. In addition, Russia's historical character, tracing back at least to Peter I, as not merely a "service state" but as one organized to mobilize military power, is now in tatters. Both the basis and the means for the militarization of society and of the country's foreign policy have disintegrated. While the detritus of this deformation is vast and hangs like a dead weight on the reform effort, it is no longer capable of defining the Russia of the future. And never before has imperial collapse been so complete. For the first time in its history, the obstacles to empire and the imperatives of the contemporary international economic setting favor the choice of Russian nationhood.

Not only is Russia different, but so too is the post–Cold War setting. At least among the developed states of the West, including Japan, some would argue, the costs of war and the benefits of cooperation have grown so large, the values of the peoples in these states have so changed, and mutual dependency among them has so expanded that war has become almost unthinkable. "Without the recurring threat of war," Robert Jervis argued, "the patterns of international politics in the developed world cannot be the same."[55]

Russia has every incentive to become a part of this world. Russia is already a part of a globalized international economy, often to its discomfort. Its reintegration into the international economy has had an important effect. The growth of Russia's global trade as a percentage of its GDP, the flow of capital in and out of the country, and its involvement with international financial institutions have made economic considerations a far larger dimension of foreign policy. This, as Celeste Wallander pointed out, helps to "normalize" Russia as a player in international politics.[56] Angry as Russian elites may be over the collapse of Russian power, impatient as they may be with the arrogance of U.S. power, jealous as they may be of their threatened position in the post-Soviet space, and frustrated as they may be by their dependency on international financial institutions and their vulnerability to international economic forces, they have no realistic alternative other than to adapt and make the best of it.

For too many other good reasons, however, this may not be the outcome. The sad truth is that the *alienated and combative* Russia begins to take shape only a few steps off the road to the moderate Russia. In the extreme case, if Russia were to recover enough of its strength to act on its discontent, if the tensions between Russia and the West were left to grow essentially unmanaged, and if the international order were to become the privileged handiwork of the industrialized democracies, rendering the other two great Eurasian powers, China and India, more receptive to talk of "strategic triangles," this alienated Russia would emerge as a plausible alternative.

Similarly, lesser versions of a disaffected Russia could appear without any of these three currently implausible preconditions. It would take only a mishandling of the mounting issues in contention between the United States and Russia to turn Russia into the odd man out among great powers, a spoiler in the sphere of great power cooperation, and a state with a grudge looking for ways to inflict damage on U.S. interests. Or the politics of despair could bring to power in Russia a leadership readier to play to popular fears and frustrations, to thumb its nose at the requirements of economic interdependence, and to place a higher priority on forcefully defending, as the phrase goes, Russia's "special interests." Or the interplay between Russia and the Western powers on the post-Soviet frontier could escalate through simple inattention into a contest that neither side wants.

If in any of these circumstances Russia remains without major allies, as is likely to be the case, it will be tempted to lash out and deal with its environment on its own. Unilateralism from a position of weakness will only add to Russia's predicament, but in the process it is also likely to create difficulty for the world outside. Were the brunt of Russia's striking out to be born by the states in its immediate vicinity, where it still has great capacity to intimidate or do harm, the disruptive effect in the larger setting would be grander than many would want to imagine.

The last Russia, *broken and collapsed*, has no parallel among the other great powers discussed in this book. None of them—with the far-fetched exception of China—can be conceived of as anything other than intact states with functioning political and economic systems coping with the challenges of a changing international environment. Russia alone among the great powers ends this century with unanswered questions about its ability to avoid a basic breakdown of its domestic order and maybe even its demise as a state. Over the centuries the central story of Russia's engagement in the outside world, as Cyril Black wrote years ago, has been its movement from the periphery to the center of the international system.[57] Russians fear that history is reversing itself, and that Russia is again receding from the center of the international system. The fear is misplaced. Though the other great powers may not always keep their minds adequately focused on the issue, whether a moderate and well-integrated Russia or an alienated and combative Russia emerges in the twenty-first century will in considerable measure determine the kind of international order we get. If, as all should pray not, the broken and collapsed Russia emerges, hazards will appear in the great space between Europe and Asia that will most certainly restore this part of the world to the center of great power attention. Either way the historical problem of finding for Russia a safe and productive location in the international system remains as pressing for the 21st century as for the three centuries that came before.

6

THE UNITED STATES

Divided by
a Revolutionary Vision

ROBERT A. PASTOR

We stand on the threshold of a new century big with the fate of mighty nations. It rests with us now to decide whether . . . we shall march forward . . . or whether we shall cripple ourselves for the contest. Is America a weakling, to shrink from the work of the great world powers? No. Our nation, glorious in youth and strength, looks into the future with eager eyes and rejoices as a strong man to run a race.

—**Theodore Roosevelt, 1900**

Events came to our assistance.

—**Henry Kissinger**

THE TWENTIETH-CENTURY arrived two years early in American foreign policy. The Spanish-American War of 1898 constituted a watershed in America's relations with the world, separating an isolationist nineteenth century from a globally engaged twentieth century. Since its independence, America had viewed itself as special and different from Europe, but Americans were often divided as to how to translate this self-image into policy. Before 1898 the debates were largely resolved in favor of America standing aloof from the world as a "promised land."[1] In the twentieth century, Americans gradually realized they had an important role to play in the world, but they still debated what that role should be—whether to be an example worthy of emulation or an activist shaping the world; whether or not to be imperialist; whether to define U.S. interests in a far-sighted or narrow way; and whether to act alone or with others.

The answers to those questions have not always been consistent, but a pattern became evident: U.S. policy was aimed not just to advance U.S. interests but to change the world. With deep roots in the country's unique heritage and favorable geography, an American idea of a new international system slowly began to crystallize. When it declared war against Spain, Washington shocked Europe by renouncing the war's main prize, Cuba. Theodore Roosevelt's goal of building a strong independent power that would open the world's doors to trade and pledge not to take its neighbors' territory added two more elements to the developing vision, but it was Woodrow Wilson who gave fullest expression to a truly revolutionary worldview.

Wilson's goal went beyond winning World War I: He wanted to prevent all future wars and at the same time make the world safe for democracy. His proposal was quintessentially American: The European balance of power system must be dismantled in favor of a "community of power"—a League of Nations—that would guarantee the self-determination of all nations and therefore eliminate the cause of wars. The countries defeated in World War I must be given a stake and a place in the new system; there must be "peace without victory"; there must be no indemnities and no colonies. These ideas were too radical to be accepted in 1918 but too compelling to be denied in 1945.

It was not just Europe that was unwilling to trade its sovereignty and self-defense for a new system based on collective security. The United States was never as committed to Wilsonianism in practice as it was in its rhetoric. Always watching the rearview mirror to make sure it wouldn't be rear-ended by the old order, the United States never allowed an international institution to replace its hands on the steering wheel or its foot on the brake pedal. America's idealism de-fined the world's mission, but its realism safeguarded its own security.

Given the nation's divisions over self-reliance versus collective secu-rity, among other issues, it is hardly surprising that U.S. diplomacy is replete with what seem to be contradictory decisions. Historians have offered a plethora of theories to explain both why the United States expanded and why it didn't; why it was an aggressive power like other nations or why and how it was exceptional.[2] Arthur M. Schlesinger, Jr. and Frank L. Klingberg believed that a "cyclical" rhythm of extrover-sion and introversion explained this paradox. Fareed Zakaria de-scribed a linear but arrested activism in U.S. foreign policy, as the state became more fully developed, and economic power translated into political influence abroad.[3]

Let me propose an alternative. Instead of visualizing the nation os-cillating from one mood to another, we can think of the United States as having two visions of itself and of its place in the world's future: a Wilsonian vision of international institutions and universal norms and a (Theodore) Rooseveltian vision of the United States as a great power acting alone.[4] Moreover, Americans have been of two minds as to whether they should reach their goals actively or passively, unilat-erally or multilaterally. Adherents of each vision and strategy have de-bated every important international issue. In remarkably balanced debates, they competed with each other and for the allegiance of a third group—those who were undecided. In the end, however, the "undecideds" were moved less by the arguments of either side than by the power of events, or what James Bryce called the "irresistible ten-dency of facts."[5]

The decision process of the undecideds is the answer to the riddle of America. The undecideds define the spirit of American pragma-tism, borrowing ideas from both activists and "passivists," both realists and idealists. This ensures that although no one is completely satisfied with the outcome, no one is entirely alienated. Some debates are harder to read because the leaders are not just debating each other; they are debating "the two tendencies" within themselves.[6]

America's divided vision is a deliberate product of the Constitution. The Founding Fathers did not mandate foreign policy goals. Instead, they designed a process by which two separate institutions with shared powers—the presidency and Congress—would define the goals. They wanted government to be divided in order to ensure that no single institution would be able to dominate the other and thereby deprive the people of freedom to participate in the debate, and they wanted to make it difficult to go to war until events compelled a unity of purpose.

Over the course of the century, and with much trial and error, a synthesis emerged because the Wilsonian and Rooseveltian visions shared the premise that the United States was an "exceptional" power with a special mission. Franklin Roosevelt and Harry Truman merged the two approaches and provided a practical design for achieving it. The institutions that America conceived during World War I, established after World War II, and rejuvenated after the Cold War embody the norms of American governance. They shape the world polity in the last decade of the twentieth century and are likely to define it well into the twenty-first century. Ironically, Americans remain halfhearted in their commitment and niggardly in their contributions to these institutions.

It has never been easy for foreigners, or even for Americans, to understand how the United States makes foreign policy, and lacking a single compelling explanation, scholars have described the many elements that compose the policy.[7] I believe that the best way to understand the process that connects the nation with the policy is to look at the national debates on the major international issues. These debates have always had vigorous advocates on both sides, but at each turning point of the twentieth century—the Spanish-American War, the protectorate era, the Great War and its aftermath, World War II, the Cold War, and the post–Cold War era—the "undecideds" ultimately determined the policy, but they did so with a logic that was not obvious at the time but that is clearer with distance. During the course of the century, U.S. foreign policy has remained stable and consistent in terms of three sets of priorities that together help explain the American design:

- **America First**. Americans might be of two minds, but with rare exceptions they have always given priority to the nation's business. There are a number of reasons for the primacy attached to domestic matters: The United States is rich in resources and land, and because its neighbors have been friendly or weak. Because the threats to the United States have been distant, Americans have used their votes to register their reluctance to fight in distant wars. The Constitution established a political system that assures that virtually every argument can be heard in Congress or in the executive branch. Although Americans accept a concentration of power during moments of crisis, they generally distrust centralized authority and want it dismantled afterwards.

- **The Americas Second**. The Monroe Doctrine functioned as the strategic bedrock of U.S. foreign policy, offering a justification for keeping foreign rivals out of the Western Hemisphere. It is not a coincidence that a hemispheric agreement—the Rio Pact—was the first regional "entangling alliance" that the United States accepted since George Washington issued his warning and that Cuba was the site where the United States came closest to fighting a nuclear war. Regardless of how far its power reached in the twentieth century, the United States always gave priority to securing its own neighborhood, and its successful policies in the hemisphere were often applied globally.
- **The World Third**. From 1898 until 1941, except 1917–1919, the United States concentrated its foreign policy on the Caribbean Basin, with occasional forays into Asia. After the bombing of Pearl Harbor, America finally turned to the world stage, and the debate in the United States shifted to such new issues as what U.S. national interests were and how should they be pursued.

The Turning Point of 1898: Background and Foreground

In his Farewell Address, George Washington warned his countrymen "to steer clear of permanent alliances" because "our detached and distant situation invites and enables us to pursue a different course."[8]

Washington's successors heeded his advice, taking full advantage of the security provided by America's two great "liquid assets."[9] Even James Monroe's landmark foreign policy message to the U.S. Congress in December 1823, subsequently hallowed as a "doctrine," was a declaration that the United States would stay out of Europe, although it is mostly remembered as a warning to Europe to keep out of the Americas.

Great Britain formally recognized the independence of the United States in the Treaty of Paris of 1783, but the young republic did not fully secure its borders from Britain, Spain, and France for another thirty-six years. Then it expanded across the continent and endured a wrenching civil war. In the final third of the nineteenth century, the country became a modern nation. It was connected by railroads and telegraphs and filled with millions of new immigrants. It developed the most productive agricultural and industrial economy in the world. A national identity took form. Proud and without a stratified society like Europe's, most Americans identified themselves as middle class, mobile, and individualists.[10]

As ocean cables and faster ships brought the world closer to home,[11] influential men urged the pursuit of a global mission and the construction of a navy. Their case was assisted by the intellectual climate of the day. Charles Darwin's theory of natural selection convinced many Americans that they had to be aggressive to survive, let alone prevail; Frederick Jackson Turner encouraged Americans to think beyond the territorial frontier to preserve their freedom and sustain the economy; and Captain Alfred Mahan urged America to build a Great White Naval Fleet. Beneath all these ideas lay a new fact: By 1900, the industrial might of the United States was more than twice that of the world's "leading power," Great Britain.[12] It was an appropriate moment for America, in the light of its new capabilities, to reevaluate its goals, to ask whether it should behave like a "great power" and seize colonies or whether it should remain different.

A generation earlier the nation had hardly noticed world events, but its new power broadened its view and intensified its reactions. The United States became exercised almost to the point of war against Germany in Samoa in 1889, against Chile in 1891 over the treatment of U.S. sailors, and against Great Britain over its territorial dispute with Venezuela in 1895. It was as if some part of this adolescent nation was looking for a fight, but another part always brought it to its senses in time.

These spats disguised a far more sensitive question that America addressed periodically after the Civil War but could not resolve: whether the United States should acquire noncontinental areas. With few exceptions, the debates in Congress on this question followed a similar pattern and led to the same outcome: Annexation was rejected, either on anticolonial or racial grounds.[13] Reflecting both the best and worst of America, Congress thought the United States should welcome states into the union on an equal basis rather than acquire colonies and that the country should not try to assimilate dark peoples who did not speak English.[14]

The debate was renewed with more passion when Cuba began fighting for its independence from Spain in 1895. Americans were sympathetic to Cuba's struggle but were of two minds as to whether and, if so, how to help. The two sides were more evenly matched and the outcome far less certain than it appears in retrospect. Both sides had forceful and eloquent leaders. The Republican Speaker of the House Thomas B. Reed did not want "to spill any American blood" unless the United States was directly threatened, which was not the case in Cuba. He felt that the United States would send a better message to the world by solving its own problems.[15]

Whereas Reed grasped every opportunity for peace, Theodore Roosevelt, recently appointed assistant secretary of the navy, seized every chance to push the country toward war against Spain. When a riot broke out in Havana, he instructed the skipper of the battleship *Maine* to proceed to Havana harbor. His nemesis, Mark Hanna, the chairman of the Republican Party, feared that if Roosevelt were assistant secretary of state rather than of the navy, "we'd be fighting half the world." Roosevelt was supported by an influential group of like-minded leaders, including Senator Henry Cabot Lodge and William Allen White, the editor of a well-known newspaper in Kansas.

President William McKinley reflected America's ambivalent desire to be a great power without having to fight. In a secret message to his government, the Spanish Minister Enrique Dupuy de Lôme accurately reported that the president was "weak and a bidder for the admiration of the crowd."[16] The message was leaked to William Randolph Hearst, who published it in his *New York Journal* with the inflammatory headline "WORST INSULT TO THE UNITED STATES IN ITS HISTORY." The leak had the effect of pushing McKinley and Americans closer to war. The next step occurred on February 15, 1898, when the *Maine* exploded in Havana harbor.

A month later a respected U.S. senator from Vermont, Redfield Proctor, reported that he had gone to Cuba as an isolationist but returned as an interventionist because of the repression and "the spectacle of a million and a half people, the entire native population of Cuba, struggling for freedom and deliverance." Three days later, the Naval Court of Inquiry reached a unanimous decision that the *Maine* had been blown up by a submarine mine. The public was incensed, and Roosevelt publicly taunted Hanna, one of the last holdouts for peace: "We will have this war for the freedom of Cuba. The interests of the business world and financiers might be paramount in the Senate," and though they might oppose the war, Roosevelt said sarcastically, he thought the public was in favor. "Now, Senator," he concluded, "may we please have war?"[17]

These events—the de Lôme letter, the explosion of the *Maine*, and the Proctor speech—pushed the undecideds toward the Roosevelt camp. After ten days of debate Congress declared war, but only after incorporating the goals of Reed and others who opposed a war of imperialism: Cuba should be free and independent, Spain should evacuate the island, and the United States would not acquire Cuba. This last point was an amendment introduced by Senator Henry M. Teller. No serious power stood in the way of the United States taking Cuba and all of Spain's possessions; the United States was deterred not by the balance of power but by its conscience. The revolutionary aspect of the Teller Amendment was noticed in Europe by no less than Queen Victoria, who urged the great powers to "unite . . . against such unheard [of] conduct. If [the Americans] declare Cuba independent, really such a precedent ought to be protested against. They might just as soon declare Ireland independent."[18]

After Admiral George Dewey sank the Spanish fleet in Manila Bay in the Philippines in seven hours and Colonel Theodore Roosevelt charged up Cuba's San Juan Hill, Europe, to use Ernest May's words, "had now to reckon with a seventh great power."[19] Americans united to defeat the Spanish and help the Cubans, but they were as divided on what to do about the other spoils of war—especially the Philippines—as they had originally been on whether to fight.

Two congressional amendments introduced by Senator Teller and Senator Orville Platt neatly reflect the nation's contradictory feelings. To those who opposed a war of imperial conquest, Teller's amendment was proof of the purity of America's motives; Samuel Bemis called it "a great and historic self-denial."[20] It should have settled the issue, but like a person finding a hundred-dollar bill in the street, the United States conveniently found a rationalization for hedging its pledge and keeping part of its new fortune. Washington did not annex Cuba, but it also did not allow it full independence. Senator Platt demanded that Cuba accept the right of the United States to intervene in its internal affairs for the purpose of protecting Cuban independence. The obvious inconsistency—how can one protect a state's independence by intervening?—escaped an America that continued to view its motives as chaste.

McKinley agonized over what to do about the Philippines for more than six months. Before the war he had opposed forcible annexation of Cuba as "criminal aggression."[21] After the war he asked his cabinet whether the United States should annex the Philippines, and they split down the middle, with the secretaries of state, treasury, and navy all opposed. He struggled for a decision until the answer finally came to him in a prayer (or at least that was what he told a group of Methodist preachers). He refused to return the Philippines to Spain or to let Germany or France take it. The only alternative, McKinley said, was "to take them all, educate the Filipinos, and uplift and civilize and Christianize them."[22]

Not all of America bought McKinley's modified "noblesse oblige" rationale or the blatantly imperialist argument offered by Senator Albert J. Beveridge. The Anti-Imperialist League was established in November 1898, largely to block the annexation of the Philippines. The movement included among its leaders former Presidents Grover Cleveland and Benjamin Harrison, Democratic presidential candidate William Jennings Bryan, Andrew Carnegie, Mark Twain, and many others. The Anti-Imperialist League condemned the proposed annexation of the Philippines by reminding Americans of their roots and their constitution:

> We regret that it has become necessary in the land of Washington and Lincoln to reaffirm that all men, of whatever race or color, are entitled to life, liberty, and the pursuit of happiness. We maintain that governments derive their just powers from the consent of the governed. We insist that the subjugation of any people is "criminal aggression" and open disloyalty to the distinctive principles of our government.[23]

During the debate on the Treaty of Paris concluding the Spanish-American War, the Senate knew that the other powers were poised to take the islands if the United States did not. Just six weeks after Dewey defeated the Spanish fleet in Manila Bay, a German fleet arrived there to ask for a naval base and land leases. The British, Japanese, and French followed. Lacking an alternative, the Senate on February 6, 1899, approved the treaty, but only by two votes (57 to 27) and mainly because of the need to formally end the war. The real test of American views on imperialism came one week later, when Americans learned that Filipinos were fighting for independence against American soldiers. Senator Augustus O. Bacon of Georgia, who had voted for the treaty to end the war, offered a congressional resolution declaring the Philippines independent. Vice President Garret Hobart had to break a tie to defeat Bacon's resolution.

William Howard Taft had opposed both the war with Spain and the annexation of the Philippines, believing that "we had quite enough to do at home" without absorbing a colony. McKinley tried to persuade Taft to be governor of the Philippines by admitting that Taft might have been right: "But we have got them, and in dealing with them, I think I can trust the man who didn't want them better than I can the man who did."[24] That comment is not easy to interpret, except as a sign that McKinley and the United States continued to want it both ways: They wanted both to keep the land and to be seen as different from Europe's imperialists.

Speaker Reed and President McKinley would have preferred to resolve the problem of Cuba without American soldiers, but in April 1898 these two experienced politicians realized that their hopes had gone down with the *Maine* and the conversion of Redfield Proctor. An easy victory seduced America into expanding its appetite for international influence beyond merely championing Cuban independence, but the debate on keeping the Philippines was even more divisive than the debate over Cuba had been. If we can interpret the Senate vote as reflecting American opinion on imperialism, the country had one foot planted in the new world and one in the old. As Lester Langley wrote: "The United States in 1898 was not considered, nor did it consider itself, an imperial power, but the nation lived in a world of competing dynamic empires."[25]

The Protectorate Era

The Caribbean Basin

On a warm August day in 1900, as the Republican National Convention began to consider nominating Theodore Roosevelt as its vice presidential candidate, Senator Mark Hanna warned his colleagues, "Don't any of you realize that there's only one life between this madman and the Presidency?"[26]

Theodore Roosevelt, a man of astonishing boldness, was determined to lift America up to the ranks of the great powers. His words and actions boosted the nation and his career. He rose in a little more than two years from a second-tier bureaucratic position to the governorship of New York and then to the highest offices of the land. But it was only after an assassin's bullet killed McKinley and put Roosevelt in the White House that people began to recognize the wisdom behind his bluster.

In 1901, in his first annual message to Congress, Roosevelt described peace as only possible if nations defended themselves and had a "just and intelligent regard for the rights of others."[27] To him, those

truths were the heart of the Monroe Doctrine. Distinguishing between the equality that characterized U.S. relations with its neighbors
and the colonialism that bound Europe to its overseas lands, Roosevelt pledged that the United States would not "secure any territory
at the expense of any of our neighbors" and would not seek any exclusive commercial arrangements. These two points—opposing territorial acquisition and favoring open trade—would be two cardinal
precepts of the American design.

The main point of Roosevelt's 1901 message, however, concerned
the Venezuelan dictator, Cipriano Castro, who refused to pay his government's debts to Europe. International law at that time permitted
creditor governments to intervene to secure their funds, but in recognition of America's new power, Great Britain, Germany, and Italy
consulted Roosevelt before taking any action. His response came in
the 1901 message: "We do not guarantee any state against punishment
if it misconducts itself, provided that punishment does not take the
form of acquisition of territory by any non-American power." Three
years later, faced with a similar crisis between the Germans and Santo
Domingo, Roosevelt sent a very different message to Congress in
what is called the Roosevelt Corollary to the Monroe Doctrine. Germany wanted a port in Santo Domingo as compensation for an unpaid
loan. This time, Roosevelt told Europe to stay out; the United States
would handle problems in its hemisphere:

> Chronic wrongdoing, or an impotence which results in a general loos-
> ening of ties of civilized society, may in America, as elsewhere, ulti-
> mately require intervention by some civilized nation, and in the western
> hemisphere, the adherence of the U.S. to the Monroe Doctrine may
> force the United States, however reluctantly, in flagrant cases of such
> wrongdoing or impotence, to the exercise of an international police
> power.

This shift in a mere three years from being a friendly neighbor to
being the region's policeman reflected a profound change not just in
tactics but in the definition of U.S. interests. There are four explanations for the change. First, after the 1901 message the three European

governments blockaded Venezuelan ports and sank several ships. The American people were horrified that Europe was allowed to attack a Latin American neighbor. Second, the Hague court gave preference to those creditors who had used force, a startling case of a court rewarding violence to resolve disputes. Third, Santo Domingo was closer to the United States than was Venezuela, and Germany was viewed with greater suspicion. And fourth, Roosevelt had just secured rights to construct a canal in Panama.

After the long voyage of the U.S.S. *Oregon* around Cape Horn during the Spanish-American War, Americans decided they needed a canal through the Central American isthmus. Roosevelt first persuaded Great Britain to revise an 1850 treaty in order to allow the United States sole authority to build and defend a canal in Panama, then a province of Colombia. The Panamanians had revolted against Colombian rule many times, but since 1850 the United States had helped Colombia suppress the revolts. When the Senate of Colombia rejected a treaty with the United States allowing it to build the canal, the Panamanians saw that their moment had arrived. They revolted again in November 1903, and this time U.S. ships prevented Colombian soldiers from landing. The United States quickly recognized the new Republic of Panama. Three days later the United States signed the Hay-Bunau-Varilla Treaty, which gave the United States the right to exercise jurisdiction "as if sovereign" over a ten-mile-wide strip of land across the middle of Panama that would allow the United States to build, operate, and defend a canal in perpetuity. The canal was the greatest technological feat of the era and the most costly investment the U.S. government had made up to that time. From its opening in 1914 until the Korean War, the canal would be America's most precious strategic asset abroad.

The canal was so important that it became the centerpiece of all U.S. policy toward Latin America.[28] Whereas Washington had largely ignored political instability in Latin America in the nineteenth century, it became obsessed with enforcing order in the twentieth, particularly in the small nations of Central America and the Caribbean. It is not hard to divine the reason: Any foreign rival could exploit the region's instability to gain a base from which it could attack the canal.

In pursuit of an elusive stability, the United States intervened about twenty times over the next three decades—in Panama, Nicaragua, Cuba, Haiti, the Dominican Republic, and Mexico. In each case, the pattern of entry and exit was similar. Marines first arrived to suppress riots. Then the United States would become embroiled in the country's internal politics. After much trial and error, Washington devised an "exit strategy": It would sponsor an election that it hoped would bring to power a strong and friendly leader with a political base. The United States would train and fund a national guard to provide order. It would recruit customs officers to run the central bank and to repay foreign loans. Then it would promote U.S. investment to develop the economy. To reassure investors, the U.S. government asked the country's government to accept a Platt-type amendment granting the United States the "legal right" to intervene in the country's internal affairs.

Between 1898 and the Great War, the most formidable external challenge the United States faced was Mexico's revolution. The revolution began when a reformer, Francisco Madero, insisted on free elections against long-time dictator Porfirio Díaz (who governed Mexico from 1877 to 1911). Díaz resigned, and Madero became president and introduced reforms. In 1913, the oligarchy collaborated with the army and foreign interests, including the U.S. ambassador, to oust and assassinate Madero. Instead of restoring the old order, however, the assassins precipitated the century's first violent social revolution.

Woodrow Wilson was inaugurated one month later on a progressive agenda, which he also applied in his foreign policy. When the U.S. ambassador argued for recognition of the military regime "on behalf of our great trade and commercial interests in the country," Wilson recalled him. Wilson was more sympathetic to Mexico's revolutionaries than to American corporate interests, and at one point he told an aide, "I have to pause and remind myself that I am President of the United States and not of a small group of Americans with vested interests in Mexico."[29] Wilson redefined U.S. interests in the region from preserving stability to promoting constitutional government. He was the first to declare that U.S. relations with a foreign government would depend not only on its respect for U.S. interests but also on its treatment of its own people.

Wilson withheld diplomatic recognition from the military regime led by General Francisco Huerta, landed troops in Veracruz to stop the shipment of arms to the government, covertly assisted the constitutionalist opposition led by Venustiano Carranza, and, finally, accepted mediation by three Latin American countries, Argentina, Brazil, and Chile. The last was a break with the U.S. tradition of acting unilaterally, but Wilson wanted to defuse charges of U.S. interventionism. The entire policy infuriated Senator Henry Cabot Lodge, who called Wilson "singularly ignorant" of foreign policy, and Theodore Roosevelt, who urged recognition of Huerta or establishment of a protectorate over Mexico.[30]

During the "protectorate period," U.S. foreign policy makers experimented in the Caribbean laboratory to find ways to advance U.S. interests abroad that were compatible with its values. Most Americans understood that the defense of the Panama Canal required a more assertive U.S. policy in the Caribbean area, but they were not persuaded of the need for military intervention. Latin America criticized U.S. policy and demanded that the Roosevelt Corollary be replaced by a new principle of nonintervention. Taft sidestepped the issue with "dollar diplomacy," encouraging Americans to invest in the region in the hopes of precluding instability. Woodrow Wilson thought promoting liberty was a better way to accomplish the same goal. These three instruments—marines, dollars, and elections—composed the "protectorate policy," America's rejoinder to imperialism. None of the three presidents' variations on the theme succeeded in implanting stable democratic institutions or promoting economic development in the region, but the United States learned from its mistakes and modified the instruments under Franklin D. Roosevelt.

Asian Doors

The United States pursued two different policies in Asia: a closed door policy with regard to the Philippines and an open door policy with regard to China. The anti-imperialist groups that were born of the debate on annexing the Philippines did not disappear after the vote. They spoke for a part of America that could not be ignored, and they seized the opportunity to reverse U.S. policy when the Senate Foreign Relations Committee held hearings on the Philippine insurrection. Their stories of American atrocities eventually caused the administration to adjust its policies. As one historian wrote, "While the United States was the last of the major powers to acquire an empire, it was also the first to become disillusioned with a formal empire, turning internal control over to Filipino independentistas by 1907 and pledging formal independence in the Jones Act of 1916, when Britain was still jailing Indians."[31]

In China the United States wed its ideals to its economic and strategic interests. The Europeans and Japanese had carved the old Chinese Empire into "spheres of influence." Despite pressure from the U.S. business community, which wanted access to the Chinese market, and despite the value of taking a slice of China as the European imperialists were doing, the United States resisted the temptation and declared an open door policy: It called on European governments to open their areas to merchants and investors from all countries and to respect China's territorial integrity. Although the United States did not treat China well, it behaved better than the European nations, and the new Chinese Republican government recognized the difference.

The Great War, the Wilsonian Plan, and the Isolationist Delusion (1916–1941)

For a century following the Napoleonic Wars, the United States benefited from Europe's general peace and localized wars. When World War I began, the United States tried to avoid being drawn into it. Wilson declared U.S. neutrality and issued ten proclamations to define the rights of neutrals. Sensitive to their need for U.S. support but also wanting to prevent goods from reaching Germany, the British took care to respect U.S. rights. Germany's ability to compete against the British Navy depended on a new weapon, submarines, whose rules of engagement had not been defined. When German U-boats began to sink ocean liners, notably the *Lusitania*, whose passengers included 124 Americans, the United States protested vehemently. In an effort to keep the United States out of the war, Germany instructed its submarine commanders not to attack neutral merchant ships or any passenger ships. Nonetheless public opinion in the United States continued to turn against Germany, though Americans still did not want to fight.

Wilson had to walk a tightrope of neutrality. He was accused by Theodore Roosevelt of being too neutral in a war between democracy and autocracy, and by William Jennings Bryan, his secretary of state, of not being neutral enough. After Wilson sent a tough message to Germany condemning U-boat attacks, Bryan resigned on June 8, 1915. Wilson later healed the rift with Bryan, who endorsed him for a second term. Wilson won in a close election that included the slogan, "He kept us out of war."

Even before Wilson's second inaugural, the German government decided to try to bring the war to a quick end. On January 31, 1917, Germany informed the U.S. government that it would begin unrestricted submarine warfare in the war zone. The Germans believed that they could defeat England in five months and that even if the United States declared war, it could not mobilize quickly enough to affect the outcome. Wilson broke off relations with Germany. The British intercepted the "Zimmerman telegram" and three weeks later, turned over to Wilson this cable from the German foreign minister to his ambassador in Mexico City in which Germany proposed an alliance with Mexico against the United States. In the event of their victory, the Germans promised to help Mexico "reconquer the lost territory in Texas, New Mexico, and Arizona."[32] The contents of the telegram were leaked to the press, and Americans were outraged.

The Zimmerman telegram and German attacks on three U.S. ships between March 12 and 18 were the events that finally convinced Wilson, his cabinet, and most Americans that they had to fight. On April 2, 1917, Wilson addressed Congress and asked for a declaration of war. He said that America must accept the "status of belligerent which thus has been thrust upon it" by German attacks on U.S. and other neutral ships. America must fight "for the rights of nations great and small and the privilege of men everywhere to choose their way of life. The world must be made safe for democracy."

Only five Senators spoke against the declaration. Senator George Norris said that he opposed entry into the war because the United States had not been completely neutral. Wall Street, in his judgment, was behind the war: "There is no doubt in my mind but the enormous amount of money loaned to the allies in this country has been instrumental in bringing about a public sentiment in favor of our country taking a course that would make every bond worth a hundred cents on the dollar." He urged his colleagues to recall George Washington's warning about entangling alliances: "Let Europe solve her problems as we have solved ours."[33] Before the Germans sank U.S. ships, many Americans shared Norris's view. In April 1917, his was a lonely voice. The Senate voted for war 82 to 6, as did the House, 373 to 50.

By this time Wilson also wanted the United States to enter the war so that he could have a hand in constructing the peace. No other leader gave as much thought or solicited and synthesized more revolutionary ideas on how the world political system should be restructured to stop future wars. From the beginning of the war, Wilson's mind turned to the fundamental questions: How to mediate an end to the war? How to assure permanent peace? He sent his principal adviser, Colonel Edward House, to Europe several times in search of an answer to the first question, but the Europeans wanted to win, not settle. Wilson therefore spent most of his time on the longer-term issue. His first thought was to try to secure mutual guarantees of territorial integrity and political independence under republican forms of government, and he decided the power of this idea could be demonstrated in the Americas. He proposed to the ambassadors of Argentina, Brazil, and Chile a "Pan-American Pact" to "mutualize" the Monroe Doctrine and to be a model that Europe could follow to end the war. Argentina and Brazil approved the idea, but Chile had reservations. In the end, Wilson's interventions in Mexico and the Caribbean precluded hemispheric agreement, but the idea would be central in his subsequent peace proposals.[34]

Beginning in May 1916 Wilson tried to awaken Americans to a new role as participants "in the life of the world" rather than as "disconnected lookers-on." In his "Peace Without Victory" address to a joint session of Congress on January 22, 1917, Wilson asked, "Is the present war a struggle for a just and secure peace, or only for a new balance of power?" He answered with a set of revolutionary principles that borrowed from James Monroe but reached all the way back to Immanuel Kant:

> There must be, not a balance of power, but a community of power; not organized rivalries, but an organized common peace . . . I am proposing, as it were, that the nations would with one accord adopt the doctrine of President Monroe as the doctrine of the world: that no nation should seek to extend its polity over any other nation or people, but that every people should be left free to determine its own polity.[35]

If all sides would acknowledge the stalemate and accept "peace without victory," not only would the war end but there would be no defeated power seeking revenge in a second war. Acceptance of self-determination would eliminate the causes of war (colonies and reparations), and a concert of powers, greater than any nation, would be able to enforce the peace. Wilson was proposing nothing less than a complete change in the way states defined their interests and the way the international system should work.

A year later, after the U.S. had entered the war, Wilson and House sat down for two hours one morning and condensed their thoughts into a fourteen-point peace plan, which Wilson delivered to Congress on January 8, 1918. The first five points set out the basic elements of "progressive internationalism": no secret treaties ("open covenants of peace, openly arrived at"); freedom of the seas; reduction of trade barriers and equality of trade conditions; reduction of national armaments to the lowest possible level; and an impartial adjustment of colonial claims based on the principle of self-determination. The next points called for the withdrawal of foreign armies to their own lands, the welcoming of revolutionary Russia "into the society of free nations," the adjustment of boundaries along clear lines of nationality, and the creation of a Polish state with access to the sea. Wilson left the most important point, his proposal for a League of Nations, for last: "A general association of nations must be formed under specific covenants for the purpose of affording mutual guarantees of political independence and territorial integrity to great and small states alike."[36]

"These are American principles," Wilson proclaimed, and he added, "they are the principles of mankind and must prevail." He also reached out to Germany: "We have no jealousy of German greatness, and there is nothing in this program that impairs it . . . We wish her only to accept a place of equality among the peoples of the world."

The speech was praised widely, and it elicited some peace feelers. But the Germans then imposed a punishing peace treaty on Russia and moved its forces west. The United States raised an army of 5 million men within one year, but they did not arrive in large enough numbers to make a difference until the autumn of 1918, when they helped blunt a German offensive. The Germans retreated to Belgium and appealed to Wilson for talks based on the Fourteen Points, but the request came at a politically awkward time. Congressional elections were approaching, and the Republicans, more attuned to American anger over 116,000 casualties, wanted Germany defeated, not accommodated. In order to win the congressional elections, the Republican leadership united behind a strategy of attacking Wilson's peace plan. Theodore Roosevelt demanded unconditional surrender and urged the Senate to reject the Fourteen Points. Henry Cabot Lodge accused Wilson of accepting "peace at any price" because his advisers were "socialists and Bolsheviks."[37] Wilson stiffened his demands to the Germans. He then tried to bring the Germans and the Allies to the bargaining table and to win the congressional elections. He succeeded only in gaining German agreement to an armistice on November 11. Five days earlier, the Republicans had won control of both houses of Congress. Henry Cabot Lodge became chairman of the Senate Foreign Relations Committee. The election campaign was so poisonous that Wilson refused to appoint Lodge or any senior Republican to advise him on the peace negotiations.

Europe's leaders dismissed Wilson's plan as naive, but they could not ignore the vast and enthusiastic crowds that met Wilson in England, France, and Italy or the popular response to his speeches urging fundamental change in the international system. Still, when Wilson sat down to negotiate, he found himself alone, asking his European counterparts to discard the rules of a 400-year-old interstate system in exchange for a set of untried, idealistic principles. The first issue on the table was the disposal of Germany's colonies, and every country except the United States made claims based on the age-old principle "To the victor belongs the spoils." Wilson listened until his patience was exhausted. Then, like a professor who was frustrasted with his students because they could not grasp the point of his lecture, he reminded the others of the purpose of their negotiations: "The world was against any further annexations. [If they occurred] the League of Nations would be discredited from the beginning." He explained his plan for ending colonialism and protecting the people "under the full view of the world, until they were able to take charge of their own affairs."[38] The English were the most indignant, but all the Allied representatives responded as if they were from a different world, as indeed they were. All the major powers except the United States also opposed small power representation on the League's Executive Council. The Japanese requested a provision on racial equality, but the English blocked it, along with two American proposals, for freedom of religion and of the seas. Wilson nonetheless negotiated with great skill and perseverance and was able to preserve enough of his points that he could present a draft to the world on February 14, 1919, and return to the United States to consult and defend it.

Between February 23 and his return to France in early March, Wilson met with numerous groups and at least thirty-four senators for intensive discussions on the draft. There was great enthusiasm among the American public for the League of Nations Covenant, but on the day before Wilson's return to Paris to continue the peace talks, Lodge offered a stiff critique that mixed vitriol with some searing substantive points. After accusing the president of abandoning George Washington in favor of "Trotsky, the champion of internationalism," Lodge displayed a round-robin letter, signed by thirty-seven senators, indicating that the treaty would not be approved in its current form. He then recommended four changes: an affirmation of the Monroe Doctrine, a provision for withdrawal from the League of Nations, explicit exclusion of domestic issues (such as immigration) from the League of Nations Covenant, and clarification of how the League would use force.

Former President William Howard Taft and the Senate Democratic leader Gilbert Hitchkock assured Wilson that if he could amend the treaty along the lines recommended by Lodge, "the ground will be completely cut from under the opposition."[39] The Allies were aware of the round-robin letter, and they were ready to amend the League Covenant in exchange for Wilson's accepting harsh provisions in the Treaty of Versailles. France wanted to annex the Saar but accepted a fifteen-year Allied occupation of the Rhineland, a separate Anglo-American defense treaty, and an exorbitant increase in reparations from Germany. The Italians demanded parts of Austria; the Japanese threatened to bolt the conference unless they received German concessions in Shandong. All insisted on a vengeful war-guilt clause against Germany. With a heavy heart, Wilson struck the compromises to accommodate Lodge. These changes diminished the enthusiasm of the progressive internationalists, the League's strongest supporters, which made selling the agreement that much harder. The Treaty of Versailles, which included the League Covenant, was signed on June 28, 1919, in the Hall of Mirrors, and Wilson turned to his next battle.

The Senate debate on the Treaty of Versailles has been described as having pitted internationalists against isolationists, but there were only twelve irreconcilably isolationist Republicans. The more interesting debate was not between them and the internationalists but between the "unilateral" and the "cooperative" internationalists. The unilateralists were thirty-seven Republican senators who supported Lodge; they wanted to constrain the League and ensure that the United States would retain the freedom to act unilaterally. The League's supporters, forty-seven Democratic senators, agreed with Wilson that international institutions should stop all wars.

Despite Wilson's success in amending the League government and making it a part of the treaty, Lodge was still not reconciled to it because, in his words, it placed "the destiny of my country under the control of a politically selected tribunal of nine . . . sitting forever upon foreign soil . . . The spirit of this plan to subordinate this great Republic into this international socialistic combine is absolutely in the face and teeth and eyes of our Constitution." His second point also had the ring of tradition: "Before I go into the stabilizing business abroad, I believe in making the foundations of a republican-democratic form of government safe and stable in my own country."[40]

President Wilson met with groups of Republican senators and realized they supported Lodge, who was stalling the debate. On September 2, despite poor health, the president decided to build support for the League around the country, and he began a national tour that would take him to twenty-nine cities to give thirty-seven speeches to rebut his opponents' arguments: "I want to call you to witness that the peace of the world cannot be established without America . . . [and] the peace and goodwill of the world are necessary to America."[41]

He returned to Washington exhausted, and on October 2 he suffered a stroke that paralyzed one side of his body. Wilson became inflexible both physically and temperamentally at the very moment compromises were desperately needed, although it is by no means clear that a compromise was possible. Lodge had crafted fourteen reservations that struck at the League's heart. For example, as a substitute for the League's collective security provision, Lodge proposed a provision stating, "The U.S. assumes no obligation to preserve the territorial integrity or political independence of any country . . . unless . . . Congress . . . by act or joint resolution [shall] so provide."[42] Other reservations were aimed at releasing the United States from commitments agreed in the League Covenant and the treaty unless Congress specifically approved. The treaty came to the Senate floor for a vote three times, the first time with Lodge's reservations, the second without, and the third with some support by Democrats for Lodge's reservations. Each time, it failed.

The tragedy was that in order to secure the League of Nations, Wilson had to compromise on so many of his Fourteen Points that the Treaty of Versailles reflected the old order more than the new.

The harsh reparations and the war-guilt clause imposed on Germany sowed seeds that were to bear bitter fruit for Europe. The decision to transfer Germany's concession in China to Japan not only alienated the Chinese from the United States but set the stage for the next war in Asia. Worse, Wilson could not deliver his own country. It was not at all clear that the League of Nations would have been able to deter or confront aggressors if the United States had been a member, but it was reasonably clear that it could not do so without the United States. Moreover, the U.S. failure to approve the agreement to defend France against German attack left France naked, with neither a new institution nor a balance of power that could prevent the next war.

Perhaps a stronger, more flexible Wilson could have won a weakened League. But it is also possible that he was just too far in front of the American people at that time. Beneath the debate among internationalists was a powerful postwar undercurrent tugging Americans home, back to "normalcy," fearful of Europe's wars and the Russian Revolution. The United States succumbed to a Red Scare in 1920 when A. Mitchell Palmer, Wilson's attorney general, launched anticommunist raids in thirty-three cities in one night. By the end of the year, Warren G. Harding won a landslide victory that reflected the nation's yearning to turn inward. Lodge interpreted Harding's victory as his as well: "So far as the United States is concerned, the League is dead."[43]

Besides the rejection of the League and the World Court, other signs that America wanted to close the door on the world included congressional approval of the country's first laws limiting worldwide immigration. The nation's leaders, predominantly Anglo-Saxon Protestants, reacted to the heavy influx of immigrants from southern and eastern Europe. Nearly 20 million people had immigrated in the two decades before the war. Congress accepted as "scientific fact" that the new immigrants were of lower quality than those who had preceded them and that a successful America required more of the original and fewer of the newer immigrants. The quotas set by the laws reflected the ethnic composition of America in 1890, before the new wave of immigration. The immigration debate coincided with an ugly mood of intolerance, reflected in the rise of the Ku Klux Klan and other nativist groups.

A debtor before the war, the United States emerged as the world's largest creditor afterwards. But it did not act like one, and the international economic system suffered as a result. With a significant trade surplus and about one-third of the world's gold, the United States should have reduced its trade barriers. Instead, because one of the core constituent groups of the Republican Party was small businesses that wanted protection against foreign competition, Congress increased tariffs in 1922 and again in 1930 to the century's highest point—52.8 percent. This slashed imports and exacerbated the depression that had begun to pull down the world's economies.

America had also become weary of Caribbean interventions and began to dismantle the protectorate policy. In 1922 Secretary of State Charles Evans Hughes announced the withdrawal of U.S. troops from the Dominican Republic and Nicaragua, but marines returned to Nicaragua in 1925 after a coup there. That second intervention proved so costly that it forced the United States to evaluate its past policies and, in a few years, to repudiate the Roosevelt Corollary. During these years, the United States also pursued arms control through the Washington Naval Treaties of 1922 and the London Treaty of 1930 aimed at limiting naval construction by the great powers. Although Japan was assured naval predominance in northeast Asia, it still abrogated the treaties in 1936.

Franklin D. Roosevelt took office in March 1933 in the midst of America's worst depression. FDR devoted most of his first two terms in office to restoring the American economy, but he also reversed course on U.S. trade policy by gaining congressional approval to negotiate bilateral, reciprocal agreements to reduce trade barriers. Those agreements served as a platform on which he would later build an open international trading system.

He completed the movement away from the protectorate policy, but instead of retreating from participation in the hemisphere he fashioned a "good neighbor policy" toward Latin America. "We are exceedingly jealous of our own sovereignty," Roosevelt wrote, "and it is only right that we should respect a similar feeling among other nations."[44] FDR withdrew the marines, leaving only those in U.S. bases in the region; he pledged to respect the principle of nonintervention, and he and Jimmy Carter are the only two elected presidents in this century who did not violate that promise.[45] He repealed the Platt Amendments, negotiated reciprocal trade agreements, and instituted regular high-level consultations with Latin American leaders. The new policy repaired much of the ill will that had resulted from U.S. interventions and improved relations with Caribbean, Central American, and Latin American nations in time to prevent Japan or Germany from gaining a foothold in the region.

Japanese aggression in Asia and the return of German militarism caused the president and Congress to renew the debate on whether and how to respond. Senator Gerald Nye picked up where George Norris had left off in his opposition to Wilson's declaration of war. Nye chaired the Senate Committee Investigating the Munitions Industry and condemned Wall Street and the arms manufacturers for having dragged the United States into World War I. This view was apparently widespread at the time. Seventy percent of the public, according to a Gallup Poll of January 1937, believed that U.S. entry in World War I had been a mistake.[46] Nye fashioned neutrality laws that barred U.S. loans and trade to belligerents. The intent was to avoid again being pulled into a European war, but the effect was to tie Roosevelt's hands and send a signal to Germany and Japan that the United States would not stand in the way of their ambitions.

Nye also became one of the leaders of the America First Committee, which opposed U.S. involvement in World War II. In a 1939 national radio broadcast, he explained that the war in Europe had nothing to do with "the cause of democracy. The cause there is that old, old one of power politics. It is a cause that we cannot meddle in unless we are ready and anxious to jeopardize the life of the one remaining great democracy, our own."[47]

Franklin Roosevelt understood, as Wilson had, that war was approaching and that at some point the United States would have to get involved, but he also knew that Americans were not ready. He therefore tried to move the country gradually; interpreting events in a way that would help Americans understand what was at stake. In his "Quarantine Speech" of October 5, 1937, the president described the "reign of terror and international lawlessness" that was spreading throughout the world and explained that it had become "impossible for any nation completely to isolate itself from economic and political upheavals." But like Wilson before his reelection, Roosevelt insisted that he was "determined to keep out of war."[48]

The American people, according to public opinion surveys from 1939 until the bombing of Pearl Harbor, were following political developments in Europe and Asia closely and believed that German and Japanese aggression endangered the security of the United States. As time passed they began to want to do more to help England, and by January 1939, 82 percent wanted to strengthen U.S. defenses, particularly the U.S. Navy to protect the coasts. But on the eve of the bombing of Pearl Harbor, only 14 percent of the American people called the war "our war" and believed we should be fighting it.[49]

Roosevelt's messages paralleled this mood. After his reelection in 1940 Roosevelt talked about the United States becoming an "arsenal for democracy"; at the same time he continued to insist that his goal was "to keep war away from our country and our people." But he was emphatic that "if Great Britain goes down . . . all of us in the Americas would be living at the point of a gun."[50] Senator Robert Taft (R.–Ohio), former President Herbert Hoover, and many others opposed Roosevelt's proposal to repeal the Neutrality Act arms embargo, fearing that would drag the United States into the war and, in Taft's words, "almost certainly destroy democracy in the United States."[51] Nonetheless, Roosevelt was able to relax the Neutrality Act in favor of France and England in 1939; in 1941 he gained approval of the Lend-Lease Act and the "destroyers for bases" deal; and the Atlantic Charter was signed by Roosevelt and Winston Churchill in August 1941—all pointing toward increasing support for the Allies.

The event that wiped out the opposition to Roosevelt was the Japanese sneak attack on the U.S. Navy fleet in Pearl Harbor. Although leaning toward war, Roosevelt probably would have failed to persuade the American people to go to war without some event as dramatic as the bombing of Pearl Harbor. He certainly could never have achieved a unified response without the Japanese attack.

The United States as World Power:
World War II and the Cold War

The world has never seen a war as global and as devastating as World War II. But of all the major powers, only the United States did not suffer attacks on its industrial base. Indeed, the U.S. economy expanded to fill its needs as well as those of its allies. As it had in World War I, the United States delayed its entry into the war until events compelled a decision, but its entry was still early enough to permit Roosevelt to be the premier strategist for the war and the postwar world. "Mindful of the ghost of Woodrow Wilson," Franklin Roosevelt was determined to avoid his predecessor's mistakes.[52] FDR had served in Wilson's administration and like many of his generation was heartbroken by Wilson's failure to gain the Senate's approval of the League. In the same month the Japanese bombed Pearl Harbor, Roosevelt set up a committee to plan for a postwar world.[53] Like Wilson, Roosevelt combined both idealism and realism, but he was a little less creative and a little more practical. With the benefit of learning from Wilson's mistakes, Roosevelt amended the revolutionary vision in several fundamental ways:

- Congress and the Republican leadership were involved in all postwar planning from the beginning. As a result, the House and Senate passed resolutions by one-sided votes in 1943 "favoring the creation of appropriate international machinery with power adequate to establish and to maintain a just and lasting peace."
- The Big Three—the United States, Great Britain, and the Soviet Union—decided to pursue an unconditional victory. This meant that the Allies could dictate the settlement and could design the political regimes in Germany, Italy, and Japan so as to prevent a third world war.
- The new United Nations would improve on the League of Nations by including a Security Council composed of five major powers (the Big Three plus France and China). The council would decide whether to use force by unanimous vote. The

United Nations would be negotiated and established during
the war so as to take advantage of the time when the unity of
purpose was greatest.

- The United States would help the Allies by Lend-Lease during the war, and it would not seek reparations from its enemies. In the end, under Soviet pressure, Germany was
  compelled to pay $20 billion in reparations, half to the Soviet
  Union. The United States did not impose reparations on the
  Japanese, and by 1946 the West had stopped trying to collect
  from Germany.

- The United States and Great Britain agreed to establish an
  open international monetary and trade system. At Bretton
  Woods, they made plans to establish the International Monetary Fund (IMF) to serve as a clearinghouse for foreign exchange and a lender of last resort, and a World Bank to assist
  Europe to recover and to promote development. A world trading system was also envisaged and approved in Geneva in 1947
  under the General Agreement on Tariff and Trade (GATT).

- A Trusteeship system would be established in the United Nations to assist colonies to prepare for independence.

Needless to say, these pieces of a peace did not all arrive, coherently
and precisely defined, on the same day. Rather, they were the products
of a complex deliberative process within the United States and among
the U.S., British, and Soviet governments.[54] Like Wilson, FDR was determined to design a postwar world that would, as he explained to Congress, "spell the end of the system of unilateral action, the exclusive
alliances, the spheres of influence, the balances of power, and all the
other expedients that have been tried for centuries—and have always
failed."[55] Roosevelt used Wilson's language, but he also understood that
the success of the United Nations would depend on whether the Big
Three would be able to collaborate after the war. He had no illusions
that that would be easy, particularly because of the harsh reality of the
Soviet army's power in Eastern Europe, but he thought it was possible.

Roosevelt, Stalin, and Churchill represented countries with distinct
interests. In addition to negotiating their common interests in win-

ning the war, establishing the United Nations, and occupying Germany, each of the leaders sought bilateral understandings. FDR was not averse to allying with Stalin against Churchill to end colonialism. Churchill joined Stalin to divide Eastern Europe along very traditional lines, although he knew his friend Roosevelt believed in open regions rather than closed spheres of influence. FDR and Churchill decided not to share the secret of the atomic bomb with Stalin.[56] These were three realists who wanted to continue their cooperation after the war but who also planned for the possibility that the hoped-for cooperation would not occur. Roosevelt, for example, instructed the Joint Chiefs of Staff to prepare a detailed military-strategic plan for a postwar era. The premise underlying the plan was that the United States would remain deeply involved in international affairs and would have bases all over the world to defend against any future attack.[57]

Harry Truman, Joseph Stalin, and Clement Attlee met in Potsdam, Germany, in late July 1945.[58] The leaders of the two English-speaking countries had changed, but the relationship between them remained close for cultural and political reasons. In contrast, both the United States and Great Britain felt growing suspicion about Soviet motives. Truman lacked his predecessor's diplomatic skills, was not adequately briefed on FDR's experiences in dealing with Stalin, and was not sensitive to the magnitude of the task the Soviet Union faced in reconstructing a devastated country and securing a strategic buffer that would prevent any future attack from the west.

Stalin's motives, however, were not solely defensive; his demands at Potsdam—for the lands obtained in the Nazi-Soviet Pact of 1939, a base on the Bosporus, Soviet trusteeship of some Italian colonies, four-power control of the Ruhr—reflected the ambition of an emerging great power following the rules of the old territorial game, energized by a revolutionary doctrine. By the time Japan surrendered, Soviet armies extended from the Korean peninsula and Manchuria to Berlin and Vienna, spanning virtually the entire Eurasian landmass. No army since Genghis Khan's had extended its reach so far. Though the United States was wrapped around the other side of the world—from Munich west to Tokyo—and though Stalin recognized U.S. power, he also knew the

United States was historically reluctant to use force. His instinct was to press his limits. Truman's mind-set was different: He felt that if governments did not uphold an agreement, they could not and should not be trusted. At Potsdam, Truman proposed the internationalization of the Danube and free elections in Eastern Europe—two examples of a new open world order that would rely on collective security.[59] Stalin accepted the rhetoric but not the reality of an open world. Truman had the option and the instinct to battle on both fronts—the new world of cooperation and the old world of confrontation.

For the United States, the victory was sweeter after World War II than after World War I because it had played a larger role and because the enemy was monstrous. But when the war ended Americans again wanted to come home and refocus. Lend-lease was ended. By mid-1946, just ten months after the war had ended, more than 8 million men and women—or roughly 75 percent of the armed forces—had been discharged and brought home. Only 1.5 million men would be in the armed forces by June 1947, and by then defense expenditures had declined from $91 billion to $10 billion.[60] Congress had already approved the Bretton Woods Agreement establishing the World Bank and the International Monetary Fund, and the Senate ratified the UN Charter on July 28, 1945, before the war with Japan had ended, by a vote of 89 to 2. The concerns of isolationists and reservationists were a mere whisper in the debate, quieted by the unified spirit of the war and by effective co-optation by the executive branch.

As tensions rose with the Soviet Union, the United States debated what to do. There were three camps: the idealists, the realists, and the Cold War crusaders. The idealists, led by Henry Wallace, who had been Roosevelt's vice president during his third term, believed that differences could be negotiated. However, they feared that if the United States backed the Soviet Union into a corner it could lead to war and would harm progressive forces for social change in the United States.

But concerns about Soviet behavior grew after the war, and in the early months of 1946 two compelling analyses gave coherence to the Cold War crusader position. On February 22, 1946, George F. Kennan, a senior official in the U.S. embassy in Moscow, sent a "long telegram" to Washington describing "the Kremlin's neurotic view of world affairs [and the] traditional and instinctive Russian sense of insecurity."[61] A few weeks later, Winston Churchill delivered a powerful speech in Truman's presence in Fulton, Missouri. Churchill warned Americans that the Soviet army had pulled an "iron curtain" down across Eastern Europe, establishing police states, extending communism westward, and threatening freedom.

The realist view was represented by Walter Lippmann, a respected national columnist, who critiqued Kennan's containment policy as a "strategic monstrosity" that "commits the U.S. to confront the Russians with counterforce 'at every point' . . . instead of at those points, which we have selected."There was not much debate over these three views because events soon convinced most Americans that the Cold War crusader view was correct: The Soviet Union suppressed human rights and prevented free elections in Eastern Europe; there was Communist subversion in Italy and France; the Soviet Union threatened Iran and Turkey[62] and occupied Manchuria; and a Communist insurgency was growing in Greece.

About one year later, in a historic passing of the baton, Great Britain informed the U.S. government that it could no longer support the Greek government's resistance to Communist aggression. It hoped the United States would fill the vacuum. On March 12, 1947, Truman addressed the U.S. Congress and painted a manichaean picture of the Communist challenge to freedom. In what became known as the Truman Doctrine, the president urged Americans to contain Soviet imperialism, beginning in Greece and Turkey. The die was cast. From then until the late 1960s, when the Vietnam War forced a later generation to rethink the assumptions of the Cold War, there was little debate as to whether the United States should be engaged in the global fight against communism. The controversial issues were where and how to fight, how much to spend, how tough the rhetoric should be, and who lost what.

The Senate debate on the Rio Pact in 1947 is a telling case of how far the American people had traveled from Washington's injunction. The Rio Pact represented the first regional entangling alliance that the United States considered. The United States and eighteen Latin American countries signed the Inter-American Treaty of Reciprocal

Assistance in Rio de Janeiro on September 7, 1947. It provided for joint action in the event of an armed attack on any member state, with collective measures to be decided by a two-thirds vote. Republican Senator Arthur Vandenberg, who had converted from isolationism during World War II, attended the Rio Conference as the chairman of the Senate Foreign Relations Committee and recommended ratification of the agreement. Only Senator Eugene Millikin (R.–Colo.) opposed the agreement, which was approved by a vote of 72 to 1 on December 8, 1947.[63]

Two years later, the Senate took up the North Atlantic Treaty. Like the Rio Pact, the North Atlantic Treaty Organization (NATO) was a group of states—originally twelve—committed to armed action in the event of an attack on a member. The treaty was opposed from the left by Henry Wallace, who feared that the military expenditures needed to implement the agreement would undermine European recovery, and by conservatives like Senator Robert Taft, who feared that "if Russia sees herself ringed about gradually by so-called defensive arms from Norway and Denmark to Turkey and Greece, it may decide that war is inevitable and that it had better come before the arming is completed."[64] Concern was also raised that the treaty would deny the Congress its legitimate constitutional role to declare war, but it was overridden, and the treaty was approved by a vote of 82 to 13 on July 21, 1949. The same issue had sunk the League of Nations just thirty years before. What had changed was the U.S. definition of its interests and its perception of the immediacy of the global threat. Although Americans wanted their government to devote more attention to domestic issues after the war, they also accepted the need to stay engaged in international affairs.[65] The Rio Pact and NATO were just the first two of several regional security alliances the United States would negotiate on the periphery of the Communist world.

Harry Truman added his own amendments to the Wilsonian vision:

- Instead of draining Europe of capital by collecting wartime debts, Truman and Secretary of State George Marshall pledged an unprecedented $17 billion to a four-year plan to promote Europe's recovery.

- He encouraged Europe to come forward with a unified plan for recovery rather than a dozen national projects. Using a traditional approach to international politics, the United States would have played one country against another, but the United States defined its interests in a more far-sighted way. Jean Monnet, the father of European unity, said that it was "the first time in history that a great power did not base its policy on ruling by dividing."[66] A decade later, encouraged by the United States, the European Economic Community was formed.
- Truman rejected the hatred that many harbored for Germany and helped it to recover and become democratic.

These three far-sighted initiatives reflected a new definition of U.S. interests based on two premises: first, that in the late 1940s U.S. power and prosperity could be enhanced more by spending money in Europe than by spending it at home, and second, that U.S. interests would be better served by a united and strong Europe than by one that was divided and weak. No doubt, this redefinition occurred in response to a dire threat, but such fears sometimes generate shortsighted reactions like McCarthyism. Leadership does matter.

The Struggle in the Third World

The civil war in China between the Nationalist government under Chiang Kai-shek and the Communists was suspended during the war with Japan but began anew after the Japanese surrender. The United States granted about $3 billion in economic and military aid to the Nationalist government; the Communists promised the peasants land reform and received weapons and aid from the Soviet Union. With the continued deterioration of the Nationalists' position, Truman sent General George Marshall to mediate between the two sides, but the effort failed. Marshall concluded that Chiang's regime was so corrupt that its fall was inevitable. The Communists won in 1949, the same year that the Soviets exploded their first atomic weapon. The Sino-Soviet alliance gave the world Communist movement momentum, if not historical inevitability, and it struck fear in the West. The Republicans attacked Truman for "losing" China, raising the political stakes of accepting any further losses in the Cold War.

The strategic threat had worsened, and Truman was under great pressure to raise the defense budget above $15 billion. In January 1950 he instructed the National Security Council to conduct a study of U.S. strategic objectives and capabilities. The result, NSC-68, was completed in March 1950. It recommended a massive U.S. military buildup to counter the expansion of Soviet-directed communism and to make credible the vast commitments the United States had made.[67] Truman accepted the logic of the Cold War, but he was not prepared to pay the price so he postponed a decision.

The event that compelled Truman to change his mind and establish a national security state occurred on June 25, 1950, when Communist North Korea invaded South Korea. Truman immediately interpreted the invasion as a test of the West's resolve—the Communist equivalent of Hitler's test at Munich. "If the history of the 1930s teaches us anything," the president told the American people, "it is that appeasement of dictators is the sure road to world war. If aggression were allowed to succeed in Korea, it would be an open invitation to new acts of aggression elsewhere."[68] The only way to prevent another world war was to respond immediately and militarily against North Korea and around the world. NSC-68 was taken off the shelf and its recommendations implemented.

Several months earlier, Secretary of State Dean Acheson had suggested obliquely that Washington might recognize the People's Republic of China and not defend Taiwan, but the invasion preempted that possibility, and Truman sent the Seventh Fleet to defend the island.[69] Truman also decided to assist the French in their colonial war in Indochina. He strengthened NATO and West Germany, a policy continued and expanded by his successor, Dwight Eisenhower. The efforts to rebuild and democratize Germany and Japan accelerated, but both countries agreed to renounce nuclear weapons and any offensive military force—two profoundly important initiatives that would contribute to the stability of both Europe and Asia.

The war in Korea signaled the shift in the struggle against communism to the Third World, where it was fought, usually indirectly and with proxies, in Guatemala, Malaya, the Philippines, the Congo, Cuba, Chile, Angola, Mozambique, Nicaragua, Grenada, and Ethiopia. Each conflict had internal causes but was exacerbated by the ideological divisions between the two Cold War camps. The relationship between internal divisions and external rivalry made resolution more difficult. To defend its clients, the United States provided economic and military aid and advice. To undermine the other's client, both the United States and the Soviet Union trained insurgents and carried out covert actions. In Cuba, Vietnam, and Afghanistan, the Cold War collided with raw nationalism, and despite America's fervent belief in democracy and the Soviets' in communism, both lost. Nationalism won.

The century began with the United States liberating Cuba from Spain. But even though Cuba was "independent," the United States controlled most of its economy and exercised more influence over its politics than did most of its presidents until Fidel Castro seized power in 1959. Castro's was a nationalist revolution, which sought to assert its independence from the United States. To defend Cuba, Castro allied with the Soviet Union. That, however, convinced Washington that Castro was a Communist, which he soon became. The most egregious violation of the Monroe Doctrine was ninety miles offshore. Soviet Premier Nikita Khrushchev offered Castro nuclear missiles for the defense of Cuba. Castro accepted them not to defend Cuba, which he believed he could do better without missiles, but to advance the cause of communism.[70] President John F. Kennedy blockaded Cuba, insisted that the Soviet Union withdraw the missiles, and threatened to invade if it did not. He pledged not to invade Cuba and to withdraw U.S. missiles from Turkey if Khrushchev agreed to withdraw the missiles from Cuba and to permit UN inspection. Castro was livid and refused to let the UN observe the withdrawal, but the Pentagon did so by aircraft. The two superpowers stepped back from the brink—the closest the world has ever come to nuclear war—agreed to a hotline and a Test Ban Treaty in the summer of 1963, and began to define the rules of détente and to negotiate agreements on nuclear disarmament.

For forty years, Cuba and Castro provoked both the best and worst of U.S. policy toward Latin America: on the positive side, Kennedy's Alliance for Progress, Carter's human rights campaign and Panama Canal Treaties, and Reagan's Caribbean Basin Initiative; on the negative side, assassinations and covert actions in Cuba, Chile, and Nicaragua.

Whereas Cuba has been a forty-year irritant to the United States, Vietnam was a deep, infected wound. In 1954, after securing a truce in Korea, President Dwight Eisenhower did not want to begin a second Asian war, and he declined the desperate request from France to prevent a Communist victory in Vietnam. Six years later, he warned incoming President John F. Kennedy that the United States could not afford to lose Indochina to the Communists. That imperative governed U.S. policy from the late 1950s until North Vietnam overran the South in 1975, imposing a humiliating loss on the United States.

U.S. policy toward the Communist world assumed and acted as if there were a unity of interests between the Soviet Union and China. Their relationship disintegrated in the late 1950s, but the United States was blind to the breakdown for more than a decade. Henry Kissinger has admitted that it was only "heavy-handed Soviet diplomacy" that alerted President Richard Nixon and him to the opportunity to change the geopolitical equation by a rapprochement with China. The Soviet ambassador visited Kissinger in the White House in 1969 and "insisted on giving me a gory account of the atrocities allegedly committed by the Chinese in an extended briefing." Kissinger mentioned the meeting to Nixon, and the two of them mused about the strategic opportunities that had not dawned on them until that moment.[71] A change in policy toward China, however, required not only an international opportunity but also a domestic political calculation. Ironically, Nixon, who had advanced his career by excoriating Democrats for losing China, was best positioned to embrace Red China in the midst of its Cultural Revolution. During the Cold War, observed Walter McDougall, the American public "breathed sighs of relief as hawkish presidents turned more dovish or dovish ones more hawkish."[72] Perhaps this was yet another indication of a public that was sure of its goals but uncertain of its tactics.

The long-term effects of the U.S.-China rapprochement have proven to be very different from what was expected in 1972. Kissinger then saw China as a lever to use on Vietnam in the peace talks and on the Soviet Union on arms control. Neither plan worked, but the new détente freed China to pursue its rivalry with the Soviet Union and allowed the United States to leave Vietnam without suffering a mortal wound in the region. When Deng Xiaoping took power in the late 1970s and established diplomatic relations with President Jimmy Carter, that opening to the world permitted fundamental economic reforms, which would alter its relations with the West and the balance of power in East Asia.

U.S. policy in the Middle East reflected an intricate balancing of political, humanitarian, and economic interests. Moved by a very close friend and business partner who was Jewish, by sympathy for the plight of the Jews, and by a recognition of the importance of the Jewish vote in the decisive state of New York, Truman overrode the objections of the State Department and oil interests and recognized the new state of Israel in 1948.[73] This, of course, did not mean that the United States could ignore the concerns of U.S. oil companies or the views of the Arab states in the region. Rather, it put Washington in the middle of the maelstrom of Middle Eastern politics, trying to maintain relations with the Arabs while protecting Israel and straining to bring each side to accept the other.

In the paradoxical politics of the Middle East, it was two wars that came to the assistance of the United States and the peace process. In 1973 the Israeli victory finally persuaded President Anwar Sadat of Egypt to make peace with Israel, and Jimmy Carter effectively mediated the 1979 Camp David Accords between Sadat and Prime Minister Menachem Begin of Israel. In 1991 the defeat of Iraq, a sponsor of the Palestine Liberation Organization (PLO), and the rise of the Intifada, a rebellion that threatened the PLO's leadership of the Palestinians, convinced PLO leader Yasir Arafat that he had no option but to follow Sadat's path. With Norway's help, Arafat and Prime Minister Yitzhak Rabin and Foreign Minister Shimon Peres of Israel negotiated the Oslo Accords, which involved mutual recognition and Palestinian autonomy in Gaza and parts of the West Bank. In 1994 Jordan joined the peace process.

The Post–Cold War Landscape

So many people had invested so much time thinking that the Cold War would end in a thermonuclear bang that they failed to notice when it ended with a whimper sometime in 1989. Mikhail Gorbachev, the first Soviet leader born after the revolution, became party secretary in 1985, determined to rejuvenate the Soviet experiment. Instead, he ended it. But he did a lot more than that. He withdrew Soviet troops from Afghanistan without securing any of his country's objectives; he encouraged Vietnam to withdraw from Cambodia and Cuba to leave Angola and Ethiopia. He repealed the Communist Party's monopoly on power in the Soviet Union and permitted free elections and dissent. Eastern Europeans adopted democracy and the private market and asked the Soviet Union to withdraw its troops and dissolve the Warsaw Pact. Germany reunited, perhaps the clearest sign the Cold War was over, and then the Soviet Union disappeared, replaced by a loose Commonwealth of Independent States led by Russia.

The United States welcomed and, when it could, facilitated these changes. President George Bush and Secretary of State James A. Baker III were unsure of the sincerity of the "new thinking," and so they repeatedly "tested" Gorbachev and his foreign minister, Eduard Shevardnadze. The biggest test came in August 1990, when the Iraqi dictator Saddam Hussein attacked and tried to annex his neighbor, Kuwait. The Soviet Union had a long-standing, close relationship with the Iraqi regime, but Bush and Baker persuaded the Soviet Union to join the United States in condemning the aggression and in threatening UN action to reverse it.[74] Bush described the UN action as the beginning of a "new world order." This was the first joint action between the two superpowers since World War II, but the unified front they presented against aggression was what Wilson and FDR had in mind when they proposed an international peacekeeping organization.

The military power of the United States legitimized by the United Nations expelled Iraq from Kuwait and compelled Iraq to accept the most intrusive system ever devised by international organizations to inspect and destroy a country's weapons. The end of the Cold War reminded the world what the United Nations could do if the major powers agreed on the norms and the strategies. Since then, the United Nations has taken actions in dozens of civil wars and crises around the world. Conflicts in the Third World were not automatically solved by the end of the Cold War, but they became easier to resolve.

The Cold War was not the only compass guiding the U.S. ship of state. Ideals, economic interests, and ethnic groups each played a role in defining U.S. policy on human rights and democracy, on investment disputes and trade and energy policies, on drug trafficking and international crime, and on the Middle East, Africa, and Eastern Europe. When the Cold War's strategic imperative ended, these other interests ascended, and Americans demanded that their leaders refocus their attention on domestic problems. The pendulum swung toward domestic interests, as it did after the two world wars. Like Woodrow Wilson in 1918 and Harry Truman in 1946, George Bush expected tributes from the people for his triumph in war; he, too, was stunned by rejection in the next election, in his case the presidential election of 1992.

Bill Clinton read the shift in the national mood. Experience in foreign policy was no longer an asset for Bush, and a lack of experience was not a liability for Clinton. A *Times Mirror* poll of October 1992 found that Americans wanted the president to give highest priority to the budget deficit, jobs, health care, education, and the environment. Another poll two years later found that crime and jobs were Americans' biggest concerns and that foreign policy had sunk to the lowest level since 1978, even among leaders. Moreover, the foreign policy goals that the public cared about were those "related to local concerns: controlling and reducing illegal migration and stopping the flow of illegal drugs into the country."[75]

At the same time, there was a consensus that the United States should continue to play a leadership role in the world, and Democrats and Republicans agreed to promote democracy and trade. President

Bill Clinton's task was to concentrate on the domestic agenda, to continue and modify slightly Bush's global policies, and to redefine U.S. foreign policy interests so as to incorporate and defend domestic interests, especially on increasing jobs and stopping drug trafficking and other crime. As with domestic politics, he opened the foreign policy door wider to ethnic and other interest groups. He modified the North American Free Trade Agreement (NAFTA) to include side agreements on the environment and labor, and Congress approved it. Some had feared that this "regionalist option" would become a stumbling block to completion of the Uruguayan Round of global trade negotiations, but NAFTA proved to be a building block and an incentive for Japan and Europe to complete GATT talks and establish the World Trade Organization (WTO) on January 1, 1995.

NAFTA had a wider significance for U.S. foreign policy. Canada was the most important U.S. trading partner, and within three years of completing the agreement Mexico had surpassed Japan to become the second most important. Half of the three countries' world trade was among themselves. This qualifies the region as the second most integrated in the world, behind the European Union.[76] In December 1994 Clinton hosted the first Summit of the Americas for thirty-four democratically elected leaders, and they agreed to negotiate a free trade arrangement for all of the Americas by 2005 and to find ways to strengthen their democracies.

Despite Clinton's efforts to de-emphasize foreign policy and to define a postwar agenda, the Republicans captured both houses of Congress in November 1994 (just as they had in 1918 and 1946) with a platform that was silent, at best, on the country's international role. When Mexico had a currency crisis a few months after the elections, Congress did not approve funding, compelling the president to act by executive order. Similar to the other postwar Congresses, the 104th passed restrictive immigration legislation; strengthened antiterrorism, anticrime, and anti–drug trafficking policies; and either reduced or suspended funding for the United Nations and the IMF. Once again, despite having the most powerful economy in the world, the United States was hampered in its role as leader by its unilateralism and postwar rhythm and blues.[77]

And yet this postwar reaction was less extreme than it had been after the two world wars. The harsher immigration restrictions were
modified within a few years, and though the United States did not
move forward on trade issues, it did not move backward either. Even
some of the most xenophobic members of Congress urged the president to be more active abroad in promoting religious freedom, preventing abortion, compensating Americans for expropriated
properties, and penalizing countries that harbor terrorists or drug-
traffickers. The United States increasingly used unilateral economic
sanctions (albeit ineffectively) to pursue these interests. Such sanctions had a history that extended back to Wilson, but their use prolif-
erated in the post–Cold War era; as many as sixty-one sanctions aimed
at thirty-five countries were passed or executed in the three-year period 1993–1996.[78]

The defining challenge of any postwar period is to integrate the losing countries into the winning system, a strategy that the Clinton administration called "enlargement and engagement"—as contrasted
with the Cold War's containment. Both Presidents Bush and Clinton
agreed on the strategic importance of opening the "community of nations"[79] to the Soviet Union and China, but both transitions were exceedingly difficult (albeit for different reasons), and U.S. policies were
not entirely consistent. Washington offered Russia conditional financial support through international financial institutions. It negotiated
further reductions in nuclear weapons and offered to help the Russians dismantle theirs, but at the same time it jeopardized these initiatives by enlarging NATO.

China's economy quadrupled in the two decades after it began its
economic reforms in 1979. Its leaders were determined to avoid Gorbachev's mistake, which they saw as undertaking political reforms before economic reforms were consolidated. In June of 1989, the
Chinese government hesitated and then violently suppressed a student
demonstration for democracy in Tiananmen Square. The American
Cold War perspective was transferred from Moscow to the "butchers
of Beijing." The United States imposed economic sanctions, but both
the Bush and Clinton administrations recognized that unilateral sanctions had little if any effect on China while putting American business

at a disadvantage. Many in Congress urged a confrontational policy, but by and large, a policy of patient engagement prevailed.

The American Synthesis

The United States had the world's strongest economy at both the beginning and the end of the twentieth century, although over the course of the century it changed from a commodity producer and manufacturer to a nation that relied on information, technology, and services. Though it was still relatively autonomous economically as compared to most of the other powers, the United States was more than twice as dependent on trade in 1996 as it was in 1970, and that was roughly twice as dependent as in 1913.[80] A century after emerging from its strategic cocoon, the United States stands alone, with a military capacity that dwarfs that of any plausible combination of rivals. The economic and military indicators, however, tell only a small part of the story of the U.S. impact on the international system in the twentieth century and its probable effect in the future. The real story is how unorthodox U.S. ideas changed the very character of the system.

In June 1914 Wilson posed the pivotal question for the United States:

What are we going to do with the influence and power of this great nation? Are we going to play the old role of using that power for our aggrandizement and material benefit only? You know what that may mean. It may upon occasion mean that we shall use it to make the peoples of other nations suffer in the way in which we said that it was intolerable to suffer when we uttered the Declaration of Independence.[81]

Wilson's answer was evident from the way he posed the question: The United States would not play the "old role." Wilson defined new goals not just for the United States but for the world, and new instruments—international institutions and norms—to secure these goals of world peace and freedom. Tapping deep roots of U.S. idealism, Wilson offered answers to the fundamental questions of why wars occur and how they could be stopped, questions that challenged the foundations of the Westphalian interstate system. Balance of power, Wilson concluded, was not the solution; rather, it was part of the problem. Wilson's proposal, despite its utopian dress, was eminently practical: to reduce the benefits and increase the costs of war by gaining universal agreement on a powerful idea, self-determination, and an institution to enforce it, the League of Nations. This norm denies war's gains, and it increases its costs by giving a voice and legitimacy to those struggling for independence.

Wilson's ideas slowly grew legs and began to walk, uncertainly at first, but within a few years after World War II territorial acquisition had virtually disappeared as a goal of states. Since 1945 only one state has tried to annex forcefully another UN member. That the violation occurred only once and only after forty-five years was not because the United Nations was powerful but because the norm of self-determination, which sits at the institution's center, was so widely accepted that almost every state understood the exorbitant cost of violating it.

Like Wilson, Franklin Roosevelt projected a liberal domestic policy abroad, first as a hemispheric good neighbor policy, and then globally. He intended for the great powers to play a larger role in his design because he understood that international institutions would be inconsequential if the Big Three did not collaborate or agree to use them. The Cold War stymied the UN Security Council, but nevertheless, colonialism was dismantled, many small states were secured, and rights were defined and defended, at least in principle. The actual securing of those rights requires a relentless struggle. But the framework within which that struggle occurred was imagined from an American dream that proved universal.

The United States and Great Britain established international economic institutions—the IMF, the World Bank, GATT—and thus replaced a closed, colonial system with one based on global rules. The norms embedded in these institutions upended the old order. Empires no longer extracted capital from poorer countries; instead, the World Bank and regional development banks provided funds and advice to help them develop. Exclusive trading regimes no longer exploited poor countries; instead, the new system had a built-in bias toward giving preferential treatment to the exports of poorer countries. European or American customs officials no longer balanced the budgets of indebted Third World countries; instead, an International Monetary Fund advised and assisted local officials to balance their own books. The principle of establishing an international institution to defend a transnational value or interest was extended to the areas of the environment, population, and women's rights. The United States was farsighted in internationalizing these tasks and in sharing the burden of financing and responsibility, although another part of the U.S. mind distrusted its international institutional offspring.

How can we explain the continuity and changes in U.S. foreign policy in the twentieth century? The continuity in U.S. foreign policy follows from both geography and political culture. Only a country sitting securely between two large oceans and weak or friendly neighbors could have afforded to devote so much time to its own affairs and so little time, relative to the other great powers, to the world. A country composed of middle-class citizens who distrust central authority and who fear that war would strengthen their government, reduce their democracy, and risk their children is a country that keeps its government out of war until a security threat compels it to act. Then it fights zealously to vanquish the foe and return home as quickly as possible. Only a country settled by refugees and blessed with distant threats and a puritan's heritage could imagine a world without war and would design institutions not just to defeat foes but to banish all war and injustice. And only a country whose reigning philosophy was pragmatism would preserve its own freedom of action even while proclaiming a new world order based on international institutions.

U.S. foreign policy in the twentieth century has undergone two kinds of change. The first is a steady progression toward greater involvement in the world except for moments of isolationist nostalgia in the interwar period. Advances in technology and transportation made the world smaller, the United States more dependent on trade and investment, and Americans more aware that distant threats could touch their country. Furthermore, the growing assertiveness of the United States was a function of its increased power and wealth. The more power a country has the more it will use—a simple but potent axiom of international politics. The United States responded to a rhythm in its international relations, but it was not a pendulum that returned to where it started. After World War I it turned inward, but it kept its bases in the Philippines and Hawaii and intervened regularly in the Caribbean Basin. After World War II it turned toward home again, but not as much as it had after World War I. After the Cold War, the United States focused on domestic concerns, but not as much as it did after World War II. Finally, the new international institutions the United States created kept it engaged in the world, stripping the postwar rhythm of some of its power.

A second kind of change can be found in policy oscillation. The examples are legion: crusades in wartime and self-preoccupation in peace, Wilson's multilateralism and Lodge's unilateralism, Roosevelt's good neighbor policy and Eisenhower's intervention in Guatemala, Truman's Marshall Plan and declining aid to developing countries since the 1980s, demilitarizing Germany and Japan and helping them to remilitarize, containing China and engaging China—the list can go on and on. The question is how to explain the variation and the differences, and the answer comes in three processes: The United States changes; the world changes; and U.S. political institutions allow it to adapt the one to the other, but only after a debate. The two political parties became relatively coherent articulators of two different perspectives of U.S. world interests, and they use the interbranch system to forge policy. The parties' views have changed over time. For example, the Republicans were the party of protectionism from 1900 until Eisenhower's term, and the Democrats were the party of freer trade throughout the century until organized labor deserted the cause in the 1970s. Since then, Democrats have been divided on this issue. Since the 1950s the Republicans have consistently urged higher defense spending; Democrats have gone up and down on the issue, but mostly they have been more diffident than the Republicans. The Democrats have championed human rights and international institutions more than have the Republicans, but there have been exceptions in both parties.

What lessons can one draw from this history of U.S. foreign policy in the twentieth century that offer some hints for the country's twenty-first century trajectory? Dean Acheson, Truman's secretary of

state, best defined U.S. interests as creating "as spacious an environment as possible in which free states might exist and flourish."[82] In the
nineteenth century, this meant keeping the world away from the
United States. In the twentieth century, it meant shaping the world.
The two-sided debate in the United States on its proper role—engaged or distant, friendly or hostile, comprehensive or selective—will
never be resolved because it is contingent on changes in the world and
alterations in the balance of political, social, and economic power in
the United States. Nonetheless, there are certain verities—not cer-
tainties—that are likely to define the U.S. role in the world:

- The United States will continue to play a major role in the
  world in the twenty-first century in virtually every field—security, economic, and cultural—but the nature of that involvement will vary and much will depend on the state of the U.S.
  economy.
- Its greatest influence will be felt in the pluralistic design of the
  international system rather than in any specific policy. (I will
  develop this point in the final chapter.)
- U.S. leadership in resolving potential security crises in north,
  south, and central Asia and in ethnically divided states or those
  with aggressive tyrants is not guaranteed, despite the fact that
  failure to address such crises could undermine the pluralistic
  international system that the United States designed. The U.S.
  reaction to these events will depend on the nature of the crisis,
  the domestic interests with a stake in the conflict, whether Europe or others will deal with it, and the nature of U.S. relations
  with the great and intermediate powers of the region. If the
  crisis is intense, if domestic interests argue for involvement, if
  Europe punts, and if Russia doesn't block, then the United
  States will get involved. Otherwise, it will be a close call.
- Though its policies will remain global, the United States will
  continue to rely and build on its economic ties in the hemisphere and retain its security ties with Europe and Japan.
  Those security ties will provide centers of stability in a world
  that will need them.

The twenty-first century will be very different from the twentieth. Testimony to the distance that the world has traveled toward America's vision is the grudging acknowledgment by Henry Kissinger, the classic realist, in his book, *Diplomacy:* "It is above all to the drumbeat of Wilsonian idealism that American foreign policy has marched since his watershed presidency and continues to march to this day."[83] The United States changed the rules and the game of international politics in the twentieth century. The world today is different because the United States is different.

7

JAPAN

Opportunism in
the Pursuit of Power

KENNETH B. PYLE

I N THE CONCLUSION TO HIS BOOK on America's unplanned rise to world power at the beginning of the twentieth century, the historian Ernest May wrote, "Some nations achieve greatness; the United States had greatness thrust upon it."[1] Japan experienced the opposite: Stature among nations was a goal to be achieved; it was not bestowed. From the time of the Meiji Restoration of 1868, Japan strove and struggled for status as a great power. Other countries in Asia were aware of their own backwardness, but nowhere else was this awareness so intense and so paramount that it drove a people to such single-minded determination. It became a national obsession in Japan to be the equal of the world's great powers. Unlike other modern revolutions, Japan's did not give rise to transcendent values or a universal ideology. Instead, the Meiji Restoration generated a nationalist struggle to gain equality with the advanced industrial nations of the West. National power, the highest goal, was to be achieved by the unremitting hard work, unity, and sacrifice of the Japanese people. Japan rose to be a great power in the twentieth century because the Meiji leaders set long-term goals to enhance the power of the Japanese nation and to overcome its status as a latecomer in the industrial world. The Japanese were a driven people.

How was it that Japan alone among Asian countries reacted so swiftly to the challenge of Western power, sacrificing so much of its own institutional heritage and restructuring its political and economic policies in order to prepare the ground for the far-reaching reforms required to build an industrial society in the course of a single generation? A compelling answer to this central question lies in the fundamental values of the new Meiji leaders. Owing to their feudal background, they instinctively gave priority to the value of power and its symbols. In the six centuries before the arrival of the West, Japan had experienced the longest period of feudalism in human history. In feudal society, maximizing military power is a condition of survival and thus an overriding concern. Power and its symbols were the source of security and prestige. As a consequence the value system contained a keen sensitivity to status and hierarchy and a profound commitment to power and its sources. This was especially true of the two outlying domains, Choshu and Satsuma, which provided most of the leadership for Japan's new government. The Meiji Restoration brought to power young samurai from these two domains, and they were the group in Japanese society who felt most keenly the need to maximize power and who best understood how it was achieved. They were not satisfied simply to consolidate their power against internal opposition. "The Meiji leaders . . . represented in an extreme form this concern of the traditional society with power," wrote Albert Craig. "In their eyes the existence on Japan's doorstep of the superior Western powers was intolerable . . . Their main task was to create a state sufficiently powerful to cope with the foreign powers of which they were so conscious . . . That the values or goals of the [feudal] period continued to function with so little change explains the strength of Japan's obsession to equal the West."[2] This primary commitment to the achievement of power imparted to Japanese foreign policy a fundamental realism that became one of its defining characteristics throughout the modern period.

The primacy of power as a value legitimated the sweeping destruction of old institutions and the adoption of new ones from another civilization. Meiji leaders cared less than did other Asian leaders about preserving the customary knowledge, values, and practices of their inherited way of life if sacrificing them was necessary to acquire national power. There was a compelling precedent for this reaction in the national experience. In the seventh century the specter of an expansive T'ang Empire and the Silla unification of Korea spurred the adoption of Chinese institutions to create the first unified Japanese state. In both the seventh and the nineteenth centuries the strategic balance in Japan's external environment catalyzed massive cultural borrowing from the very source of the outside threat. This continued to be so throughout the modern period as Japan persistently absorbed the most advanced knowledge from abroad. But this cultural borrowing on such a massive scale was not without cost, for it weakened the nation's self-esteem and increased its preoccupation with Japan's status in the world and with overtaking the West.

Because it was so strongly influenced by realist considerations, Japanese foreign policy lacked a decisive commitment to transcendent ideals. The ideological justifications given for foreign policies were more pretext than motivation. Pan-Asianism appealed to some Japanese intellectuals, but Japanese political leaders rejected identification with Asia in a century in which Asia was dominated by the West. Japan was guided more by pragmatic nationalism than by fixed principles. In 1992 a U.S. journalist asked Ambassador Okazaki Hisahiko, one of Japan's leading strategic thinkers, if there were any fixed principles in Japan's foreign policy. "The histories of our two countries are different," he responded. "Your country was built on principles. Japan was built on an archipelago."[3] Japan, an island nation farther from its continent than England is from Europe, has a homogeneous population and few natural resources. Its modern outlook on world affairs has been shaped by its geography as well as by the unique history that was its legacy. Japan was not created by drawing lines on a map, nor was it constructed from common beliefs. Rather, it is a natural nation-state, the result of a homogeneous ethnic group living alone within an archipelago. Ambassador Okazaki doubtless also had in mind that Japan could not afford to take a stand on principle. Its island economy and geopolitical position made it too vulnerable, and its peculiar dependence on trade gave it a feeling of insecurity that engendered an ambitious and opportunistic foreign policy.

Pursuit of its own autonomous, self-sufficient sphere has been a persistent but elusive goal for the modern state. With an almost religious sense of its own distinctive identity, Japan, alone among East Asian states, unyieldingly resisted inclusion in the Sinocentric world order. On only one brief occasion through the premodern millennium had Japan acknowledged subordination to the Chinese emperor. Thus, from the outset of the modern period, the Meiji leaders stressed that self-reliance was essential because Japan was surrounded by predatory imperial powers. One of the Restoration leaders wrote to his fellow oligarchs in 1869, describing the world Japan had entered, "All countries beyond the seas are our enemies."[4] Before the West arrived Japan was wholly self-reliant. But the industrialization that was intended to restore national independence actually increased Japan's reliance on the external world. Japan is almost devoid of the raw materials required for modern industry and had to import them; it became the world's largest importer of raw materials and had to export finished goods to pay for them. Overcoming the resulting vulnerability and restoring its independence and self-mastery became a paramount objective. The Pacific War was fought to establish Japan's economic autonomy. When that failed, Japanese leaders formulated a political-economic strategy designed to assure it access to the raw materials, markets, and technology required to provide maximum autonomy. No matter how persistent the pursuit or how brilliant the strategy, the goal ultimately proved elusive. Toward the end of the twentieth century, in the words of one economist, "[Japan's] dependence on foreigners for the necessities of life is greater than that of any other major industrial country."[5]

Resource poor and a late arriver in the modern world, Japan was uniquely vulnerable to shifts in the international system, which accordingly exercised a striking influence on both the formulation of Japanese foreign policy and the shape of domestic political-economic institutions. Because international conditions beyond the reach of its policymakers determined Japan's international role to an extraordinary degree, Japan became a reactive state. Opportunistic adaptation to international conditions is a principal recurrent characteristic of Japanese foreign policy. Japan repeatedly demonstrated a tendency to adapt and accommodate to fundamental changes in its external environment.

In addition to the economic dependence that industrialization imposed, there are cultural, historical, and geopolitical reasons for this distinctively Japanese way of interacting with the world. Since the Meiji Restoration Japanese leaders have been keenly sensitive to the forces controlling the international environment, which they referred to as *sekai no taisei* (trends of the world), *jisei* (trends of the time), or *hitsuzen no ikioi* (inevitable force of circumstance). All these terms denote a kind of dynamic force in human affairs, a force that impels events through an inevitable progression. The Japanese judged their leaders by their capacity to gauge the trend of the times and to react to opportunities that presented themselves. Japanese leaders tried to operate in accord with these trends and to use them to their own advantage.

To some extent this accommodative approach to the international system may be the result of historical timing. That is, as a late developer, Japan learned to be responsive to conditions established by the Western powers. In the middle of the nineteenth century, when the West demonstrated its power by imposing unequal treaties upon the countries of East Asia, Japan quickly adapted to the rules and mores of imperialism. When the international system was transformed after World War I, Prime Minister Hara Kei declared that Japan must act in accord with the trend of the times, and the Japanese accepted the Wilsonian redefinition of international order and its new norms. Only once, in the 1930s, did Japan appear to abandon this reactive and accommodative approach, but even then many of its leaders thought they were acting in accord with the trend of the times: Other powers were forming closed regional spheres, the international system was collapsing, and fascism seemed to be the wave of the future; they did not want Japan to miss the bus. In the Cold War Japan adapted shrewdly to the Pax Americana and formulated policies and institutions designed to pursue its national interest within the expanding international free trade order. As a vice minister in the Ministry of

International Trade and Industry (MITI) remarked, "Japan has usually considered the international economic order as a given condition and looked for ways in which to use it."[6]

Although this accommodative approach may be attributable in part to Japan's late development, it may be even more deeply embedded in Japan's historical experience. The late Professor Kosaka Masataka, a leading authority on Japanese postwar foreign policy, emphasized the passive, situational, and reactive patterns in the Japanese approach to international norms. "Japan," he observed,

> is a natural nation-state; the idea that the state is created by a common will and contract has not existed in Japan. Japan has existed and will exist, regardless of the will and action of its people. Hence, norms are considered to be created by nature, not men ... The logical conclusion from such a view is that the task of the Japanese is to adapt wisely to the international situation, to secure its national interests, and not try to change or create the mysterious framework.[7]

In other words, in Japan's historical experience, whether in domestic or international society, norms are "either given from above or called forth by the situation. They are not created by men through multilateral action. Therefore, Japanese will observe norms when they are given in a clear form." The distinguished political scientist Kyogoku Jun'ichi observed in the same vein that in Japan's experience, "the world has been a 'given' surrounding Japan, which makes a real impact on Japan, but which cannot be modified by the efforts of the Japanese. The world is nothing but the 'framework' or the setting which can change only mysteriously."[8]

The persistent and recurrent characteristics of Japanese foreign policy—its realism and pragmatic nationalism, its relative lack of ideals, its persistent pursuit of self-sufficiency, its adaptive and accommodative character—produced an extraordinarily self-absorbed tradition of international behavior in the twentieth century. From the time Japan attended its first international conference with the major powers at Beijing in 1901, when they gathered to deal with the consequences of the Boxer Uprising, Japanese leaders rarely offered any suggestions for shaping the rules and institutions of the international system. Neither in the League of Nations nor in the United Nations has Japan played the active role befitting a major power. As a matter of self-interest Japan has repeatedly allied itself with the dominant ascendant power: with Great Britain from 1902 to 1922, with Germany from 1936 to 1945, and with the United States since 1952. Even though short-term tactics required cooperation with the foreigners, Japan has been a uniquely lone player among the world powers.

The Meiji Vision

The Meiji period (1868–1912) provides the archetype of the accommodative, adaptive Japanese approach to the international system. Domestically, the Meiji Restoration returned the emperor to the center of government, did away with Tokugawa feudalism, centralized the government, and undertook sweeping reforms to build military and industrial power. But the Restoration was also a revolutionary event designed to accommodate to the norms, rules, mores, and institutions imposed by the imperialist order in East Asia. The Meiji leaders went to great lengths to accommodate to the international system. For the first twenty-five years of the Meiji period the primary goal of foreign policy was to win revision of the unequal treaties imposed by the imperialist powers and thus to escape from semicolonial status. In order to win recognition from the Western powers that it was a nation in its own right, Japan had to avoid foreign entanglements and concentrate its energy and resources on domestic reforms. It adopted Western legal codes in order to impress on the imperialist powers Japan's civilized progress and so to hasten treaty revision. Many of the other Meiji reforms, including the constitution, were motivated by the effort to win revised treaties. The Meiji leaders were shrewdly pragmatic in adopting the long-range view that however humiliating accommodation might be, it was nevertheless the path to national power. And they fully understood the Western demand that Japan reform its laws and institutions. "After all," said Inoue Kaoru, who served as foreign minister early in the Meiji period, "would we expect Japanese subjects to subject themselves to Korean law and courts?"[9] He summed up the oligarchs' agenda: "What we must do is transform our empire and our people, make the empire like the countries of Europe and our people like the peoples of Europe. To put it differently, we have to establish a new, European-style empire on the edge of Asia."[10]

In a striking illustration of the pattern of accommodation, the new Meiji government, even while itself encumbered by unequal treaties and burdensome restrictions on Japanese sovereignty, quickly sought to impose the very same restrictions on its neighbors. In 1870 the government sent an envoy to China to seek most favored nation privileges reserved for the imperial powers. Although the Chinese foreign minister angrily dismissed the request, several years later in 1876 the Japanese succeeded in imposing an unequal treaty on Korea that gave the Japanese the full array of privileges reserved for the imperial powers.

Throughout its modern history Japan's foreign and domestic policies have been driven by its ambition to catch up with the advanced industrial powers. This vision was formed at the outset of the Meiji period, taking shape in the years following a remarkable, nearly two-year-long mission led by the oligarch Iwakura Tomomi. Iwakura and almost the entire leadership visited the advanced countries in order, as Iwakura said, "to discover the great principles which are to be our guide in the future."[11] The most striking aspect of the 2,000-page chronicle of the mission's observations is its pervasive optimism. One might suppose that the visitors would have been overwhelmed by Western civilization and the task of trying to match its achievements. Instead, one finds a bold self-confidence that the West's material strength was of recent origin and that Japan, through careful planning and by mobilizing its hard-working populace, could catch up.

Free trade theories were quickly rejected for mercantilist views. The young Meiji leaders were influenced by the German historical school of economics, with its unabashed nationalism and its emphasis on a systematic industrial policy for developing the economy. It resonated with their earlier experiences in their own domains when they recognized the importance of a state role in the production of wealth. The imperative of self-reliance was widely accepted, and trade was seen as a means of vanquishing the foreigners. "The only real difference between us and [the xenophobic swordsmen of yesteryear]," a Mitsubishi official has said, "is that we fight [foreigners] by means of economics and trade." The Maruzen Company's founding statement expressed the same patriotic fervor:

> The foreigners did not come to our country out of friendship . . . Their main object is solely to seek profits through trade. When we sit idly by and allow them to monopolize our foreign trade, we are betraying our duty as Japanese. If we once allow them to take over our foreign trade, if we are aided by them, if we rely on them, if we borrow money from them, if we are employed in their companies, if we invite them into our companies, if we respect and admire them, if we run around at their orders, if we fall into that kind of condition, there could not possibly be a greater disaster to our country. A country in that situation is not a country.[12]

The Meiji leaders implanted the vision of catching up at every occasion. Thus, for example, Takahashi Korekiyo, who later became finance minister and prime minister, exhorted his students in an 1889 farewell address at Tokyo Agricultural College, "Gentlemen, it is your duty to advance the status of Japan, bring her to a position of equality with the civilized powers and then carry on to build a foundation from which we shall surpass them all."[13]

The pursuit of national power, the realist imperative that guided Japanese foreign policy, legitimated the sweeping rejection of the nation's institutional heritage and cultural identity. So extreme was Japan's cultural submission that the great advocate of these reforms, Fukuzawa Yukichi, wrote in 1875, "There is not one thing in which we excel . . . In Japan's present condition there is nothing in which we may take pride vis-à-vis the West. All that Japan has to be proud of . . . is its scenery."[14] Westernizers like Fukuzawa were, of course, fundamentally anti-Western. For them Westernization was a means to an anti-Western end: By adopting the techniques and institutions of Western society, they hoped to eliminate from their country all manifestations of Western power, especially the unequal treaties. They also often had in the back of their minds a long-range ambition toward leadership of Asia. As Fukuzawa confided in 1882, "We are

Japanese and we shall some day raise the national power of Japan so that not only shall we control the natives of China and India as the English do today, but we shall possess the power to rebuke the English and to rule Asia ourselves."[15]

The First Phase of Japanese Imperialism, 1894–1918

The 1890s marked a watershed for Japan: It became a full-fledged participant in the international system that prevailed in East Asia. The generation of reforms designed to modernize and strengthen the state, the military, and the nation's economic base had born fruit. Japanese perseverance in adhering to the rules of the game was rewarded in the agreements reached with Britain and the other powers in 1894 that provided for the termination of the unequal treaties. The fourth edition of Wheaton's *Elements of International Law*, published in 1904, described the great significance of the "acquisition by Japan of full international status" in a new section entitled "The International Status of Non-Christian Nations."[16]

Little more than two weeks after revision of the unequal treaties was achieved, Japan declared war on China and embarked on its first great foreign adventure in three centuries. The Sino-Japanese War of 1894–1895 was immensely important in the history of international relations because it revealed the full extent of China's weakness and set off an intense competition among the imperial powers for control of the resources and markets of East Asia. Japan was inevitably swept into this maelstrom and was obliged to subordinate all its other concerns to the protection and extension of its interests.

Several factors led to the strong imperialist drive that emerged at this time. One important factor was the nationalist ambition for equality with the advanced industrial powers of the West. The Meiji ambition to make Japan a "first-class country" helped inspire expansionism. Together with constitutional government, industrialization, and a modern military, a colonial empire was a mark of status in the

civilized world. Japan's mission was to be the leader of Asia and to uplift its neighbors by instructing them in civilization. The young journalist Tokutomi Soho declared in 1895 that Japan's destiny was to
"extend the blessings of political organization throughout the rest of
East Asia and the South Pacific, just as the Romans had once done for
Europe and the Mediterranean."[17]

In addition to this distinctive nationalism, another factor motivating
Japanese imperialism was the economic motivation of maintaining access to the raw materials and markets of East Asia, which might be denied them if neighboring countries fell under the domination of one
or another of the Western powers. Furthermore, one of the oligarchs'
fundamental objectives was to build a modern economy as the basis of
national power, and this meant establishing a strong export market for
the products of its light industry. Asia and the Pacific, which lacked indigenous modern industry, were seen as the most promising market
for Japanese textiles, cement, canned goods, and other products.

The most important factor in the imperialist drive, however, was
strategic. The prevailing political instability of East Asia outside of
Japan created both problems and opportunities. In Korea and China
old impotent governments were being undermined by revolutionary
movements at the end of the nineteenth century. The impending collapse of these weak governments caused consternation in Japan. If
they were to be replaced by Western control, Japan's security would
be jeopardized. Given Japan's more rapid development and the institutional backwardness of the other countries in East Asia, Japan could
almost inevitably expect to dominate its neighbors. As a consequence,
to the extent that one can separate strategic and economic objectives,
it was the need for security that was the primary motive for imperialist expansion. In fact, as the historian Mark Peattie wrote,

> No colonial empire of modern times was as clearly shaped by strategic
> considerations . . . Many of the overseas possessions of Western Europe
> had been acquired in response to the activities of traders, adventurers,
> missionaries, or soldiers acting far beyond the limits of European inter-
> est or authority. In contrast, Japan's colonial territories . . . were, in each

instance, obtained as the result of a deliberate decision by responsible authorities in the central government to use force in securing territory that could contribute to Japan's immediate strategic interests.[18]

The empire grew by a kind of inexorable strategic logic that was implied by Japan's leading military strategist, Yamagata Aritomo. In an address to the Diet as prime minister at its opening session in 1890, he explained his security strategy:

> The independence and security of the nation depend first upon the protection of the line of sovereignty and then the line of advantage . . . If we wish to maintain the nation's independence among the powers of the world at the present time, it is not enough to guard only the line of sovereignty; we must also defend the line of advantage . . . and within the limits of the nation's resources gradually strive for that position.[19]

In other words, Japan's security depended not only on protecting the actual territorial limits of the nation but also on establishing dominance in the areas beyond. In 1890 Yamagata was thinking of Korea as the neighboring area that fell within the "line of advantage." Subsequently, when Japanese control of Korea was achieved, the line of advantage extended into southern Manchuria, where, to ensure the security of Korea, Japan also had to establish its dominance. Such strategic thinking was not unique to Japanese leaders. But it was unusually influential among them, partly because Japan's empire, unlike the far-flung European and U.S. empires, was close to the home islands.

Even in the premodern period changes in the strategic balance of power on the Asian continent affected Japan in significant ways, but in the nineteenth century the strategic balance was critical. In the 1880s it became a cardinal principle of Japanese foreign policy that the security of the Japanese islands depended on preventing Korea from falling under control of a third country. As the Prussian adviser to the Meiji army put it, the Korean peninsula was "a dagger thrust at the heart of Japan."[20] The Meiji General Staff concluded that the "independence" of Korea could only be secured by Japanese control of neighboring Port Arthur and the Liaotung Peninsula. With those strategic objectives in mind, the government steadily built up the nation's military power. By 1894 intrigue and chaotic politics in Korea had created tense relations between China and Japan, each seeking to assert influence over the course of Korean politics. The Japanese foreign minister moved to resolve the situation. In a personal memoir he wrote that "I sensed that the wisest course to follow now was to precipitate a clash between ourselves and the Chinese."[21] The superior planning and readiness of the Japanese military brought quick victory. The Treaty of Shimonoseki of 1895 enmeshed Japan in the framework of the imperialist system. In addition to ceding Taiwan and the Liaotung Peninsula to Japan and recognizing Korean independence, the treaty also gave Japan an impressive array of commercial concessions, which through the most favored nation clause were also accorded to the other powers.

Japan's triumph, however, was short-lived. Soon after the peace treaty was concluded, Japan suffered one of the most devastating experiences in its modern diplomacy. The Triple Intervention, by which Germany, France, and Russia insisted that Japan return the Liaotung Peninsula to China, had a lasting impact on Japanese diplomacy—especially since three years later Russia seized the southern part of the peninsula for itself. It indelibly reinforced the leaders' preoccupation with power, which became the preeminent national concern. The young journalist Tokutomi Soho, who had formerly been a Christian and an admirer of the West, wrote of the Triple Intervention, "I was baptized to the gospel of power."[22] In addition this lesson in power politics demonstrated the need for alliances. Japan had been vulnerable because it was isolated. Japanese diplomats set out to overcome this isolation, and the conclusion of the Anglo-Japanese Alliance in 1902 was a triumph that set a pattern in Japanese foreign policy. Through most of the twentieth century, Japan sought alliance with the ascendant world power.

Japanese imperialism in its first phase was unique in the degree to which it was prompted by the international system. The uneven development of Asia and the scramble for concessions made it imperative that Japan look to its strategic interests. Elsewhere, forces unleashed by industrial society played a more prominent role in impelling imperialism. The search for markets and investment opportunities, the growing involvement of the masses in politics, and the influence of a nationalist press prodded expansionism. Some of these same forces became evident in Japan, though they were less influential than they were elsewhere, on the eve of the Russo-Japanese War. A coalition of journalists, businessmen, and politicians added their support to the Meiji leaders. The popular press became a factor, and by the end of the war a nascent public opinion was expressing itself on foreign policy.

Still, these were secondary influences. The Meiji leaders were above all pursuing strategic advantage as they sought to displace and preempt Russian influence in Korea and southern Manchuria. Although they held differing opinions on tactics, the Meiji leadership was a tightly knit elite, fully in control of the institutions they had built for the explicit purpose of pursuing national power. In the decade following the Sino-Japanese War and the Triple Intervention, the government laid comprehensive plans for military buildup, intelligence penetration, and diplomatic cover for what was regarded as an almost inevitable conflict.

The Russo-Japanese War, which established Japan's sphere of interest in southern Manchuria, brought Japan great power status and won it worldwide acclaim. Throughout Asia the leaders of subjected peoples drew inspiration from the Japanese example. Jawaharlal Nehru described the Japanese victory as "a great pick-me-up for Asia"[23] that kindled his nationalism, and Sun Yat-sen, recalling the profound impression made on Chinese revolutionaries, said, "We regarded that Russian defeat by Japan as the defeat of the West by the East."[24] Japanese leaders, with their realist outlook, were never strongly attracted to the ideals of pan-Asianism. They were preoccupied with augmenting their strategic advantage. They had little sympathy or even understanding of nationalist movements elsewhere in Asia. They crushed a nascent Korean nationalism to ensure their control of the Korean peninsula, which Japan annexed in 1910.

Despite having fulfilled the Meiji vision by escaping the unequal treaties, joining the ranks of the great powers, and acquiring substantial overseas possessions, Japan was beset by a sense of insecurity and

vulnerability. The strategic requirements of Japan's empire were becoming formidable. It included both island possessions, which required a strong fleet, and continental territory, which required a
strong army. The fearful demands that industrialization and imperialism were placing on Japanese society created a pervasive sense of un-
easiness. Officials emphasized that Japan was now also engaged in a
"peaceful war," by which they meant economic conflict with other
countries for trade advantage. Young men, old men, children, even
women, they declared, were needed for this economic warfare. The
Meiji novelist Natsume Soseki, despairing of the pace his country was
setting itself, prophesied "nervous collapse" and admonished his
countrymen not to be deluded into thinking that Japan was capable of
competing on an equal footing with the great powers. Other writers
favored a shift to a less assertive international position, a "little
Japanism," that would stress the development of industry and trade to
improve meager living standards at home. But theirs was a minority
opinion. The majority strongly favored improvement of Japan's imperial position. National power remained the paramount goal. The navy
sought imperial sanction for an "eight-eight fleet"—that is, eight
dreadnought battleships and eight armored cruisers—and the army
insisted, as Lieutenant General Tanaka Giichi of the army General
Staff wrote in 1906, "We must disengage ourselves from the restrictions of an island nation to become a state with continental interests."[25] The Imperial Defense Policy of 1907, which defined Japan's
grand strategy, recognized the priorities of both services. The army
was accorded force levels necessary to pursue a forward position on
the Asian continent and to prepare for conflict with a revanchist Russia, which became its prime hypothetical enemy. At the same time, the
navy was allowed to prepare for conflict with the United States, which
it designated as its primary hypothetical enemy.

The Washington Treaty System

World War I transformed the international system in East Asia. On
the eve of the war, East Asia enjoyed the stable order among the im-

perial powers that had been achieved in the two decades since the Sino-Japanese War. Isolated and outmaneuvered in the Triple Intervention of 1895, Japan had since worked its way into the power structure by skillful diplomacy, backed on occasion by military force. The Anglo-Japanese alliance established a pattern of cooperation with Britain, which in turn contributed toward the development of an understanding with the United States. In a series of agreements the latter acknowledged Japan's position in northeast Asia. At the same time, Russia and Japan had by war delimited their spheres of interest, with the former now relegated to protecting its remaining hold on northern Manchuria. Japan had consolidated its colonial administration in Korea and developed its newly won concessions in southern Manchuria. The East Asian international system was in rough equilibrium and the interests of each power were more or less acknowledged: the United States in the Philippines, France in Indochina, Britain in the Yangtze Valley and in south China, Germany in the Shantung Peninsula, and Russia and Japan in northeast Asia.

World War I upset this balance, and eventually the East Asian power structure collapsed. Japanese unilateralism was partly responsible for destroying the old order. After war broke out, the preoccupation of the European powers allowed Japan, under the guise of the Anglo-Japanese alliance, to seize the German sphere in China and German-held islands in the Pacific. Hard on the heels of those swift maneuvers, Japan in 1915 delivered its Twenty-One Demands on China. Their demands not only intervened in Chinese sovereignty but also infringed the spheres of interest of the European powers. Although U.S. protest compelled Japan to modify its demands, this incident was a critical moment, fraught with significance for the international relations of East Asia. Japan's unilateral pursuit of strategic advantage, an aberration from its customary caution and circumspection, exacted a heavy cost for its future course. First, it upset the equilibrium that had been established among the powers and thereby undermined the system that protected and legitimated Japan's imperial prerogatives. Second, it provoked Chinese nationalism, which took on an increasingly anti-Japanese tone, thus prefiguring the problems that beset Sino-Japanese relations for the remainder of the century. Third, it marked a growing estrangement between Japan and the United States and the emergence of the United States as protector of the new Chinese Republic.

It is of course possible to place the origins of the estrangement between Japan and the United States a decade earlier, in the racial tensions raised by Japanese immigration. But the Twenty-One Demands outlined the clash of national interests more sharply, for the United States increased its determination to maintain an open door for U.S. trade and investment in order to oppose Japan's continental aspirations. Wilson's "new diplomacy" proclaimed the self-determination and the sovereign rights of every people, and he made plain his opposition to international power rivalries at China's expense. He told his European counterparts at the Paris Peace Conference that there was "nothing on which the public opinion of the United States of America was firmer than on this question that China should not be oppressed by Japan."[26] The balance of power among the imperialists in East Asia would have to be replaced by a new order, in which all would refrain from military and political expansion.

At Versailles, Japan had little to propose for a new order other than a racial equality clause to be included in the League of Nations Covenant. The clause would state that "the principle of equality of nations and the just treatment of their nationals . . . [shall be] a fundamental basis of future international relations in the new world organization." When this proposal was blocked by England, Japan successfully demanded that it be allowed to keep the German concession in Shantung. Japan was a founding member of the League of Nations, seeking the international recognition that such participation brought; but it was the only great power not to submit a draft proposal for the League. Despite its status as one of the five permanent members of the League's council, it never took an active role in the new organization. By 1928 the low level of Japan's participation in the personnel of the Secretariat was indicative of its skeptical attitude toward the League: the Japanese contributed 5 members; the Italians, 23; the French, 100; the Swiss, 126; and the British, 143.

Nevertheless, Hara Kei, who was prime minister after the war, from 1918 to 1921, and other Japanese leaders acted in a characteristic

Japanese fashion, accommodating to the emerging new system in East Asia, which was a regional expression of the framework of international affairs formulated in the League Covenant. They acknowledged the "new world trends" and came to feel it was inevitable that Japan should move in accord with them. There were few genuine Wilsonians, that is, Japanese who were genuine adherents of the Fourteen Points. Instead, Japan's "internationalists" were believers in the diplomatic tradition established by the Meiji leaders, who had consistently held that Japan's interests were best pursued by circumspect policies and realpolitik that adapted to the prevailing international mores. It was better to work within the system, using it to achieve Japan's purposes, than to resist it. The rising young diplomat Yoshida Shigeru, for example, described himself as a member of the "clique that makes use of Britain and the United States."[27] Japan's postwar leaders signaled their willingness to trim Japan's continental aspirations, accept the disappearance of the former imperialist diplomatic structure, and participate in a redefinition of mutual relations among the powers.

A conference for this purpose was convened on U.S. initiative in Washington in 1921–1922. Believing that the Japanese had used the Anglo-Japanese alliance as a cover for unilateralism, the Americans insisted that it be replaced by an innocuous Four-Power Treaty in which the United States, Britain, France, and Japan agreed to confer should there be threats to peace in the Pacific. A Nine-Power Treaty laid down the principles that were to guide the new order in East Asia. It condemned spheres of influence in China, pledged equal opportunity for commerce and industry, and promised to respect China's territorial and administrative integrity. The conference sought to forestall a runaway naval arms race and to provide mutual security in the Five-Power Naval Limitation Treaty, which restricted competition in battleships by setting a ratio of 5:5:3 for Britain, the United States, and Japan respectively.

The Japanese navy was deeply divided by the decision to limit Japan's naval strength in capital ships to 60 percent of U.S. naval strength. The navy minister supported it because he believed Japan could not sustain an escalating arms race with the United States and that it would be prudent to cooperate with the Anglo-American naval powers. Younger, hard-line naval officers, however, were bitter because they believed that a minimum ratio of 70 percent was essential to Japanese security interests.

Japanese acceptance of the radically revised rules and norms was embodied in the policies of Shidehara Kijuro, who served as ambassador to Washington (in 1924–1927) and then as foreign minister (1924–1927 and 1929–1931). He steered Japanese foreign policy toward the U.S. vision of a liberal capitalist world order that emphasized economic interdependence and cooperation with the United States (which was Japan's largest source of capital and best trading customer, purchasing 40 percent of Japan's exports in the 1920s). Shidehara therefore held that Japan should abstain from aggressive pursuit of its political interests in China and should instead concentrate on economic advancement in China in the framework of international agreement. U.S. policymakers were pleased. Franklin Roosevelt, who had served in the Wilson administration as assistant secretary of the navy, wrote in 1923 that Japan and the United States "have not a single valid reason, and won't have as far as we can look ahead, for fighting each other."[28]

But such optimism was misplaced. The Washington Treaty System was a house built on sand. Founded on idealism, it had inadequate enforcement powers and depended instead on voluntary abstention from the use of force. As Akira Iriye observed, "It was more a state of mind than an explicit mechanism; it expressed the powers' willingness to cooperate with one another in maintaining stability in the region."[29] It relied on the hopeful expectation that peaceful commercial competition would replace armed rivalries. If the new regional order were to be stable and enduring, however, it had to reflect the distribution of power in the region. That is, the institutions governing the system had to be fully rooted in the interests of the region's major powers. The major states had to accept the framework of the international order as fair and legitimate. They had to accept the existing territorial, political, and economic arrangements, that is, the norms and rules of the system. There could be no nation with a revolutionary foreign policy.

The Washington Treaty System failed to enhance international security because the United States, after establishing the system, ulti-

mately failed to support it, much less give it leadership. Moreover, it
failed to accommodate an ascendant Japan, which was never fully assimilated into the new order. From the outset there were powerful
forces within Japan that regarded the system as illegitimate and unfair
to Japanese interests. Because it obliged Japan to withdraw its troops
from Siberia (where they had been dispatched as part of an Allied expedition at the end of World War I), return the Shantung concession
to China, and abandon its ambitious naval building plan, Togo
Shigenori, who later served as foreign minister in the Tojo cabinet,
described it as a "second Triple Intervention."[30] Throughout the
1920s there was a strong undercurrent of opposition to Shidehara's
cooperation with the new order. Within the navy senior command
there was a deep split between those who agreed with civilian leaders
of the government that Japan could not compete with the United
States in an all-out naval building program and those who increasingly
viewed conflict with the United States as inevitable and demanded the
right to build to parity.

Beginning with the Versailles Peace Conference, many Japanese
had regarded Wilsonian principles with suspicion. A new generation
of influential political figures saw the League of Nations as part of an
Anglo-American effort to preserve the status quo. The young Konoe
Fumimaro, who became Japan's most important political leader in the
1930s, denounced the League and the Washington Treaty System as
embodying high-sounding principles to mask Anglo-American self-
interest. He saw their universalism as nothing more than an ideology
of Western imperialism, and from 1918 on he consistently argued that
Britain and the United States were trying to contain Japan's legitimate
aspirations on the continent. Konoe and a growing number of other
"revisionists" said that the Washington Treaty System had to be revised in order to ensure an equitable distribution of land and resources among the world's great powers. Japan, they argued, as a late
developer was being denied its place by the Anglo-American powers,
who were pitting the "have nations" against the "have-not nations."
Late-developing countries such as Japan, said Konoe, were condemned "to remain forever subordinate to the advanced nations" and
unless something was done to allow Japan "equal access to the markets

and natural resources of the colonial areas," Japan would be forced to "destroy the status quo for the sake of self-preservation."[31]

Japan's military increasingly saw U.S. policy as an impediment to Japanese interests. Kato Kanji, soon to be appointed commander in chief of the Combined Fleet, regarded the naval arms limitation as an "unreasonable" demand to freeze the status quo and to "deprive the Imperial Navy of its supremacy in the Far East." By "dictating" an "unequal treaty" to Japan, the United States was trying to establish its own "hegemony."[32] In 1923, in a revision of the Imperial Defense Policy, Kato and other military leaders insisted upon inserting the view that "the United States, by its limitless economic resources, by its policies of economic aggression, and, in China in particular, by its provocation of anti-Japanese activities, threatens the Japanese position in China for which our nation has risked its destiny."[33]

The U.S. decision to press for an end to the Anglo-Japanese alliance at the Washington Conference left the Japanese without restraints. The British foreign secretary, Lord Curzon, had favored renewal of the alliance because it made it easier "to keep a watch upon [Japan's] movements in China . . . and to exercise a moderating influence on her policy generally."[34] In Japan Yoshida Shigeru, who was to serve as prime minister during most of the first decade following World War II, subsequently saw the dissolution of the alliance as destabilizing Japanese diplomacy and allowing China to play one power against another: "Without the stabilizing influence of the Alliance, our military men saw fit to overrun Manchuria and China; the Second World War started . . . and everybody knows what happened to us."[35]

There were other flaws in the liberal U.S. international vision. One appeared in 1924, when Congress passed an immigration act which excluded Japanese as "aliens ineligible for citizenship." Secretary of State Charles Evans Hughes was "greatly depressed" by it and wrote that Congress "has undone the work of the Washington Conference and implanted the seeds of an antagonism which are sure to bear fruit in the future."[36] The Japanese media saw the new legislation as a national affront and interpreted it as evidence of U.S. perfidy.

A more fundamental flaw in the liberal vision was its high hopes for and dependence on economic expansion. But foreign trade did not perform up to expectation. There were many obstacles. The United States followed a strongly protectionist course. Britain was making preferential tariff agreements within its empire that were detrimental to Japanese exports. In China, too, the nationalist movement demanded tariff autonomy and increasingly opposed Japanese economic interests. When to all these obstacles was added the onset of the Great Depression, the discontent and restlessness with Shidehara's internationalist diplomacy mounted.

In addition, Japan was now faced with a hostile Soviet Union, which repudiated earlier agreements, negotiated with the tsarist government, acknowledging Japan's special position in Korea and Manchuria. Even more ominous, Japan faced a rising tide of Chinese nationalism that threatened Japan's strategic position in China. As the Kuomintang embarked on its campaign of national unification and demanded an end to imperialist privilege, Japan's treaty rights and interests in Manchuria were jeopardized.

The Abortive Japanese East Asian Order

The Great Depression and the international failure to deal with the Manchurian issue proved to be the combination of circumstance that brought down the Washington Treaty System. Japan's military leaders were determined not only to resolve the uncertainty of Japan's position in Manchuria but also to create a self-sufficient economic bloc that would provide the economic and industrial potential to fight the wars of the future. Much of this strategic thinking was drawn from German total-war theories, which held that twentieth-century warfare would require the full mobilization of a nation's resources and a self-sufficient industrial base not vulnerable to economic pressure from other countries. Army strategists concluded that if Japan hoped to maintain its great-power status, it must pursue autarky and control of such resource-rich territories as Manchuria.

By 1930 the opportunities for avoiding a clash between Japanese and Chinese nationalisms were fast disappearing. Party government in Japan was vulnerable. As one authority wrote, "A strong government

in Japan might have restrained army action in Manchuria and post-
poned a showdown with China on the basis of some compromise settlement on the issue of Japanese treaty rights. But the government in
Tokyo was too weak and too unwilling to risk its existence by a strong
stand."[37] The political community was characterized by drift and loss
of mastery and could address neither the nation's severe social and
economic problems nor the major crisis in foreign relations. This set
the stage for the demise of party supremacy and for the increased
power of military and bureaucratic elites, which had the technical expertise and the nationalist agenda to fit the times. The weakness of
party government, the diffuseness of decisionmaking power, the general uncertainty attending both domestic and foreign turmoil—all
created an opportunity for Japan's Kwantung Army (which had been
stationed in Manchuria since the Russo-Japanese War in order to protect Japan's concessions) to take independent action to provoke an incident and provide a rationale for seizing Manchuria. Key members of
the army General Staff were privy to the plot and did not object. On
September 18, 1931, Kwantung Army officers blew up a short strip of
rail line of the South Manchurian Railway and, blaming Chinese
saboteurs, pushed ahead to conquer all of Manchuria. The government in Tokyo acquiesced in the fait accompli, and the following year
the Japanese established the puppet state of Manchukuo.

The Japanese, rarely comfortable in international meetings, did a
poor job of defending themselves to the League of Nations and in the
court of world opinion. Lord Lytton, who chaired the League's commission investigating the Manchurian Incident, wrote to his wife from
Shanghai, "The Chinese are so articulate—they talk beautiful English
and French and can express themselves clearly. With the Japanese it
was a surgical operation to extract each word."[38] The commission
tried to find a middle ground by recognizing China as the suzerain
power while acknowledging Japan's treaty rights and interests in
Manchuria and the general absence of law and order. Given the weakness of the internationalist point of view in Japanese foreign policy
and the balance of forces in Japanese domestic politics, Lytton's efforts to achieve a constructive peace were foredoomed. The nuances
of the commission's report were lost on Japan's foreign ministry. Op-

portunities to probe conciliatory approaches in the League Council, Japan's best hope, were ignored. The issue was consequently referred to the League of Nation's Assembly. In the assembly small countries exercised their influence, and it issued a report that was firmer than the Lytton Commission's and condemned Japanese aggression. When the resolution was adopted by 42 to 1, Japan opposing and Thailand (Siam) abstaining, Japan withdrew from the League in March 1933.

The Manchurian Incident thus proved to be a turning point. Japan abandoned the general policy of cooperation with the powers, which had for the most part controlled its international behavior since 1868, and chose to pursue its own destiny in East Asia, to trust its own strength to protect and advance its interests. The Manchurian Incident constituted Japan's testing of the viability of the Washington Treaty System as a stable international system. If the sea powers had acted jointly to resist the seizure of Manchuria and thereby to underwrite the principles of the system the outcome could have been different.

Western historiography on the origins of the Pacific War has focused its attention on Japan's internal politics, especially on the military's increased influence in the domestic political order following the Manchurian Incident, as the source of Japan's aggressive foreign policy in the 1930s. "An 'inside-out' explanation of Japanese political behavior," as Michael Mandelbaum observed, "gained wide acceptance" after World War II.[39] Indeed, as the influence of the political parties receded, the military and the bureaucracy gained the upper hand because they had complementary strategies to deal with the national crisis. Total-war planners committed to mobilizing the economy joined with "reform bureaucrats" who were advocating a state industrial policy and a managed economy as a strategy for surviving the depression.

But this change in the domestic political order, a shift in power from the parties to the military and bureaucratic elites, was a response to the changing international environment. Japanese leaders were convinced that the liberal international order was collapsing. In fact, as Peter Duus wrote, "The rules of the old order were being abandoned, even by the Anglo-American powers that had established them. The gold standard was giving way to managed currencies, free trade was being supplanted by rising tariffs and trade quotas, and open economic borders were being pushed aside by the creation of exclusive economic blocs."[40] The formation of exclusive economic blocs appeared to be the wave of the future, the trend of the times to which Japan must adapt to protect its interests. The United States had imposed a staggering increase in its tariff rates, and

> Britain had abandoned the gold standard and the venerable commitment to international liberalism in 1931; the Ottawa Preference System of 1932 appeared to be a first step toward the conversion of the empire from the free trade area that it had been since the nineteenth century to a closed economic unit. The French had their empire. German economic policies were designed to create a dependent economic sphere in Central Europe. The Bolsheviks had closed Russia's borders.[41]

In the uncertainty accompanying the crumbling of an international order, strategic concerns and security objectives now resumed their paramount role in determining Japanese foreign policy. In contrast to the first phase of Japanese imperialism (1894–1918), when imperialism had constituted a recognizable system with its own rules and mores among the imperial powers, Japan's external environment now seemed anarchic and devoid of rules or enforcers. But the trend of the times seemed to many Japanese leaders to lie in the formation of regional blocs. They were drawn to German geopolitical thinking, which maintained that "the world would come to be divided into a few blocs, each under a dominant power. In this process of 'global redivision,' the powers would engage in a deathly struggle for supremacy. Each great power would have to acquire more resources, mobilize its people, and drive out other nations' economic and political influences from the region under its control."[42] The leadership now spoke of an "Asian Monroe Doctrine," declaring Japan's responsibility for maintaining peace in Asia.

In thus choosing to withdraw from the Washington Treaty System, Japan set formidable requirements for the nation's defense. To maintain the strategic posture demanded by its "Monroe Doctrine" and by its commitment to Manchuria, Japan now needed military power sufficient to accomplish three major tasks: to defeat the Soviet army, whose strength on the border of Manchuria had been vastly augmented; to guarantee the security of the home islands against the U.S. fleet; and to compel the Chinese to accept Japan's position in Manchuria and northern China. These three strategic objectives required a military capability that Japan was never able to achieve. The Meiji oligarchs would have been appalled at the incautious commitments to policies that exceeded the nation's capacities.

Why did Japan's leaders in the early 1930s embark on so perilous a course? In part the answer lies in the fragmented nature of decision-making in the Japanese government, which at that time lacked a strong, central controlling leadership able to impose its will on all factions of the administration and able to coordinate and develop prudent and balanced policy goals. In part too it lies in the combination of ambition for Asian leadership, the vacuum of power and confusion in the region, frustration with the Washington Treaty System and with events in China, and a keen sense that the changing international order offered Japan an opportunity to acquire the greater power and self-sufficiency it had always sought.

In the summer of 1937, during the prime ministership of Prince Konoe Fumimaro, Japan found itself at war with China as a result of an unplanned incident at the Marco Polo Bridge outside of Beijing. Unlike the Manchurian Incident of six years earlier, this was not a war the army General Staff wanted, for the total-war planners were acutely aware that it would be some time yet before Japan had developed an industrial structure capable of supporting an all-out war. They felt that it was critical to avoid hostilities and to concentrate on a fully coordinated effort to develop Japan's economy. But having chosen to abandon the principles of the Washington Treaty System, and operating in an atmosphere dominated by ultranationalist goals and a readiness to resort to military solutions, the government was ill-prepared to restrain itself. A minor skirmish between Japanese and Chinese soldiers at the Marco Polo Bridge escalated into all-out conflict.

Konoe, an erratic and ineffectual politician and the leading spokesman of revisionism, proved to be an inept leader. He had been chosen by the emperor's advisers to become prime minister because he was a widely respected figure from an old noble family who might, it was thought, succeed in uniting the country and restraining the military. He had ties to the army, the political parties, and big business, but he turned out to be weak and indecisive. During his first tenure as prime minister (1937–1939) the nation stumbled into war with China and during his second tenure (1940–1941) the fateful steps were taken toward war with the United States.

Japanese of all persuasions looked at Japan's position in China as sanctioned by economic need and by their destiny to create "a new order in Asia." Western influence would be expelled, and the Japanese would establish a new structure based upon what they vaguely termed "Asian concepts" of justice and humanity. In 1938 Konoe declared a determination to establish a new self-sufficient order in East Asia and a new political and economic order at home to support it. Efforts to centralize Japanese government power and decisionmaking never succeeded. The leadership was inept and power remained diffused. Japan's war effort was severely handicapped by a lack of coordination and coherency, consistency, and unity both in its economic policies at home and in its foreign policies and military strategies abroad.

It is common to label the Japanese political system in the 1930s as "fascist" because its policies and ideologies resembled those of Germany and Italy. In significant ways, however, the Japanese experience was different. The 1930s produced no Japanese mass leader, no Hitler or Mussolini haranguing the crowds. There was, rather, an awed reverence for the emperor, who remained a distant symbol of national identity. No vanguard or mass movement succeeded in overthrowing the Meiji Constitution and establishing a new political order. To be sure, military and bureaucratic elites increased their power, but they were long established. Japan's leading post–World War Two political scientist, Maruyama Masao, termed the new policies "fascism from above" because it was the bureaucratic elites who directed Japan's precipitous response to the multiple crises.[43] On the face of it, Japan appeared to have a totalitarian political-economic structure inspired by contemporary regimes in Europe. As Gordon Berger wrote, however,

severe schisms within bureaucratic and military leadership groups prevented any individual or faction from achieving a dictatorship or degree of political control analogous to that of contemporaneous wartime regimes in Germany, Italy, and the Soviet Union. Conservative forces in parliament, business, the bureaucracy, the right wing, and traditional elites in the countryside blunted [all] attempts to reorganize the state . . . and establish a monolithic system of government controls over all political and economic activities.[44]

The dilemma that Japanese diplomacy had struggled with ever since the Manchurian Incident now became still more difficult, for as the conflict in China expanded, the nation was less prepared to deal with the Soviet army on the Manchurian border and the U.S. fleet in the Pacific. A succession of border skirmishes with the Red Army revealed the vulnerability of the Kwantung Army; at the same time, the U.S. Navy was now embarked on a resolute program of building additional strength in the Pacific. By the spring of 1940 the Japanese navy General Staff had concluded that America's crash program would result in its gaining naval hegemony in the Pacific by 1942 and that Japan must have access to the oil of the Dutch East Indies in order to cope with U.S. power.

Konoe's impulsive and unstable foreign minister, Matsuoka Yosuke, set out to resolve the impasse by a swift démarche. Matsuoka disastrously misread world trends. As Nazi victories multiplied, it appeared to him and to many other Japanese leaders that fascism was about to triumph in Europe and that Japan must not miss the bus. As Holland and France fell and the defeat of England seemed imminent, opportunism ruled the day. The U.S. ambassador in Tokyo, Joseph Grew, reported that the Japanese were "unashamedly and frankly opportunist."[45] In the autumn of 1940 Matsuoka signed the Tripartite Pact with Germany and Italy, in which the signatories pledged to aid one another if attacked by a power not currently involved in the European war or the fighting in China. Matsuoka thereby hoped to isolate the United States and to dissuade it from conflict with Japan, thus opening the way for Japan to seize the European colonies in southeast Asia, grasp the resources it needed for self-sufficiency, and cut off Chinese supply lines. Furthermore, to free his northern flank he signed a neutrality pact with the Soviet Union in April 1941; and when Hitler attacked Russia in June the Manchurian border seemed secure.

Matsuoka was surprised by the strength of U.S. reaction to the Tripartite Pact. President Roosevelt forbade any further shipment of scrap iron to Japan, and after Japanese troops entered Indochina, he embargoed oil. Japan's resources were more and more stretched. Japan had a gross national product (GNP) of $6 billion and a per capita income of $86. Nearly 50 percent of the government's annual budget went to military expenditures. Courting conflict with the United States, a country at least ten times as wealthy, was perilous. Moreover, the United States was Japan's primary source of the materials and resources crucial for war. At the end of the 1930s the United States furnished 80 percent of Japan's fuel, 75 percent of its scrap iron imports, 93 percent of its copper imports, and more than 60 percent of its machine tool imports. Heavily dependent on trade with the United States, Japan had the choice of maintaining good relations with the Americans or, alternatively, establishing a self-sufficient empire.

The oil embargo, which left Japan with reserves that would be exhausted in two years, decisively clarified the alternatives facing the nation. As the Japanese ambassador in Berlin wired the foreign minister, "There are only two possible attitudes we can take: either to preserve the spirit of the Tripartite Pact and cooperate with Germany and Italy to construct a new world order, or to abandon the alliance, submit to the Anglo-American camp, and seek friendly relations with England and America."[46] Military and many civilian leaders saw the same kind of opportunity for Japan in the current situation as had existed in World War I: It could take advantage of conflict in Europe to seize colonial possessions in Asia; moreover it could secure the status, autonomy, and self-sufficiency it had pursued for a century. The risks, however, were much greater. U.S. policy was stiffening. Belatedly, Konoe recognized that Japan and the United States were on a collision course and sought a summit meeting with Roosevelt. Secretary of State Cordell Hull, however, believed there was little likelihood that the army would approve any solution acceptable to the United States and advised Roosevelt against the meeting. In October 1941 Konoe, recoiling from the crisis he had done so much to create, resigned. He was replaced by the army minister, General Tojo Hideki.

At the heart of the emerging conflict was a clash between U.S. liberal internationalism and Japanese late-development nationalism, which implied radically different views of Japan's role in East Asia. Negotiations between Hull and Japan's ambassador to Washington, Nomura Kichisaburo, foundered in a morass of confusion and ineptness. It is doubtful that negotiations had much opportunity for success in any case at this juncture, given the positions taken by the two sides. Hull restated the principles of the Washington Treaty System—self-determination, territorial integrity, equal commercial opportunity, and peaceful alteration of the status quo, as the basis for international order—and insisted on Japanese withdrawal from China. To Japanese leaders imbued with pervasive nationalist sentiment this was unthinkable and tantamount to reducing Japan to a second-class power.

The main theme of this nationalist sentiment was a determination to establish not only Japan's strategic autonomy in East Asia but also its cultural autonomy and independence from the West and a sphere of influence in which its culture would predominate. This preoccupation with Japan's unique cultural identity had been a central theme of modern Japanese nationalism since the 1890s. Partly to compensate for the massive borrowing from the West that industrialization entailed, nationalism asserted Japanese moral superiority. Nationalists characterized Anglo-American values of individualism, liberalism, and capitalism as motivated by materialism and egocentrism. In contrast, Japanese society was held to have its foundations in spiritual commitments of selfless loyalty to the welfare of the entire community. As a result, society attained a natural harmony and solidarity in which everyone found his or her proper place. This moral order had divine origins in the unique imperial line, and the Japanese consequently had a mission to extend its blessing to other peoples. Japan's purpose in the war was to create a "new world order" that would "enable all nations and races to assume their proper place in the world, and all peoples to be at peace in their own sphere."[47] As the "leading race" of Asia, Japan would create a Greater East Asian Co-prosperity Sphere in which there would be a division of labor, with each people performing economic functions for which their inherent capabilities prepared them.

Nationalist writings often contained themes of pan-Asianism and the liberation of Asians from Western imperialism, but a report produced by Japanese bureaucrats privately described the goal of the new order as the creation of "an economic structure which would ensure the permanent subordination of all other peoples and nations of Asia to Japan."[48] Asianism was little more than window dressing for the pursuit of national power. Japanese foreign policy had never been marked by a strong identification with Asian interests.

In the face of U.S. demands for a return to the principles of the Washington Treaty System, Japanese leaders were prepared to take risks rather than turn back. "Nothing ventured, nothing gained," Matsuoka concluded. "We should take decisive action."[49] And the new prime minister, General Tojo Hideki, was quoted as saying, "Sometimes people have to shut their eyes and take the plunge."[50] The navy General Staff in particular pressed for war, arguing that oil reserves were limited and that U.S. naval strength was increasing. Ultimately its reasoning was accepted, and the president of the Privy Council explained to the emperor a month before Pearl Harbor,

> It is impossible from the standpoint of our self-preservation to accept all of the American demands . . . If we miss the present opportunity to go to war, we will have to submit to American dictation. Therefore, I recognize that it is inevitable that we must decide to start a war against the United States. I will put my trust in what I have been told: namely that things will go well in the early part of the war; and that although we will experience increasing difficulties as the war progresses, there is some prospect of success.[51]

Unwilling to submit to Hull's terms, which they regarded as an ultimatum, Japan's leaders determined on a bold and crippling blow at the main U.S. battle force in the Pacific. A surprise, preemptive strike on the Pacific Fleet at Pearl Harbor would give the Japanese time to sweep through southeast Asia, consolidate their control, and seize the resources necessary for total war. It might also break U.S. morale, lessen the chances of a disastrous war of attrition, and improve Japanese prospects in a prolonged war. The strategy was a gamble worthy of its mastermind, Admiral Yamamoto Isoroku, commander in chief of the fleet. Admiral Yamamoto had deep misgivings about prolonged conflict with a power whose superior resources, strategic reserves, and latent energies he knew from many years of study and service in the United States. "If I am told to fight regardless of the consequences," he said, "I shall run wild for the first six months or a year, but I have utterly no confidence for the second or third years."[52]

Japan paid a terrible price for its leaders' bold gamble. Tragically miscalculating the trends of the time, the nation entered into a conflict that cost it the lives of nearly 3 million Japanese and its entire overseas empire and led to the destruction of one-quarter of its machines, equipment, buildings, and houses. Generations were left physically and psychologically scarred by the trauma.

Japan did run wild in the first months of war, seizing Hong Kong, Malaya, the Dutch East Indies, Burma, and the Philippines. French Indochina and Thailand, though supposedly neutral, submitted to Japanese hegemony. By the end of 1942 Japan had established dominion over 350 million people in a vast area, from the Solomon Islands in the mid-Pacific to the borders of India, and from the rain forests of New Guinea to the icy shores of the Aleutians, embracing a population three-quarters that of the British empire.[53] Japan had carried out its earlier forays in northeast Asia over a number of years. In contrast, it made its sudden thrust into southeast Asia in the midst of war and with little preparation for administration and development of the new territories. In November 1942, belatedly recognizing the need for a blueprint or comprehensive design for a new order, Tojo established a Greater East Asia Ministry over the strenuous objections of the Foreign Ministry, which thereby lost many of its remaining functions. Initially the new ministry, which was dominated by the army, gave little place to pan-Asian goals; the strategic demands of the war were paramount. As Tojo put it, "the whole of Greater East Asia, whether independent countries or newly occupied lands, must be made one with Japan, each being brought to contribute its own strength for the sake of Japan."[54]

Only when the tide of war turned against Japan the following year did Tojo's cabinet decide to make political concessions in the occupied lands. The situation compelled Japanese leaders to articulate the benefits of a new order to rally Asians to the goal of liberation from Western colonialism. By November 1943, when a Great East Asia Conference was convened in Tokyo, the earlier emphasis on Japan "at the core" of the new order, with other Asian peoples being allowed to "find their respective places," had been replaced by declarations of "voluntary cooperation," "respect for mutual autonomy and independence," and "creation of an interdependent order."[55] The Japanese were especially anxious to reach a settlement with China, where they had critical resources tied up in the ongoing conflict with the Nationalist regime, but efforts to reach an accord with Chiang Kai-shek were fruitless.

By 1944 the war effort had reached a desperate stage. When Saipan fell in July and the home islands came within range of U.S. bombers, Tojo resigned and thought was given in some quarters to finding a means to terminate hostilities. Most senior statesmen, though they recognized the cause was lost, felt that the time was not yet right to sue for peace, that military and civilian fanatics had to be propitiated, that too abrupt and humiliating an end to fighting could lead to social revolution at home, and that only after a battlefield victory was achieved should peace negotiations be undertaken. This indecisiveness in the face of growing pessimism prolonged the war another disastrous year. Moreover, Japanese diplomats now embarked on a tragically misguided approach to the Soviet Union to request it to act as a mediator, believing this strategy would help disengage it from the Anglo-American war effort and preserve its neutrality. The Yalta Conference in February 1945 demonstrated the folly of this strategy and led Konoe, the veteran diplomat Yoshida Shigeru, and other conservatives to directly approach the emperor urging immediate measures to end the war. The emperor, the majority of senior statesmen, and military leaders remained convinced that fighting must continue until the right opportunity presented itself. Above all, the army, recognizing that the unconditional surrender the Americans demanded would mean its destruction, was adamant that fighting must continue until acceptable terms were offered. They demanded not only that the imperial system be preserved, but also that the military be allowed to demobilize itself and that there be no enemy occupation.

The allies meeting at Potsdam in July listed their objectives as dismantling the Japanese empire, punishing war criminals, and establishing a democratic order. Partly because the Potsdam Declaration left unclear the fate of the imperial institution, the Japanese rejected its terms. Only after the atomic bombs were dropped and the Soviet Union entered the war against them did the emperor intervene and insist that fighting cease. Japan was to be occupied by enemy soldiers for the first time in its history.

Japan's Unique Cold War Foreign Policy

Unconditional surrender, occupation, and demilitarization appeared to mark an end to Japan's status as one of the traditional great powers. Determined to strip Japan of militarism and the capacity to wage war, the American occupation forces set out to revolutionize the Japanese political structure and society. A democratic system, never achieved by the Japanese people themselves, was imposed. The military and political elites were purged, and a new constitution provided for popular sovereignty and included an article renouncing war and rearmament. All vestiges of nationalist doctrine were erased, and the education system was given the new purpose of contributing to "the peace of the world and the welfare of humanity by building a democratic and cultural state."[56] In every way imaginable the Occupation Forces sought to ensure that the Japanese state would not be motivated by its traditional pursuit of national power. In fact, the trauma of defeat and occupation did leave a radical legacy of pacifism and revulsion from prewar nationalism in the Japanese populace.

Nonetheless, the postwar political order was not so radically new as many observers thought at the time. The Americans largely spared the civilian bureaucratic elite from the purge, thereby permitting an unexpected continuity of a key part of the prewar conservative elite. Insensitive to the potential power of an independent bureaucratic elite, which in the prewar period had drafted over 90 percent of the legislation submitted to the Diet, the Occupation Forces kept the bureaucracy intact to run the day-to-day business of government. Seasoned bureaucrats emerged in a dominant position in the postwar order. In addition to their traditional power base in the ministries, they moved into leadership positions in postwar political parties and provided a continuity of both personnel and purpose. Despite the fact that the postwar political regime was, in many respects, quite distinct from its predecessor, the values of the prewar state thereby survived in a new setting.

Postwar Japan withdrew from international politics and became in effect a military protectorate of the United States. For decades it had no role in international strategic affairs as ordinarily defined. What is notable, however, is that the strategic principles and patterns of Japanese foreign policy reappeared in a new context. The realist pursuit of national power, the swift adaptation and skillful accommodation to the workings of a new international order, the absence of ideological commitment, alliance with the ascendant power, and the obsession to equal the advanced Western industrial nations, all were reconfigured in the formulation of a new and unique foreign policy. U.S. Secretary of State Henry Kissinger was said to have privately derided Japanese diplomats as "prosaic, obtuse, and unworthy of sustained attention"[57] because they were not party to great power politics, but Japan had as clear a foreign policy strategy as any of the major powers, and Kissinger himself was later forced to conclude in his memoirs that "Japanese decisions have been the most farsighted and intelligent of any major nation in the postwar era."[58] The postwar conservative leaders who survived despite the Occupation's radical reforms revived the prewar purpose of achieving national power, but they focused sharply on economic and industrial goals. "Japan," observed the political scientist Samuel Huntington in 1993, "has accepted all of the assumptions of realism but applied them purely in the economic realm."[59]

Postwar Japanese foreign policy, which may be best characterized as "mercantile realism," grew out of the lessons of defeat.[60] A remarkably revealing anecdote about Okita Saburo, postwar Japan's leading economic planner—who, significantly, also served as foreign minister in the 1970s—illustrates how the war influenced postwar foreign policy choices. In the spring of 1945, as the last months of the war were unfolding, Okita visited an old friend who was an engineering professor at the Tokyo Imperial University. Knowing the war was lost, the two men fell to talking about the lessons learned and about Japan's postwar prospects. The engineer recorded in his diary that Okita felt that not all was lost if Japan drew the proper lesson from its tragic experience, namely, that "Japan, poorly endowed with natural resources, must shape its future around precision engineering." In other words, Okita believed that Japan must concentrate its energies on taking imported raw materials and fashioning them into high quality products for export:

> Okita made himself comfortable and we spoke for a long time. He told me this story from around 1882 which an Englishman—it might have been Bagehot—used to tell as a warning to the people of his time. A poor warrior wanted to buy a splendid suit of armor but had no money, so he cut down on the amount of food he ate and little by little saved enough to buy a fine suit of armor. A war broke out and courageously he left to fight, but because his body had become so weak from his years of semi-starvation, he could not bear the weight of his armor and was soon slain by the enemy. This was just what happened to Japan. He did not think that a defeated Japan would be allowed to rearm at all, but this would probably be a blessing in disguise. I completely agreed with all he said. I will actually be happy if rearmament is completely prohibited. An army in uniform is not the only sort of army. Scientific technology and fighting spirit under a business suit will be our underground army.[61]

As it turned out, the postwar international system provided Japan with extraordinary opportunities for a newly focused national purpose of building Japan into a great economic power.

The key figure in reshaping Japanese foreign policy to achieve its long-standing purposes in the circumstances of a new international system was Yoshida Shigeru, who was prime minister during most of the first decade of the postwar period and who served concurrently as foreign minister during much of this time. A realist and nationalist and a product of the prewar foreign policy elite, Yoshida had a keen sense of the possibilities that changes in international politics might offer. When he formed his first cabinet in the spring of 1946, he observed to a colleague that "history provides examples of winning by diplomacy after losing in war."[62] Yoshida perhaps compared himself to Talleyrand, who at the Congress of Vienna won back with diplomatic skill what France had lost in the Napoleonic wars. Yoshida sensed that the defeated nation might use to its own advantage disputes between victors over the postwar settlement. In fact, the outbreak of the Cold War offered just such an opportunity.

The critical moment for the determination of Japan's postwar strategy arrived with the beginning of the Korean War in 1950. The Soviet-U.S. rivalry presented Japan with both dangers and opportunities. The dangers were that Japan would be drawn into Cold War politics, expend its limited and precious resources on remilitarization, and postpone the full economic and social recovery of its people. Conversely, the opportunities arose from Yoshida's perception that the Cold War made Japan strategically important to the United States and gave him bargaining leverage. When John Foster Dulles, special emissary of the secretary of state, arrived in Japan on the eve of the Korean War to negotiate a peace treaty and end the Occupation, he urged Japanese rearmament (which would have entailed revision of the constitution that the United States had only recently imposed). Dulles envisioned Japan joining a regional defense alliance, similar to the North Atlantic Treaty Organization (NATO), that would facilitate Japanese rearmament under international auspices, along the lines chosen by Germany.

Yoshida resisted. He was convinced that the Cold War would require the United States to maintain its presence in Japan, which would suffice to deter a Soviet attack. He would therefore give exclusive priority to pursuing Japanese economic recovery and maintaining political stability in a society deeply split over foreign policy issues, deferring indefinitely the task of preparing the Japanese people for a return to the hard realities of international politics. As Yoshida confided to his young aide, Miyazawa Kiichi:

The day [for rearmament] will come naturally when our livelihood recovers. It may seem devious, but let the Americans handle our security

until then. It is indeed our Heaven-bestowed good fortune that the constitution bans arms. If the Americans complain, the constitution gives us
a perfect justification. The politicians who want to amend it are fools.[63]

In protracted negotiations with Dulles, Yoshida traded a post-Occu-
pation continuation of U.S. bases on Japanese soil for a U.S. guarantee of Japanese security. Japan would remain as lightly armed as
possible so as to allow the nation to concentrate all its energies on
economic growth. Japan would avoid all foreign entanglements. It became an idée fixe of postwar Japanese diplomacy to avoid any collective security commitments. This stance was often very costly in terms
of Japanese amour propre. Japan became a subordinate to the United
States in international affairs. On the same day the San Francisco
Peace Treaty was signed, Japan also signed a Mutual Security Treaty
with the United States. For nearly four decades after 1954, when the
Self-Defense Forces (SDF) were organized under U.S. pressure, the
Japanese government maintained the position that the constitution
did not permit deployment of the SDF abroad.

This policy of shunning international political-military commitments while concentrating on economic growth, which became
known later as the Yoshida Doctrine, was elaborated by his successors
in the 1960s with the adoption of the three non-nuclear principles
(never to produce, possess, or permit the entry of nuclear weapons),
the three principles proscribing arms and military technology exports
(never to export arms to countries in the Communist bloc, to countries covered by UN resolutions on arms embargoes, and to countries
involved in armed conflicts), and the limitation of defense spending to
1 percent of the GNP. The Yoshida Doctrine proved much more
durable than its author had anticipated because it dealt so effectively
with the international as well as the domestic political environment.
As Japanese economic recovery gave way to high economic growth,
the doctrine took on a life of its own. At home it served to maintain a
balance among widely diverse views on foreign policy. It was a political compromise between the pacifism of opposition groups and the security concerns of the right-wing conservatives. This broad consensus
in favor of a mercantile role in international affairs prevailed in the

mainstream of political, bureaucratic, and business elites as the policy best suited to Japanese national interests. During the Vietnam War, for example, whereas South Korea was induced to dispatch more than 300,000 troops to fight alongside the Americans, the Japanese avoided direct military involvement and battened on procurement orders as they had in the Korean War.

This strategy was a carefully crafted adaptation to the conditions in Japan's international environment. The Pax Americana that followed World War II provided a liberal international economic order in which a defeated and outcast nation could take refuge, focus its sights on economic growth, and seek to rise again as a great power. More than any other country, Japan was the beneficiary of the postwar international order. For more than twenty-five years after the end of the war, Japan operated in extraordinary and uniquely favorable political-economic circumstances. Until the late 1960s Japan benefited from a special relationship with the United States under which the latter sponsored Japanese recovery and development by keeping the U.S. market open to Japan's goods while at the same time allowing Japan to limit severely the import of goods into its own economy. The expanding world trade that the United States was promoting through the International Monetary Fund and the General Agreement on Tariffs and Trade permitted a vigorous expansion of Japanese manufactured goods and the ready purchase of abundant and cheap raw materials. Moreover, Japan had easy access to new, inexpensive, and highly efficient Western technology.

The realist goal of maximizing power that had always characterized Japanese foreign policy strategy was now concentrated exclusively on economic competition, in which the instruments of power were productive efficiency, market control, trade surplus, strong currency, foreign exchange reserves, advanced technology, foreign direct investment, and foreign aid. Japanese leaders reshaped their domestic institutions in order to pursue their mercantilist policies. Working hand in glove with business interests, the bureaucrats built a system in which the Ministry of Finance (MOF), the Ministry of International Trade and Industry (MITI), and the Economic Planning Agency constituted the principal guiding forces. The Foreign Ministry was heavily constrained by

Japan's subordinate position in the U.S. alliance, and the Defense Agency lacked ministerial status and was the captive of the MOF. As two Japanese economists who worked for the government described it, "the banks and economic bureaucracy functioned as a general staff behind the battlefield in this second 'total war' called high economic growth."[64] Thus adherents to the Yoshida Doctrine determined to profit from the international order even while flouting its liberal norms.

Among Japanese leaders there was a growing conviction that in the nuclear age military power carried less advantage in the calculus of state power. A fundamental part of the emerging strategy was the nurturing of technological supremacy. As a key Mitsubishi official observed, "Although national supremacy was once a product of military power, it is now decided primarily by economic power. Economic power is, for its part, decided primarily by the ability to generate technology."[65] It therefore became a vital element of Japan's national security strategy to maintain an autonomous industrial capacity, preventing penetration of Japanese markets by foreign manufactured goods and foreign investment in key areas of fundamental technological strength. Japan's dependence on raw material imports and its consequent strategy gave it the world's most skewed import-export balance. Whereas manufactured goods made up 50 to 65 percent of other industrial countries' imports, they amounted to only 30 percent of Japan's imports in the mid-1970s. At the same time, 95 percent of Japan's exports were manufactured goods. Success in preventing foreign direct investment was evident in that only 1 percent of Japan's assets in the 1980s were foreign-owned. As one authority observed, "Japanese strategists have been more willing to accept U.S. military on their soil than they have U.S. bankers or manufacturers."[66]

Japanese planners thereby renewed their commitment to the elusive goal of autonomy and self-sufficiency that had been central to pre–World War II planning, but they now defined the goal in more focused economic terms. The oil crisis in the 1970s demonstrated that Japan must have unimpeded access to raw materials, especially oil. The lesson of defeat was that it could not gain this by military power. Instead it must depend on industrial policy and a shrewd diplomacy with no room for adherence to abstract ideals. Japan should maintain

cordial relations with all countries through an "omnidirectional foreign policy" to ensure supplies of energy and raw materials and to
protect trade. Okita Saburo, postwar Japan's leading economic planner and later foreign minister, wrote in 1974, "'being friends with
everyone' may be justified as the basic principle of Japan's diplomacy
in the present and future decades."[67]

Even where its fundamental interests were involved Japan maintained
a low posture. At the United Nations Law of the Sea Conferences in
the 1970s, although Japan accounted for a fourth of the world's catch of
fish, a sixth of the merchant shipping, and a fifth of the maritime freight
and was heavily dependent on seabed minerals, "Japan," an observer remarked, "championed no significant causes, took no major initiatives,
was not a key consensus-builder, and was not associated with any major
formulation."[68] As one prominent foreign affairs commentator advocated in 1980, Japan should avoid becoming entangled in international
disputes by deliberately "missing the boat"; that is, when controversial
international issues arose, Japan should always "go to the end of the
line" and wait quietly, unnoticed, while other nations stepped forward
to declare their positions. This was a "diplomacy of cowardice," he admitted, but it served Japan's interests.[69]

Japanese foreign policy had never been guided by abstract principles. Now, however, this nonideological nature was made explicit.
Miyazawa Kiichi, Japan's most durable postwar leader and an
unswerving adherent of the Yoshida strategy, maintained that Japan's
constitution made it a "special state" and precluded it from normal
participation in international politics. Accordingly, Japan could not
justify promoting any point of view other than its own self-interest.
Japan's foreign policy, he told an interviewer in 1980, "precludes all
value judgments. It is a pretense of a foreign policy. The only value
judgments we can make are determining what is in Japan's interests.
Since there are no real value judgments possible we cannot say anything." When challenged politically, Japan could only defer: "All we
can do when we are hit on the head is pull back. We watch the world
situation and follow the trends."[70]

By the 1980s Japan's century-long goal of overtaking the West
seemed to have been achieved. By many measures of economic and

technological strength Japan had come abreast of the United States, a chorus of foreign commentators praised the Japanese achievement, and in an official government poll, for the first time a majority of Japanese responded that Japanese were superior to Westerners.[71] There was widespread conviction that economic power would be increasingly important in determining the primacy or subordination of states. The chairman of the Sony Corporation, Morita Akio, was confident that "we are going to have a totally new configuration in the balance of power in the world."[72]

Nowhere did the economic instruments of power appear to be more effective in maximizing Japanese influence than in Asia. As Asian economic growth developed in the 1980s, Japanese economic bureaucrats working closely with business formulated an Asian strategy to pursue the goals of autonomy and self-sufficiency, seeking to carve out a sphere of economic dominance. Amassing trade and current account surpluses year after year, Japan became the world's largest creditor and largest aid donor. As a consequence, Japan was prepared to offer other Asian countries a persuasive set of economic inducements to follow its leadership: foreign aid, commercial loans, technology transfer, direct investment, and preferential access to the Japanese market. A government study in 1988 recommended a comprehensive integration of the economies of Asia in which the Japanese bureaucracy would serve as the "Asian brain" that would mastermind the region's economic development.[73]

As the success of Japanese developmentalist policies and institutions became obvious in the 1970s and 1980s, Japan's deviance from neoclassical international norms became a matter of growing controversy. Beginning with the "Nixon shock" of August 15, 1971, when President Richard Nixon announced his New Economic Program, which included the abandonment of the gold standard. The United States sought to cope with Japan's trade success by ending fixed exchange rates, imposing a surcharge on all Japanese imports, and forcing the Japanese to increase the value of their currency. As trade friction increased, Japan's distinctive economic strategy was stigmatized in the West as illiberal, unfair, and illegitimate. Critics saw Japan as a free rider on the international system, and the U.S. Congress increasingly regarded the alliance with Japan, where 50,000 U.S. troops were still garrisoned, as one-sided in its benefits.

The United States was ambivalent, however, about whether it wished to encourage Japan to undertake a greater defense effort. Rearmament would increase Japanese autonomy. This ambivalence was evident at the time Richard Nixon carried out his surprise opening to China in 1971. When the Chinese leaders met with Nixon and Kissinger, the specter of a resurgent Japan was one of their greatest concerns. Chou En-lai said to Nixon, "Japan's feathers have grown on its wings and it is about to take off . . . Can [the] U.S. control the 'wild horse' of Japan?"[74] Nixon reassured Chou and Mao Zedong that the United States intended to maintain the security treaty with Japan; otherwise, he said, Japan would build the capability to defend itself.

The U.S.-Japanese Security Treaty had originally been aimed at containing the Communists, but now Nixon was telling the Chinese that though the treaty continued to be targeted at a potential Soviet threat, it also served to contain Japanese nationalism, or as Kissinger called it in his memoirs, "Japanese unilateralism."[75] Nixon and Kissinger convinced the Chinese leadership to see the security treaty in a favorable light. In fact, two years later, in 1973, at one of their meetings Mao lectured Kissinger on the need to be more attentive to the Japanese. "When you pass through Japan, you should perhaps talk a bit more with them. You only talked with them for one day [on your last visit] and that is not good for their face."[76] Mao, until recently an anathema to the Americans, was telling them to be more accommodating to their Japanese ally! Kissinger wrote in his memoirs that "the Chinese, indeed, came to stress that U.S.-Japanese relations were more important than U.S.-Chinese relations."[77]

The U.S.-Japanese alliance was increasingly beset by tensions as Americans began to resent Japanese economic success achieved at their expense. In 1985 an esteemed American journalist, Theodore White, likened the Japanese drive for markets to their earlier pursuit of empire: "Today the Japanese are on the move again in one of history's most brilliant commercial offensives, as they go about dismantling American industry."[78] Nonetheless, the United States continued to provide for Japan's security not only because of the demands of the

Cold War but also because of deep ambivalence about Japanese rearmament. The top U.S. Marine Corps general in Japan said U.S.
troops must remain in Japan indefinitely because "no one wants a
rearmed, resurgent Japan. So we are a cap in the bottle."[79]

The growing negative reaction to its mercantilist policies and its
dramatic rise in the world stimulated a reassessment of Japanese foreign policy in the 1980s. A neoconservative agenda formulated during
the administration of Prime Minister Nakasone Yasuhiro (1982–1987)
proposed a new and broader sense of the national interest. Acknowledging that Japan could no longer be merely a follower in the international system, Nakasone's agenda included a self-generated, rather
than merely accommodative, activist foreign policy that would convert Japan to international leadership. On the eve of assuming office
in 1982, the colorful and forceful Nakasone wrote, "The first necessity is a change in our thinking. Having 'caught up,' we must now expect others to try to catch up with us. We must seek out a new path
for ourselves and open it up ourselves."[80] Always opposed to the
Yoshida Doctrine's low-profile stance in foreign affairs and subordination to the United States, Nakasone concluded that having caught up
with the West, Japan needed a new and broader definition of national
interest. Japan must no longer adhere to the narrow mercantilist policies of the past: They had been the means of Japan's catch-up struggle. Japan must increasingly be a leader in the international system.

Nakasone was aware that he was seeking a systemic change that was
not simply a revolution in Japan's foreign policy. It meant changing
Japan's economic structure, its political system, its educational and social goals—in fact, the people's way of thinking. During his five-year
tenure he embarked on a grand strategy to achieve these extraordinary
ambitions. These were heady days of close association with Ronald
Reagan and Margaret Thatcher, world acclaim for Japan's miracle,
and expectation of future achievement. Nakasone used the diplomatic
responsibilities of his office to promote an activist foreign policy. He
talked about revision of the constitution, and he tried to change policies that limited Japan's defense spending.

Accomplishing such a historic shift of national purpose proved to be
exceedingly difficult. The institutional legacy of the nation's long strug-

gle to overtake the West hobbled the systemic transformation that Nakasone envisioned. The balance of power in Japanese politics was still with the adherents of the Yoshida strategy. Because of the powerful momentum created by its modern history, the principal motive force of national life continued to be the economic dynamism of Japanese firms, the existing political-economic framework within which they operated, and the values of economic rationality that drove them.

The Post–Cold War Era

In the 1990s East Asia entered what we might call an interregnum, a period of flux and uncertainty when the shape of a new order was not yet apparent. There were many explanations for this interregnum: The Cold War ended suddenly, unanticipated, by massive implosion of the Soviet system rather than by victory on the battlefield. Nevertheless, despite total Soviet collapse in Europe, Cold War issues persisted in East Asia, including a divided Korea, the Taiwan issue, the lack of a peace treaty between Japan and Russia owing to the territorial dispute over the southern Kurile Islands, and the continuation of Communist governments in China and Vietnam as well as in North Korea. No new threat appeared that might impel the formation of a new system, and the region's powers, China, Russia, Japan, and the United States, were each for its own reasons mired in domestic issues and lacked a strategic vision for the region. China was still an emergent power of uncertain purpose, preoccupied with the immense tasks of economic development. Like China, Russia had to make the transition from a command economy. Japan, at the end of a long catch-up struggle, had to deregulate its economy, extricate itself from developmentalist institutions, and establish a more mature political economy. The United States had yet to formulate a new strategic vision for the region, preferring to adhere to Cold War strategies with modest amendments, while concentrating on long-deferred domestic economic renewal.

There are many puzzles in Japan's post–Cold War foreign policy: A country known for its strong national spirit continues to rely on a foreign power to guarantee its security; it preserves its foreign-imposed constitution, which it interprets as forswearing the right of collective security; it resists the widely recognized need to reform its troubled political-economic institutions; it has yet to come to terms with the historical burdens of its imperialist past; its policymaking is opaque and painstakingly slow. Most studies of how Japan might change its foreign policy in the post–Cold War era concentrate on the domestic determinants, particularly the internal debates about Japan's future international role. They look at Japan's foreign policy from the inside out.

But if we look at the pattern of the past and note that Japan has tended to be adaptive to major changes in its international environment and that it has been guided by a shrewd opportunism, then it becomes clear that in East Asia's present interregnum period, examining Japan's domestic determinants is not sufficient to understand Japan's future role. Through the modern century there has been an intimate link between the domestic institutional structure and Japan's external environment; Japan has typically adjusted its domestic institutions to suit the needs of a new international order. Therefore, it is probable that until the structure of the post–Cold War order becomes clear Japan will not make fundamental choices; rather, it will move slowly and with strategic caution. Henry Kissinger was on the mark when he observed in his 1994 book, *Diplomacy*, that "the role of Japan will inevitably be adapted to . . . changed [post–Cold War] circumstances, though following their national style, Japanese leaders will make the adjustment by the accumulation of apparently imperceptible nuances."[81]

Throughout its modern history, an opportunistic adaptation to the prevailing international order to enhance Japan's national power has been a principal recurrent characteristic of Japanese foreign policy. The Yoshida Doctrine, both in its foreign policy and in its supporting domestic institutions, was a brilliant adaptation to the structure of the international system during the Cold War. But the sudden, unanticipated end of the Cold War and the "interregnum" that followed in East Asia has left Japan disoriented. A tide of troubles swept over the country in the 1990s. The economy experienced its worst recession since the 1930s, and the political system, which had been shaped by and attuned to the unique circumstances of the Cold War, collapsed in

1993. The Liberal Democratic Party (LDP) was overthrown after thirty-eight years of uninterrupted rule; parties experienced a dizzying succession of realignments, leaving politics rudderless. In the face of these troubles Japan showed a bewildering lack of purpose and direction that paralyzed its policymaking. The Japanese system, which worked so well under the Cold War and which had been widely expected to provide world leadership, foundered. As a consequence of Japan's long failure to develop a political role in world affairs and the unexpected failure of its once highly praised economic institutions, it suffered a dramatic diminution of its international stature.

A succession of crises made it apparent that the Yoshida Doctrine's abstention from participation in strategic issues had become outmoded. The Persian Gulf conflict was the first great international crisis of the post–Cold War period. When an international coalition was organized in 1990 under a UN resolution, it was expected that Japan, as a great economic power dependent on the Middle East for two-thirds of its energy needs, would take an active part in supporting the coalition. But the debate that ensued in Japan over its proper role revealed a mixture of self-complacency, isolationism, and reluctance to abandon the status quo. Decades of withdrawal from international politics immobilized the Japanese political scene. Eventually the government decided to send no personnel but instead to make a $13 billion contribution to support the coalition. This sizable sum was scorned in many foreign quarters as "checkbook diplomacy," and many considered it a failure on Japan's part to meet its responsibilities as a country deeply dependent on the stability of the international system.

A crisis much closer to home raised the same kind of issues. In 1994, when a showdown with North Korea over its nuclear weapons program made war appear imminent, the U.S. forces based in Japan requested Japanese backup in the event of conflict, and Japanese officials were unable to accommodate their request. Had conflict ensued without such assistance, U.S. Secretary of Defense William Perry later said, "it would have been the end of the alliance."[82] Japan has much at stake in how the Cold War division of the Korean peninsula is resolved, and not only because it will determine the nature of its strategic relationship with its closest neighbor. So central is the issue of

Korean unification to the future structure of international relations in the region that it will bear heavily on Japan's relations with China, Russia, and the United States, all of whom have interests that intersect on the peninsula. A unified Korea might retain nuclear weapons or be tilted toward China or refuse to countenance a continued security relationship with the United States, including some continued U.S. presence, or be resolutely hostile toward Japan in its vision of the future—any of these scenarios would represent a major foreign policy defeat for Japan and would be a problem of immense concern for the nation's future. Yet despite having so great a stake in the outcome of Korean unification, Japan took no lead in the diplomacy to resolve the division of the peninsula. Constrained by the legacy of its Cold War foreign policy, Japanese policymakers maintained a low posture. Reactive and adaptive to the process of unification, they generally deferred to U.S. leadership.[83]

Japan would have seemed well suited to offer leadership in the resolution of the Asian financial crisis that began in 1997. But again its system was found wanting. In the midst of a prolonged economic slump in which its institutions—designed to catch up with the advanced industrial countries—were no longer appropriate or effective, Japan was unable to muster the leadership to stimulate its economy, reform its financial institutions, and help lead Asia out of the regional contagion.

In the changed environment of the new era one of the most perplexing problems for Japan was the rise of China. Nothing has been so psychologically jarring to those Japanese who think about their future strategic role and their aspirations for leadership in Asia. Nothing in Japan's international environment clouds the future so much as the rise of China. In the modern period Japan had never had to deal with a strong China. Throughout history, the emergence of a new great power has been destabilizing. Not only does a newly emerging power challenge the political and strategic status quo, it may also capture a substantial share of trade in a relatively short time, giving rise to intense economic conflicts. It was so with Germany's rise. Similarly, the emergence of Japan as a major power was a disruptive process that was not successfully managed and thus led to the greatest and most calamitous conflict in the history of Asia.

The potential size of China's economy, the uncertainty about its future power and purpose as a nation, the potential magnitude of its environmental degradation, its competition for resources, and the possible political and social turmoil as it rapidly industrializes have all justifiably alarmed the Japanese. Japan approached an emergent China with caution and circumspection. Policymakers sought to separate economics from politics in their relations with China, leaving it to the United States to press the controversial political issues of human rights reform and Taiwan with Beijing. Japan was not simply concerned to exploit the huge China market. It also hoped to use aid, its principal foreign policy tool, to gain leverage and to moderate Chinese behavior. Japan had a delicate and complex role to play in its relations with China, in part because it involved triangular relations with the United States. In its policy toward China, Japan sought the maximum autonomy it felt that Washington would tolerate. Japan must rely on the United States to balance China because it cannot do this itself. Therefore, preserving its alliance with the United States is critical to Japan.

At the same time, Japan does not want to be hostage to U.S. China policy, which has been notoriously inconsistent, driven as it is by multiple purposes and the uncertain currents of domestic politics. To the extent that U.S. China policy is incoherent and confrontational, Japan will want to keep as much distance as is compatible with maintaining its alliance with the United States. Following the Taiwan Straits crisis in 1996, when China fired missiles into waters close to Taiwan to demonstrate its displeasure with Taiwan's assertions of greater independence, Japan under U.S. pressure agreed to an increased defense role in the event of a regional crisis. As a consequence, for the first time since the Nixon and Kissinger opening to China in 1971, the Chinese eyed the U.S.-Japanese alliance with suspicion, regarding it as increasingly aimed at containing China's growing power and influence. As it did in its low-posture stance toward Korean unification, Japan is likely to move cautiously on political issues that arouse the Chinese.

The Japanese are clearly limited in their foreign policy options by the legacy of the institutions that remained from the catch-up period and by the unique role that Japan played in the international system during the Cold War. The political system worked efficiently in pursuing economic catch-up but faltered when challenged to make changes in the nation's goals and in the development of new policies and institutions. The process of reorienting Japanese purpose will be arduous and time-consuming, demanding an institutional revolution. Developing a foreign policy with greater symmetry between the economic and political dimensions of its international role will challenge the institutional and informal practices sanctified by decades of success in purely economic matters. Concentrating exclusively on economic growth during the entire post–World War II period has left many political-strategic institutions undeveloped. The weak prime ministership, the lack of crisis management practice, and the inexperience in deploying armed forces were glaring examples. As a matter of self-interest, Japan has repeatedly allied itself with the dominant ascendant power, and it is likely to continue to rely on its alliance with the United States in light of its undeveloped political-strategic institutions and the uncertain nature of the East Asian power balance. There is a growing recognition, however, that this alliance will have to be more reciprocal, more balanced in its obligations than was the case during the Cold War.

The Japanese have historically tended to make fundamental changes in their domestic institutions as part of their adjustment to a changed international system. In Japan's post–Cold War environment there are huge uncertainties, including the future role of the United States in Asia, the globalization of capitalism, the rise of China, and the prospect of Korean unification. Japan is not disposed to international leadership. It is typically reactive and adaptive, opportunistic and pragmatic in its pursuit of the national interest. Historically, in times of uncertainty Japan often moves with circumspection, waiting for trends to clarify, in part because of the nature of the decisionmaking process. The late Professor Kosaka Masataka, an astute observer of Japanese political behavior, stressed the difficulty in reaching consensus in situations of great uncertainty in the framework of Japan's in-

ternational environment: "Consensus is obtained without great difficulty when the nature of the task is clear. Often, for instance, the
Japanese have been good at adapting to strong, decisive pressures
from outside. But when the situation is blurred they are in trouble."[84]
Accordingly, the combination of systemic gridlock and strategic caution in Japanese politics at the end of the twentieth century is likely to
prevail so long as the present flux in the East Asian order continues.
But once the structure of its external environment becomes clear,
Japan is likely to accommodate itself to the new order of things.
Moreover, if the past is a reliable guide, it will accommodate with a
speed that will surprise those who look only at its present immobility.

8

◆

CHINA

A Tortuous Path onto the World's Stage

MICHEL OKSENBERG

Even today, the view is spectacular from the summit of Qingshan, or Coal Hill, in Beijing.[1] Situated within the former grounds of the Imperial Palace, it straddles the north-south axis that was so cosmologically important to Chinese imperial capitals for more than 2,000 years. To the south stretch the dazzling acres of golden-tiled, rectangular roofs covering the hundreds of vermilion-plastered palace buildings. The largest of these is the Hall of Great Harmony, where the emperor, facing southward on his throne astride the axis, met his bureaucratic officials and the tribute-bearing foreign dignitaries who, according to ritual, performed the *koutou*—the three kneelings and nine knockings of the head against the floor—"with ashen face and trembling knees."

The emperor and those in his privileged retinue were the only people on earth who could climb Coal Hill and see the architectural wonders below and beyond to the rest of the city. Arising in the southeast quadrant of the city was the blue-tiled circular roof of the Temple of Heaven, where the emperor performed the annual rituals that helped to harmonize the realms of the heavens and the earth so that his earthly realm would enjoy order and bounty. From Coal Hill one could see the other ritualistic centers of Beijing: in the east, the Temple of the Sun; to the west, the Temple of the Moon; to the southwest, the Temple of Agriculture; and to the northwest, the elegant Confucian Temple. There, engraved marble tablets listed the name of every candidate to pass the highest-level civil service examination, which had been administered triennially since the founding of the Ming dynasty in 1368. Beyond the Confucian Temple was the Yong-he-gong, the large ornate temple complex that the Qianlong emperor had erected as part of his patronage of Tibetan Buddhism. Scattered about both within and without the walled capital city were thriving Daoist and Chinese Buddhist temples and mosques serving the city's substantial Muslim community.

In the late 1700s the northern extension of the Grand Canal outside the city's eastern walls was filled with barges bringing rice, silk, pottery, and other commodities from the south; the goods were stored in the huge warehouses located just inside the eastern gates of the city. Some of these goods, especially spices, came from southeast Asia. And at the city's northwestern gates, camels and their herders gathered at the end of the caravan routes that reached to the old Silk Route linking China to the Middle East. On the frequent clear days in the eighteenth century—there were few such days in the polluted air of late-twentieth-century Beijing—one could see from Coal Hill to the mountains that stretch to the north and west of the city. Farther in the distance, though not visible from Coal Hill, was the Great Wall, rebuilt in Ming times, which was designed to protect China against what was traditionally its greatest vulnerability: invasion from central Asia. Messages could be conveyed rapidly along the wall from tower to tower to the northeast and the far northwest.

In the late 1700s the Qianlong emperor's immediate realm stretched from the island of Taiwan in the east to oases in the arid regions of the far west and from the tropical south to the nomadic regions of today's Mongolia and Manchuria (from whence the emperor's Manchu ancestors had marched southward and established the Qing dynasty in 1644). Beyond the imprecisely delineated domain, various kingdoms, nomadic groups, and theocracies engaged in periodic ritualistic relations with the Qing court that the Chinese saw as acknowledging the moral superiority of the emperor. Those who offered the tribute did not necessarily see the relationship in the same light. Indeed, the actual conduct of Qing diplomacy was a good deal more flexible than the hierarchical ritual suggested. For example, the Qing dealt differently with inner Asian states than with its neighbors to the east. Its relations with Tibet were purposefully ambiguous, suggesting that the emperor was both a secular patron and a religious disciple of Tibetan Buddhism. Its relations with Korea were strained. When necessary, it had entered into agreements as an equal.

Nonetheless, whether from the serenity of Coal Hill or amid the noise of the dusty Beijing streets, in the late 1700s the imperial capital possessed such a sense of majesty, power, ritual, and continuity that neither resident nor visitor could easily imagine that anything could overwhelm it as long as the emperor ruled the realm wisely and benevolently and kept the nomadic Mongol, Islamic, and Tibetan peoples of the interior under control.

By the late 1700s, however, the forces that would destroy the Qing Empire in the nineteenth and early twentieth centuries had already arrived. The expanding Russian and British Empires had knocked on Chinese doors. Already nestled against the northeast corner of the city wall was a Russian ecclesiastical mission, the result of a treaty signed between emissaries of the emperor and the tsar at Kiakhta in 1727. And the British had begun to make their presence felt in the Himalayas, in Canton where the British East India Company had opened offices in the 1780s and temporarily in Beijing itself when Lord McCartney led a mission from King George III to the emperor in 1793. Chinese exports of silk, porcelain, and tea to western Europe via India or the New World had assisted Canton to thrive on the periodic, state-regulated commerce channeled through that city. But the West was suffering from a severe trade imbalance, and its traders had begun to bring small amounts of opium from India to China in the late 1700s. By the 1830s opium use had reached epidemic proportions. The first missionary did not appear in Canton until 1807, and he soon retreated to Malacca. But within two to three decades Protestant missionary activity had begun in earnest, posing an ideological challenge to the Confucian order. The triple threat posed by the West—its military might, its commerce, and its ideologies—was in the wings. At least as important, serious domestic strains that would shake the Chinese state—peasant uprisings, fueled in part by rapid population increase and inadequate governmental response—were beginning to be evident by the end of the eighteenth century, though they were not yet really felt in Beijing.

Within a century foreign forces and the marauding Chinese accompanying them had ransacked portions of Beijing twice, first in 1860 and then in 1900. The Qing Empire was defeated in a series of wars, especially the Opium War of 1839–1842, the Anglo-French War of 1858–1862, the Sino-Japanese War of 1894–1895, and the multinational military expedition that lifted the 1900 siege of Beijing. It was forced to sign treaties surrendering portions of Chinese territory and granting foreign powers special privileges. Moreover, massive peasant rebellions had shaken the empire to its core: the Taiping, the Nian, and extensive Muslim uprisings in the southwest.

With perhaps the exception of Russia, no other of the seven nations that were major powers at the end of the twentieth century suffered such a traumatic and tragic entry into the modern era. Indeed, of the world's major belief systems (Confucianism, Christianity, Hinduism, Buddhism, and Islam) only state-sponsored, orthodox Confucianism failed to survive the twentieth century. To be sure, many Confucian values have endured among the Chinese populace, but the Western onslaught, coupled with the domestic crisis of governance, demonstrated the ineffectiveness of the imperial system and of the state-sponsored, orthodox Confucianism in which the system was rooted.

Thus as the twentieth century dawned, modern China had begun to confront the great paradox that has weighed heavily upon its leaders throughout the ensuing 100 years: China has the most ancient and continuous civilization among today's major powers, but it was the only one among them to suffer a total eclipse of the official ideology and institutions that had sustained that continuity. To a considerable extent, Chinese foreign policy in the twentieth century involves a quest to redress national grievances and to restore the lost greatness.

This search for wealth and power defined the tasks facing China's twentieth-century political leaders: how to reconstitute the Chinese state; on what system of beliefs to root that state; what its territorial and political domain should be; and how to attain wealth, power, and security for their country. Indeed, by the end of the nineteenth century such intellectuals as Liang Qichao and Yan Fu had identified the four underlying issues that would define much of the political debate of the twentieth century: What from the West had to be absorbed by China in order to achieve wealth and power? What from the Chinese past had to be jettisoned because it precluded a Chinese renaissance? What from the past had to be preserved because it defined the Chinese essence and bestowed its distinctiveness? And what from the West had to be firmly rejected because it would destroy the Chinese essence? Sometimes implicitly but usually explicitly, these questions have framed the debate over the broad contours of Chinese foreign policy in the twentieth century.

China's Global and Regional Geostrategic Environment

By the end of the nineteenth century the regional geostrategic environment that China would inhabit for the next hundred years had basically taken shape.[2] China's world, that is, the region in which its security interests are directly involved, stretches from the Kamchatka Peninsula and Hokkaido in northeast Asia to the south Asian subcontinent and from the Pacific islands to central Asia. From the 1500s until the late 1700s a unified China dominated the region's core. However, the 1800s brought enormous change to the region, and by the end of that century a new strategic configuration had emerged that persisted throughout the twentieth century. Namely, the region has contained five major powers: two indigenous to the region, China and Japan; two inextricably intertwined with it, Russia and the United

States; and one peripheral to it, Britain and its successor India as the dominant power of south Asia.

The five-power regional system came into being as Qing imperial power waned and as British naval dominance over maritime Asia eroded while it contended with Germany's assertiveness elsewhere. Russia's expansion into central Asia and its building of the trans-Siberian railroad enhanced its ability to project its power into the region. With its acquisition of Hawaii and the Philippines in 1898, the United States became a full-fledged Pacific power. Most significantly, the rise of an expansionist Japan, demonstrated in stunning victories over China in 1894–1895 and Russia in 1904–1905, introduced a new power into the equation. The constantly changing distribution of power among these five countries and the evolving interrelations among them have defined the strategic configuration in the region ever since.

In the last two decades of the twentieth century, however, the five-power Asian regional system has exhibited two important new qualities. First, from the beginning of the century until the late 1980s, at least two of these five powers found themselves locked in bitter rivalry, with the contestants seeking allies and clients. For much of the twentieth century, at least one major tension-producing fault line divided one part of the region from another. However, with the end of the Cold War, all the five major powers have basically constructive relations with one another; no fault line divides the region. Second, until the 1980s, the Asian regional configuration, rivalries, and alliances were largely the product of global developments. Anglo-German rivalry, World War I, the Great Depression, and the Soviet-American Cold War profoundly affected Asian alignments. By century's end, the situation had changed. Asia, China and Japan in particular, had begun to affect global concerns, alignments, and balances. The region's economic dynamism and its growing technological and military capabilities are transforming the international system. Such developments as Asia's economic performance and China's currency management and nuclear weapons strategy shape the global balance.

Moreover, by the early 1900s the regional strategic chessboard had become clear, and it has remained the same throughout the twentieth century. The interests of the major powers have intersected in a number of locales: the Pacific islands, Taiwan, the Indochina peninsula and the South China Sea, the Strait of Malacca, the Himalayas and Tibet, central Asia and Xinjiang, Mongolia, Siberia, Manchuria, the Sea of Okhotsk and its surrounding territory, and Korea. None of the five major powers has had vital security interests in each of these locales. In only one of them—Korea—have the interests of four of the five powers intersected. Most of the wars involving the major powers have arisen over their competition for influence and control of these locales.

Because of China's size and central geographic location, its security is affected by the arrangements made in most of these locales, especially in those places that an adversary can use as a base from which to launch aggression against China. Taiwan, Indochina, the Himalayas and Tibet, central Asia and Xinjiang, Mongolia, Manchuria, the Russian Far East, and Korea were all used for such purposes, both in China's distant past and during the past 150 years. As a result, the leaders in Beijing are especially vigilant and quick to assert China's interest when a hostile power seeks to dominate any one of these places.

This setting has defined the strategic choices that the leaders of China have faced in the twentieth century, particularly in light of China's own weakness. For much of the century, China's leaders have had to react or respond to an environment that they could only marginally influence. They had to calculate which of the major powers was the least threatening to them and which potentially offered the most assistance. Conversely, they had to decide who posed the greatest threat to their rule and to national security. They had to assess how they could take advantage of the rivalries among the other powers. Moreover, they had to assign priorities among the many and often divergent threats on their periphery. Were the threats from the coast or the interior more serious? How should China's limited military capabilities be deployed? Indeed, what kind of military capability should be acquired to cope with the threats? And what priority should be attached to the acquisition of military strength, compared to allocation of resources for the development of an economic infrastructure?

The strategic decisions confronting China's leaders throughout the twentieth century have gone beyond the choices of alignment and the threat assessment that any set of leaders must face. Each of the major powers who offered protection and assistance to a weak China also sought to intervene in Chinese internal affairs. Each foreign power brought with it a vision of how China should solve its domestic problems; each sought to integrate China into its own regional or global socioeconomic order. Britain wished to weave China into its commercially oriented world of colonies and neocolonies. The United States sought to nurture an open, democratic, and possibly Christian China. Japan during the 1930s and early 1940s desired to incorporate China into its designs for a Greater East Asian Co-prosperity Sphere. The Soviet Union wanted to create a Leninist state that was integrated into the Soviet commercial and military bloc.

As they formulated their integrated economic developmental and national security strategies, China's leaders had to consider how to adjust and temper their strategies in light of the demands their preferred external partner sought to impose upon them. From this perspective, Chinese foreign policy throughout the twentieth century has been an object of negotiation between its Chinese designers and the external power from which they chose or were forced to seek assistance. China's leaders have had to calculate whether the demands that a foreign power made upon their domestic rule were worth the benefits they received from cooperation. On the eve of the twenty-first century, however, China's leaders have accrued sufficient might to enable them to challenge other countries in similar fashion.

Objectives

The Stated Goals

Chinese foreign policy objectives have flowed from its historical legacy and its strategic context.[3] Throughout the twentieth century, China's diverse leaders have voiced a strikingly similar set of objectives at the most general rhetorical level. Similar themes exist in Sun Yatsen's Three People's Principles (nationalism, democracy, and socialism), Chiang Kai-shek's call in *China's Destiny*, the speeches and essays assembled in the selected works of Mao Zedong and Deng Xiaoping, and Jiang Zemin's 1997 call for a strong, unified, prosperous, socialist, democratic, and culturally advanced China.

Each of China's often-stated objectives is rooted in its modern history. The stress upon unity and stability arises from the protracted period of fragmentation and civil war. The yearning for independence springs from China's subservience to outside powers and the positions of privilege that foreigners had obtained within China. The emphasis upon strength and security stems from the penetration and perceived exploitation of a weak China by each of the major powers. The search for wealth and prosperity flows from the poverty that gripped so much of the country, made all the more bitter by memories of a previously abundant land. The quest for an equitable society and new political arrangements grows from a widespread recognition that previous societal and political patterns, even in imperial times, promoted much injustice and often prevented an effective response to the challenges the outside world posed. The demand for respect, dignity, and a voice in the councils of nations originates in the humiliations heaped upon China not only in the treaties forced upon its rulers in the nineteenth century but in its lack of voice at Versailles at the end of World War I and Yalta at the end of World War II. China had contributed to the winning side in both world wars, but its interests were neglected in the postwar arrangements because of its weaknesses.

Different Interpretations of the Goals

Though China's leaders, political thinkers, and strategists have exhibited considerable continuity and consistency in the national goals and foreign policy objectives they have articulated, they have struggled over the precise meaning of their words, and they have often given different priorities to conflicting objectives. For example, though all leaders have sought a unified China, they have differed over what its precise territorial domain should be. The Kuomintang, the Nationalist Party of Chiang Kai-shek, for example, continued to claim that all of Mongolia, including Outer Mongolia, or the Mongolian Republic, was a part of China; Mao Zedong and the Chinese Communist Party (CCP), however, did not assert that Mongolia rightfully belonged to

China. And though Mao laid claim to Taiwan after coming to power, he did not include it in his listing of Chinese irredenta in interviews with the Western journalist Edgar Snow in 1935.

At issue is the Chinese sense of identity and its territorial domain. China's ethnic minorities, the roughly 8 percent of its populace who inhabit its border regions, who do not speak any form of Chinese, and who are non-Han, pose particular difficulties for the national identity. The Han leaders of the twentieth century have tended to claim the territory these people inhabit (the Mongolian Republic is the exception), but they have voiced different views about whether the state should seek to assimilate the minorities into the dominant culture or to grant them considerable autonomy. Policies toward ethnic minorities have considerable foreign policy implications, since the lands inhabited by most ethnic minorities cross Chinese borders.

Issues of identity also arise with respect to Han peoples who reside outside of China. Tens of millions of such "overseas Chinese" reside in southeast Asia. Their ancestors migrated to what is today Indonesia, the Philippines, Vietnam, Thailand, and the Malay Peninsula. In some places, especially Thailand and the Philippines, most citizens with ethnic Han background have joined the mainstream culture, but elsewhere the process of assimilation has proceeded slowly if at all. What responsibility does the Chinese state have toward these people, particularly when they suffer from discrimination? Do Han Chinese have a right to return to their ancestral homeland? And does the Chinese state have any rightful claim upon their loyalties? Such questions have foreign policy consequence, and they are still quietly contested in China.

The priority given to national autonomy, independence, and sovereignty is full of the same ambiguity, particularly when balanced against the equally strongly voiced desire for international respect, participation in the councils of nations, and access to world markets. What are the defining characteristics of sovereignty, and precisely what erodes it? What policies represent an unacceptable foreign presence on Chinese soil, symbolizing exploitation by the outside world? To give an example of the policy disagreements that can arise from such questions, many Maoists firmly opposed joint venture arrangements with multinational energy corporations in which China would sell equity holdings in its petroleum and coal reserves in order to acquire the capital and technology to develop those natural resources. But Deng Xiaoping and his associates did not view this policy as yielding to imperialist exploitation; they formed joint ventures with such companies as Exxon and British Petroleum.

Some Shared Beliefs

Although superficially it appears that Chinese foreign policy has been characterized by a high degree of consensus over national goals, a cursory examination of the oft-stated objectives reveals deep divisions. But not all has been problematic. Five widely held beliefs—derived from both China's distant and more recent past and reinforced by its exposure to the West—have decisively affected foreign policy in the twentieth century.

The first is a deep and abiding faith in the greatness of China, even though this confidence is often accompanied by a gnawing doubt that China can swiftly recover its greatness. A strong streak of Great Han chauvinism exists among the populace, which the leaders can easily rouse for their purposes.

Second, there is general agreement that China's eras of greatness have coincided with its periods of unity and strong central governments and at moments when its territorial domain has been at a maximum. China's heroes are those who unified the realm; its villains are those who contributed to its fragmentation and foreign penetration.

Third, most believe that China's structure of authority should be indivisible and concentrated, residing in a single institution. Separation of powers, as in the U.S. Constitution, is inappropriate for China because such a constitution would lead to chaos, fragmentation, and, potentially, civil war. To be sure, some Chinese intellectuals at various times in the twentieth century have become enamored of the American model. They advocated creating federalist or commonwealth arrangements and allowing organized religions whose heads are not selected by China's political rulers. A few have even seen merit in permitting international bodies to dictate internal economic arrangements, or placing Chinese military forces under foreign command. Each of these has been at issue on more than one occasion in the conduct of Chinese foreign policy in the twentieth century. But for the most part, Chinese rulers have been loathe to permit encroachments upon their authority; they have guarded their prerogatives jealously.

Fourth, though the quest for wealth, power, and security demanded considerable adjustments within the country, most Chinese attribute their country's century of humiliation to the machinations of the outside world rather than to domestic causes. Different views exist over the extent of the disruption, and many acknowledge the benefits that the Western incursion brought to China—especially new ideas, a system of higher education, investment, and a stimulation of commerce. But the searing lesson is unmistakable: Although China has foreign friends and possesses resources and ideas that are useful for China's development, malevolent forces in the outside world are always eager to exploit China, possibly to divide it, and to take advantage of its weaknesses. As a result, alliances should be joined only warily; China's destiny must remain in the hands of its rulers.

And last, the Chinese believe that China must acquire military might in order to be a great nation again. This is a question not of "whether" China will become strong militarily but of "when" and "how." China is not home to many pacifists. Its entire modern history suggests that as its economy develops, as its technological base improves, and as its government revenue increases, its leaders will devote a significant portion of this increased capability to the development, acquisition, and deployment of modern weaponry. Mao Zedong and his colleagues amply demonstrated this commitment in their nuclear weapons program. This does not mean that China's leaders will emulate the USSR and swiftly seek parity with the leading power of the world. Deng Xiaoping revealed as much in placing military modernization fourth among his priorities, behind agriculture, industry, and science. In keeping with tendencies in traditional strategic thought, China's leaders are more likely to probe for the weak links in a potential adversary's strategy and capability and then to develop the means to disrupt that strategy. And they will seek the ability to deter an adversary from operating with impunity in adjacent regions where Chinese security is at stake. This is the course to which Jiang Zemin and his associates committed themselves in the 1990s.

Strategic Thought

Thus far I have focused on three of the broad factors shaping Chinese foreign policy in the twentieth century: the historical legacy of the nineteenth century; the global and Asian strategic setting; and its leaders' goals and intentions. These considerations shaped but did not determine the choices available to the leaders. I turn now to the strategic thought on which the leaders have drawn in the twentieth century, that is, to the repertoire of ideas about how to harness and use power and influence in pursuit of their objectives.[4]

A generation ago, the predominant view among analysts of China was that Chinese leaders in the early 1900s had only a rather limited and confining repertoire of strategic thought available to them. To be sure, a few practitioners of statecraft had demonstrated considerable insight and skill during the 1800s. But according to these analysts, Confucian traditions did not equip the elite to conceive an appropriate national security strategy in response to the interstate system the imperialist powers were imposing upon them. That narrowness of vision, coupled with the splendor and isolation of the Beijing bureaucracy, explained their obtuseness and rigidity. Only when their range of ideas had been widened through extensive and intensive contact with the outside world were Chinese leaders able to understand their new security environment and to develop appropriate strategic responses.

More recent scholarship, however, calls that interpretation into question. First of all, it is argued, Chinese leaders did far better in comprehending and responding to Western challenges than was previously thought. They were constrained not so much by a lack of conceptual weapons as by the domestic political, economic, and military conditions around them. The Qing state was less awesome than the imposing architecture of Beijing suggested. For example, according to the estimates of economic historians, the Qing state mobilized less than 5 percent of the empire's gross national product (GNP).[5] And the mobilizational capacity of the state remained low throughout the first half of the twentieth century as well.

Moreover, the development of a modern army and armaments industry and the economic infrastructure to sustain it probably matched Japan's, at least until China's defeat in the 1894–1895 Sino-Japanese War. But the lack of national communications and transportation systems, as well as the need to keep local forces in place to maintain domestic order, made it impossible to concentrate their troops at the places of foreign incursions. For example, the Sino-Japanese War of 1894–1895 was essentially a local war; the Qing state was unable to deploy all its forces against Japan. Similarly, historians are reappraising the progress that China made under Chiang Kai-shek and the Kuomintang (KMT) from 1927 to 1937, asserting that his foreign policy strategies were more adept than earlier historians have suggested. Even the Dowager Empress Tz'u Hsi, previously seen as an archconservative and a manipulator of the Boxer Uprising, and Yuan Shikai, the previously widely condemned militarist who sought to become emperor after the overthrow of the Qing dynasty, have found sympathetic biographers who explained their strategies as rational and perhaps even enlightened in their contexts.

But perhaps most important, recent scholarship has discovered that traditional Chinese strategic thought was a good deal more sophisticated and varied than earlier interpretations allowed. A generation ago the literature was filled with such conventional formulas as "The Chinese tradition in foreign affairs emphasized hierarchical relations and left no room for dealing with others as equals," "Chinese statecraft slighted the role of military force and considered power as an outgrowth of virtuous rule," and "The traditional East Asian order, with its emphasis on ritual and imperially prescribed conduct, did not prepare China's rulers for a world of realpolitik and balance of power." Such generalizations frequently could be traced to the complex set of myths that the Chinese bureaucrat-scholar-gentry class and their descendants perpetuated about their pivotal and civilizing role in the governance of the empire. They assigned primacy to their role and denigrated that played by the military and commercial sectors. These interpretations were not wrong, but they were not complete. The actual doctrines that guided foreign policy were a good deal more complicated and varied.

As more recent writings have stressed, Confucianism was hardly a monolithic system of thought, and when Legalist and Daoist thought were added to the mix, Chinese intellectual traditions were rich, diverse, and wide-ranging. In particular, traditions of statecraft draw not only on the periods of Chinese unity but also on the many instances in which a divided Chinese domain hosted an interstate system somewhat akin to the international system of the twentieth century. Balance of power arrangements, alliances and their avoidance, preemptive attacks, the amassing and use of military might under the guise of morality, deception in diplomacy—all were widespread practices in China during periods of disunion, and they were well known to the many Chinese familiar with the popular novels, theatrical plots, and folklore that drew on these eras for their material.

Moreover, as Chinese leaders and their strategic thinkers came in contact with the West, their ideas about the purposes and techniques of foreign relations changed. Their strategies were affected by such Western concepts as international law, sovereignty, and the modern nation-state with delineated boundaries. By the time of the Versailles Peace Conference of 1919, China was represented by well-trained diplomats. And soon after the Russian Revolution, Marxist-Leninist thought spread in China, bringing with it theories of imperialism and the organization of a garrison or developmental state. The original diversity in available national security policies, which ranged from "soft" and accommodationist to "hard" and confrontational, was therefore enriched and broadened throughout the twentieth century.

In the last two decades of the twentieth century, many Chinese involved in the formulation of the nation's foreign policy have absorbed Western strategic theories on nuclear deterrence, the revolution in military armaments, methods for attracting foreign capital, and international financial markets. They have had to grapple with the concepts of an interdependent global economy. As a result, the repertoire of strategic thought available to Chinese leaders has been even further enriched since the early 1980s. But even so, one wonders to what extent the new ideas are genuinely understood. The ideas from abroad (such as nuclear doctrine) have been grafted onto indigenous strands of thought and existing institutional arrangements. Chinese strategic thought has therefore not been the inevitable product of a doctrinal straitjacket, it still grows out of institutions and beliefs that originated in a deeper past.

Twentieth-Century Discontinuities

Thus far, this essay has dwelled upon the sources of continuity in Chinese foreign policy: shared memories of a nation fallen from greatness; an immutable geostrategic context; a common rhetoric on national aspirations; and a somewhat continuous but evolving strategic culture. Yet the responses of China's leaders to their strategic choices and hence their foreign policies have undergone continual change. I will first review the record of changes in Chinese foreign policy and then seek to explain them.[6]

Sometime Friend, Sometime Foe

China has found it difficult to sustain alliances and has had no permanent friend and no permanent enemy during the past 100 years. At some point during the twentieth century the national government has aligned itself with each of the other major powers in the region; at other junctures it has been at war with each. Japan invaded and occupied large portions of China from 1931 to 1945, participated in a U.S.-led embargo of China from 1950 to 1971, but entered into a Treaty of Peace and Friendship in 1978 and extended massive development assistance loans in the 1980s and 1990s. The United States attached little importance to China from 1900 to the late 1930s, when it became its ally during World War II, fought its forces in Korea from 1950 to 1953, considered it an enemy from 1950 to 1970, then assisted it in its resistance to Soviet expansionism in the 1970s and 1980s, and sustained a partially cooperative and partially confrontational posture in the 1990s. China's national government sought to use Russia early in the century as a balance against Japan. The KMT viewed the revolutionary Soviet Union both as a threat and as an ally against militaristic Japan. After the Communist ascent to power in 1949 China became a Soviet ally, but by 1960 the relationship had become acrimonious, and it culminated in fierce border clashes in 1969 and a massive Soviet military buildup along the border. But the rancor faded in the Gorbachev era, and by the 1990s, following the collapse of the Soviet Union, Russia was a major arms supplier to China. Relations with Britain and India have also been unsteady. In the Communist era Sino-Indian relations were at first quite close, but in 1962 the two fought a border war. Relations between the two remained strained for more than two decades, improving in the late 1980s and 1990s, but deteriorating again following India's 1998 nuclear test.

Changes Toward Its Neighbors

Not only have China's relations with the major powers been tortuous throughout the twentieth century, but its relations with its immediate and smaller neighbors have also exhibited marked changes in the past fifty years. (During the first five decades of the century, most of China's neighbors were colonies of Japan, Britain, France, or the United States; moreover China lacked the capacity to pursue coordinated policies toward its neighbors.) In northeast Asia the People's Republic of China was a close ally of North Korea until the 1980s, supporting Pyongyang's invasion of the south in 1950 and sending troops to save the regime when the United States was on the eve of annihilating it. China remained hostile toward South Korea until the 1980s. Since then, Beijing has cultivated a wide-ranging relationship with the south at the cost of its relations with the north.

In southeast Asia Beijing was an ally of North Vietnam from its founding in 1954. But relations between them deteriorated during the late 1960s and 1970s, partly as a result of Hanoi's increasingly close relations with Moscow and partly as Beijing came to recognize Hanoi's ambition to dominate the entire Indochina peninsula. In 1977 Hanoi began a campaign against Han Chinese residing in both the north and the recently captured south. Massive numbers of them fled

from the country both by sea and by land to China. The animosity between the two culminated in the Chinese incursion into Vietnam in
1979 in reprisal for Hanoi's invasion of Cambodia that overthrew the
Beijing-backed Pol Pot regime. Relations between China and Vietnam improved only after Vietnam withdrew from Cambodia in the
1980s.

Relatedly and at the same time, China ceased its support of Communist insurgency movements in Thailand, with which it previously
had adversarial relations, and throughout the 1980s and 1990s the two
have enjoyed close relations. A similar turnabout occurred in China's
relations with Malaysia and Singapore. But perhaps the greatest fluc-
tuations have occurred in China's relations with Indonesia, where,
through the 1950s and 1960s, the mercurial Sukarno initially welcomed, then distanced himself from, and finally tightly embraced
China. The military leaders who replaced Sukarno in 1965 sought to
rid Indonesia of Chinese Communist influence, leading to the slaughter of tens of thousands and perhaps hundreds of thousands of inno-
cent ethnic Chinese. Sino-Indonesian relations remained frozen until
the late 1980s, at which point President Suharto of Indonesia warily
improved relations with Beijing.

Only in south Asia have China's foreign relations been more consistent. From the mid-1950s on, it has managed to sustain constructive relations with Pakistan, Burma, Sri Lanka, and, after its separation from
Pakistan in 1971, Bangladesh despite the many changes in government
in all these states. It has been a major arms supplier to Pakistan, Burma,
and Bangladesh. China's objective appears to be to prevent India from
achieving dominance over the subcontinent, and all the countries surrounding India seem to have shared in this objective.

The Complicated KMT-CCP and PRC-Taiwan Relationship

Finally, there are the twists and turns in relations between the two political parties—the KMT, which traces its origins to the late 1800s,
and the CCP, founded in 1921—that have vied to rule China in the
twentieth century. Since 1928 each has been in control of a different
portion of Chinese territory, and each has pursued its own foreign

policy. The two were allied from 1923 to 1927, were at war from 1927 to 1936, were uneasy and reluctant partners during the resistance against Japan, and then engaged in civil war on the mainland from 1945 to 1949. The KMT was favorably inclined toward the United States, where many of its leaders had been educated; the CCP had a natural ideological affinity for the Soviet Union. During the war of resistance and the civil war, the Communists gradually developed the organizational capacity, military savvy, and popular appeal that propelled them to victory in 1949. When the KMT retreated to Taiwan, it transferred the government of the internationally recognized Republic of China to Taipei, and the CCP established the People's Republic of China (PRC) with its capital in Beijing. The two then competed for recognition and supremacy in the international arena.

The Korean War enabled the Republic of China (ROC) on Taiwan to resurrect its links with the United States, culminating in the U.S.-ROC security treaty in 1954. From 1950 until 1962 the ROC and the PRC were in a state of continual military buildup and confrontation in the Taiwan Strait, including the PRC's 1954 and 1958 shelling of Taiwan-held islands close to the mainland and persistent KMT raids and plans for invasion of the mainland. Gradually the military confrontation stabilized, and the battleground shifted to the United Nations and the capital of every country in the world, as the two competed for recognition as the legitimate government of all of China.

In the 1970s the PRC made major gains in the competition: It wrested the China seat in the United Nations away from Taiwan in 1971, won diplomatic recognition from Japan in 1972 and the United States in 1979, and obtained membership in the World Bank and the International Monetary Fund in 1980. Cross-strait relations were transformed in the 1980s, as the two sides permitted trade, tourism, and capital flows. Each still claimed to be the legitimate government of all of China, however. But this was altered in the 1990s, when the government on Taiwan dropped its claim, acknowledged the reality of Communist rule on the mainland, and sought to be recognized internationally as a government of equal status in a temporarily divided country. The PRC is unwilling to grant this claim. It seeks to prevent Taiwan from declaring independence and is unwilling to have formal diplomatic relations with any country that establishes diplomatic relations with Taiwan.

What has caused the frequent seismic shifts in Chinese foreign policy? Three interrelated factors have been involved: changes in China's strategic environment, differences among China's paramount leaders, and significant discontinuities in the nature of the Chinese state.

The Evolution of Chinese Foreign Policy

The changes in China's strategic environment can be outlined briefly, if too simply. In the first three decades of the twentieth century, China's leaders presided over a weak and divided China. They had to steer a course between an ascendant Japan, a declining but still powerful Britain, a rising United States, and a faltering Russia. From the late 1920s to the end of World War II, they sought to maneuver within an intensifying U.S.-Japanese rivalry, coping with a Japan that sought to dominate China and a United States that generally wished China well but was unwilling to act upon its benevolent impulses. After the defeat of Japan in 1945, China had to seek security within a world largely shaped by the U.S.-Soviet Cold War. And with the collapse of the Soviet Union, it has sought security in a world of unchallenged U.S. military might and in which no major power rivalries exist in Asia.

A Divided China, 1912–1927

Following the collapse of the Qing dynasty in 1912, China entered a period of disunion and civil war. A weak central government existed in Beijing, but this central government (called "the Republic of China") was controlled by whatever local militarists had achieved dominance in the Beijing area. Other military rulers—dubbed *junfa* (warlords)—dominated other regions of the country. This situation persisted until the late 1920s. Although the warlords in Beijing retained a Foreign

Ministry and pursued a nominal foreign policy, in reality this weak government was not able to control most of the transactions that flowed across China's borders, and it had little power to project beyond its borders. The central government had a foreign policy, but it did not control the nation's foreign relations. The rest of the world treated China with scorn.

The world's disdain became particularly evident at the Versailles Peace Conference at the end of World War I. China had joined the Allied cause, sending workers to Europe to replace French and other factory workers who had joined the fight at the front. China got nothing for its effort. At the conference it sought the return of the territories and privileges that Germany had obtained earlier from the Qing. Though the conference's guiding principles ostensibly included "self-determination" for nationalities, in reality the victors divided the spoils. In the ultimate humiliation, the Allies assigned the German-ruled territories in China to Japan. Demonstrations erupted in Beijing, initiating a popular social movement—the May Fourth movement—that is often cited as heralding the birth of modern Chinese nationalism. Among the movement's many consequences was the founding of the Chinese Communist Party in 1921 and the heightened determination of the Kuomintang Party to acquire the might to reunify the country under its aegis.

During this period Chinese foreign policy consisted of attempts by each of the various warlords and political parties both to enlist support from one or more of the outside powers for its effort to unify the country under its rule, and also to seek popular support through nationalistic pledges to rid China of foreign privileges. Hence warlords both welcomed financial support and military advice from foreign powers and also supported anti-foreign protest movements. Both the KMT and the CCP embraced the advice and assistance of the agents dispatched from Moscow. And within the divided nation, the contending Chinese factions joined hands with some and resisted other foreign businessmen, missionaries, educators, journalists, and philanthropists, who had spread across China seeking to nurture the nation's current and future elite.

Torn Between Japan, the United States, and the USSR, 1927–1950

From the late 1920s until the end of World War II, the most signifi-cant events in East Asia revolved around Japan's drive to be the hege-monic power in the region; the U.S. response, at first acquiescing to and then opposing their ambitions; and the resulting war between them. Then, in the late 1940s, the Cold War extended to Asia as the United States fashioned a Japanese ally against Communist forces on the Asian mainland. China had to seek its security within this chang-ing context.

In the late 1920s, in a complicated sequence of events, the KMT partially achieved its objective of unifying China. Under the leader-ship of Chiang Kai-shek, the KMT and its armies had established a more effective central government than that of its predecessors. Con-tinuing to call the central government the "Republic of China (ROC)," in 1927 the KMT shifted its capital from Beijing to Nanjing (Nanking), roughly 100 miles up the Yangtze River from Shanghai. Chiang's actual control over large portions of the country was tenu-ous, however, since many of the warlords had remained in place, their troops still under their command, and had only pledged their loyalty to Chiang. And in other parts of the former Qing Empire, especially the areas inhabited by ethnic minorities, such as Tibet, the local lead-ers no longer considered themselves under Chinese rule.

Nonetheless, Chiang had garnered enough strength to pursue an active foreign policy. He aligned himself primarily with British, U.S., German, and French interests. He hoped these powers would assist him to resist the Japanese advance and consolidate his control over the country. He hoped in vain, however, for he found little international support to oppose the Japanese occupation of Manchuria in 1931. The other foreign powers were preoccupied with their own domestic problems in the midst of the Great Depression.

Moreover, Chiang attached higher priority to unifying China than to fighting the Japanese. He thought that a divided China would surely lose to Japan, and therefore, until 1936, he concentrated upon defeating his domestic Communist adversaries. Many in Chiang's entourage sought a close relationship with the United States, but Washington was preoccupied with the Great Depression. Chiang therefore turned to Germany for assistance in his largely successful campaign against the CCP. The closer Chiang came to achieving a united China under his Nationalist banner, however, the more Japan feared that its interests would be adversely affected. Japan's militaristic leaders believed that increasing pressure upon a unified but still weak China would compel Chiang to accommodate their interests, and they pursued that course from 1931 onward. In 1936, however, a rising tide of nationalism and anti-Japanese sentiment among the populace and demands from within the ranks of previously pro-Chiang military officers forced the still reluctant Chiang to resist Japan without an external ally.

Japan invaded the core of China in 1937, and the Sino-Japanese War began in earnest. The KMT resumed its alliance with a greatly weakened CCP so that the nation could devote its full attention to Japan's occupation of coastal China. Outside support for Chiang was initially limited. Indeed, Japan had established collaborating Chinese governments in both Manchuria in 1931 and Nanjing in 1937, forcing Chiang to retreat to the interior. He located his wartime capital in Chongqing in southwest China. Slowly and painfully, Chiang began to acquire outside assistance, especially after Japan's alliance with Nazi Germany, when the outside world (including the Soviet Union) concluded that China could play a constructive role in the worldwide struggle against fascism. Not until 1941 and the Japanese attack upon Pearl Harbor, however, did Chiang find an ally, the United States. But the United States attached less priority to assisting Chiang in the China theater than it did to defeating the Germans in Europe or to rolling back Japan through the island-hopping campaign in the Pacific. After the defeat of Japan, the Kuomintang became embroiled in a civil war with the Chinese Communists. Chiang—militarily inept and receiving only limited U.S. assistance—was unable to defeat the Communists. (It is very unlikely that massive U.S. assistance would have altered the outcome.) The KMT government then retreated to Taiwan, from which Chiang hoped eventually to launch a counterattack and reconquer the mainland.

Alliance with the Soviet Union, 1950–1960

Mao Zedong, the leader of the victorious Communist Party, proclaimed the founding of the People's Republic of China on October 1, 1949. He stated that China had stood up; it would no longer be humiliated in world affairs. He did so facing south, standing astride the same north-south axis on which the emperor once received visitors, Coal Hill in the distance behind him, thereby symbolically drawing upon the strength of the imperial past as he launched the new China. But he also broke with the imperial past. He brought his office to the southernmost gate of the Imperial Palace, the Tiananmen, or Gate of Heavenly Peace, and, signifying a different relationship between leader and led, he allowed the masses to gaze directly at him. Previously, the populace was far from the center of power; now they were accessible to the rulers, available for mobilization. Further, Mao and his colleagues launched the new regime not in isolation from the world but with a foreign alliance structure in hand.

The new leaders needed external assistance to get their nation back on its feet. Throughout 1948 and 1949 Mao had made it clear that he intended to orient Chinese foreign policy toward the Soviet Union, and by the spring of 1949 the Soviet Union and the Chinese Communists were negotiating the size of the aid package that Moscow would provide to the government that would be soon established. Earlier Mao had hoped that his ideological affinity for the Soviet Union would not preclude a limited economic relationship with the United States, but Mao recognized that in the bipolar world that had dawned neither Joseph Stalin nor Harry Truman would accept such a posture. Stalin acted swiftly to incorporate the new Communist government into his alliance system.

The United States began the process of disentangling itself from the Republic of China, but it did not rapidly reach out to the new regime, wishing to see how closely aligned they became with Moscow and how the new leaders behaved toward the Americans still in China.

Mao signed a treaty of alliance with the Soviet Union in February 1950, and the Korean War of 1950–1953 then sealed the alignment. When North Korea invaded the south in June 1950, the United States feared the attack was a prelude to wider Communist aggression. (We now know that the attack was not part of a worldwide military offensive, but it did occur with the foreknowledge and grudging support of both Stalin and Mao.) To the surprise of the north and its backers in Beijing and Moscow, the United States rushed to the south's assistance, and after U.S. forces crossed what had been the dividing line between the north and south in an effort to unify the peninsula, China intervened to preserve the government in the north. Chinese and U.S. troops then fought a bitter war in Korea for more than two years, and the enmity persisted for nearly another twenty years. In addition, at the outset of the Korean War the United States dispatched ships from its Seventh Fleet to the Taiwan Strait to protect the Chinese Nationalist government there from a possible Communist invasion and imposed an economic blocade that was to last until 1970. The United States had become reengaged in the Chinese civil war, and by 1954 it entered into a security treaty with the Republic of China. Hence the mainland government was aligned with the USSR, and the island of Taiwan was under U.S. protection.

The Sino-Soviet alliance extended far beyond the foreign policy domain. It integrated the two nations' national security and economic development strategies, entailing Chinese emulation of Stalin's model of economic development: a command, planned economy, centralized bureaucracies, collectivized agriculture, a high rate of capital accumulation, priority for heavy industry, and monopoly rule by the Communist Party. Stalin evidently believed that his alliance with China served his interests, and he generously poured assistance into the country. For a brief time the alliance worked well, and Soviet assistance greatly aided the initial stages of China's industrialization effort.

At no time during the decade of the alliance, however, did Mao and his colleagues allow their nation to become a total client of Moscow politically, economically, militarily, or diplomatically. The privileged positions that Mao reluctantly granted Stalin were of limited duration, and Mao later resisted and resented Soviet efforts to obtain military installations in China. Economically, the Chinese leaders refused the Soviet invitation to join COMECON, the Soviet economic bloc. Militarily, Mao ordered his aides to begin research and development of nuclear weapons, missiles, and nuclear submarines. Diplomatically, China sought to escape from the rigid bipolar world in Asia that the Korean War had created. When it ended Mao and his advisers sought an independent opening toward the United States, initiating ambassadorial talks in Geneva that soon floundered over the Taiwan issue. They also vigorously sought to establish links with newly independent, nonaligned countries in the developing world. The 1950s overtures toward the developing world and the United States were harbingers of the alternate strategies Beijing pursued in subsequent decades.

Confrontation with Both the USSR and United States, 1960–1972

Crises in 1956 over the Suez Canal and the Hungarian uprising, in 1958 in Lebanon, in 1960 over the Russian downing of a U-2 spy plane, in 1961 in Berlin, and in 1962 in Cuba underscored to both Washington and Moscow the fundamental importance of their bilateral relationship. Each could destroy the other in a matter of hours. Each was reluctant to allow its allies to intrude into the management of this tension-filled relationship. To Mao's repeated annoyance, Moscow especially proved reluctant to subordinate its relationship with Washington to accommodate the interests of its junior, Chinese partner. Further, the breakthrough 1963 Nuclear Test Ban Treaty suggested that the two could cooperate to prevent a nuclear war, and thereby led both the United States and the USSR to believe that China, over the long run, would pose a greater danger to world peace.

Mao grew disenchanted with his Soviet backers, and they wearied of him. By the late 1950s, many Chinese leaders—especially Mao—had concluded that the Soviet model was not entirely suitable to Chinese conditions. And as the Chinese began to depart from it, the Soviets became more reluctant to support them. The dispute, fed by personal animus between Mao and Khrushchev, spiraled first into a full-fledged ideological rivalry; then into an economic rupture when, in 1960, Moscow withdrew its advisers and ceased its aid program; and finally into an increasingly tense military confrontation on the Sino-Soviet border. Mao turned to his guerrilla origins and championed a developmental strategy of self-reliance both in international affairs and at local levels. To vastly oversimplify: In order to forge a regime capable of mobilizing China's labor power, Mao first sought a simultaneous transformation of the county's economic base and its ideological and political superstructure during the Great Leap Forward (1957–1960). When that effort ended in an economic disaster for China, he attempted to transform the political institutions and thoughts of the Chinese people during the Cultural Revolution (1966–1976). Both efforts essentially entailed simultaneous defiance of both the Soviet Union and the United States.

Mao did seek external support, primarily from the developing world and among revolutionary forces. He cautiously assisted revolutionary movements in countries whose governments were allied with the United States and had diplomatic relations with Taiwan (such as Thailand and South Vietnam), and he offered aid to national liberation movements that were opposed to the Soviet Union. As a result, in such places as Angola, Mozambique, and Southern Rhodesia (now Zimbabwe), Chinese-backed and Soviet-backed movements competed with each other. And China cultivated relations with countries that neither recognized Taiwan nor had good relations with Moscow. (Albania and Iran were the leading examples.)

The strategy endangered China's national security. Both the massive Soviet military buildup along the Sino-Soviet border and U.S. involvement in Vietnam were a response to a seemingly irrational, nuclear, and increasingly erratic China. By the late 1960s China confronted the possibility that it would become involved in a war with either the USSR or the United States, and if war came, it would have to fight its battle essentially alone.

Alignment with the United States, 1972–1989

Leonid Brezhnev's 1968 assertion that the Soviet Union had the right to intervene militarily in any state that was abandoning socialism—a doctrine he had acted upon in the invasion of Czechoslovakia—and border clashes along the Sino-Soviet border in 1969 set the stage for yet another change in China's strategic alignment, which began to tilt toward the United States to counterbalance the increasing possibility of a war with the Soviet Union. The United States, weakened in Asia by the Vietnam War, was ready to accommodate some of the long-standing Chinese demands on Taiwan. The Soviet Union, on the other hand, not only staunchly refused to yield on a wide range of Chinese ideological and territorial demands but intensified its military buildup along the border.

Although the tilt toward the United States began under Mao, China's full realignment occurred after his death in 1976, under his successor Deng Xiaoping. Once again, China's leaders sought to link their national security policy with their economic development strategy. Mao's strategy, with its emphasis on ideological change, had left the people weary and impoverished. Meanwhile, China's East Asian neighbors, including Taiwan and Hong Kong, had forged ahead economically during the 1960s and early 1970s. The solution was to reorient China toward the United States, Japan, and Western Europe, seeking access to their markets, capital, equipment, and technology in order to accelerate China's economic growth and to draw upon their strength to resist Soviet pressures. Mao's limited opening yielded considerable gains: It complicated Moscow's strategic concerns, removed the U.S. economic embargo, enabled diplomatic relations with U.S. allies (especially Japan), and eased China's entry into international organizations.

The profound consequences of China's reorientation became more evident in the Deng era. Domestically it led to the opening of China to foreign investment, to the creation of special economic zones in which foreign firms could operate under favorable conditions, and to a recognition that economic reforms were necessary. It enabled China to alter its previously hostile relations with U.S. allies ranging from South Korea and the Philippines to Thailand and even Israel and Saudi Arabia. In the process, China ceased to support revolutionary movements, and in international forums such as the World Bank it often served as an intermediary between the developed and the developing world. And it tangibly joined the United States in resisting the Soviet Union. At the peak of their animosity, the USSR deployed roughly 30 percent of its total Soviet defense effort against China and its Far Eastern theater. China assisted the United States in gathering intelligence about Soviet military developments, cooperated with the United States in training and equipping Afghan resistance fighters, and began a modest program of arms purchases from the United States. By the early 1980s, the two were unofficial, quasi allies.

A Region Without Major Power Rivalries, 1989 to the End of the Century

In the mid- and late 1980s, as Moscow's foreign policy changed under Gorbachev, it became possible for China to modify its strategic orientation once again. Gorbachev concluded that security was an interdependent concept; he explicitly condemned Moscow's previous policy of seeking to attain its security by engendering a sense of insecurity among its neighbors. He sought rapprochement with China largely on the terms that Deng Xiaoping had set: a lessening of Soviet military forces on the border, settlement of the boundary dispute, cessation of ideological polemics, and reduction of Soviet assistance to Vietnam.

Then, with the fall of the Soviet Union and the end of the Cold War in Asia, for the first time since the regional system came into being in the late 1800s, no fault line sharply divided one set of Asian countries from another. For the first time in a century, all the major powers had good relations with the others. China no longer had to seek security within a conflict-ridden context. For the first time since the Opium War, China confronted no imminent threat to its security. It could cultivate constructive relations with all the major Asian powers simultaneously, but also it could not play off one rival against another. Moreover, with its increasing economic influence and its gradually increasing military capacity, it could play a more active role in shaping the strategic environment that it inhabits. It could seek to influence the arrangements in those peripheral locales where its interests are engaged.

The late 1980s and 1990s offered hope that China's leaders would exploit their new position well and wisely. They improved relations with all the countries on their periphery. Despite their reservations and their veto power as holders of one of the permanent five seats in the UN Security Council, they refrained from impeding various UN peacekeeping operations, and participated actively in the successful multinational effort to bring peace to Cambodia. They joined international nuclear nonproliferation regimes and pledged to limit their sales of missiles. They played a constructive role in helping to maintain stability on the Korean peninsula by expanding relations with the south, and they apparently acted behind the scenes to constrain the north. They cautiously supported the creation and expansion of various regional forums, such as the Asia Pacific Economic Cooperation (APEC) process, the annual summit of leaders of Asia Pacific nations, and the security dialogue of the Association of Southeast Asian Nations Regional Forum (ARF). Following the reversion of Hong Kong to Chinese rule in 1997, they meticulously adhered to their pledges to honor the "one country, two systems" formula. In the early stages of the Asian economic debacle that began in 1997, they contributed to the financial bailout packages for Thailand and Indonesia and managed their own currency in a responsible fashion.

Yet, in June 1989, China's leaders also shocked the world by their brutal suppression of demonstrators who had occupied Tiananmen Square. They vigorously asserted their territorial claims in disputed waters and over uninhabitable islands in the East and South China Seas. They bullied Taiwan, going so far as to hold missile tests in 1996, timed to coincide with the island's first democratic election of a president. Their sale of weapons and technology to Pakistan and several Middle Eastern countries prompted concerns over proliferation of weapons of mass destruction and ultimately contributed to India's decision in 1998 to test a nuclear weapon. Their suppression of Tibetan Buddhism damaged their international reputation, partly because the Dalai Lama mounted a successful campaign to raise the visibility of this issue. Their rising trade deficits with the United States and what most Americans saw as a poor human rights record introduced strains in Sino-American relations.

Finally, weapons purchases from Russia and their own weapons development program raised concerns among some Americans about China's longer-term designs in the western Pacific.

As a result of this ambiguous record, the Sino-American relationship became more difficult for both sides to manage in the 1990s.[7] In the mid-1990s some Americans, including some members of Congress, began to speak of China as the next U.S. enemy, and China's leaders began to believe that the United States was returning to its 1950s policies of seeking to encircle and isolate China. State visits by President Jiang Zemin to the United States in 1997 and President Bill Clinton to China in 1998 dispelled some of these fears. But at century's end the Sino-American relationship remains fragile, and China's leaders could easily adopt policies concerning Taiwan, Korea, arms sales, trade, or human rights that would place them on a collision course with the United States.

The Leaders

Not only has China's pattern of alignment continually shifted in the twentieth century, but the widely divergent characteristics of its four preeminent leaders—Chiang, Mao, Deng, and at century's end, Jiang—have had major and diverging impacts upon foreign policy. To be sure, they shared common traits as well. Each sought to preserve China's national independence and its national essence, although they differed in their definitions of that essence. Each was deeply committed to the unification of the country. Each was willing, to varying degrees, to use force against both domestic and foreign adversaries who threatened to divide the country. Each demanded to be treated with dignity. Each sought to reconcile and deflect a somewhat similar set of conflicting domestic pressures upon them. And each employed similar tactics: free riding, playing upon the expectations of China's future greatness, seeking the moral high ground by proclaiming that China's position was principled, threatening to defect from alignments unless China's partner provides additional incentives, and claiming special consideration because of past injustices.

Yet the differences among the four are equally noteworthy. Chiang Kai-shek lived in two conflicting worlds. In many respects he was a traditional Confucian. He also felt comfortable both with the militarists and the leaders of the interior and with xenophobic ideologues. At the same time, his wife was a Christian and a graduate of Wellesley College. His coterie of Chinese advisers included some of the most sophisticated, cosmopolitan, and effective diplomats and some of the most knowledgeable financiers in the world—all foreign trained. His attempt to bridge these two worlds of the Chinese interior and the Chinese coast made it difficult for him to pursue a coherent and credible policy. The nativists and the underworld figures in his coterie alienated the foreign supporters of his cosmopolitan Chinese. Where he actually stood among the mélange he had assembled was never very clear; he remained an aloof enigma. As a result, Chiang's relationship with his U.S. allies entailed considerable wariness, tension, and mistrust. But as Chou Enlai noted approvingly at the end of their respective careers, Chiang never let the Americans control him.

Mao Zedong clearly was the most domineering of the four. He dwarfed his lieutenants and dispensed with those who could have emerged as a rival. His willfulness made it impossible for him to sustain cooperation as an equal, much less a subordinate, to any foreign leader. He also was the least familiar of the four with the outside world, and made only two brief journeys outside China, both to Moscow, in 1950 and 1957. He was curious about the outside world, read widely about it, met with many foreigners, and received extensive briefings from his many associates who were familiar with international affairs. But in essence he inhabited a pantheon populated by the heroes and villains of his nation's past. He applied their stratagems and statecraft on the international stage. Though an isolated China dismayed the many internationally oriented Chinese in his entourage, Mao himself relished dwelling within an exclusively Chinese world.

Like Mao, Deng Xiaoping was a son of the interior, but he had been exposed to the West in his youth, as a factory worker and student in France. Mao thought in terms of epochs and sought cultural transformations. Deng thought at most in terms of decades and sought practical results. Both Mao and Deng were very tough, but Mao was more self-indulgent. Deng knew how to discipline himself and subordinate his desires to greater purpose. Although Mao had a strong pragmatic streak (evidenced, for example, in his tolerance of continued British rule in Hong Kong), Deng's foreign policy exhibited a consistent pragmatism and strategic calculation that Mao's policies often lacked. The opening of China to foreign investment, the sale of its natural resources through joint venture arrangements, and the creation of special economic zones where foreigners enjoyed special privileges were Deng initiatives that Mao would have had great difficulty accepting.

Jiang Zemin brings new qualities to office: He has had extensive training as an engineer and a lengthy education abroad, his career has been exclusively within the Communist era, and he has a greater understanding of the modern world than did any of his three predecessors. He is the first of the four not to have commanded military forces. While he has yet to decide upon the legacy that he wishes to bequeath, clearly he is committed to China's integration into the global economy on terms that do not threaten his country's stability or unity. He also seems less impulsive and more cautious than either Mao or Deng, but his caution may be due less to his personality than to the fact that he is politically weaker than either Mao or Deng. Thus far, he has consulted widely and has been a consensus builder. His foreign policy—methodical, considered, and evolutionary—has not been marked by sudden or unexpected departures.

The Growth of Bureaucracy

In the preceding sections I have shown how China's regional strategic context and the personal characteristics of its leaders have contributed to the many changes in twentieth-century Chinese foreign policy. But another major factor has also been at work: the dramatic strengthening of the Chinese state and the growth of Chinese foreign policy bureaucracies.[8] In the late 1700s the imperial system lacked agencies that specialized in foreign policy. Only in the mid- and late 1800s did the Qing establish a professional bureaucracy for managing foreign affairs and dispatch permanent emissaries abroad. It is indicative of the Qing Empire's weakness that it had to rely on the British to organize and manage its customs service, which became a major source of the Qing court's revenue. And the Qing military, which greatly expanded in the

second half of the 1800s, was organized more for domestic than foreign policy purposes.

Not surprisingly, although the new foreign policy bureaucracies were
staffed by many very competent diplomats, they did not thrive in the
warlord era. They began to expand in the Nationalist era, and Chiang
Kai-shek did a great deal to create a modern state apparatus during his
Nanjing years. But an extensive foreign policy bureaucracy was created
only after the founding of the People's Republic of China. In many
functional areas—including finance, agriculture, and education—the
Communists built upon the governmental agencies that the KMT had
developed. Not so in the national security area. In 1949 Mao assigned
Premier and Foreign Minister Chou En-lai the task of creating a totally
new Ministry of Foreign Affairs. It drew its senior personnel from three
sources: the army, the corps of Party officials who had worked with
Westerners in KMT-held areas during World War II or in Hong Kong
after the war, and a group within the CCP who had studied in Moscow
and who therefore had extensive experience with the Russians. Chou
recruited younger foreign affairs officials with excellent foreign-lan-
guage skills from such leading Western-oriented universities as St.
John's in Shanghai, and he wooed bright, patriotic Chinese then studying abroad to return to the motherland.

The communists established a navy and an air force, and a system of
attachés was established in the military. (The CCP lacked these in
their guerrilla days.) A Chinese covert intelligence service, which had
already been active abroad, expanded its foreign presence and analytical capabilities. The Liaison Department of the CCP established
contacts with the expanding, worldwide Communist movement. The
Ministry of Foreign Trade and state-owned trading companies were
established to conduct the newly established state monopoly in foreign trade. One commission was established to implement unofficial
economic relations and another to engage in foreign aid. A commission was created to manage issues relating to ethnic Chinese living
overseas. Another agency supervised the Soviet and Eastern European
advisers who poured into China as part of China's alignment with the
Soviet bloc. Foreign affairs bureaus were established in every ministry
and provincial government; they were considered part of Chou's for-

eign affairs system. And universities were established to train the human resources for these expanding organizations.

In short, by the mid- to late 1950s, under the demanding tutelage of Chou En-lai and a talented group of senior associates, China had acquired an extensive, professional foreign policy apparatus for the first time in its history. For the first time since the British arrived along the China coast, Chinese foreign policy largely coincided with the country's foreign relations. The Chinese state controlled almost all transactions that crossed its borders. There were exceptions: The KMT and the United States carried out covert operations inside China's coastal and southern border regions; nomadic tribes wandered across the western borders; and Overseas Chinese made surreptitious contact with their kin at home. But these were minor compared to the newly established organizational strength of the Chinese state that enabled it to carry on both formal and informal relations with other nations even as the United States sought to isolate it.

Mao never fully trusted this foreign policy apparatus, and he frequently circumscribed or ignored it in the conduct of his diplomacy. But it was there to respond to his command. Its efficacy greatly strengthened the conduct of Chinese foreign policy. Even during the Cultural Revolution, when attacks inspired by Mao greatly weakened the apparatus, it was still able to direct the diminished flow of ideas, people, and material across China's borders. Only once was China briefly unable to conduct an orderly foreign policy: In 1968 marauding Red Guards, under the sponsorship of radical personnel in the Foreign Ministry, besieged some foreign legations, and Chinese embassies abroad were paralyzed by their own strife and by the lack of guidance from Beijing. The system was swiftly restored, and it was fully functioning by the late 1970s. In short, the national security apparatus that Mao and Chou built enabled China to project its power and influence beyond its borders in a way that had simply been unavailable to China's rulers in the first half of the century. The apparatus greatly expanded the leaders' range of strategic choices and enabled them to be actors rather than victims on the world stage.

However, the administrative decentralization of the Deng era, the opening to the outside world, and the introduction of a partial market economy have made it more difficult for the top leaders and the central state apparatus to control the flow of goods, people, and ideas across China's borders. That is, the foreign policy bureaucracies of the central government have increased the top leaders' ability to project power, but at the same time, as China's exchanges with the outside world have increased, the proportion of the exchanges the top leaders can control has decreased. For example, more than 50,000 foreigners now reside in Beijing, and the Chinese government estimates that 150,000 Chinese scholars and students are studying in universities in the United States, Japan, Europe, and Australia. This movement of people is an opportunity for the Chinese state to expand its influence. The foreign residents in China are susceptible to pressures and enticements by the state, many of the Chinese scholars and students studying abroad serve the purposes of Chinese governmental policy, and even those individuals opposed to their political leaders expand the influence of Chinese society, if not of the state.

The economic realm has undergone a similar shift since the Mao era, when the roughly 5 percent of GNP that fell in the foreign trade sector was entirely controlled by Beijing's state trading companies. Today, more than 30 percent of GNP falls in the foreign trade sector, and GNP has quadrupled since the Mao era.[9] China's foreign trade is an astounding twenty-five times larger in 2000 than it was in 1980, measured in real dollars. But a very substantial portion of that trade is outside the control of the central state apparatus. It is either smuggled, in the hands of local governments that pay scant attention to central directives, or carried out by foreign-owned firms with special privileges that cannot be easily retracted.

In short, since the early 1980s China's boundaries have become more porous, its foreign affairs apparatus more fragmented, and its growing engagement in world affairs less susceptible to coordinated direction from the center. In the Mao era China's foreign relations were the disciplined product of the policies and guidelines that its leaders set. At century's end, this is no longer the case. Rather, the leaders adjust policies and create new institutions in a frequently vain attempt to channel, contain, or legitimate relations that developed outside their control.

The top leaders have lost much of the initiative. With their country more deeply immersed in world affairs, they must devote more of their energies to formulating policies that cope with unanticipated consequences of their previous decisions that their foreign affairs and national security bureaucracies implemented. Chinese weapons sales to Pakistan and Iran are one such example. The national security bureaucracies gave China's leaders weapons they had never had before. The leaders then sought to advance China's interests by selling weapons in the Middle East and south Asia. The ensuing negative reaction from the United States dragged the reluctant leaders into arms control arrangements it originally had no intention of joining. Another example is the development of an intellectual property rights regime in China. The decision to invite foreign direct investment and the creation of a vast domestic institutional infrastructure to host them, though remarkably successful, has also made it necessary to create yet additional institutions to which the leaders were originally opposed.

Thus, the large bureaucratic apparatus that the leaders created in the 1950s and have expanded since the mid-1970s have had a dual effect. The growth of the Chinese state has given the leaders levers of influence that they previously lacked. But those same bureaucracies have become mechanisms through which the outside world can reach, act upon, and constrain them.

State Capacity

Even though the consequences of creating a stronger state apparatus may not have been all positive from China's leaders' point of view, without question the Chinese state is stronger at century's end than it was at the beginning.[10] By most objective indicators, its strength has grown even as China has become more integrated into international affairs in the last twenty years. And the leaders have an increased capacity to apply that strength for carefully targeted and controlled purposes. The extractive capacity of the entire Chinese state apparatus has increased dramatically during the twentieth century, from an estimated maximum of 2–5 percent of GNP in 1900, to 10–15 percent in the 1930s, nearly 40 percent at the peak of the Mao era, and roughly 30 percent in the late 1990s. The state has amassed more than US $150 billion in foreign currency reserves. The leaders have nuclear weapons at their command. The People's Republic is a permanent member of the UN Security Council. The leaders are in constant and direct contact with their counterparts in other countries and are consulted on matters that most affect their interests. And they have the capacity to project their power and to influence events in each of the subregions around their periphery.

Qualifications are again necessary. Much of state revenue remains at lower levels, beyond the reach of the central state apparatus, and a high proportion of state revenue is not extracted through regular taxation but is collected in an ad hoc fashion, by levying fines and fees and as profits from state-run enterprises. The central state apparatus acquires roughly 10 percent of GNP from the taxes it levies. This is very low compared to the revenue available to the central governments of the other major powers. Moreover, China is still only in the process of building an effective central banking system. And even though it has substantial foreign currency reserves, its foreign indebtedness is also growing and exceeds US$130 billion.

China's military strength is also limited. Even though it has advanced weaponry and is improving the quality of its missiles, the People's Liberation Army has glaring vulnerabilities that can not be swiftly or easily remedied. To its neighbors to the south, China is a looming military giant. The threat that the PRC military presents to Taiwan is gradually increasing, but Taiwan is determined to maintain the capacity to inflict major damage should China use force against it, and the United States is obligated via the Taiwan Relations Act to assist Taiwan to maintain its self-defense capability. But compared to the United States and its South Korean and Japanese allies, China is still weak and vulnerable, a situation that is likely to persist for the foreseeable future.

And the Chinese state has little to offer in the realm of ideas and culture. Its official ideology of Marxism-Leninism is bankrupt. In the Mao era the Chinese state waged war on the indigenous culture, which still bears the scars. China today is a massive importer of ideas from high technology to popular culture. In this context, international nongovernmental agencies are affecting Chinese thought on such issues as the environment, women's rights, human rights, religion, ethnic identity, and democratization. The telecommunications transformation is making China even more accessible and vulnerable to foreign ideas.

In short, a hard-nosed assessment of China's state capacity—and hence of the capacity of its rulers—reveals that it is not as strong as it appears on paper. Many vulnerabilities and weaknesses are cloaked in secrecy and hidden behind bravado, and the existing strengths are maximized by a generally intelligent leadership that draws heavily upon and fuels the expectations of China's future greatness.

Looking to the Future

What does this excursion into the Chinese past tell us about its future? What does an understanding of China's tortuous twentieth century lead us to expect in the next ten to twenty years? Does its previous trajectory suggest that China is a looming giant and threat? China's difficult journey onto the world stage in the twentieth century reveals that its future is open and amenable to influence. Neither China's historical legacy nor the geostrategic context nor the intellectual milieu have predetermined China's trajectory. But the past century does illuminate the factors that will shape its foreign policy as well as their uncertainties.

The first factor is the management of the Sino-American-Japanese triangle and the strategic orientations and economic policies that each of the three nations adopts. The generally good relations that have existed among the three since the early 1970s have brought unprecedented stability to the region. But it is by no means assured that this propitious situation must continue. Washington's and Tokyo's policies toward Beijing will significantly affect China's course, and China's trajectory will also influence their behavior toward Beijing. Whether all three capitals will demonstrate the wisdom to manage the triangle well is uncertain.

Second are the developments within those locales where the interests of the major powers intersect, and these are largely outside

China's control. Chinese security interests may impel a reaction that brings it in conflict with one of the other major powers. Taiwan, Korea, or the Tibetan/Himalayan/south Asian regions are the obvious places of concern. In addition, several predictable developments on China's periphery will have major but uncertain consequence for Chinese national security policy. Within the next twenty years, Korea is likely to be reunited; such an event will transform the Asian strategic context. The strategic orientation of a united and independent Korea will have a tremendous effect upon alignments throughout the region. Further, inner Asia, from Afghanistan through the central Asian republics to Mongolia and the Russian Far East, will become increasingly intense focal points of great power competition. China's interests are vitally engaged in the outcome of this competition and will consume considerable attention, greatly affecting China's relations with Russia, India, and Iran—but in what direction is unclear.

Third is the probable growth in China's state capacity, but the growth is likely to be slow and is easily subject to reversal. How China's leaders will seek to use their increased capacity is unclear. And the collapse of the Soviet economy, Japan's protracted recession, and the economic debacle in Indonesia in 1997 are reminders that economic growth should not be assumed anywhere. The ramifications of an economic crisis in China are very unpredictable.

Fourth are the uncertain foreign policy consequences of China's integration into the international economy. Potentially, foreign policy may be very constrained, especially if China's leaders decide to embark upon an even deeper integration through membership in the World Trade Organization. But China's leaders would thus also acquire a larger voice in international economic and political affairs.

Fifth is the fact that the humiliations of the disastrous nineteenth and early twentieth centuries will probably have less influence on foreign policy decisions. Leaders are coming to the fore who did not experience those humiliations, but such memories fade very slowly. The complex nationalism of the twentieth century, aggrieved yet eager to join the world, is likely to yield to a different form of nationalism whose contours are not yet evident.

The final factor, probably more significant than any of the other factors, will be the quality of China's leaders and the nature of their domestic governance. Will they eschew the temptation to unify their country through a militant or assertive nationalism? Will they embark upon a process of democratization? Will they introduce the rule of law? Will they fully join an open international economic system? What balance will they strike among the somewhat conflicting goals of stability, growth, equity, and increasing opportunities for political participation? Will they tolerate cultural diversity and draw upon the talents of their country's ethnic minorities? Will they be able to manage the tensions created by growing income disparities between urban and rural areas? Will they develop universities of international excellence and reward creativity?

Here is where the greatest uncertainty about Chinese foreign policy arises. Unless China is governed effectively and its leaders respond wisely to the daunting domestic challenges, the leaders will be unable to pursue a steady course at home or abroad. An ineffectively governed China will be a source of regional instability and will pose difficulties for the world. But if its leaders' increased resources and wider repertoire of strategies enable them to govern their own society well, they are likely to behave responsibly in international affairs. China has become a major player on the world stage, and all the major powers have a stake in its effective governance in the twenty-first century.

9

LOOKING BACK AND FORWARD

The Trajectories of the Great Powers

ROBERT A. PASTOR

THE DISTANCE TRAVELED by the great powers in the past century can be measured by the chasm that separates their goals then and now: They sought empires at the beginning of the twentieth century and markets at its end. The world was different, in part, because the goals had changed. At the turn of the last century empires were ruled by monarchs and all the great powers except the United States had empires. Markets—both private and public—respond to changes in consumer and voter preferences, to the price of a product and the performance of leader. All the powers today respond, albeit in different ways and degrees, to market forces. The two worlds are more than just a century apart. The old world was hierarchical and territorial; it was a world of conquest and spheres of influence. The new world is more pluralistic and depends on interaction between leaders and people, between firms and consumers, between great powers and other states. Markets adjust to change peacefully; they provide space for entrepreneurs at all levels—individuals, firms, non-governmental organizations, states—to grow and find their place without disrupting the system.

What accounts for the fact that the great powers booked passage on a train to an imperial destination but arrived one hundred years later at a global marketplace? "Two gigantic and insane wars," in Hoffmann's words, together with the implosion of the Soviet Union made space for a new power with a radical idea. America was the switchman that put the train onto new tracks. With startling pre-science a century ago, Woodrow Wilson wrote: "A new age has come which no man may forecast. But the past is the key to it, and the past of America lies at the center of modern history."[1]

Of the three emerging powers at the beginning of the century, Germany and Japan sought to displace the older powers, and the United States sought to overturn the entire imperial balance-of-power system. The ideas first developed by Wilson were based on such princi-ples as self-determination, the rule of law within and between nations, juridical equality of states, and collective security through interna-tional organization. These ideas were implanted in the international institutions established after World War II. The passing of the Cold War permitted those institutions to operate, almost as they had origi-nally been intended. With the end of superpower rivalry, a Liberal Epoch emerged that relied on private markets and public arenas and allowed states to define their space on the world's canvas. Not all states accept all the norms and the rules, and the system is still strug-gling to find appropriate ways to enforce the rules, but violations and uneven enforcement are true of any system. Whether the Liberal Epoch expands and endures will depend on the continued collabora-tion of the great powers; the acceptance, at least in principle, of the norms; and effective enforcement of the rules.

Confucius once told a student that his wisdom derived from his hav-ing grasped "one thread that links up the rest." The authors of this volume searched tenaciously for that "one thread" that could explain the impulses that move each country. This was no mean feat, given the abrupt and often violent changes in government and policy in sev-

LOOKING BACK AND FORWARD

eral of the countries. Most of us found the thread of continuity in a curious combination of the country's geography and its national psychology. Our point of departure, then, for identifying the trajectories of the great powers will be the headwaters where geopolitics and collective perceptions merged.

The Thread

For Germany, in the center of Europe, geography has been a "curse," and its strategic challenge was to prevent the "nightmare of coalitions." Yet the psychological need to dominate the system led Germany twice in this century to provoke the very coalition it feared.

France's geostrategic problem throughout the twentieth century was Germany combined with a generalized fear of decline. Though the twin obsessions did not change, France's policies toward Germany ran the gamut from bitter war to friendly embrace, with all the nuances one would expect from a country that wrote the dictionary of diplomacy. At critical moments when its strategic options were limited, France's internal weakness left its leaders either grabbing for the wrong option or groping for ones that did not exist. On the eve of World War I, faced with the choice of supporting or restraining Russia in the Balkans, France chose the first option and found itself careening into Europe's abyss together with the other powers. It emerged from the war exhausted and demoralized, facing an angry Germany that would soon exact its revenge by bringing the French army to its knees in a week. Since 1940, in Hoffmann's words, France "has not been a major player," but that did not mean that it did not have an important role to play. Indeed, in its pursuit of European integration France finally found the most constructive formula for dealing with its twin obsessions. Its new policy toward Europe permitted France to modernize its industrial economy while locking Germany into a tight embrace that was reinforced by the security framework of the North Atlantic Treaty Organization (NATO). By the end of the century, France had a nuclear force and economy.

England and Japan were island nations with transoceanic ambitions.
Both needed strong navies to defend their islands, to secure sea-lanes
and protect their commerce, and to venture abroad. Beyond that geographical imperative, England viewed itself as a balancer, adding its
weight against any power that tried to dominate the European continent. After two debilitating world wars, Great Britain's burden was to
adjust to decline; the nation that had ruled one-quarter of the world's
territory and people now barely maintained the unity of a kingdom
the size of Oregon. Its skilled diplomats demonstrated that an effective strategy—in this case, as the principal adviser to the Western superpower—could compensate for a lack of hard power. An economic
revival in the 1980s permitted it to project power that, according to
Lieber, was second only to that of the United States. Its ties to Europe
grew stronger, and in a world in which information is power and the
language of the world is English, the island finds itself in an advanta-
geous position.

Beyond the geopolitical need to defend its islands, Japan used its
might to try to control the Asian continent. This represented a curious but not unfamiliar reaction by a country that viewed itself as trying to accommodate a system that refused to accept it as an equal.
Pyle locates the thread of Japan's foreign policies in its pursuit of national power. At critical points in the century its specific objectives
were shaped by the current international system and the nature of its
regime. It pursued territorial power in an age of imperialism and economic power in the age of a global market system.

China and Russia shared a similar geopolitical challenge, one that
lurked on and within their borders: how to defend a huge landmass
while maintaining the unity of a diverse and dispersed people. The answer came in the form of large standing armies that could ensure domestic order and, if provoked or enticed, extend the empire into new
lands.

At the beginning of the century China was more an object of international politics than an actor. In 1900 all the great powers descended
on Beijing, ostensibly to suppress the Boxer Uprising and to secure
their legations. But each arrived with its own vision of how to shape
the once-proud Middle Kingdom. Britain, Germany, and France had

commercial designs on China; Russia had territorial objectives; Japan wanted to incorporate China into its Asia sphere; U.S. missionaries preached Christianity and its diplomats lectured on democracy. An accumulation of catastrophes—both imposed by the great powers and self-induced—kept China's leaders preoccupied with trying to unify the nation and restore its stability and self-respect. In order to secure these objectives, China allied with or made war against each great power at some point during the century. The wars left the country weaker, but the triumph of the Communist Party in 1949 offered the first chance in the century to unite the nation.

The "burden of China's past," as Oksenberg shows, was of a Middle Kingdom where foreigners performed the *koutou* before the emperor, who was convinced that China's strength derived from its isolation. This perspective reached its nadir during Mao's Great Leap Forward and the Cultural Revolution, which reduced the country to chaos. Deng Xiaoping, Mao's successor, was prepared to risk a strategy at odds with China's history but in line with the contemporary world. By lowering the country's economic barriers and opening itself to the world, China's leaders quadrupled the size of its economy. "Without question," Oksenberg concludes, "the Chinese state is stronger at century's end than it was at the beginning ... [and] its strength has grown even as China has become more integrated into international affairs in the last twenty years." China had arrived as an actor on the world stage. The "thread" that Oksenberg sees connecting China's different regimes is the shared belief in its greatness and the common goals of achieving unity, stability, and respect.

Russia had the century's wildest ride. Before World War I ended, Imperial Russia was defeated, dismembered, and then reassembled into an ideologically driven, multinational empire that reigned as one of two superpowers for forty-five years before plummeting again, this time, economically, into the Third World. None of the authors here has searched more intensely for a country's soul than Legvold. He concludes that geography is less important in explaining the three Russias' foreign policies than the authoritarian character of its regimes and the fact it never had an empire; it was one. Modern Russia therefore still lacks a national identity and structures that can con-

nect its leaders with society. Past ideologies, a history of social upheaval, continued suspicion of the West—all leave the country with a
"basic insecurity" about whether it will survive intact, making it difficult to construct a modern approach to the world. For these reasons,
the future direction of this declining state is the least clear and the
most potentially explosive.

If geography was a curse for Germany, it was a blessing for the
United States, which took its favorable geographical position as a sign
of divine recognition and manifested its appreciation with hubris. With
distant threats and uncontested power, the United States took its place
on the world stage in the twentieth century with so little experience and
so much confidence that it acted as if no other country had ever made
war for a just cause or tried to secure a permanent peace. It dreamed of
new ways to order the planet so that it conformed to U.S. ideals. But
the thread connecting a century of oscillating U.S. foreign policies is
not undiluted idealism but ambivalence, the product of a divided revolutionary vision. The United States emerged from the Spanish-American War determined to be a great power different from the others. It
liberated Cuba (though not completely) and then acquired the Philippines. After World War I it designed the League of Nations and other
international organizations to keep the peace and promote prosperity,
but did not join the League, and its support for the United Nations has
been sporadic and conditional.

Geography provides a map, and collective psychology suggests the
national impulse, but neither tell us which path a country takes or why
it changes course or climbs or falls. Germany faces the same geographical "curse" at the end of the century as it did at the beginning,
and yet it has responded with policies as different as peace is from war.
In the 1930s Germany's trade policy was based on exclusive, discrimi-
natory trading blocs; three decades later, its policy was based on a European Common Market and an open global trading system. Its
geography did not change, but its policy did.

What explains the change? The foreign policies of Germany and
Japan seem to parallel each other: the challenge to the established empires, the rise of militarism, the unconditional defeat, and then the
mutation into pacifist, democratic trading states. Pyle describes Japan-

ese determination to be recognized and succeed, and Joffe sees a similar drive in Germany. But in both cases the need to be accepted blurred into a drive to dominate, and their neighbors were forced to defend themselves and their interests. After World War II, security alliances with the United States and the change to democratic regimes allowed each to rebuild its economy and grow without threatening themselves or their neighbors. Moreover, their neighbors were reassured by their renunciation of nuclear weapons and by commitments prohibiting the offensive use of their armed forces. The security treaties reinforced the position of those in both Germany and Japan who were committed to peaceful goals and made it more difficult for those who wished to change them. Thus changes in regime and a security umbrella explain Germany's and Japan's turn toward more pacific and economically rooted foreign policies.

England and France provide a neat contrast of two powers that were compelled to adapt to diminished roles. Both resisted the anticolonialist policy of the United States, but both succumbed to its logic. Britain adjusted relatively smoothly, devolving its empire gradually and in a manner that permitted some of its colonies to emerge democratic and desirous of joining the Commonwealth. In contrast, France fought two nation-shaking, futile wars over a sixteen-year period (1946–1962) trying to retain Indochina and Algeria. France, however, was quicker than its island neighbor to recognize the tides of history pulling toward European integration. By the time Great Britain decided to join the Common Market in 1961, it was no longer welcome, at least by France. Britain did not become a member until 1973, and even then it remained a reluctant participant.

What explains the difference between the policies of England and France on decolonization and European integration? The English always seemed more attached to the "idea" of empire than to the colonies themselves, from which they kept a patrician distance. The reverse seemed to be true for France. Letting its colonies become independent was much more traumatic for the French, who imagined they had assimilated their colonies into a single grand country and culture. The differences in the two nations' policies on European integration could be explained by the different options they had. England felt it had two alternatives to European integration, the United States and the Commonwealth. France understood that its continental location denied it the option of following a separate path and, indeed, that European integration was the answer to its problems.

Oksenberg explains that China's abrupt change in external alliances was due to three factors: The principal threat has, at different times, come from different nations, Japan, the United States, and the Soviet Union. The personalities of China's four paramount twentieth-century leaders has affected the nation's course. And the nature and direction of the Chinese state has changed from a divided nationalist regime to a Communist regime, and then from one that was consumed by Cultural Revolution to one that was looking to integrate into the world political economy.

Geography, in brief, helps explain policy, but it is not destiny. It fails to explain why countries with similar geographical predicaments—England and Japan; China and Russia—pursued different policies, and it also cannot explain the many shifts in policy during the century. One such explanation is a change in regime—as occurred in Germany, Japan, Russia, and China. Second, leadership within the context of a particular regime is important for the way in which a country's interests are defined and defended. The differences between Konrad Adenauer's strategy to reassure the West and Willy Brandt's policy to reduce tensions with the Soviet Union are significant, but they pale when both policies are compared to those of Adolf Hitler. Third, policies are affected by the changes in the international system. Japan made war in Asia in part because it felt squeezed by the international system; after the war it was secured by the United States and could therefore channel its energies to economic purposes. The variations in French policy toward Germany during the century are partly explained by the different alliances, first pulling it into the two world wars and then, since the late 1940s, promoting a new relationship.

Each country, in brief, has responded to the world's challenges in different ways because they draw from different national experiences that vary with a nation's geography, collective psychology, regime, and leadership. But these national experiences are not static. William

Faulkner once wrote that "the past is never dead; it's not even past." Similarly, the national experience evolves over time as leaders pass the baton, as new generations take the place of old, as regimes change and rewrite the nation's history and its future, and as power is redistributed between countries. With the benefit of a century of hindsight, we were all impressed by the continuity—the threads connecting different leaders and regimes—and by the way in which domestic politics intersected with compelling international events to produce sharp changes in policy. Most local actors see the external events of their time as determining their policies; they fail to recognize how much decisions in different countries connect, either for good or bad.

Hindsight also reveals how much the seven powers and the world were affected by the three major wars—World Wars I and II and the Cold War. A sharp line distinguishes victory from defeat, but the line blurs as one steps back from the battlefield and views the suffering of both sides. In that regard, Charles de Gaulle did not exaggerate when he concluded, "All the countries of Europe lost the war, but only two were defeated."[2] He was speaking of Europe in World War II, but the comment could be applied to World War I, to most of Asia in World War II, and to the Communist governments in the Cold War. Given the calamitous history, it is remarkable that the seven major powers that stood astride the world at the dawn of the twentieth century are still there a century later. None of them stood still, however, and their place in line changed. The only great power to have escaped the wars' devastation was the United States, and this explains, in part, why the last power standing defined the contemporary era.

The Liberal Epoch

The great artist Georges Braque once explained that he created the space in his paintings before he drew the actors. That is a good way to think about the world. Since the seventeenth century states have defined the world's space. The great powers drew their own figures, and until recently they also drew most of the other figures on the global canvas.

In 1900 Great Britain and France held sway over immense empires, and Germany and Japan felt that their time had come. Collisions between the great powers were unavoidable. China, on its knees, was an object of Japan's ambitions; France and Russia, of Germany's. The United States was divided about whether to board the imperialist train. Not long after it annexed the Philippines, the United States recognized that it had made a mistake—colonialism was wrong not only for the colonies but also for the colonizers and the international system.

Woodrow Wilson developed this idea into a vision of a world order very different from anything in history. Wilson believed that acceptance by the international community of the principle of self-determination was not only the best alternative to colonialism, it was the answer to the primordial question of how to prevent wars between states. If all countries respected the rights of others to determine their future "under Republican forms of government," then this principle would eliminate the causes (that is, the spoils) of war while raising the costs by ennobling nationalism. From this simple idea flowed many others: Self-determination meant governments should be independent and accountable to their people; democracy within nations would increase the prospect of peaceful relations between them; countries, like people, should be juridically equal, not divided or dominated by the great powers into spheres of influence; security should be defended collectively by international organizations, not by a balance of power; markets should be open to all, not parceled out to each power; international relations should be defined by rules freely negotiated by states; and barriers to trade and investment should be dismantled.

In brief, the new world—the Liberal Epoch—would not be defined from above by emperors or dictators but from below, by citizens and consumers. Citizens would choose their leaders in a free political market within their state, and consumers would choose their products in a free economic market that would expand as technology shrank the world. In the old world, leaders ruled by divine right. In the new epoch, leaders would be compelled to respond to popular preferences or lose elections. Citizens would be shareholders in the state, just as they might own stock in a business. To stay in business, firms would need to respond to their shareholders' demand for profits and to the changing preferences of their consumers. The world of empires and monopolies would be replaced by one of democratic governments and private markets.

The U.S. vision was enunciated during World War I, institutionalized during World War II, and crowned after the Cold War. The key to the century's riddle and the U.S. vision, however, is not in the wars but in the peace that followed. The wars altered the distribution of power, but the peace sketched the space within which states and other actors worked.

The peace of 1919 was resented, and it sowed the seeds of the next war. The peace of 1945 was decisive in one sense, divisive in another, and visionary in a third. It was decisive in its success in remaking the three defeated countries—Germany, Japan, and Italy—into solid, pacific democracies. It was divisive in its failure to forge a durable consensus among the Big Three, making it impossible during the Cold War for the UN Security Council to fulfill its role. It was visionary in the establishment of international economic institutions that permitted the most rapid and widespread growth in world history and a fifteenfold expansion of world trade.

The peace after the Cold War was ambiguous, but its challenge was similar to that of the others: to integrate the losers into the winner's system, in this case, a market-oriented international system composed of mostly democratic states. The victory was not unconditional, and so the victor's ability to influence the losers was limited and varied considerably. The Eastern European governments broke from the Soviet Union and sought new economic ties with the European Union (EU) and security within NATO. The Soviet Union disappeared and was replaced by fifteen independent republics. All suffered difficult transitions, but virtually all sought a path toward democratic modernity. China is moving toward its vision of these two goals in its own way—first expediting the economic reforms it had begun in 1978, then experimenting with local elections as the Berlin Wall fell, and finally, as the century closed, quietly and reluctantly debating wider political reforms. Vietnam pursued limited economic reforms. Cuba and

North Korea, like satellites orbiting a planet that had disappeared, could not break their circular paths and have condemned themselves either to irrelevance or roguishness.

The two distinguishing characteristics of the post–Cold War peace are implicit in the awkward transitions of the former Communist governments. First, all claimed to accept the goals of democracy and free markets, and virtually all began to move towards those goals, albeit with varying speeds and degrees of commitment. Second, the great powers have all sought good relations with each other; none has viewed another as irredeemably hostile. This may be the first time in history that the major powers—both winners and losers—accepted the same goals and desired good relations. These two features establish the foundation on which the Liberal Epoch rests.

To return to Braque's canvas, the Liberal Epoch allows the actors to define the size and shape of their place. That is the vision's real power and durability: New challengers can overtake established powers by what they produce or invent; they do not have to go to war or seize their colonies to displace them. All states have a voice and a vote in the international institutions. Any of the regional powers that can sustain a high rate of economic growth over an extended period of time will accumulate the influence that will permit it to join the great powers. Whereas the funeral of Queen Victoria, with its attending royalty, symbolized the ruling cabal at the beginning of the century, Group of Seven summit meetings and the inauguration of newly elected presidents are symbols of governance at the century's end. Any state with free elections can join the democratic club, and the criterion for membership to the Group of Seven is not divine right but gross domestic product. The incentive system embedded in the Liberal Epoch encourages states to grow and be democratic, and it permits a peaceful reordering of power.

The test of a democratic system is whether it permits the people to change leaders or policies peacefully. The test of the international system is how it reacts to ascending powers. Most historians agree that the greatest danger to world peace occurs when a rising power believes the established powers are preventing it from achieving its destiny. At that point the established powers feel threatened and compelled to take a stand, resulting in a conflict in which all the powers use force for defensive reasons. One indication of the relative effectiveness of the Liberal Epoch is the way in which two of the three ascending powers in the twentieth century—Germany and Japan—responded to the Westphalian system and to the Liberal Epoch today. Both forcefully challenged the old system several times in the century. Today, Joffe writes that "the rules of the international game *favor* Germany," and Pyle concludes that "more than any other country, Japan was the beneficiary of the postwar international order." Although many believe that the existing system favors the United States, the second- and third-wealthiest powers, according to these two authorities, think the system favors them. This is the operational definition of a stable system: one in which principal challengers believe they have more at stake in preserving the system than topling it.

The Liberal Epoch has a private market and a public arena and laws for each. In the early part of the twentieth century, countries defined their economic goals in terms of acquiring gold, minerals, and natural resources; that is why colonies were so vital. Today the economic goals that are most important are jobs, markets, capital, and technology. As Joffe notes, "It is welfare, not warfare, exports rather than expansion that animate most European states."[3] To achieve these economic goals, states must pursue very different policies than they did when they sought to defeat their rivals. Instead of threatening their neighbors, they need to reassure them. Instead of dictating the terms of trade, they need to negotiate rules of access to markets that apply to everyone. Instead of hoarding gold, they need to encourage investments by assuring stability and rule of law. Instead of freezing capital, they need to avoid frightening investors. If they fail, capital flees, the budget is out of balance, unemployment grows, and leaders are reminded of the first law of economics: People or countries that live beyond their means will have to pay for their excesses by reducing their consumption and their independence.

James Carville, Bill Clinton's campaign manager in 1992, learned this law quickly in the White House when some of his expensive proposals were rejected by those responsible for maintaining Wall Street's confidence. "I used to think that, if there was reincarnation, I wanted to come back as the president or the pope," Carville quipped. "But now I want to be the bond market: you can intimidate everybody."[4] This is what is meant by the discipline of the market.

A simple law also governs the public arena: Leaders who lose touch with the needs and aspirations of their people will be replaced. Perhaps the biggest difference between the dawn and the dusk of the twentieth century is the degree to which the goals of states are now defined by these two interlocking public and private markets and their dual systems of accountability.

The Liberal Epoch is an open, self-correcting system that replicates several characteristics of a pluralist democracy at an international level. A pluralistic system puts a premium on process as distinguished from goals, which are shared and therefore not debated. Everyone wants prosperity and peace; the hard questions are "how" questions: how to achieve these shared goals? There are no magic answers to the "how" questions, and there are many views. In a pluralistic system, decisions are made both within states and among them on the basis of elections and democratic debate. The outcome is usually a compromise among contending interests. The process is often messy, but by trying to draw together the various interests and perspectives, it instills civility in a body politic. This is evident, however, only when one compares it to a system in which rulers are selected by divine right or by force. The latter regimes appear the most stable, particularly at moments when authority is unquestioned, but they are the most brittle when new actors demand seats at the table. That is the strength of the Liberal Epoch because its canvas allows new actors to emerge in both the private sector and civil society and to channel their influence at each level of governance—local, national, and international. It has made possible the flourishing of a transnational society in which the multinational enterprises (MNEs) in the private market and the nongovernmental organizations (NGOs) in the public arena of one nation can link arms with their counterparts in other countries and can thus challenge states to alter their policies or make good on their promises.

NGOs are often entrepreneurs in the public arena. Like MNEs in the private sector, NGOs seek niche issues that have been neglected (for example, the banning of landmines) or a value that is not being advanced (for example, the rights of indigenous peoples) and they mobilize groups and other NGOs to lobby governments to address the problem (for example, to approve a convention on biodiversity or protecting children's rights). NGOs have spread beyond their activities in economic development and human rights to work in such areas as democratization and disarmament, areas that were long believed to be the sole prerogative of states.

U.S.-based NGOs transpose the adversary relationship that interest groups have with the U.S. government onto the international landscape. Coalitions of NGOs, led by Americans, sought approval of the Landmines Treaty and the International Criminal Court by concentrating their criticism against the United States. By questioning the authority of the superpower, U.S.-based NGOs establish their credentials as autonomous entities and encourage foreign groups to do what they do, that is, to hold their governments accountable. Their challenge also refutes those who charge that U.S.-based NGOs are extensions or tools of U.S. power.

There are those who believe that state power and sovereignty have diminished as a result of the spread of these NGOs, the increasing authority of intergovernmental organizations (IGOs), and the pressing nature of globalization. Jessica Matthews saw a "power shift": "The steady concentration of power in the hands of states that began in 1648 with the Peace of Westphalia is over."[5] Susan Strange argued that globalization has fundamentally changed the nature of production and the source of finance and has begun to change beliefs, perceptions, ideas, and tastes. These forces and ideas and the international institutions established to manage them have eroded the traditional attributes of sovereignty and accountability and have allowed a shift in power from states to firms.[6]

These trends toward greater influence by the market and transnational groups are real, but their effect on the states' role as the principal actors in the international system is debatable and, we believe, exaggerated. "After all," as Daniel Yergin and Joseph Stanislaw remind us in their book on the battle between government and the marketplace in the twentieth century, "there is no market without governement to define the rules and the context. The state creates and maintains the parameters within which the market operates."[7]

States are increasingly influenced by NGOs and constrained by international regimes, but states decide the rules that IGOs enforce, and the great powers retain a veto on the most important decisions related to the use of force. Beyond security issues, IGOs serve multiple purposes, from regulating the world economy and environment to deflecting criticism. When the International Monetary Fund (IMF) compels a government to tighten its fiscal belt, the U.S. secretary of the treasury breathes a sigh of relief that it is the IMF managing director who is the target of discontent (although not all foreign governments are impressed by the distance between the two institutions).

The great powers do not exercise the same kind of control over the international system today as they did 100 years ago, when monarchs, for the most part, ruled centralized empires. Forty-six nations signed the UN Treaty in July 1945; the organization today includes 185 countries. Power is not as concentrated as it was then, but it is also not as diffuse as one might expect from a quadrupling in the number of states. In 1946 the top four powers in the world accounted for roughly three-quarters of the world's domestic product; fifty years later the top seven accounted for 65 percent. In 1950 the top five powers accounted for 82 percent of the world's military spending; in 1993 seven accounted for nearly 70 percent.[8]

The influence that the great powers can wield depends on the particular institution and decision. Weighted voting in most economic institutions gives the great powers more influence than other states, but not enough to direct the institutions. The Group of Seven summit meetings offer the great powers (except China and only sometimes including Russia) an opportunity to negotiate common responses to current problems. In the World Trade Organization (WTO), the United States and the European powers have comparable influence in determining whether a country like China has satisfied the conditions for entry, but the dispute-settlement mechanism is autonomous and frequently makes judgments against one or more of the great powers. In the UN Security Council, each of the permanent five members has the power to veto decisions.

Whether the great powers have more or less power today than they did in 1900 is not easy to determine because power is more difficult to measure. But there is no question that the great powers continue to exert substantial influence over the full range of issues on the contemporary agenda, and sometimes their influence is greatest when it is least recognized. For example, since 1986 the total amount of capital sloshing around the financial markets of the world increased eightfold, to $1.5 trillion a day. Many writers attributed this surge in globalization to market forces. This confuses cause and effect. The dramatic increase in foreign investment is the result of concerted efforts by U.S. and other Western governments to persuade developing and former Communist governments to liberalize their financial markets. When the state barriers were dismantled, so much capital began to flow that states felt rich or became poor almost overnight.[9]

One way to think about the distinctiveness of the U.S.-designed Liberal Epoch is to contrast it with the painting of the world that would have been drawn by Nazi Germany or Soviet Russia. Each power had a global vision based on one of the three big ideas of the twentieth century—Nazi Germany on fascism and monopoly capitalism, Soviet Russia on communism and state capitalism, and the United States on democracy and private enterprise.[10] Each idea has weight and explains part of the reason for the influence of each of the three states. But the state's power explains the global success of the idea rather than the other way around. If Germany had prevailed in World War II or the Soviet Union in the Cold War, the world today would be nasty and brutish. That was George Orwell's nightmare. Instead, the United States prevailed, and the world awoke to Woodrow Wilson's dream.

The Twenty-First Century: Trajectories, Threats, and Opportunities

Before trying to peer into the future we should recall the unpredictability of recent history. In the late 1980s the conventional wisdom held that the two superpowers would continue their struggle into the next century. Then, overburdened by excessive defense spending, the two superpowers would be overtaken by Japan. Some even thought the scenario had already occurred. "The Cold War is over," proclaimed the Asian scholar Chalmers Johnson, "and Japan won."[11] But suddenly the Japanese "bullet train" stalled, and throughout the 1990s it had trouble restarting. The Soviet Union imploded, and Russia sank so low that by 1996 its economy was overtaken by those of Brazil and India. Two years later Japan's stock market suffered a one-day drop in which it lost more value than the Russian economy produced that year. Although many believed that a country's economic growth was harmed when it spent too much on defense, U.S. military spending was roughly equal to the total spent by the other six powers in the mid-1990s, and yet its economy outdistanced those of its competitors.[12] So much for the conventional wisdom. The only safe prediction is that when the economy of a great power grows faster than the others, people will look to it as a model. The three great capitalistic economies offer different prototypes for those searching for the holy grail of development. The United States' model is the most laissez-faire; Japan's, the most collusive between government and business; and Germany's, the most concerned about social welfare.

The Liberal Epoch is a unique moment in history, both in terms of the world's economic and political openness and the degree of cooperation among the great powers. The contemporary world is closer to Wilson's vision than it is to the world that he tried to convert, but we should be under no illusion that his dream is today's reality. There are still wars, tyrants, and protectionism, and some countries still covet their neighbors' lands. Moreover, Wilson's core idea of self-determination, like many worthy goals, has been tarnished by its evil twin, "ethnic cleansing," the assertion of one group's identity by denying another's. Nonetheless, states pursue different ends today than they did 100 years ago. A century ago states used force to acquire territory and resources; today that's the exception. And wars have changed as well. In the first five years after the Cold War ended in 1989, two scholars identified ninety-six conflicts, but only five were between two internationally recognized states. The rest were within states.[13] Each state maintains an army to defend its security, but it pursues economic goals as much and, in some ways and cases, more than before.

Whether the Liberal Epoch will endure, deepen, and expand will depend in part on the direction U.S. leadership takes, on the trajectories of the other great powers, and on the nature of tomorrow's challenges and opportunities.

National Trajectories

France and Great Britain reflect a century of imperial decline and national rejuvenation. France, according to Hoffmann, is focused on fostering European integration. If it succeeds, Europe's influence as a model and center of power could be restored. Great Britain, as Lieber sees it, will continue to collaborate closely with the United States, but it also leans toward greater involvement in Europe. Germany, according to Joffe, is more comfortable and less threatened in its neighborhood than it has ever been. Because it has benefited so much from the European Union, it has a stake in resolving the seemingly endless disputes that stem from trying to deepen integration and extend it. If Eastern Europe could be brought smoothly into the European Union, there would be less need to reassure those countries or to antagonize Russia by enlarging NATO any further.

One theme that weaves its way through the stories of these three European nations, as well as the others', is the degree to which each is still attached to its own interest, even as it surrenders large chunks of its decisionmaking to EU institutions. In the case of Germany, Joffe acknowledges the historical impulse to "overreach ... [to] always try to dominate the system." The stronger Germany has become, the more it has frightened its neighbors, causing them to coalesce into the "nightmare of coalitions." Joffe believes that even if a new German generation is more assertive, the old dynamic is unlikely to recur because Germans have learned history's lessons, and the country is flourishing under the "wondrous ... permissive" Liberal Epoch. Moreover, three sets of constraints—democracy, European integration, and the U.S. security treaty—will keep it from succumbing to a temptation to dominate.

Japan's history reflects a paradoxical combination of pursuing power and accommodating it. Since World War II, the U.S. security treaty has freed Japan to concentrate on economic goals. But the economic crisis of the 1990s and the end of the Cold War have left it bewildered. Pyle believes that Japan will soon break loose of its immobility "with a speed that will surprise." Less clear is its direction.

When asked to project each country's policy into the twenty-first century, the authors paused and asked what they should assume about U.S. foreign policy because it was central to other countries' calculations. Joffe and Pyle, in particular, were aware not only of the constructive roles Germany and Japan have played since World War II but also of the destructive impulses that have been restrained. The subterranean bedrock that has kept Europe and Asia stable has been the U.S. security treaty with both countries and the renunciation by Germany and Japan of nuclear weapons and of an offensive military posture.

If the United States closed its military bases in Japan, South Korea, and Europe, the habits learned during the past fifty years might survive the immediate tectonic shift, but the consensus among the authors of this book was that the U.S. withdrawal would eventually be profoundly destabilizing. In Europe, the relationship between France and Germany could become strained, and Eastern Europe would feel more vulnerable from both the east and the west. If the United States were to withdraw its troops from Japan and South Korea, the Japanese would probably rearm, leading to an arms race with China. In brief, what seems to be a stable new world of economic interdependence might look very different if one element—a security guarantee—were withdrawn, and no other confidence-building, compensatory structure replaced it. It is hard to envision a post-NATO security arrangement in Europe at this time, but it would have to include a combination of disarmament and a new structure that would credibly assure the independence of central Europe. In Asia the powers would have to overcome a mountain of suspicion before discussing the parameters of a quadrilateral security guarantee involving the United States, Japan, China, and a united Korea.

The two countries whose future trajectories are hardest to predict are, of course, China and Russia. President Bill Clinton posed the problem diplomatically: "How Russia and China define their own greatness will have a lot to do with how the twenty-first century comes out."[14] The central questions facing both countries are whether they will remain united, and whether and how long it will take them to complete their transitions to democratic market economies.

Oksenberg describes a China whose rapid growth is creating a need to find a new equilibrium between an insular tradition and its new commitment to the modern world. The challenge of guiding 1.2 billion people into the modern era would be formidable even if the country were not surrounded by such regional flash points as North Korea, Taiwan, India-Pakistan, and central Asia. Although some in the United States fear that continued economic success could make China a threat to U.S. interests in the region, Oksenberg's analysis suggests that the far greater threat stems from economic recession or political instability. Instability within China could generate an authoritarian and nationalist response and exacerbate its relations with its neighbors. Conversely, border crises could unsettle the delicate balance within the country.

China's future, however, seems almost crystalline compared to Russia's, whose twenty-first-century foreign policy depends on what kind of nation-state emerges and how it chooses to relate to the other former states of the Soviet Union. Legvold finds few people from the old Soviet Union who believe it could be restored, fewer who will relinquish the idea of a restored Soviet Union, and fewest of all who are interested in reassuring the new states that Russia wants to build constructive relations with them. With regard to future scenarios, Legvold thinks the chances that Russia will emerge as a liberal democracy are slim. He thinks the chances are considerable that it will emerge as a "modern and well-integrated" nation with some democratic features. It is plausible that it could become an "alienated and combative" state with "a grudge looking for ways to inflict damage on U.S. interests"; and finally, the least likely but the most frightening scenario is that Russia emerges as a "broken and collapsed" country that becomes the object of great power competition. "Russia," Legvold concludes, "has every incentive to become a part of this [modern, market-oriented, democratic] world," but it might also suffer a systemic breakdown. Whatever happens, however, "will in considerable measure determine the kind of international order that we get."

What will the United States do? In the short and medium terms, the United States is committed to keeping its armed forces in both the European and Asian theaters and in playing a leadership role in the world, with some caveats and reservations. If the United States were asked to withdraw its armed forces, which is unlikely but not impossible, it would do so, but until the transitions in Russia and China are clearer a departure of U.S. forces would create more problems than it would resolve. The need for broader leadership by the United States was acknowledged by none other than Hubert Vedrine, the French foreign minister. Asked to comment on the sex scandal that led to President Bill Clinton's impeachment, Vedrine said, "With 25 regional conflicts involving 40 countries, states in the process of disintegration, a spreading financial crisis, what we need is strong leadership in all our countries, starting with the United States."[15] The comment is telling because it's so unexpected from a leader of a country that has been the most critical of U.S. leadership.

What does history suggest for the U.S. trajectory? It will be erratic: often unilateral, niggardly, and small-minded in its support for its international institutional offspring; occasionally organizing its allies in an effective approach to a problem but mostly focusing on its own social and economic concerns and the external dimension of these concerns. The foreign policy agenda pursued by the United States thus far in the Liberal Epoch is closely tied to such domestic issues as drugs, immigration, corruption, crime, trade, and jobs, and it is driven by domestic groups, either ethnic (Cuban, Jewish, Eastern European) or issue-based (abortion, religious persecution, human rights). Divided government—with presidents and Congresses of different parties—reinforces the incoherence of the policy, particularly as the two political parties move further apart in their constituent bases and their philosophies. Despite these centrifugal pressures and, indeed, perhaps because of the way they interact, U.S. foreign policy will continue to pursue Wilsonian goals of a world based on democracy and collective security. Public opinion surveys consistently reflect this perspective. The American public wants their government to concentrate on domestic issues because they feel relatively secure from external dangers, and they understand that U.S. power requires solving domestic prob-

lems, invigorating the economy, and maintaining the attractiveness of
the U.S. model. The public believes that the United States should
play an active role in the world, but in the post–Cold War era more
than before, we ought to seek partnerships and not confront problems
unilaterally.[16]

An activist America, however, will encounter problems. The sheer
power of the United States carries within it the seeds of its own opposition, not just from those governments, like Yugoslavia, Libya, Iraq,
or Cuba, with which the United States is at war or virtually at war.
Some allied or friendly governments will disagree with particular policies, will resent unilateral U.S. "police" actions, or will want to carve
out some space for their own leadership. France, in particular, wants
the EU to serve as a balance to U.S. power. That is one reason that
Samuel Huntington has argued that the world is moving toward a
"uni-multipolar" world, that is, one in which the United States needs
to approach problems with "some combination of other major states."
The United States retains veto power on some actions, but if it acts
unilaterally, it risks stimulating new alliances against it.[17] The Liberal
Epoch not only provides space for criticizing authority, it encourages
it. This is the strength of the system because by encouraging criticism,
it defuses its destructiveness, provided that the great powers, especially the United States, respond in an appropriate fashion. Some criticism of the superpower is inevitable. Lord Carrington once advised
the United States that the burdens of power need to be borne: "You're
always in a hiding to nowhere if you're the big boy in town. You simply can't in that position hope for your reward on earth. The British
had a lot of practice at that."[18]

On the eve of World War I, Norman Angell, in a widely read book,
predicted that interdependence had advanced so far that war was inconceivable.[19] Even in the middle of World War II, Wendell Willkie,
the 1940 Republican presidential candidate, flew around the world and
returned deeply impressed at how "the world has become small and
completely interdependent."[20] This argument has been heard again in
the post–Cold War era, but in a survey of world history Donald Kagan
dismisses it: "This is not the first time that new conditions and ideas
have led many to believe that a unique prospect of lasting peace was at

hand, and yet over the past two centuries the only thing more common than predictions about the end of war has been war itself."[21]

Despite the profound changes in the world during this century, our review of the trajectories of the great powers suggests that Kagan's point remains potent. Conflicts cannot be ruled out, although nuclear weapons will remain an important deterrent to conflict among the great powers. Still, Russia and China are on edge; they seem as likely to totter toward a nationalistic authoritarianism as to complete their transitions to modern democratic polities, and there are many potential security problems on their borders. Deepening ties of economic interdependence raise the costs of conflicts, but they do not preclude them. Democratic restraints can inhibit new conflicts, but two of the seven great powers are not consolidated democracies.

Since the Cold War's end, the great powers have collaborated more than at any other time in the century, but this trend toward cooperation was impeded by NATO's enlargement and suffered a serious setback because of the conflict in Kosovo. The foreign dimension of the Kosovo conflict was not delimited by religion but by states, as this book suggests, and the defining crevice was between democratic and undemocratic states. To understand the reaction by the great powers to the crisis, one needs to be cognizant of both the democratic divide and the impulses and interests that drive each state—in short, the national trajectories. To Europe, the United States, and Japan, the cause of the crisis was Serbia's genocidal suppression of ethnic Albanians in Kosovo. The NATO countries differed as to whether ground troops were necessary or desirable, but they agreed that the international community needed to respond strongly to Serbian behavior.

The view in Russia and China was quite different; both opposed the use of force by the international community. They proposed a resolution in the UN Security Council condemning NATO's air war. After an unprecedented public debate among the great powers, the council rejected the resolution by a vote of 12 to 3. Nonetheless, because Russia and China could veto a UN peace-keeping force, the NATO countries did not seek such authorization.[22]

What led Russia and China to take an opposing approach? Both saw the events through the prism of their own experience, and information was filtered to reinforce images that were different from those seen in the West. Russians and Chinese learned about the "terrorism" of the Kosovo Liberation Army and the Serbian victims of NATO bombing, while NATO governments focused on the victims of Serbian aggression. Russia and China are traversing dangerous political, economic, and ethnic transitions, and both fear that if the UN or NATO could intervene legitimately in Yugoslavia, they could do so in Russia and China too. Moreover, the Russians have a long history of sympathy with the Serbs, and the Chinese government viewed the (accidental) bombing by NATO of its embassy as a deliberate act aimed to humiliate or intimidate it. All of this led to a dangerously divergent perception between NATO and China and Russia, a division that was reminiscent of the Cold War but actually had older and newer causes.

The tragedy in Kosovo reflects the century's journey. Globalization or, in this case, the desire to become part of Europe, will not stop seemingly senseless and destructive conflicts. But Kosovo was a new kind of war. "The first war," in the words of President Vaclev Havel of the Czech Republic, "that has not been waged in the name of national interests, but rather in the name of principles and values. Kosovo has no oilfields to be coveted; no member nation in the alliance has any territorial demands . . . [They are] fighting out of concern for the fate of others."[23] Both the cause of the conflict—the violent suppression of the rights of an ethnic group—and the response of the international community—are two sides of a new century's conflicts.

Challenges and Opportunities

A new world has not emerged, but the outlines of one, a Liberal Epoch, are becoming visible. Many architects and builders are constructing it piece by piece without a master plan. They are guided by both humanitarian and realistic instincts, shards of a collective memory, and the need to respond to awful events. Sometimes, there is a feeling of disorder or even chaos, but what is more remarkable is that the project has any coherence at all, and that is partly because the new epoch rests on the firm foundation of international norms. These have been articulated in the UN Charter, the Universal Declaration of Human Rights, and the International Covenants. They define universal values.

Four pillars, still unfinished, will hold up the Liberal Epoch. The first pillar is international law—treaties, conventions, and rules that embody the universal norms. The body of international law is expanding rapidly in international commerce, finance, and intellectual property rights, but also in human rights (of gender, minorities, children, labor, refugees), environmental rights, democratization, and disarmament. The second pillar is composed of international courts, tribunals, or panels that try to judge violations of the laws or settle disputes. The strongest panels are at the World Trade Organization, but the world is experimenting with new venues for trying international crimes, whether torture by a former Chilean dictator or genocide by a sitting Yugoslavian president.

The third pillar relies on monitoring and incentives to encourage compliance, and the fourth pillar is punishment for violating the rules. These two pillars of enforcement are essential for maintaining a Liberal Epoch, but they remain weak.

NGOs have worked with small and middle powers, like Canada and Norway, as rule-makers and monitors. They have provided expertise and popular support to transform norms into treaties and to construct new institutions to judge behavior or settle disputes. They monitor state actions and helped victims petition the courts and international organizations for redress or to correct an injustice.

Effective and legitimate enforcement requires a decision by the UN Security Council and thus the approval or acquiescence of the great powers. The weakness of the last two pillars stems from the absence of political will and a unifying vision among the great powers. Most of the contemporary challenges to the international system emerge from within failed states or by the actions of "rogue" states. Either because they lack the capacity or are democracies, the great powers are reluctant to risk their peoples's lives in conflicts where their direct security interests are not threatened. That explains why the international community has not found a successful formula for coping with such problems. But the great powers are the gatekeepers to the UN Security council, and the success of the Liberal Epoch rests ultimately on their power.

When power is exercised in ways that the system and the major states view as legitimate, such as in the Persian Gulf War, then existing institutions—notably the United Nations—become stronger. When the great powers use force for self-interested purposes that other states do not consider legitimate, international institutions are diminished and the fragile collective security system, such as it exists, is eroded. Kofi Annan, the secretary-general of the United Nations, put this point most sharply when he wrote that the United Nations "will have the potential to advance the interests of all the states only so long as it does not appear to serve the narrow interests of any one state or group of states."[24] The United Nations will be tested periodically by the tyrants of pariah regimes. The more credible its threat the less likely that force will be needed to compel compliance with UN resolutions, but assembling a coalition time and again to meet the threats of incorrigible tyrants is taxing, in all senses of that word.

These are all reasons why the United States must pursue a new and different kind of leadership if the Liberal Epoch is to succeed. Unilateral U.S. imposition of sanctions combined with its unwillingness to contribute or fulfill its obligations to international organizations weakens the very system it has established. Washington must lead by example and take action with multilateral authority.

Beyond the steps necessary to establish, manage, and sustain a liberal system, our picture of the future depends on how a number of challenges are addressed. The most important and dangerous set of problems arises among the great powers. World war can only occur if one or more of these powers fight another. Whether this is likely depends, to a great degree, on whether the transitions in China and Russia toward market democracies succeed and whether the other great powers can forge partnerships with these two governments. *There is no challenge more important than this one!*

The industrialized democracies must open space on the international landscape for Russia and China to play important roles; if either feels excluded or cornered, the authoritarians in both states will be stengthened and the prospect for successful transitions would be diminished.

World war is not inevitable if the transitions fail and one or two countries revert to an authoritarian mode, but cooperation and an effective United Nations collective security system is unlikely. World peace is not assured if the transitions succeed, but the prospects for cooperation on dealing with global security problems are much improved.

Assuming that Russia and China make the transition, and the great powers devise a new system of collaboration, then they will face a host of pressing security issues, including proliferation of weapons of mass destruction; instability in the Caspian area (the "Eurasian Balkans" of Central Asia, as Zbigniew Brzezinski called them in a provocative analysis)[25]; revolutionary fundamentalism in the Middle East; rivalries between India and Pakistan, China and India, Iran and Iraq; North Korea; ethnic conflicts; and rogue and failed states. "Regional powers" may have more influence in their areas than do the great powers. Such powers include India, Nigeria, South Africa, Indonesia, Brazil, and Iran, and the states in Europe, Asia, and the Americas that are stable democracies but do not have the reach of the great powers. Constructive roles need to be found for these countries, and they should be encouraged to build "security communities,"[26] where states are assured that their differences will be settled short of war.

A second challenge concerns the growing gap between rich and poor countries. The World Bank and regional development banks have been the principal instruments for promoting development and narrowing the widening gap between rich and poor, and these institutions should continue to focus on the poorest countries. While an increasing proportion of the world's population is born in the poorest countries, an increasing share of the world's wealth is produced and consumed in the European Union, Japan, and the three NAFTA countries.

The question is whether these three pan-regions can be enlarged in a manner that integrates poorer countries. Only the European Union has had a concerted "regional" strategy for raising the living standards of the poorer countries and regions in its community. The transfer of resources to the four poorest countries ranges from roughly 2–4 percent of the gross domestic product of the countries—a not insignificant sum—and there is evidence that the policies have narrowed the disparities in income.[27] NAFTA lacks such a policy, but should consider drawing some lessons from the European experience.

Each pan-region should not be a fortress that excludes other governments or products; rather, each should be a laboratory, experimenting with ideas and rules that can subsequently be applied globally. But a critical problem is to prevent marginalization of those countries, especially in Africa, that are outside each region.

The third challenge—after the transitions in Russia and China and the enlargement of the three pan-regions—is to develop more effective means for global governance. The UN Security Council needs to be expanded to include Japan, Germany, and several regional powers. At the same time, the voting process needs to be changed; if each of these countries has a veto, the Security Council will return to an earlier era of paralysis. Single-country vetoes should expire (except in a few cases in which a permanent member is directly engaged); each of the permanent members should find partners if they want to stop UN actions. The European Union faced a similar problem and decided, in 1986, to discard the unanimity rule in order to accelerate integration.

This question of decision making is part and parcel of the pivotal issue of how much control states should delegate to international organizations and how much should they retain. Yogi Berra is reported to have once said that "when you reach a crossroads, you should take it!" At the crossroads between unilateralism and collective action, the United States has hesitated, torn by advocates of each option. However, progress towards the goals identified by Wilson and FDR is not possible without unequivocal U.S. leadership.

*   *   *

In perusing the daily headlines, one cannot help but think that nothing has changed. Massacres in Kosovo, ethnic holocaust in Rwanda/Burundi, the intransigence of an Iraqi dictator, population pressures in South Asia, AIDS in Africa—we've seen all of this before, albeit in different terrain.

There are threads that connect our contemporary problems to all that has gone before, but there are also new elements to our current predicaments that could not have been conceived, let alone predicted, even a few days before they occurred. We cannot escape our history, and although we seem to come close, we never quite repeat it either.

The overpowering lesson of the twentieth century is that leaders can take us down a path that appeals either to mankind's basest instincts or to its highest values. Institutions and rules can make it more difficult to take the first path and easier to take the second. To paraphrase Winston Churchill, we make the institutions, and then they make us. Although international institutions and norms can constrain countries' leaders, there is no question but that national institutions provide the most potent restraints and incentives on their behavior. Domestic and international constraints relate to each other sometimes in counterintuitive ways. It is generally believed that a country with great influence internationally will be more independent domestically, but China's recent growth suggests that these two factors might be inversely related. China's opening to the world made it more dependent, but also stronger. The fear of diminished sovereignty might simply miss the point that the traditional definition is obsolete. Joffe finds the same paradox in Germany's recent history. Germany has been more successful and influential abroad when it has accepted the constraints imposed by its neighbors than when it tried to go it alone.

In this decentralized Liberal Epoch, the great powers are important not because they are trying to direct traffic but because they provide a stable and secure framework within which others can drive their ships of state. When a financial crisis occurs, as it did in the summer of 1997, or when a security or humanitarian problem emerges, great powers can lend their weight to stabilize the currency or restrain the warring factions. This does not mean they can necessarily solve the problem, but international solutions are not possible without their active involvement.

No single power has ever exercised the kind of influence in the world that the United States does at the end of the century. The source of its power is both its national assets and the international system that it helped establish. That system, that space on the canvas of the world, is the Liberal Epoch in which living standards are improved and states and other actors can define their own place in the sun. Whether it survives and succeeds will depend on several factors. First, the United States must maintain a security presence in Europe and Asia, and it must be prepared to use force at key moments on behalf of international norms, not just on behalf of its own interests. Second, the survival of the Liberal Epoch will depend on whether Russia and China make the transition to some semblance of a democratic, market economy and are prepared to approach global issues in a collaborative way with the other powers. This, in turn, requires that the other powers provide room for Russia and China to play constructive roles in addressing international issues. Third, new forms of partnerships need to be developed among the great powers. The European Union should be prepared to shoulder the burden of primary responsibility in the Balkans and Eastern Europe, and Japan needs to join with the United States and China to provide a bedrock of security in East Asia. If the great powers seek good relations with each other, and if their goals and values can converge, the twenty-first century will be markedly different from the past, and the entire world would benefit.

States have ruled throughout the twentieth century and will do so in the twenty-first, but their goals have changed. Their roles in the economy will evolve as they seek ways to integrate with others without losing full national control. Their primacy in the area of foreign policy will remain unchallenged. The great powers will lead but not dominate the institutions that will set the rules for the twenty-first century. If they can sustain the Liberal Epoch, the scope for world conflict will narrow and the perimeter of a global civilization can be extended.

NOTES

Chapter 1: The Great Powers

1. The gross product of all European governments in 1900 has been estimated by Paul Bairoch at $188 billion (in 1960 U.S. dollars); see Paul Bairoch, "Europe's Gross National Product: 1800–1975," *Journal of European Economic History* 5 (July 1976): 281. General Motors had revenues of $178 billion in 1997; see Keith Bradsher, "Forget Microsoft: GM Is Still the Biggest Kid on the Block," *New York Times*, July 26, 1998, E4.

2. Kenichi Ohmae, *The End of the Nation State: How Capital, Corporations, and Communications Are Reshaping Global Markets* (New York: Free Press, 1995), viii.

3. Samuel P. Huntington, *The Clash of Civilizations and the Remaking of World Order* (New York: Simon and Schuster, 1996). At one point Huntington refers to 7 or 8 major civilizations (21), but his map (26–27) shows nine. This in itself should suggest that the dividing lines may not be as clear as one would expect of the most significant world divisions.

4. For President George Bush's description of this new world order, see his addresses to Joint Sessions of Congress before and after the Gulf War. The first, on September 11, 1990, was reprinted in *Foreign Policy Bulletin*, November-December 1990; the second was reprinted in the *New York Times*, March 7, 1991.

5. For an instructive essay on the growing "incongruence" between the state system and global activities and on ideas for ways to respond, see Seyom Brown, *New Forces, Old Forces, and the Future of World Politics* (New York: HarperCollins, 1995).

6. The literature on this thesis is vast, but the reader could begin with the following: Michael W. Doyle, "Liberalism and World Politics," *American Political Science Review* 80, no. 4 (December 1986): 1151–1169; Bruce Russett, *Grasping the Democratic Peace: Principles for a Post–Cold War World* (Princeton: Princeton University Press, 1993); James Lee Ray, *Democracy and International Conflict: An Evaluation of the Democratic Peace Proposition* (Columbia: University of South Carolina Press, 1995).

7. Robert A. Pastor, "The North American Free Trade Agreement: Hemispheric and Geopolitical Implications," *The International Executive* 36, no. 1 (January-February 1994): 3–31.

8. Organization for Economic Cooperation and Development, *The World in 2020: Towards a New Global Age* (Paris: OECD, 1997), 29. World exports as a percentage of world product increased from about 7 percent in 1950 to 21 percent in 1995. World

Bank, *World Develomment Report, 1998/1999* (Washington, D.C.: Oxford University Press, 1999), p. 23.

9. Raymond Vernon, *In the Hurricane's Eye: The Troubled Prospects of Multinational Enterprises* (Cambridge, Mass.: Harvard University Press, 1998).

10. For the most insightful exploration of the many-sided effects of globalization, see Thomas J. Friedman, *The Lexus and the Olive Branch: Understanding Globalization* (New York: Farrar, Straus, Giroux, 1999).

11. Raymond Vernon, *Sovereignty at Bay: The Multinational Spread of U.S. Enterprises* (New York: Basic Books, 1971), 249.

12. World Bank, *World Development Report, 1997: The State in a Changing World* (New York: Oxford University Press, 1997), 2, 22–23.

13. Vernon, *In the Hurricane's Eye.*

14. See Benjamin R. Barber, *Jihad Versus McWorld: How Globalism and Tribalism Are Reshaping the World* (New York: Ballantine Books, 1996). To see how these forces interact within North America, see Robert A. Pastor and Rafael Fernandez de Castro, eds., *The Controversial Pivot: U.S. Congress and North America* (Washington, D.C.: Brookings Institution Press, 1998), chapters 1, 9.

15. For a discussion of the prospects of a stronger new world order after the end of the Cold War, see John Gerard Ruggie, "Third Try at World Order? America and Multilateralism After the Cold War," *Political Science Quarterly* 109 (Fall 1994): 553–570.

16. Barbara Crosette, "The World Expected Peace. It Found a New Brutality," *New York Times*, January 24, 1999, IV, 1.

17. Edward D. Mansfield and Jack Snyder, "Democratization and the Danger of War," *International Security* 20, no. 1 (Summer 1995): 5–38. This article is reprinted, together with thirteen others, in *Debating the Democratic Peace*, ed. Michael E. Brown, Sean M. Lynn-Jones, and Steven Miller (Cambridge: MIT Press, 1996).

18. Spencer R. Weart, *Never at War: Why Democracies Will Not Fight One Another* (New Haven: Yale University Press, 1998).

19. Bruce Russett, John R. Oneal, and David R. Davis, "The Third Leg of the Kantian Tripod for Peace: International Organizations and Militarized Disputes, 1950–85," *International Organization* 52, no. 3 (Summer 1998): 441–467.

20. See Robert A. Pastor, "The Centrality of Elections: A Global Review," *New Perspectives Quarterly* 13, no. 4 (Fall 1996). The number of democratic countries—117—is from Freedom House Survey Team, *Freedom in the World: The Annual Survey of Political Rights and Civil Liberties, 1997–98* (New York: Freedom House, 1998), pp. 607–608.

21. Huntington, *The Clash of Civilizations*, 21.

22. Thomas L. Friedman, "A Manifesto for the Fast World," *New York Times Magazine*, March 28, 1999, 61.

23. World Bank, *World Development Indicators, 1998* (Washington, D.C.: World Bank, 1998), 188–203, 326–329.

24. See Martha Finnemore, *National Interests in International Society* (Ithaca: Cornell University Press, 1996).

25. Robert O. Keohane and Joseph S. Nye Jr., "Power and Interdependence in the Information Age," *Foreign Affairs* 77, no. 5 (September–October 1998): 82.

26. Joseph S. Nye Jr., *Bound to Lead: The Changing Nature of American Power* (New York: Basic Books, 1990), 25.

27. Paul Kennedy, *The Rise and Fall of the Great Powers: Economic Change and Military Conflict from 1500 to 2000* (New York: Vintage Books, 1989).

28. Al Gore, "Information Technology for the Twenty-First Century," White House press release, January 24, 1999, 1.

29. Richard Rosecrance, "The Rise of the Virtual State," *Foreign Affairs* 75, no. 4 (July-August 1996): 45–61. See also Keohane and Nye, "Power and Interdependence in the Information Age."

30. Hans Morgenthau's definition of power was comprehensive, including geography, natural resources, industrial capacity, military preparedness, population, national character, national morale, the quality of diplomacy, and the quality of government; see Hans J. Morgenthau, *Politics Among Nations* (New York: Knopf, 1978), 117–154.

31. Robert A. Dahl, *Who Governs? Democracy and Power in an American City* (New Haven: Yale University Press, 1961).

32. Morgenthau, *Politics Among Nations*, 5–6. He writes, "It is futile because motives are the most illusive of psychological data, distorted . . . by the interests and emotions of actor and observer alike. Do we really know what our own motives are?"

33. Nye, *Bound to Lead*, 30. Nye's book is a superb analysis of the subjective and relative qualities of power and informs this section of my chapter.

34. Quoted in Henry A. Kissinger, *Diplomacy* (New York: Simon and Schuster, 1994), 632.

35. Table 1.1 uses most of the categories developed by Joseph S. Nye Jr. in the 1980s; see his *Bound to Lead*, 109.

36. The data on population are from Arthur S. Banks, *Cross-National Times Series, 1815–1997* [computer file] (Binghamton, N.Y.: Computer Solutions Unlimited, 1998); World Bank, *World Development Indicators, 1998* (Washington, D.C.: World Bank, 1997).

37. The data on GNP—rank and share—are from Banks, *Cross-National Times Series, 1815–1997*; World Bank, *World Development Indicators, 1998*.

38. The data on research and development spending is from *OECD in Figures* (1997), cited in *The Public Perspective*, February-March 1998, 80; the data on patent applications is from World Bank, *World Development Indicators, 1998*, 298–300.

39. Kissinger, *Diplomacy*, 400.

40. *Imperial Séance*, June 7, 1815, quoted in World Bank, *World Development Report, 1997*, 29).

41. Jules Cambon, "The Foreign Policy of France," in Council on Foreign Relations, ed., *The Foreign Policy of the Powers* (New York: Harper and Brothers, 1935), 3–24.

42. See, for example, Ronald Inglehart and Marita Caballo, "Does Latin America Exist? (And Is There a Confucian Culture?): A Global Analysis of Cross-Cultural Differences," *PS: Political Science and Politics*, vol. 30, 30 March 1997, 34–47. Based on a World Values Survey, they suggest that the differences between countries influence a people's civic attitudes and presumably foreign policy, but the source or permanence of the differences is not clear.

43. For a superb essay on how the international system shapes and constrains the security policies of five states, see Michael Mandelbaum, *The Fate of Nations: The Search for National Security in the Nineteenth and Twentieth Centuries* (New York: Cambridge University Press, 1988).

44. Arthur M. Schlesinger Jr., "Foreign Policy and the American Character," *Foreign Affairs* 62, no. 1 (Fall 1983): 1.

45. For a collection of essays representing a wide range of foreign policy theories, see G. John Ikenberry, ed., *American Foreign Policy: Theoretical Essays* (Boston: Scott, Foresman, 1989).

46. Kennedy, *The Rise and Fall of the Great Powers*.

Chapter 2: Great Britain

1. The figures for the major colonizing countries as of 1900 are from data compiled by H. C. Morris, *The Statesman's Yearbook* (London, 1900), as published in J. A. Hobson, *Imperialism: A Study* (London: Allen and Unwin, 1902).

2. At the turn of the century, the world's thirteen leading colonial powers controlled 22.3 million square miles of territory and 521 million people. Of that total, Britain alone ruled 11.6 million square miles and 345 million people (my calculations, from data in Morris, *The Statesman's Yearbook*, and Hobson, *Imperialism*).

3. A useful definition of grand strategy is provided by Christopher Layne: "Grand strategy is a three-step process: determining a state's vital security interests; identifying the threats to those interests; and deciding how best to employ the state's political, military, and economic resources to protect those interests" (Christopher Layne, "From Preponderance to Offshore Balancing," *International Security* 22, no. 1 [Summer 1997]: 88). See also the related definition employed by Barry Posen, *The Sources of Military Doctrine: France, Britain, and Germany Between the World Wars* (Ithaca: Cornell University Press, 1984), 13.

4. Viscount Castlereagh, *Correspondence, Dispatches, and Other Papers*, ed. Marquess of Londonderry (London, 1848–1852), 12:394, quoted in Henry A. Kissinger, *Diplomacy* (New York: Simon and Schuster, 1994), 89.

5. Paul Kennedy, *The Rise and Fall of the Great Powers* (New York: Random House, 1987). However, Aaron L. Friedberg has argued that at the turn of the century Britain could have enhanced its power through modest government intervention in the economy, somewhat higher tax rates and defense spending, and peacetime conscription. While he concluded that by 1900 a return to primacy was no longer possible, more could have been done to preserve the country's position. See *The Weary Titan: Britain and the Experience of Relative Decline, 1895–1905* (Princeton: Princeton University Press, 1988).

6. The total land area of the United Kingdom is 94,525 square miles; Oregon, the tenth-largest state in the United States, covers 97,073 square miles; see *The New York Times 1998 Almanac* (New York: Penguin, 1997), 192, 690.

7. In the 1590s Spain's population was 8.4 million. In 1717, 125 years later, its population had dropped to 7.6 million; see John Lynch, *The Hispanic World in Crisis and Change, 1598–1700* (Oxford: Blackwell, 1992), 173. Harmful commercial and tax poli-

cies damaged Spain's textile, shipbuilding, and metal industries; discouraged agriculture; and contributed to emigration and rural depopulation in parts of the country.

8. Claude Cockburn, *I Claude: The Autobiography of Claude Cockburn* (Harmondsworth, Middlesex, Eng.: Penguin, 1967), 37–38. See also my chapter, "Britain," in *Contemporary Politics: Europe*, ed. Alexander J. Groth, Robert J. Lieber, and Nancy I. Lieber (Cambridge, Mass.: Winthrop Publishers, 1976), 38–41.

9. See the account in Chaim D. Kaufman, "When All Else Fails: Ethnic Population Transfers and Partitions in the Twentieth Century," *International Security* 23, no. 2 (Fall 1998): 126–131.

10. *Times* (London), October 1, 1938, 14; also see Charles Loch Mowat, *Britain Between the Wars, 1918–1940* (Chicago: University of Chicago Press, 1955), 619.

11. Quoted in David Butler and Jennie Freeman, *British Political Facts 1900–1967*, 2nd ed. (London: Macmillan, 1968), 271.

12. *Hansard Parliamentary Debates*, 5th series (Commons), vol. 476 (June 13, 1950), cols. 35–36.

13. Address at West Point, December 5, 1962, quoted in James Chace, *Acheson: The Secretary of State Who Created the American World* (New York: Simon and Schuster, 1998), 406.

14. The three circles concept, as well as the reasons for Britain's long delay in coming to terms with Europe, are analyzed in Robert J. Lieber, *British Politics and European Unity: Parties, Elites, and Pressure Groups* (Berkeley: University of California Press, 1970), especially 16–27.

15. Winston Churchill explicitly placed the three relationships in this order; See *Hansard Parliamentary Debates*, 5th series (Commons), vol. 476 (June 27, 1950), cols. 2157–2162.

16. For a more detailed account of this problem and its implications, see Robert J. Lieber, *No Common Power: Understanding International Relations* (New York: HarperCollins, 1995), 313–314; also Benjamin J. Cohen, "Beyond EMU: The Problems of Sustainability," *Economics and Politics* 5, no. 2 (July 1993): 187–203.

17. In 1990, for example, the figures for defense spending as a percentage of GDP were, for Britain, 4.1 percent; Germany, 2.2 percent; Japan, 1.0 percent (for purposes of comparison, the figure for France was 2.9 percent and for the United States, 5.3 percent); see International Institute for Strategic Studies, *The Military Balance, 1992–1993* (London: Brassey's, 1992), 218–220. With the end of the Cold War, these figures dropped sharply, so that by 1997 Britain was spending 2.8 percent; Germany, 1.6 percent; Japan, 1.0 percent; France, 3.0 percent; and the United States, 3.4 percent.

18. For a summary of British general election results from 1945 through 1997, see Anthony King, et al., *New Labour Triumphs: Britain at the Polls* (Chatham, N.J.: Chatham House Publishers, 1998), 249.

19. Data for 1960 are from U.S. Department of Commerce, *Statistical Abstract of the United States* (1971), cited in David Calleo, *The Imperious Economy* (Cambridge, Mass.: Harvard University Press, 1982), 204. Data for 1980 are from U.S. National Foreign Assessment Center, *Handbook of Economic Statistics, 1981* (Washington, D.C.: GPO, 1981), 14.

20. Data for 1960–1973 are from Calleo, *The Imperious Economy*, 204, and for 1971–1981, *OECD Economic Outlook*, no. 34 (Paris: Organization for Economic Cooperation and Development, December 1983), 18.

21. Samuel H. Beer provides a valuable account of Tory paternalism in *British Politics in the Collectivist Age* (New York: Vintage, 1969). In a much more recent work, he assesses its subsequent rejection as well as the dramatic change in Labour's ethos represented by Tony Blair; see "The Roots of New Labour: Liberalism Rediscovered," *The Economist*, February 7, 1998, 23–25.

22. For a compelling account of Keith Joseph's role, Thatcher's approach, and the measures taken during her eleven years as prime minister, see Daniel Yergin and Joseph Stanislaw, *The Commanding Heights* (New York: Simon and Schuster, 1998), 92–124.

23. *New York Times*, May 9, 1999; also see *OECD Economic Outlook*, no. 63 (Paris: Organization for Economic Cooperation and Development, June 1998), 245. Data are from Annex Table 21, Unemployment Rates: Commonly Used Definitions.

24. Statement by the trade secretary, Lord Cockfield, quoted in British Information Service (New York), *Survey of Current Affairs* 12, no. 8 (August 1982): 266.

25. *New York Times*, July 2, 1982, and *Washington Post*, September 11, 1982.

26. Quoted in Jonathan Clarke, "The Thatcher Debacle: Is Thatcher to Blame?" *The National Interest* 50 (Winter 1997-1998): 22.

27. Clarke, "The Thatcher Debacle," 22.

28. Tony Blair, "Third Way, Better Way," *Washington Post*, September 27, 1998. Also see Tony Blair, "The Third Way and Modernizing Britain," *The Independent* (London), January 8, 1999, reprinted in British Information Services (New York), Press Release PR 5/99, January 8, 1999. For a critique of the "Third Way" concept, see Robert Wade, "The Coming Fight over Capital Flows," *Foreign Policy*, no. 113 (Winter 1998-1999): 42–45.

29. Beer, "The Roots of New Labour."

30. Polling data as reported in *The Economist*, 28 March, 1998, 52.

31. Karl Marx, *The Eighteenth Brumaire of Louis Bonaparte* (New York: International Publishers, 1963), 15.

32. *New York Times*, October 1, 1998.

33. Blair was referring to Europe's role in Kosovo; quoted in the *New York Times*, October 26, 1998.

34. *The Economist*, April 29, 1989, 19.

Chapter 3: France

1. The best analysis of France's external relations during this period is by Jean-Baptiste Duroselle in his two volumes *La Décadence* (Paris: Imprimerie Nationale, 1979) and *L'abime* (Paris: Imprimerie Nationale, 1982).

2. Some of the most useful works for the period covered in this chapter are Anthony Adamthaite, *France and the Coming of the Second World War* (London: Frank Cass, 1977), and *Grandeur and Misery* (London: Arnold, 1995); Joel Blatt, ed., *The French Defeat of 1940* (Providence, R.I.: Berghahn Books, 1998); Frédéric Bozo, *Deux stratégies pour l'Europe* (Paris: Plon, 1996); Maurice Couve de Murville, *Une politique étrangère,*

1958–1969 (Paris: Plon, 1971); Guy de Carmoy, *Les politiques étrangères de la France, 1944–1966* (Paris: Table Ronde, 1967); Samy Cohen, ed., *Mitterrand et la sortie de la guerre froide* (Paris: Presses de la Fondation Nationale de Sciences Politiques, 1998); Robert Frank, *La Hantise du déclin* (Paris: Belin, 1994); Pierre Gerbet, *Le Relèvement* (Paris: Imprimerie Nationale, 1991); Philip Gordon, *A Certain Idea of France* (Princeton: Princeton University Press, 1993); Alfred Grosser, *La Quatrième République et sa politique extérieure* (Paris: A. Colin, 1961); William Hitchcock, *France Restored* (Chapel Hill: University of North Carolina Press, 1998); Edward Kolodziej, *French International Policy Under de Gaulle and Pompidou* (Ithaca: Cornell University Press, 1974); Maurice Vaïsse, *La Grandeur* (Paris: Fayard, 1998); Arnold Wolfers, *Britain and France Between Two Wars* (New York: Harcout Brace, 1940); Robert J. Young, *In Command of France*, (Cambridge, Mass.: Harvard University Press, 1978); Robert J. Young, *France and the Origins of the Second World War* (New York: St. Martin's Press, 1996).

3. I have dealt with some of the issues covered in this chapter in *Decline or Renewal? France Since the 1930s* (New York: Viking, 1974); George Ross, Stanley Hoffmann, and Sylvia Malzacher, eds., *The Mitterrand Experiment* (New York: Oxford University Press, 1987), chapters 18, "Mitterrand's Foreign Policy," 21, "Conclusion"; "The Nation, Nationalism, and After: The Case of France," *Tanner Lectures*, vol. 15 (Salt Lake City: University of Utah Press, 1994); Gordon Craig and Francis Lowenheim, eds., *The Diplomats, 1939–1979* (Princeton: Princeton University Press, 1994), chapter 8, "The Foreign Policy of Charles de Gaulle"; Gregory Flynn, ed., *Remaking the Hexagon* (Boulder, Westview Press, 1995), chapter 13, "Thoughts on Sovereignty and French Politics."

Chapter 4: Germany

1. The first Reich was the Holy Roman Empire.

2. Friedrich der Grosse, "Das politische Testament von 1752," in *Die politischen Testamente der Hohenzollern*, ed. Kuntzel and Hass (Leipzig and Berlin: B. G. Teubner, 1911), 2:43.

3. Quoted in R. B. Mowat, *A History of European Diplomacy* (London: Edward Arnold, 1928), 142.

4. Thus the title of a book on the Seven Years' War by Johannes Kunisch: *Das Mirakel des Hauses Brandenburg* (Munich: Oldenbourg, 1978).

5. Ludwig Dehio, *Deutschland und die Weltpolitik im 20. Jahrhundert* (Munich: Oldenbourg, 1955), 15.

6. This is precisely how Frederick thought Prussia should proceed. In his "Political Testament of 1752," he advised his successors to eschew grand planning. It is better, he wrote, "to profit from favorable constellations rather than to prepare them in advance. This is why I counsel you not to conclude treaties that would anticipate uncertain events, but to keep your hands free [*garder les mains libres*] so that you may take action according to time, place, and situation" (my translation from the French original in Friedrich der Grosse, "Das politische Testament von 1752," 2:46).

7. A. J. P. Taylor, "Conquest of Germany by Prussia," chapter six, covering the period 1862–1871, in his *The Course of German History* (London: Hamish Hamilton, 1945).

8. Dispatch to the German ambassador in St. Petersburg, dated February 28, 1874. Quoted in Johannes Lepsius, Albrecht Mendelssohn-Bartholdy, and Friedrich Thimme, eds., *Die Grosse Politik der Europaischen Kabinette*, vol. 1, *Der Frankfurter Friede und seine Nachwirkungen, 1871–1877* (Berlin: Deutsche Verlagsgesellschaft für Politik und Geschichte, 1924), 240.

9. The Kissinger Diktat (dictation) was formulated in Bad Kissingen, a German spa, on June 15, 1877; Lepsius, Mendelssohn-Bartholdy, and Thimme, *Die Grosse Politik der Europaischen Kabinette*, vol. 2: *Der Berliner Kongress, seine Voraussetzungen und Nachwirkungen* (Berlin: Deutsche Verlagsgesellschaft für Politik und Geschichte, 1924), 154.

10. Bismarck untiringly professed that Germany was not a threat, as, for example, in a letter to the British prime minister, Lord Salisbury, of November 22, 1887; see his *Gesammelte Werke*, ed. Wolfgang Windelband and Werner Frauendienst (Berlin: Deutsche Verlagsanstalt, 1924–1935), vol. 14, part 2, 890.

11. Cited in Richard Fester, "Saburow und die russischen Staatsakten über die russisch-deutschen Beziehungen, 1879 bis 1890," *Die Grenzboten* 80 (1921): 60.

12. Quoted by Walther Frank, "Der Geheime Rat Paul Kayser," *Historische Zeitschrift* 168 (1943): 320, as quoted in Gordon A. Craig, *From Bismarck to Adenauer* (New York: Harper and Row, 1965), 21.

13. Quoted in Frank A. Golder, ed., *Documents of Russian History, 1914–1917* (New York: Century, 1927), 18.

14. For a lengthy exposition of the Memorandum, see Sybil Crowe and Edward Corp, *Our Ablest Public Servant: Sir Eyre Crowe, 1864–1925* (Braunton, England: Merlin Books, 1993), 110–119.

15. For the tables, see *A Short History of Germany, 1815–1945* (Cambridge: Cambridge University Press, 1969), 105, 107, 112.

16. Much has been made of the *Sonderweg* ("path of separate development") as a prime cause of World War I. According to this argument, the ruling aristocracy withheld political rights from the rising middle and working classes. Following the advice of Shakespeare's Henry IV to "busy giddy minds with foreign quarrels," the ancien régime sought to deflect discontent by provoking conflict abroad and to rally the masses around the flag of nationalism. The problem with this theory is that Wilhelmine Germany, with a strong parliament, an independent judiciary, and a free and diverse press (at least by the then prevailing standards) was hardly less democratic or liberal than Britain or France. Nor were chauvinism, expansionism, and imperialism peculiarly German traits. Even the most perfect democracy of the time, the United States, turned expansionist under Presidents William McKinley and Theodore Roosevelt after going through a similarly stormy industrialization and growth phase.

17. N. V. Tcharykow, as quoted in Kissinger, *Diplomacy*, 210.

18. Witt Bowden et al., *Economic History of Europe Since 1750* (New York: American Book Co., 1937, 1970), 690–691 (page citations are to the 1970 edition).

19. From a letter to the German crown prince, of September 7, 1925; Gustav Stresemann, *Vermächtnis* (Berlin: Ullstein, 1932), 2:555.

20. For the draft and the actual agreement, see the exhaustive treatment of Russo-German relations in the 1920s by Herbert Helbig, *Die Träger der Rapallo-Politik* (Göt-

tingen: Vandenhoeck and Rupprecht, 1958), 73–83. For a briefer but excellent account, see Theodor Schieder, *Die Probleme des Rapallo-Vertrags* (Cologne: Westdeutscher Verlag, 1956).

21. The Germans explained—or rationalized—their actions at Rapallo as being preemptive. Ago von Maltzan, head of the Foreign Office's Ostabteilung (Eastern Department), claimed the Russian deal was a sheer necessity. Had it remained unsigned, he said, "on the Tuesday after Easter we might have been confronted with the fact that Russia had concluded a deal with the Entente behind our backs, leaving us to suffer the present and future consequences of this association" (quoted in Helbig, *Die Träger der Rapallo-Politik*, 99).

22. E. H. Carr, *German-Soviet Relations Between the Two World Wars, 1919–1939* (Baltimore: Johns Hopkins University Press, 1951), 66.

23. Quoted in an anonymous article in the *Hamburger Fremdenblatt*, April 10, 1925, as reproduced in Stresemann, *Vermächtnis*, 2:95.

24. Michael Freund, *Die Gegenwart* 8, no. 11 (1953): 329. Chancellor Adenauer's strategy after World War II was a virtual replay of this one: pacification in the west, an "open," that is, movable, status quo in the east.

25. Soviet objections (and blandishments) were summed up in an aide-mémoire by Deputy Foreign Minister Litvinov to the German chargé d'affaires in Moscow, Radowitz on September 23, 1924. The League constituted a "system which eternalizes the existing frontiers, especially those of the Treaty of Versailles. This includes the present border of Silesia as well as the borders which touch us more closely. The League of Nations is an association for the victors, a mutual insurance agreement of those who have gained something. The *beati possi dentes* form in this way a common defense organization . . . By its entry into the League of Nations, Germany joins a definite coalition; Germany hereby becomes a satellite, renounces its independent policy by subjecting its policies to those of the coalition. Germany's policy thereby comes into collision with the policy of Rapallo. Contrary to its own wishes . . . Germany thus might be drawn into combinations and actions which will lead it into conflict with us . . . Germany itself will decline to a mere pawn in the power politics of the Entente" (quoted from *Nachlass des Reichsministers Dr. Gustav Stresemann*, Serial 2860 H, Roll 1407, Frame 556, Records of the German Foreign Ministry and the Reich Chancellery, National Archives Records Group 242 [Washington, D.C.: National Archives] in Kurt Rosenbaum, *Community of Fate* [Syracuse, N.Y.: Syracuse University Press, 1965], 115).

26. Annex F of the Locarno Treaties, in Fritz Berber, ed., *Locarno: Eine Dokumentensammlung* (Berlin: Junker and Dunnhaupt, 1936), 63.

27. Ibid., 65–66.

28. From a conversation with Karl J. Burckhardt, the League of Nations' high commissioner for Danzig, quoted in Sebastian Haffner, *Von Bismarck zu Hitler* (Munich: Kindler, 1987), 287.

29. From an addressing to the commanders of the Wehrmacht on May 23, 1939, *Akten zur Deutschen Auswärtigen Politik, Series D, Vol. VI* (Göttingen: Vandenhoeck and Ruprecht, 1968), 479.

30. On Hitler's war aims, see Hugh Trevor Roper, "Hitlers Kriegsziele," in *Nationalsozialistische Außenpolitik*, ed. Wolfgang Michalka (Darmstadt: Wissenschaftliche

Buchgemeinschaft, 1978), 31–48; Andreas Hillgruber, *Hitlers Strategie, Politik, und Kriegführung* (Munich: Bernard and Graefe, 1982), 564–578.

31. The former Reich was divided into seven parts: West Germany and West Berlin (under the control of the United States, Britain, and France), East Germany and East Berlin (under Soviet control), the Saar (under French administration), and the German lands in the east incorporated into Poland and Soviet Russia. The Sudetenland ceded to Hitler in Munich in 1938 was returned to Czechoslovakia.

32. "I offered complete union between France and Germany, commending this as a means for settling all differences on the Saarland" (Konrad Adenauer, *Erinnerungen, 1945–1953* [Stuttgart: Deutsche Verlagsanstalt, 1965], 312). That bold gamble actually worked, forcing the French to respond with a unity proposal of their own. This was the "Schuman Plan" for the integration of Western Europe's coal and steel industries, which blossomed into the European Coal and Steel Community, the forerunner of the European Union. Thus Adenauer managed to persuade Paris to postpone autonomy for the Saar. A few years later, France agreed to a referendum. When the population of the Saar rejected autonomy, the area became a *Land* (federal state) of the Federal Republic in 1957.

33. Quoted by Dieter Schröder in *Süddeutsche Zeitung*, January 7, 1960, 3.

34. From an interview with John Leacacos, *Cleveland Plain Dealer*, December 4, 1949; see Adenauer, *Erinnerungen, 1945–1953*, 341–344.

35. The bargain (called *Deutschlandvertrag* in Germany) was enshrined in a series of agreements signed in London and Paris in the fall of 1954. For the documents, see "London Conference" and "Paris Conference" in Council on Foreign Relations, ed., *Documents on American Foreign Relations, 1954* (New York: Harper Brothers, 1955).

36. For the German pledge, see Council on Foreign Relations, ed., *Documents on American Foreign Relations, 1954*, 115–117.

37. Council on Foreign Relations, ed., *Documents on American Foreign Relations, 1954*, 116, 117, 139.

38. Pierre Hassner, "Europe West of the Elbe" in *Europe and the Superpowers*, ed. Robert S. Jordan (Boston: Allyn and Bacon, 1974), 103.

39. Though the three Western powers, the United States, Britain, and France, gave statehood to West Germany in 1949, they maintained the occupation regime while reserving critical residual powers for themselves.

40. From a broadcast interview with Ernst Friedländer on June 11, 1953, Presse- und Informationsamt der Bundesregierung, *Mitteilungen an die Presse*, no. 561/53, 3–4.

41. *Verhandlungen des Deutschen Bundestages*, July 16, 1952, 9853.

42. Speech to the Bundestag on February 23, 1972. *Verhandlungen des Deutschen Bundestages*, February 23, 1972, 9740.

43. *Verhandlungen des Deutschen Bundestages*, May 17, 1972, 10,897.

44. See *The Treaty of August 12, 1970 Between the FRG and the USSR* (Bonn: Presse- und Informationsamt der Bundesregierung, 1970). Nonetheless, elements of the open status quo, as they had been laid down in the 1954 settlement with the West, still remained. The Moscow Treaty declared the postwar borders "inviolable," but a resolution of the Bundestag on May 17, 1972, affirmed that the treaties "do not establish a

legal foundation for currently existing borders." The Warsaw Treaty stated that the Oder-Neisse Line "constitutes the Western state border of the People's Republic of Poland," yet the same compact also affirmed the continued validity of earlier "international agreements" pertaining to Poland and Germany, such as those of 1954 reserving the final determination of Germany's boundaries for a comprehensive peace settlement.

45. The fine distinction between de facto and de jure was mainly semantic: Both states opened "permanent missions" rather than "embassies" in each other's capitals.

46. Speech to the Bundestag on November 6, 1974; *Texte zur Deutschlandpolitik*, series 2, vol. 2 (Bonn: Bundesministerium für innerdeutsche Beziehungen, 1976), 295.

47. Address to the Bundestag, July 25, 1975; *Bulletin des Presse-und Informationsamtes der Bundesregierung*, July 29, 1975.

48. *Verhandlungen des Deutschen Bundestages*, February 23, 1972, 9791.

49. For an elaboration of the logic of *Ostpolitik*, see Josef Joffe, "The Tacit Alliance: West German Policy Toward Eastern Europe," in *Eroding Empire: Western Relations with Eastern Europe*, ed. Lincoln Gordon (Washington, D.C.: Brookings Institution Press, 1987).

50. Interview with Norddeutscher Rundfunk (North German Radio), November 4, 1981, as translated by Foreign Broadcast Information Service (FBIS), *Western Europe Daily Report*, November 5, 1981, J2.

51. Mutatis mutandis, that was also the Achilles heel of Bismarck's alliance structure; the Reich's long-term inability to balance the conflict between its ally Austria and its quasi-ally Russia.

52. From a speech to newspaper publishers in Bonn, November 10, 1981, as translated in FBIS, *Western Europe Daily Report*, November 12, 1981, J1. Later on he described his services as transcending mere translation: "We have indeed played the interpreter. But beyond that, we have an important role to play to the effect that the two world powers . . . observe moderation and a sense of perspective in the pursuit of their interests toward each other" (address to the Bundestag on December 3, 1981; *Bulletin*, December 4, 1981).

53. This was what Schmidt told me (in a taped conversation on March 1, 1985) he had tried to achieve in Moscow. He thought he had gotten Brezhnev to accept negotiations on the SS-20s. Within the next two weeks, however, the Kremlin, speaking through *Pravda*, reneged. If there were negotiations, these "should center principally on American forward-based systems," *Pravda* editorialized on July 8. On July 15, it was brutally explicit in "For the Sake of International Security." Was Moscow ready to deal, as some Westerners "pretend"? Evidently, the message was addressed to Schmidt, and so, "nothing could be further from the truth." (In Berlin in 1878, Bismarck *had* persuaded the Russians to accept "parity" with Britain in the Near East and hence to relinquish many of the gains won in their war against Turkey.)

54. In German usage, *Deutschlandpolitik* refers to relations between the FRG and GDR; *Ostpolitik* designates the policy toward Eastern Europe and the Soviet Union.

55. "Die deutsche Frage im europäischen Rahmen," address before the Swedish Institute for International Relations, May 15, 1986, as published in *Europa-Archiv* 41 (June 1986): 341–348.

56. Genscher tells how he reenacted Stresemann's game—being of the West but not always with the West—in his "Der Kampf gegen die Modernisierung der nuklearen Kurzstreckenraketen," chapter 15 in his *Erinnerungen* (Berlin: Siedler, 1995).

57. The best account of U.S. policy is Philip Zelikow and Condoleeza Rice, *Germany Unified and Europe Transformed: A Study in Statecraft* (Cambridge, Mass.: Harvard University Press, 1995).

58. This fictional account and the following discussion are based on my "Don't Count on the Euro," *New York Review of Books*, December 4, 1997, 26–31 [p. 26].

59. The most important convergence criteria were deficit to GDP ratios of no more than 3 percent, national debt to GDP ratios of no more than 60 percent, stable parities, and declining interest and inflation rates.

60. This term was coined by Joseph S. Nye Jr. in *Bound to Lead: The Changing Nature of American Power* (New York: Basic Books, 1990). See Chapter 1 of this book.

61. For a fuller version of this argument, see Josef Joffe, "One-and-a-Half Cheers for German Reunification," *Commentary*, June 1990.

62. The euro, essentially a Franco-German invention, is often portrayed as a competitor to the dollar and as the means of Europe's self-assertion against the United States.

63. "Uns die Last erleichtern," interview with *Der Spiegel*, January 4, 1999, 44.

64. Interview with *Welt am Sonntag*, 28 February 1999, 33.

Chapter 5: The Three Russias

1. For the latest example, see John P. LeDonne, *The Russian Empire and the World, 1700–1917: The Geopolitics of Expansion and Containment* (New York: Oxford University Press, 1997).

2. Martin Malia, *Russia Under Western Eyes: From the Bronze Horseman to the Lenin Mausoleum* (Cambridge, Mass.: Harvard University Press, 1999), 19.

3. The phrase "Russian idea" traces back to an 1889 lecture given by the Russian philosopher Vladimir Solovyev. It was made famous by Nikolay Berdyayev in his book *The Russian Idea* (published in English in 1948). An excellent contemporary study is Tim McDaniel, *The Agony of the Russian Idea* (Princeton: Princeton University Press, 1996).

4. As quoted in Lindsey Hughes, *Russia in the Age of Peter the Great* (New Haven: Yale University Press, 1998), 56.

5. F. Martens, *Recueil des traités et conventions conclus par la Russie avec les puissances étrangères*, 2:228–235, quoted in LeDonne, *The Russian Empire and the World*, 58.

6. Michael T. Florinsky, *Russia: A History and an Interpretation* (New York: Macmillan, 1953), 2:687. My emphasis.

7. Henry A. Kissinger, *A World Restored* (New York: Grosset and Dunlop, 1964), 131.

8. See, for example, Jonathan Haslam, *Soviet Foreign Policy, 1930–33: The Impact of the Depression* (London: Macmillan, 1983) for the first view; Jiri Hochman, *The Soviet Union and the Failure of Collective Security, 1934–1938* (Ithaca: Cornell University Press, 1984) for the second.

9. For a fuller elaboration of the argument, one informed by new archival material, see Vladislav Zubok and Constantine Pleshakov, *Inside the Kremlin's Cold War: From Stalin to Khrushchev* (Cambridge, Mass.: Harvard University Press, 1996), 9–77.

10. Paul Schroeder, in "Did the Vienna Settlement Rest on a Balance of Power?" *American Historical Review* 97 (June 1992): 683–706, makes the argument that at and after the Congress of Vienna in 1815 the British and the Russians were Europe's only two hegemonic powers, but this characterization is disputable in a way that the post–World War II one is not.

11. An excellent recent treatment of the subject, with a post-Soviet Russia in mind, is Geoffrey Hosking's *Russia: People and Empire* (Cambridge, Mass.: Harvard University Press, 1997).

12. See Richard Pipes, *Survival Is Not Enough* (New York: Simon and Schuster, 1984), 37.

13. The fullest account is still Richard Pipes, *The Formation of the USSR* (Cambridge, Mass.: Harvard University Press, 1964).

14. Hosking, *Russia: People and Empire*, 478.

15. S. Yu. Witte, *Vospominaniya* (Moscow, 1960), 3:274–275.

16. Gerhard Simon, *Nationalism and Policy Toward the Nationalities in the Soviet Union* (Boulder: Westview, 1991), xv.

17. Ibid.

18. Now, after the fact, they sound rather like Eduard Beneš, the post–World War II Czechoslovak president, who in a pre–World War I dissertation wrote, "People have often spoken of the dissolution of Austria. I do not believe in it. The historic and economic ties which bind the Austrian nations to one another are too powerful to let such a thing happen" (Arthur James May, *The Hapsburg Monarchy, 1867–1914* [New York: Norton, 1968], 437, as quoted in Ivan T. Berend, *Decades of Crisis: Central and Eastern Europe Before World War II* [Berkeley: University of California Press, 1998], 47).

19. Hosking, *Russia: People and Empire*, 484–485.

20. A good illustration is Molotov's role in shaping the Soviet response to the Marshall Plan. Western observers have long wrongly assumed that his imperious behavior in that regard could only have been Stalin's diktat; see Zubok and Pleshakov, *Inside the Kremlin's Cold War*, 103–108.

21. Recent accounts may be found in Jeffrey T. Checkel, *Ideas and International Political Change* (New Haven: Yale University Press, 1997); Robert G. Herman, "Identity, Norms, and National Security: The Soviet Foreign Policy Revolution and the End of the Cold War," in *The Culture of National Security: Norms and Identity in World Politics*, ed. Peter J. Katzenstein (New York: Columbia University Press, 1996); and Allen Lynch, "Changing Soviet Elite Views on the International System and Foreign Policy," in *Soviet Foreign Policy: Classic and Contemporary Issues*, ed. Frederick J. Fleron, Erik P. Hoffmann, and Robbin Laird (New York: Aldine De Gruyter, 1991), 385–405.

22. For Afghanistan, see Sarah Mendelson, *Changing Course: Ideas, Politics, and the Soviet Withdrawal from Afghanistan* (Princeton: Princeton University Press, 1998); and for Germany, see Hannes Adomeit, *Imperial Overstretch: Germany in Soviet Policy from Stalin*

to Gorbachev (Baden-Baden, Germany: Nomos Verlagsgesellschaft, 1998); and Angela Stent, *Russia and Germany Reborn* (Princeton: Princeton University Press, 1999).

23. Hosking, *Russia: People and Empire*, 447.

24. This is a theme in Adam Ulam's general treatment of Soviet foreign policy; see his *Expansion and Co-existence* (New York: Praeger, 1968), especially 129, 347.

25. Michael T. Florinsky, *Russia: A History and Interpretation* (New York: Macmillan, 1963), 2:1028.

26. This is all from Foreign Minister Edvard Shevardnadze's address to a conference of scholars and practitioners in the Ministry of Foreign Affairs, July 21, 1988. It is the single most elaborate and substantial foreign policy speech he gave; see "Nauchno-prakticheskaya konferentsiya MIDSSSR, 'XIX vsesoyuznaya konferentsiya KPSS: Vneshnyaya politika i diplomatiya,'" *Vestnik Ministerstva inostrannykh del* no. 12 (August 15, 1988): 27–46.

27. Ibid., 32.

28. See Seweryn Bialer, *The Soviet Paradox: External Expansion and Internal Decline* (New York: Knopf, 1986).

29. Quoted in Baron M. de Taube, *La Politique russe d'avant guerre et la fin de l'empire des tsars, 1904–1917* (Paris, 1928), 130.

30. Ye. M. Primakov, "Rossiya: Reformy i vneshnaya politika," *Mezhdunarodnye otnosheniya* 44, no. 4 (1998): 3. (This is his address in Winterthur, Switzerland, June 2, 1998.)

31. S. N. Prokopovich, *Narodnoe khozyaistvo SSSR* (Moscow: Chekhova, 1952), 1:174–175.

32. David Kotz, *Revolution from Above: The Demise of the Soviet System* (London: Routledge, 1997), 174.

33. In the United States, where the share of gross domestic product spent on national government is among the lowest, it is still nearly 20 percent.

34. This comparison holds notwithstanding the Soviet regime's secret military collaboration with Germany in the 1920s, or more accurately, with a portion of its military command and former military-industrial complex.

35. Laurence Freedman, "Traditional Security," in *Russia and the West: The 21ˢᵗ Century Security Environment*, ed. Alexei Arbatov, Karl Kaiser, and Robert Legvold (Armonk, N.Y.: M. E. Sharpe, 1999).

36. "Note from Chicherin to the British, French, and Italian Governments on the Genoa Conference," (March 22, 1922), in *Soviet Documents on Foreign Policy*, ed. Jane Degras (New York: Oxford University Press, 1951), 1:293.

37. A. Pushkov, "'Doktrina Primakova' i novyi poryadok v Evrope," *Mezhdunarodnye otnosheniya* 44, no. 2 (1998): 4.

38. Samuel P. Huntington, "American Ideals Versus American Institutions," *Political Science Quarterly* 97, no. 1 (Spring 1982): 10.

39. Quoted in Louis Fischer, *Russia's Road from Peace to War* (New York: Harper and Row, 1969): 44.

40. Ibid., 46.

41. Stalin, who must be seen as among the more cynical among the leadership, sent a note to the German Communist leader August Thalheimer on the eve of the 1923

events: "The approaching revolution in Germany is the most important event of our time. The victory of the revolution in Germany will have a greater importance for the proletariat of Europe and America than the victory of the Russian revolution six years ago . . . From the bottom of my heart I wish the *Rote Fahne* new, decisive successes in the struggle ahead, for the conquest of power by the proletariat, for the unity and independence of a Germany about to be born" (quoted in Werner T. Angress, *Stillborn Revolution: The Communist Bid for Power in Germany, 1921–1923* [Port Washington, N.Y.: Kennikat Press, 1963], 428).

42. See Edward Hallett Carr, *The Bolshevik Revolution 1917–1923* (New York: Macmillan, 1961), 3:95–98, 175–176. The "Kerensky period" refers to the interlude between the fall of the Russian monarchy in the March 1917 revolution and the Bolshevik *coup d'état* in November. Alexander Kerensky headed the shaky provisional government during these months.

43. See Max Beloff, *The Foreign Policy of Soviet Russia, 1929–1941* (New York: Oxford University Press, 1947), 1:60–67.

44. Gennady Zyuganov, *My Russia* (Armonk, N.Y.: M. E. Sharpe, 1997), 14.

45. Sergei Kortunov, "Kakaya Rossiya nuzhna miru?" *Pro et Contra* 2, no. 1 (February 1997): 21–37.

46. Malia, *Russia Under Western Eyes*, 412.

47. Sergei Kortunov, "Russia's National Identity in a New Era," monograph, Strengthening Democratic Institutions Project, John F. Kennedy School of Government, Harvard University (September 1998), 9.

48. "Russia's Strategy in the Twenty-First Century," report by the Council on Foreign and Defense Policy, *Nezavisimaya gazeta*, June 18, 1998, 8.

49. Yevgeny Primakov, "Rossiya v mirovoi politike," *Mezhdunarodnye otnosheniya* 44, no. 3 (1998): 7–12.

50. Ibid., 11.

51. Ibid., 10.

52. Rajneesh Darshan, "The Strategic Triangle vis-à-vis the Chinese Viewpoint," *Delhi Jansatta*, January 4, 1999, 4, in Foreign Broadcast Information Service (FBIS) *Daily Report*, FBIS-NES-99-005, January 5, 1999.

53. See, for example, the commentary of Nikolai Paklin, "Treugolnik: Moskva-Pekin-Deli," *Rossiskaya gazeta*, December 22, 1998, 7.

54. See, for example, Zhou Xiaohua, "Covert and Overt Russia-U.S. Rivalry in Central Asia," Xinhua Domestic Service, December 28, 1998, in FBIS *Daily Report*, FBIS-CHI-990004, January 4, 1999.

55. Robert Jervis, "The Future of World Politics: Will It Resemble the Past?" *International Security* 17, no. 3 (Winter 1991–1992), 39–73.

56. Celeste Wallander, "The Economization, Rationalization, and Normalization of Russian Foreign Policy," Program on New Approaches to Russian Security Policy Memo Series, no. 1 (July 1997).

57. Cyril E. Black, "The Pattern of Russian Objectives," in *Russian Foreign Policy Essays in Historical Perspective*, ed. Ivo J. Lederer (New Haven: Yale University Press, 1962), 3–38.

Chapter 6: The United States

1. Walter McDougall, *Promised Land, Crusader State: The American Encounter with the World Since 1776* (New York: Houghton Mifflin, 1997).

2. For the expansionist thesis, see William Appleman Williams, *The Tragedy of American Diplomacy* (New York: World Publishing Company, 1959); Walter LaFeber, *The New Empire: An Interpretation of American Expansion, 1860–98* (Ithaca: Cornell University Press, 1963). For the thesis on American exceptionalism, see Seymour Martin Lipset, *American Exceptionalism: A Double-Edged Sword* (New York: W. W. Norton, 1996); Louis Hartz, *The Liberal Tradition in America* (New York: Harper Books, 1955).

3. Arthur M. Schlesinger Jr., *The Cycles of American History* (Boston: Houghton, Mifflin, 1986); Frank L. Klingberg, *Cyclical Trends in American Foreign Policy: The Unfolding of America's World Role* (Lanham, Md.: University Press of America, 1983). For succinct descriptions of twenty-two cases between 1865 and 1899 in which the United States had an opportunity to expand—an opportunity it rejected in all but six cases—see Fareed Zakaria, *From Wealth to Power: The Unusual Origins of America's World Role* (Princeton: Princeton University Press, 1998). Zakaria describes Congress's decision to annex Alaska as "such a Herculean task that it can be regarded only as an exception to the general pattern."

4. Henry Kissinger also identified these two great presidents as representing two poles in U.S. foreign policy, although he sees Theodore Roosevelt as a classic balance of power realist, much like Richard Nixon and himself. I would disagree with his interpretation of Roosevelt, although I understand why he thought it was a more effective literary device to use Roosevelt as a model than Nixon; see his *Diplomacy* (New York: Simon and Schuster, 1994).

5. James Bryce, *The American Commonwealth* (New York: Macmillan, 1911), 2:574.

6. Hartz argues that "the two tendencies [an isolationist and a crusader impulse] have usually fought it out within the single American mind" (*The Liberal Tradition in America*, 287). I think he meant "mind" in a collective way, whereas I think many individuals fight it out within themselves.

7. In *Promised Land, Crusader State*, McDougall identifies eight such elements: liberty, unilateralism, the American system, expansionism, progressive imperialism, Wilsonianism, containment, and global meliorism.

8. "George Washington's Farewell Address," in *Major Problems in American Foreign Relations*, ed. Thomas G. Paterson and Dennis Merrill, vol. 2, *To 1920: Documents and Essays* (Lexington, Mass.: D. C. Heath, 1995), 76–78. Henceforth referred to as Paterson and Merrill.

9. Thomas A. Bailey, *A Diplomatic History of the American People*, 10th ed. (Englewood Cliffs, N.J.: Prentice-Hall, 1980), 4.

10. For the sociological and ideological roots of the American identity, see Hartz, *The Liberal Tradition in America*. The perception, though not necessarily the reality, of being in the middle class distinguishes Americans from other nationalities. When asked their class, eight of ten Americans describe themselves as middle class; see Sam Roberts, "Another Kind of Middle-Class Squeeze," *New York Times*, May 18, 1997, E1.

11. Whereas in 1861 it took ten weeks to bring the U.S. fleet home from Europe, in 1873, after ocean cables were introduced, it took one day to send a message to the fleet and five weeks to sail home (James A. Field Jr., "American Imperialism: The 'Worst Chapter' in Almost Any Book," *The American Historical Review* 83, no. 3 [June 1978]: 661–664).

12. From 1870 to 1900 Great Britain's industrial output (gross national product estimates) nearly doubled, from $19.6 billion (in 1960 U.S. dollars) to $36.3 billion, while that of the United States grew nearly fivefold, from $16.6 billion to $78.4 billion (estimates from Paul Bairoch, "Europe's Gross National Product, 1800–1975," *Journal of European Economic History* 5, no. 2 [Rome: Banco di Roma, Fall 1976], and B. R. Mitchell, "The Americas," table J1 in *International Historical Statistics* [London: Macmillan Reference, 1998], with conversion formulas from Scott Derks, *The Value of the Dollar, 1860–1989* [Detroit: Gale Research, 1994]).

13. The most important case of annexation was Alaska, which was purchased from Russia in 1869 mainly because Russia was viewed favorably for having supported the Union in the Civil War and Great Britain, which was a likely purchaser for the territory if the United States rejected the offer, was viewed negatively.

14. There is, of course, a vast literature on whether the United States was imperialistic in intent and policy. One of the neatest debates on the subject can be found in James A.Field "American Imperialism," with comments by Walter LaFeber and Robert L. Beisner, and reply by Field, *The American Historical Review* 83, no. 3 (June 1978): 644–688. For understanding U.S. policy, Field suggests that a far better question than why the United States annexed Hawaii in 1898 would be why it did not annex Hawaii earlier (646), and why it rejected or failed to respond to so many offers for coaling stations (from Korea, Peru, Liberia, Denmark, or Portugal; 654) or, I might add, of territory (El Salvador, Dominican Republic, or the Virgin Islands).

15. William A. Robinson, *Thomas B. Reed: Parliamentarian* (New York: Dodd, Mead, and Company, 1930), 351–376. James Bryce captured this perspective very well in his book. He noted the widely held view in the United States that the balance of power politics of the old world was bad "and that the true way for the model Republic to influence the world is to avoid its errors, and set an example of pacific industrialism" (Bryce, *The American Commonwealth*, 566).

16. Quoted in Ernest May, *Imperial Democracy: The Emergence of America as a Great Power* (New York: Harcourt, Brace, and World, 1961), 137.

17. Quoted in Edmund Morris, *The Rise of Theodore Roosevelt*, 606–608.

18. Quoted in May, *Imperial Democracy*, 218.

19. Ibid., 221.

20. Samuel Flagg Bemis, *The Latin American Policy of the United States: An Historical Interpretation* (New York: Harcourt, Brace, 1943), 279.

21. Lester H. Brume, *Chronological History of United States Foreign Relations* (New York: Garland Publishing, 1985), 1:428.

22. "William McKinley's Imperial Gospel, 1899," in Paterson and Merrill, vol. 2, 424.This is an excerpt from a speech he gave to a visiting delegation of Methodist Church leaders on November 21, 1899.

23. "American Anti-Imperialist Program, 1899," quoted in Paterson and Merrill, vol. 2, 422–423.

24. Quoted in Paterson and Merrill, vol. 2, 442.

25. Lester Langley, *The United States and the Caribbean in the Twentieth Century* (Athens: University of Georgia Press, 1982), 4.

26. Quoted in Morris, *The Rise of Theodore Roosevelt*, 724.

27. For Roosevelt's presidential messages from 1901–1904, see *The Evolution of Our Latin American Policy: A Documentary Record*, ed. James W. Gantenbein (New York: Octagon Books, 1971), 359–365.

28. Bemis called our entire policy the "Panama Policy"; see his *The Latin American Policy of the United States*, 185–189.

29. For Ambassador Wilson's comment, see U.S. Department of State, *Foreign Relations of the United States, 1913* (Washington, D.C., Government Printing Office), 808; and for President Wilson's, see Joseph P. Tumulty, *Woodrow Wilson as I Know Him* (New York: Doubleday, 1921), 146.

30. Thomas J. Knock, *To End All Wars: Woodrow Wilson and the Quest for a New World Order* (Princeton: Princeton University Press, 1992), 25–30.

31. Stuart Creighton Miller, "Racism and Military Conquest: The Philippine-American War," in Paterson and Merrill, 442.

32. For the text of the telegram, see Paterson and Merrill, 533.

33. *Congressional Record* (Senate), 65th Congress, 1st session, April 4, 1917, vol. 55, part 1:212–215.

34. Knock, *To End All Wars*, 70–84. Chile opposed the idea because it feared that its neighbors would object to its acquisition of some of their territory in the War of the Pacific and because it was concerned that the pact's reference to "republican forms of government" would permit international interference in a country's domestic affairs.

35. "Peace Without Victory," 64th Congress, 2nd session, January 22, 1917, in *Papers of Woodrow Wilson*, ed. Arthur Link (Princeton: Princeton University Press, 1982), 40:533–539.

36. For the full text of the Fourteen Points, see Paterson and Merrill, *Major Problems in American Foreign Relations*, 1:538–539. For interpretation and background, see Knock, *To End All Wars*, 142–145.

37. Knock, *To End All Wars*, 168–176.

38. Quoted in ibid., 211.

39. Ibid., 247.

40. "Senate Debate on the League of Nations," *Congressional Record* (Senate), 66th Congress, 1st session, November 19, 1919, vol. 58, part 9:8774–9777.

41. Excerpts from speeches that Wilson gave in 1919 in Indianapolis (September 4), St. Louis (September 5), South Dakota (September 8), and San Francisco (September 17–18), in Paterson and Merrill, 1:540–545.

42. Quoted in Knock, *To End All Wars*, 258.

43. Quoted in ibid., 269.

44. Franklin D. Roosevelt, "Our Foreign Policy: A Democratic View," *Foreign Affairs* 6 (July 1928): 584–585.

45. Despite pledges to the contrary, every president since Roosevelt except Carter has intervened in the hemisphere, either by military force or by covert interference in the internal affairs of at least one country. The only one who merits a "caveat" is President Bill Clinton, whose intervention in Haiti in September 1994 was under the auspices of a UN Security Council resolution.

46. *The Public Perspective*, August-September 1997, 21.

47. Senator Gerald Nye (R.–N.D.), "Save American Neutrality," Republican rally, reprinted in *Vital Speeches* 5, no. 23 (September 15, 1939).

48. "Address Delivered by President Roosevelt at Chicago, October 5, 1937," in *Peace and War: U.S. Foreign Policy, 1931–41* (Washington, D.C.: GPO, 1943), 383–387.

49. "The Roper-Fortune Survey Series," *The Public Perspective*, December-January 1998, 40–46.

50. "Arsenal of Democracy," December 29, 1940, in *Peace and War,* 599–600.

51. "Let Us Stay Out of War," address before the American Forum of the Air, January 22, 1939, reprinted in *Vital Speeches* 5, no. 8 (February 1, 1939): 254–256.

52. Robert E. Sherwood, *Roosevelt and Hopkins* (New York: Universal Library, 1950), 756–757.

53. For a superb study of the postwar planning, see Townsend Hoopes and Douglas Brinkley, *FDR and the Creation of the UN* (New Haven: Yale University Press, 1997).

54. For the United Nations, see Hoopes and Brinkley, *FDR and the Creation of the UN*; for the negotiations for the international economic system, see Richard N. Gardner, *Sterling-Dollar Diplomacy: Anglo-American Collaboration in the Reconstruction of Multilateral Trade* (Oxford: Clarendon Press, 1956).

55. From Roosevelt's statement before Congress after the Yalta meeting in February 1945, quoted in Warren F. Kimball, *The Juggler: Franklin Roosevelt as Wartime Statesman* (Princeton: Princeton University Press, 1991), 200.

56. During his meeting in Moscow in October 1944, Churchill passed a note to Stalin dividing up Eastern Europe and then confided, "It was better to express these things in diplomatic terms and not to use the phrase 'dividing into spheres,' because the Americans might be shocked" (quoted in Kimball, *The Juggler,* 162). On the atomic secret, see Kimball, *The Juggler,* 16, 87.

57. Melvyn P. Leffler, "The American Conception of National Security and the Beginnings of the Cold War, 1945–1948," in *American Foreign Policy: Theoretical Essays*, 2nd ed., ed. G. John Ikenberry (New York: HarperCollins, 1996), 140–167.

58. Churchill started the meeting but had to return for elections, which he lost. Attlee replaced him as prime minister and at the conference.

59. Kissinger saw Potsdam as "a dialogue of the deaf," the end of the new world order even before it had a chance to begin. "In the end, each side exercised a veto wherever it had the power to do so" (Henry Kissinger, *Diplomacy* [New York: Simon and Schuster, 1994], 434–436).

60. James Stokes Ballard, *The Shock of Peace: Military and Economic Demobilization After World War II* (Lanham, Md.: University Press of America, 1983), 100, 198; and

Samuel P. Huntington, *The Common Defense: Strategic Programs in National Politics* (New York: Columbia University Press, 1961), 278–280.

61. For the entire text, see Appendix C in George F. Kennan, *Memoirs, 1915–1950* (Boston: Little, Brown and Company, 1957), 547–559; excerpt on 549.

62. See Eduard Mark, "The War Scare of 1946 and Its Consequences," *Diplomatic History* 21, no. 3 (Summer 1997): 383–415. Based on documents from Soviet and U.S. archives, Mark concludes that the Truman administration's fears of a Soviet invasion of Turkey in the summer of 1946 were justified and that the main reason Stalin did not invade Turkey was that Truman demonstrated he was prepared to go to war if he did.

63. Congressional Quarterly, *Congress and the Nation, 1945–64, Vol. I-A* (Washington, D.C.: Congressional Quarterly, 1965), 99.

64. Speech at Bard College, May 22, 1948, reprinted in Caroline Thomas Harsberger, *A Man of Courage: Robert A. Taft* (Chicago: Wilcox and Follett Company, 1952), 217.

65. These views began to prevail in the United States during World War II. In March 1943, 77 percent of the public said the United States should play a larger role in world affairs after the war than it had before (*The Public Perspective*, December-January 1998, 46).

66. Quoted in Geir Lundestad, *"Empire" by Integration: The United States and European Integration, 1945–1997* (New York: Oxford University Press, 1998), 3 (I modified the translation). One could argue that the Marshall Plan divided Western from Eastern Europe, but despite serious reservations, the United States invited the Soviet Union and Eastern Europe to participate. Stalin rejected the invitation.

67. Melvyn P. Leffler, "The American Conception of National Security and the Beginnings of the Cold War," in *American Foreign Policy*, ed. Ikenberry, 158–163.

68. "Radio and Television Report to the American People on the Situation in Korea," in *Public Papers of the Presidents: Harry S. Truman, 1950* (Washington, D.C.: GPO, 1965), 609–610.

69. Nancy Tucker, *Patterns in the Dust: Chinese-American Relations and the Recognition Controversy, 1949–50* (New York: Columbia University Press, 1983).

70. Castro described his motives and exchanges with the Soviets in 1961 and 1962 at a conference in Havana that I attended; see James G. Blight, Bruce J. Allyn, and David A. Welch, *Cuba on the Brink: Castro, the Missile Crisis, and the Soviet Collapse* (New York: Pantheon Books, 1993).

71. Henry A. Kissinger, *White House Years* (Boston: Little, Brown, 1979), 172.

72. McDougall, *Promised Land, Crusader State*, 170.

73. For the various factors influencing Truman's decision, see David McCullough, *Truman* (New York: Simon and Schuster, 1992), 595–620; and for the politics of the Jewish vote, see Clark Clifford's "Memorandum to the President," written in 1947 and published in *Major Problems in American History Since 1945*, ed. Robert Griffith (Lexington, Mass.: D. C. Heath, 1992), 147–153. Truman later said that the influence of his good friend Eddie Jacobson was of "decisive importance," and McCullough concluded that "for Truman, unquestionably, humanitarian concerns mattered foremost." Secretary of State George Marshall, on the other hand, believed that the threat from the Soviet Union was grave, that the United States needed secure access

to oil, and that recognition of Israel would put that access at risk (McCullough, *Truman*, 599, 596, 605).

74. Baker began his memoir by describing the negotiations that led to the cooperative approach between the Soviet Union and the United States on Iraq; see James A. Baker III, *The Politics of Diplomacy: Revolution, War, and Peace, 1989–92* (New York: G. P. Putnam's Sons, 1995).

75. "Review of Times Mirror Poll of October 1992," *National Journal*, November 21, 1992, 2697; and Chicago Council on Foreign Relations, *American Public Opinion and U.S. Foreign Policy* (Chicago: Council on Foreign Relations, 1995), 6.

76. See Robert A. Pastor and Rafael Fernandez de Castro, eds., *The Controversial Pivot: The U.S. Congress and North America* (Washington, D.C.: Brookings Institution Press, 1998).

77. Robert A. Pastor, "The Clinton Administration and the Americas: The Postwar Rhythm and Blues," *Journal of InterAmerican Studies and World Affairs* 39, no. 1 (Winter 1996-1997): 99–128.

78. The data are from a National Association of Manufacturers study, cited by Richard N. Haass, "Sanctioning Madness," *Foreign Affairs* 76, no. 6 (November-December 1997): 74–85. For a rebuttal to Haass's argument, see Jesse Helms, "What Sanctions Epidemic?" *Foreign Affairs* 78, no. 1 (January-February 1999): 1–8.

79. Bush's words, quoted in Warren Kimball, *The Juggler*, 183.

80. The value of total U.S. trade was 13 percent of the nation's gross domestic product in 1970 and 30 percent in 1996. Cited by the U.S. Trade Representative, *Annual Report of the President of the United States on the Trade Agreements Program* (Washington, D.C.: GPO, 1996). The figure for 1913 is extrapolated from 3.7 percent for exports/GDP, from a table in Angus Madison, *Monitoring the World Economy, 1820–1992* (Paris: Organization for Economic Cooperation and Development [OECD], 1995), 38.

81. "Address at Niagara Falls, June 30, 1914," quoted in E. Robinson and V. West, *The Foreign Policy of Woodrow Wilson, 1913–1917* (New York: Macmillan, 1917), 39.

82. Dean Acheson, *Present at the Creation* (New York: Signet, 1970), 923.

83. Henry A. Kissinger, *Diplomacy* (New York: Simon and Schuster, 1994), 30.

Chapter 7: Japan

1. Ernest R. May, *Imperial Democracy: The Emergence of America as a Great Power* (New York: Harcourt, Brace, 1961), 270.

2. Albert M. Craig, *Choshu in the Meiji Restoration* (Cambridge, Mass.: Harvard University Press, 1961), 373–374.

3. Okazaki Hisahiko, "Ajia chotaiken e no shinsenryaku," *This Is Yomiuri*, August 1992, 42–90; translated as "Southeast Asia in Japan's National Strategy," *Japan Echo* 20 (special issue 1993), 61.

4. Marius B. Jansen, "Modernization and Foreign Policy in Meiji Japan," in *Political Development in Modern Japan*, ed. Robert E. Ward (Princeton: Princeton University Press, 1968), 158–159.

5. Isaiah Frank quoted in Michael Mandelbaum, *The Fate of Nations: The Search for National Security in the Nineteenth and Twentieth Centuries* (Cambridge: Cambridge University Press, 1989), 336n.

6. *Look Japan*, September 10, 1986, 4.

7. Masataka Kosaka, "The International Economic Policy of Japan," *The Foreign Policy of Modern Japan*, ed. Robert A. Scalapino (Berkeley: University of California Press, 1977), 224.

8. Quoted in ibid., 224.

9. Jansen, "Modernization and Foreign Policy in Meiji Japan," 175.

10. Ibid.

11. Quoted in Marlene J. Mayo, "Rationality in the Meiji Restoration," in *Modern Japanese Leadership: Transition and Change*, ed. Bernard S. Silberman and Harry D. Harootunian (Tucson: University of Arizona Press, 1966), 356.

12. Quoted in Arthur Tiedemann, "Japan's Economic Foreign Policies, 1868–1893," in *Japan's Foreign Policy, 1868–1941: A Research Guide*, ed. James W. Morley (New York: Columbia University Press, 1974), 130.

13. Quoted in E. Sydney Crawcour, "Industrialization and Technological Change," in *The Twentieth Century*, ed. Peter Duus, vol. 6 of *The Cambridge History of Japan*, ed. John Whitney Hall (Cambridge: Cambridge University Press, 1988), 389.

14. Albert M. Craig, "Fukuzawa Yukichi: The Philosophical Foundations of Meiji Nationalism," in *Political Development in Modern Japan*, ed. Ward, 120–121.

15. Quoted in Kenneth B. Pyle, *The Japanese Question: Power and Purpose in a New Era*, 2nd ed. (Washington, D.C.: American Enterprise Institute, 1996), 18.

16. Gerrit Gong, *The Standard of "Civilization" in International Society* (Oxford: Clarendon Press, 1984), 27–28.

17. Quoted in Kenneth B. Pyle, *The New Generation in Meiji Japan: Problems of Cultural Identity, 1885–1895* (Stanford: Stanford University Press, 1969), 181.

18. Mark Peattie, "The Japanese Colonial Empire, 1895–1954," in Duus, *The Twentieth Century*, 218.

19. Quoted in Roger F. Hackett, *Yamagata Aritomo in the Rise of Modern Japan, 1838–1922* (Cambridge, Mass.: Harvard University Press, 1971), 138.

20. Quoted in Ramon H. Myers and Mark R. Peattie, eds., *The Japanese Colonial Empire, 1895–1945* (Princeton: Princeton University Press, 1984), 15.

21. See Mutsu Munemitsu, *Kenkenroku: A Diplomatic Record of the Sino-Japanese War, 1894–95*, ed. and trans. Gordon Mark Berger (Tokyo: University of Tokyo Press, 1982), passim.

22. Quoted in Pyle, *The New Generation in Meiji Japan*, 180.

23. Quoted in Kenneth B. Pyle, "The Technology of Japanese Nationalism: The Local Improvement Movement, 1900–1918," *Journal of Asian Studies* 33 (November 1973): 51.

24. Quoted in Marius B. Jansen, *The Japanese and Sun Yat-sen* (Cambridge, Mass.: Harvard University Press, 1954), 211.

25. Quoted in David C. Evans and Mark R. Peattie, *Kaigun: Strategy, Tactics, and Technology in the Imperial Japanese Navy, 1887–1941* (Annapolis, Md.: Naval Institute Press, 1997), 148.

26. Quoted in Charles E. Neu, *The Troubled Encounter: The United States and Japan* (New York: Wiley, 1975), 99.

27. Quoted in John W. Dower, *Empire and Aftermath: Yoshida Shigeru and the Japanese Experience, 1878–1954* (Cambridge, Mass.: Harvard University Press, 1979), 97.

28. Quoted in Neu, *The Troubled Encounter*, 117.

29. Akira Iriye, *The Origins of the Second World War in Asia and the Pacific* (London: Longman, 1987), 2.

30. See the review of Matsumoto Shigeharu, *Showashi e no ichishogen*, by Marius Jansen in *Journal of Japanese Studies* 14, no. 2(Summer 1988): 468.

31. Quoted in Yoshitake Oka, *Konoe Fumimaro: A Political Biography*, trans. by Shumpei Okamoto and Patricia Murray (Tokyo: University of Tokyo Press, 1983), 10–13.

32. Quoted in Sadao Asada, "From Washington to London: The Imperial Japanese Navy and the Politics of Naval Limitation, 1921–1930" in *The Washington Conference, 1921–1922: Naval Rivalry, East Asian Stability, and the Road to Pearl Harbor*, ed. Erik Goldstein and John Maurer (Newbury Park, England: Frank Cass, 1994), 153.

33. Quoted in Evans and Peattie, *Kaigun*, 200.

34. Quoted in W. G. Beasley, *Japanese Imperialism, 1894–1945* (Oxford: Clarendon Press, 1991), 166.

35. Quoted in Dower, *Empire and Aftermath*, 36.

36. Quoted in Neu, *The Troubled Encounter*, 124.

37. Akira Iriye, *After Imperialism: The Search for a New Order in the Far East, 1921–1931* (Cambridge, Mass.: Harvard University Press, 1965), 295–296.

38. Quoted in Ian Nish, *Japan's Struggle with Internationalism: Japan, China, and the League of Nations, 1931–1933* (London: Keagan, Paul, 1993), 240.

39. Mandelbaum, *The Fate of Nations*, p. 341.

40. Peter Duus, Ramon H. Meyers, and Mark R. Peattie, eds., *The Japanese Wartime Empire, 1931–1945* (Princeton: Princeton University Press, 1996), xvi.

41. Mandelbaum, *The Fate of Nations*, 343–344.

42. Akira Iriye, *Japan and the Wider World: From the Mid-Nineteenth Century to the Present* (London: Longman, 1997), 65.

43. This section draws on my *The Making of Modern Japan*, 2nd ed. (Lexington, Mass.: D.C. Heath, 1996), 192–204.

44. Gordon M. Berger, "Politics and Mobilization in Japan, 1931–1945," in *The Twentieth Century*, ed. Duus, 105.

45. Quoted in Waldo H. Heinrichs Jr., *American Ambassador: Joseph C. Grew and the Development of the American Diplomatic Tradition* (New York: Oxford University Press, 1966), 317–318; see also John H. Boyle, *Modern Japan: The American Nexus* (New York: Harcourt, Brace, Jovanivich, 1993), 206.

46. Quoted in Akira Iriye, *Power and Culture: The Japanese-American War, 1941–1945* (Cambridge, Mass.: Harvard University Press, 1981), 31.

47. An imperial rescript of September 27, 1940, announcing the Tripartite Pact. Quoted in Dower, *War Without Mercy*, p. 281.

48. John W. Dower, *War Without Mercy: Race and Power in the Pacific War* (New York: Pantheon, 1986), 288–290.

49. Quoted in Marius B. Jansen, *Japan and China: From War to Peace, 1894–1972* (New York: Rand McNally, 1975), 404.

50. Maruyama Masao, *Thought and Behavior in Modern Japanese Politics*, ed. Ivan Morris (Oxford: Oxford University Press, 1969), 85.

51. Quoted in Jansen, *Japan and China*, 405.

52. Quoted in John Hunter Boyle, *Modern Japan: The American Nexus* (New York: Harcourt Brace, 1993), 211.

53. Duus, Myers, and Peattie, *The Japanese Wartime Empire, 1931–1945*, xii.

54. Quoted in Beasley, *Japanese Imperialism, 1894–1945*, 237–238.

55. Iriye, *Power and Culture*, 117–119.

56. The Fundamental Law of Education of 1947 as quoted in Kenneth B. Pyle, *The Making of Modern Japan* (Lexington, Mass.: D. C. Heath, second ed., 1996), p. 223.

57. Quoted in Pyle, *The Japanese Question*, 94.

58. Henry Kissinger, *White House Years* (Boston: Little, Brown, 1979), 324.

59. Samuel Huntington, "Why International Primacy Matters," *International Security* 17, no. 4 (Spring 1993): 72.

60. Eric Heginbotham and Richard J. Samuels, "Mercantile Realism and Japanese Foreign Policy," *International Security* 22, no. 4 (Spring 1998): 171–203.

61. Saburo Okita, *Japan's Challenging Years: Reflections on My Lifetime* (New York: George Allan and Unwin, 1986), 26.

62. Quoted in Dower, *Empire and Aftermath*, 312.

63. Quoted in Miyazawa Kiichi, *Tokyo-Washington no mitsudan* (Tokyo: Jitsugyo no Nihonsha, 1956), 160.

64. Sakakibara Eisuke and Noguchi Yukio, "Okurasho—Nichigin ocho no bunseki," *Chuo koron*, August 1977, 113.

65. Quoted in Heginbotham and Samuels, "Mercantile Realism and Japanese Foreign Policy," 201.

66. Ibid., 199–200.

67. Quoted in Michael Blaker, "Evaluating Japan's Diplomatic Performance," in *Japan's Foreign Policy*, ed. Gerald Curtis (Armonk, N.Y.: M. E. Sharpe, 1993), 6.

68. Ibid., 15.

69. Matsuoka Hideo, "'Nori-okure' gaiko no susume," *Chuo koron*, March 1980.

70. Quoted in Pyle, *The Japanese Question*, 130.

71. Ibid., 50.

72. Quoted in Huntington, "Why International Primacy Matters," 75.

73. See Pyle, *The Japanese Question*, 133.

74. Walter LaFeber, *U.S.-Japanese Relations Throughout History* (New York: Norton, 1997), 355–356.

75. Kissinger, *White House Years*, 1089.

76. LaFeber, *U.S.-Japanese Relations Throughout History*, 358.

77. Kissinger, *White House Years*, 1089.

78. Theodore H. White, "The Danger from Japan," *New York Times Magazine*, July 29, 1985.

79. Quoted in Pyle, *The Japanese Question*, 16.

80. Quoted in ibid., 89–90.

81. Henry Kissinger, *Diplomacy* (New York: Simon and Schuster, 1994), 827.

82. Quoted in Don Oberdorfer, *Changing Context of U.S.-Japan Relations* (New York: Japan Society, 1998), 39.

83. Michael H. Armacost and Kenneth B. Pyle, "Japan and the Unification of Korea," *NBR Analysis* 10, no. 1 (March 1999), 5–38.

84. Kosaka, "The International Economic Policy of Japan," 222.

Chapter 8: China

1. This section draws particularly on John Fairbank and Merle Goldman, *China: A New History* (Cambridge, Mass.: Belknap Press, 1998); John Fairbank, ed., *The Chinese World Order: Traditional China's Foreign Relations* (Cambridge, Mass.: Harvard University Press, 1968); Joseph Levenson, *Confucian China and Its Modern Fate* (Berkeley: University of California Press, 1968); Frederick Wakeman Jr., *The Fall of Imperial China* (New York: Free Press, 1975); Pamela Crossley, *The Manchus* (London and New York: Blackwell, 1997).

2. This section benefits from Michael Yahuda, *The International Politics of the Asia Pacific, 1945–1995* (Routledge, 1996); Francois Godement, *The New Asian Renaissance: From Colonialism to the Post–Cold War* (Routledge, 1997); Akira Iriye, *China and Japan in the Global Setting* (Cambridge, Mass.: Harvard University Press, 1992); and Suisheng Zhao, *Power Competition in East Asia* (New York: St. Martin's Press, 1997).

3. See Michael H. Hunt, *The Genesis of Chinese Communist Foreign Policy* (New York: Columbia University Press, 1996).

4. See especially Alastair Iain Johnston, *Cultural Realism: Strategic Culture and Grand Strategy in Chinese History* (Princeton: Princeton University Press, 1995); Andrew Waldron, *The Great Wall of China: From History to Myth* (Cambridge, 1990); Michael Pillsbury, ed., *Chinese Views of Future Warfare* (National Defense University, 1998); Harold Jacobson and Michel Oksenberg, *China's Participation in the IMF, the World Bank, and GATT: Toward a Global Economic Order* (Ann Arbor: University of Michigan, 1990).

5. This estimate comes from Dwight Perkins, *Agricultural Development in China, 1368–1968* (Chicago: Aldine, 1969), and Albert Feuerwerker, "Economic Trends in the Late Ch'ing Empire, 1870–1911," in *The Cambridge History of China*, ed. John Fairbank and Kwang-ching Liu (New York: Cambridge University Press, 1980), 11:1–69.

6. For elaboration of this and the next section, see Thomas W. Robinson and David Shambaugh, eds., *Chinese Foreign Policy: Theory and Practice* (Clarendon, 1994); Harry Harding, ed., *China's Foreign Relations in the 1980s* (New Haven: Yale University Press, 1984); Samuel Kim, *China and the World* (Boulder: Westview, 1998); and John Garver, *Foreign Relations of the People's Republic of China* (Prentice Hall, 1993).

7. See Ezra Vogel, ed., *Living with China* (New York: W. W. Norton, 1997).

8. This section draws upon Immanuel Hsu, *China's Entrance into the Family of Nations* (Cambridge, Mass.: Harvard University Press, 1960); Masataka Banno, *China and the West, 1858–1861: The Origins of the Tsungli Yamen* (Cambridge, Mass.: Harvard

University Press, 1964); Julia C Strauss, *Strong Institutions in Weak Polities: State Building in Republican China, 1927–40* (Clarendon, 1998); Hung-mao Tien, *Government and Politics in KMT China, 1927–37* (Stanford: Stanford University Press, 1972); Kenneth Lieberthal, *Governing China* (New York: W. W. Norton, 1995); Lu Ning, *The Dynamics of Foreign Policy Decision Making in China* (Boulder: Westview, 1997); Donald W. Klein, "The Origins of the Ministry of Foreign Affairs," in *Management of a Revolutionary Society*, ed. John Lindbeck (University of Washington, 1971); A. Doak Barnett, *The Making of Foreign Policy in China: Structure and Process* (Boulder: Westview, 1985).

9. For China's role in the world economy, see Susan Shirk, *How China Opened Its Door* (Washington, D.C.: Brookings Institution Press, 1994); Nicholas Lardy, *China in the World Economy* (Washington, D.C.: Institute of International Economics, 1994); *China Engaged: Integration with the Global Economy* (The World Bank, 1997).

10. China's economy is analyzed in *China 2020* (Washington, D.C.: World Bank, 1997). Its military capabilities are analyzed in C. Dennison Lane, Mark Weisenbloom, and Dimon Liu, eds., *Chinese Military Modernization* (Washington, D.C.: AEI Press, 1996) and David Shambaugh and Richard H. Yang, eds. *China's Military in Transition* (Oxford: Clarendon, 1997).

Chapter 9: Looking Back and Forward

1. Woodrow Wilson, "The Significance of American History," preface to *Harper's Encyclopedia of the United States*, quoted in Thomas J. Knock, *To End All Wars: Woodrow Wilson and the Quest for a New World Order* (Princeton: Princeton University Press, 1992), 14.

2. Quoted in William Safire, "Mr. Comeback," *New York Times*, April 25, 1994, A11.

3. Josef Joffe, "The Foreign Policy of the Federal Republic of Germany," in Roy C. Macridis, ed., *Foreign Policy in World Politics* (Englewood Cliffs, New Jersey: Prentice Hall, 1992, eighth edition), 100.

4. Carville was Bill Clinton's campaign manager in 1992. Quoted in *The Economist*, October 7, 1995, 15.

5. Jessica T. Matthews, "Power Shift," *Foreign Affairs* 76, no. 1 (January-February 1997): 50. Lester Salamon also sees a historic transformation: "We are in the midst of a global 'associational revolution' that may prove to be as significant to the latter twentieth century as the rise of the nation-state was to the latter nineteenth" ("The Rise of the Non-Profit Sector," *Foreign Affairs* 73, no. 4 [July-August 1994]: 109).

6. Susan Strange, *The Retreat of the State: The Diffusion of Power in the World Economy* (Cambridge: Cambridge University Press, 1996). For a brief summary of her thesis, see her article "The Erosion of the State," *Current History*, November 1997.

7. Daniel Yergin and Joseph Stanislaw, *Commanding Heights* (N.Y.: Simon and Schuster, 1998), 373.

8. The data is compiled from several sources, including J. David Singer and Melvin Small, *Natonal Material Capabilities Data, 1816-1993* (Ann Arbor, Michigan: ICPSR, 1996, computer file); International Institute for Strategic Studies, *The Military Balance, 1997/98* (Oxford: Oxford University Press, 1997); Arthur S. Banks, *Cross-*

National Time Series, 1815-1997 (Binghamton, New York: Computer Solutions Un-limited, 1998, computer file); and World Bank, *World Development Indicators, 1997* (Washington, D.C.: World Bank, 1998).

9. Nicholas D. Kristof with David Sanger, "How U.S. Wooed Asia To Let Cash Flow In," *New York Times*, February 16, 1999, 1, 10–11. Also Nicholas D. Kristof and Edward Wyatt, "Who Sank, or Swam, in Choppy Currents of a World Cash Ocean," *New York Times*, February 15, 1999, A1, 10–11.

10. For a fascinating essay on this theme, see Amos Perlmutter, *Making the World Safe for Democracy* (Chapel Hill: University of North Carolina Press, 1997).

11. Quoted in Nicholas D. Kristof, "Changing Fortunes: Hubris and Humility as U.S. Waves and Asia Wanes," *New York Times*, March 22, 1998, 12; Paul Kennedy, *The Rise and Fall of the Great Powers: Economic Change and Military Conflict from 1500 to 2000* (New York: Vintage Books, 1989).

12. U.S. Arms Control and Disarmament Agency, *World Military Expenditures and Arms Transfers, 1995* (Washington, D.C.: ACDA, 1997).

13. Peter Wallensteen and Margareta Sollenberg, "The End of International War: Armed Conflict, 1989-1994," *Journal of Peace Research* 33, 3 (August 1995), 353-370.

14. President Bill Clinton, "Interview with Tom Brokaw of MSNBC's 'In-terNight,'" July 15, 1996, in *Public Papers of the Presidents of the United States: William J. Clinton, 1996* (Washington, D.C.: GPO, 1997), 1246.

15. Quoted in R. W. Apple, "View from Abroad: U.S. Policy Sapped by Scandal," *New York Times*, September 25, 1998, A6.

16. John E. Reilly, ed., *American Public Opinion and U.S. Foreign Policy, 1999* (Chicago: Chicago Council on Foreign Relations, 1999). 61% of the public and 96% of the leaders believe the U.S. should "take an active part in world affairs," and 72% of the public and 48% of the leaders believe the U.S. should not act alone. (pp. 4-5)

17. Samuel P. Huntington, "The Lonely Superpower," *Foreign Affairs* 78, no. 2 (March-April 1999), 36.

18. Quoted in *New York Times*, January 12, 1984, 2.

19. Norman Angell, *The Great Illusion* (New York, Putnam, 1910).

20. Wendell L. Willkie, *One World* (New York: Simon and Schuster, 1943), 1.

21. Donald Kagan, *On the Origins of War and the Preservation of Peace* (New York: Doubleday, 1995).

22. Judith Miller, "Russia's Move To End Strikes Loses; Margin Is A Surprise," *New York Times*, March 27, 1999, p. A7.

23. Quoted in Anthony Lewis, "Which Side Are We On?" *New York Times* May 29, 1999, p. A27.

24. Kofi A. Annan, "Walking the International Tightrope," *New York Times*, Janu-ary 19, 1999, A23.

25. Zbigniew Brzezinski, *The Grand Chessboard* (New York: Basic Books, 1997).

26. Emanuel Adler and Michael Barnett, eds., *Security Communities* (Cambridge, United Kingdom: Cambridge University Press, 1998).

27. See Loukas Tsoukalis, *The New European Economy Revisited* (N.Y.: Oxford University Press, 1997), Chapter 9, "Cohesion and Redistribution;" European Commission, *Sixth Periodic Report on the Social and Economic Development of the Regions of the European Union* (Brussels: European Commission, 1997).

ABOUT THE EDITOR
AND AUTHORS

Robert A. Pastor is the Goodrich C. White Professor of International Relations at Emory University. From 1985 to 1998 he was a fellow and founding director of the Carter Center's Latin American and Caribbean Program. He also developed the center's democracy and China programs and organized international missions to monitor elections in twenty countries. He is the author or editor of eleven books on U.S. foreign policy and other issues, including *Whirlpool: U.S. Foreign Policy Toward Latin America*. He served on the National Security Council from 1977 to 1981 and has been a consultant to the Departments of State and Defense. He received his Ph.D. from Harvard University.

Stanley Hoffmann is the Paul and Catherine Buttenweiser University Professor at Harvard University, where he received his Ph.D. and has taught since 1955. He was the chairman of the Center for European Studies at Harvard from its inception in 1969 until 1995. The author of numerous books on French and international affairs, he is also an essayist for the *New York Review of Books* and the Western Europe review editor for *Foreign Affairs*.

Josef Joffe is editorial page editor and columnist of the *Suddeutsche Zeitung*, West Germany's largest daily newspaper. He is Associate at the Olin Institute for Strategic Studies at Harvard University. The author of *The Limited Partnership: Europe, the United States, and the Burdens of Alliance*, he has written on German diplomacy, arms control and strategy, U.S. foreign policy, and European security. He received his Ph.D. from Harvard University.

Robert Legvold is professor of political science at Columbia University and was director of the Harriman Institute for East-West Studies from 1986 to 1992. From 1978 to 1984 he was senior fellow and director of the Soviet Studies Project at the Council on Foreign Relations in New York. He is the coeditor of *After the Soviet Union: From Empire to Nations* (1992) and the author of "The Russian Question." He received his Ph.D. from the Fletcher School of Law and Diplomacy.

Robert J. Lieber is professor of government at Georgetown University. He has previously taught at Harvard, Oxford, and the University of California at Davis. He is the author of six books, including *No Common Power: Understanding International Relations* (1995) and the editor of *Eagle Adrift: American Foreign Policy at the End of the Century* (1997). He received his Ph.D. from Harvard University.

Michel Oksenberg is senior fellow at Stanford University, at the Asia Pacific Research Center where he is also professor of Political Science. He was president of the East-West Center and before that professor of political science at the University of Michigan and director of the Center for Chinese Studies there. From 1977 to 1980 he served on the National Security Council, where he played a central role in the normalization of relations between the United States and China. He received his Ph.D. from Columbia University.

Kenneth B. Pyle is professor of history and Asian studies at the University of Washington, where from 1978 to 1988 he was also director of the Henry M. Jackson School of International Studies. He is president of the National Bureau of Asian Research and the author of many books on Japan, including *The Japanese Question: Power and Purpose in a New Era* (1992) and *The Making of Modern Japan* (1996). He was founding editor of the *Journal of Japanese Studies* (1974–1986). He received his Ph.D. from Johns Hopkins University.

INDEX